RANDI'S PRIZE

Robert McLuhan gained a First in English Literature at Oxford, then worked as a foreign correspondent for *The Guardian* in Spain and Portugal. He now works as a freelance journalist. He has been a member of the Society for Psychical Research since 1993, blogging and lecturing on paranormal topics.

RANDI'S PRIZE

What sceptics say about the paranormal,
why they are wrong
and why it matters

ROBERT McLUHAN

Matador
5 Weir Road
Kibworth Beauchamp
Leicester LE8 0LQ, UK
Tel: 0116 279 2299
Fax: 0116 279 2277
Email: books@troubador.co.uk
Web: www.troubador.co.uk/matador

ISBN 978 184876-494-1

British Library Cataloguing in Publication Data.
A catalogue record for this book is available from the British Library.

Cover design by David Wardle (www.designedbydavid.co.uk)
Designed and typeset in Minion Pro by Maria Hampshire at Shoreline
Printed in the UK by TJ International Ltd, Padstow, Cornwall

Matador is an imprint of Troubador Publishing Ltd

For Ana Bandeira

CONTENTS

ACKNOWLEDGEMENTS

The research for *Randi's Prize* was largely a matter of toiling in libraries, and it was sometimes easy to forget that the subject derives from human experience. So I'd like to thank all those people – friends, colleagues, strangers in pubs – who over the years, on hearing about my interest, offered stories of their own, reawakening in me a sense of surprise that something so potentially significant still remains in the shadows.

When I started my blog *Paranormalia* I hoped readers would find it a useful informational service, but it turned out to be a two-way thing. My thanks to regular visitors, sceptics included, who in the comments threads have suggested angles that had not previously occurred to me and added new information and links. They have greatly enriched my understanding of the subject.

Several people helped out in the later stages of the book. Guy Lyon Playfair read the penultimate draft, while Chris Roe, Rupert Sheldrake, Pam Smart, David Rousseau, Julie Rousseau, John Poynton, Matt Colburn and Mary Rose Barrington all read chapters. My thanks to them for their valuable corrections and comments, and of course I take full responsibility for the book's remaining shortcomings. Thanks also to those in the SPR who helped in various ways: Peter Jenkins, Eleanor O'Keefe and the late Wyllys Poynton.

I owe a big debt of gratitude to Maria Hampshire, who went beyond the call of duty in getting the book through the final stages of editing and typesetting. My sister Janie was a constant source of encouragement and slogged through more than one draft. Last but not least, thanks to my dear wife Ana, without whose support – as is often said, but never so feelingly – this book could not have been written.

INTRODUCTION

James 'The Amazing' Randi is a Canadian stage magician well known to scientists as a debunker of paranormal claims. Since the 1960s he has pledged a cash prize to anyone who can convince him that they possess psychic powers. The amount on offer has grown to a tempting one million dollars, but he says no one has ever come close to winning it.

The invincibility of Randi's Million Dollar Challenge doesn't surprise scientists at all, for such things as telepathy and psychokinesis don't fit with their understanding of how the world works. In general, science long ago abandoned the idea that humans possess an immortal mind or soul – a 'ghost in the machine'. And if you think about it, how could the grey goo in our skulls possibly cause objects to move at a distance, or divine another person's thoughts? How can we continue to have feelings and experiences when we are dead and our brain has decomposed?

It took me a while to grasp the conflict here. Like many people educated in nominally Christian schools, I put religion behind me as soon as I could think for myself. The natural world seemed much more interesting than superstition, and I became an avid reader of popular science books. Yet I saw myself more as a free-thinking agnostic than a committed atheist, as I believe many scientists themselves do. It wasn't obvious to me that scientific knowledge rules out the existence of the non-material reality described in Eastern philosophy, and I was curious about the religious visions reported by some hospital patients and accident victims.

However I began to realize this ambivalence won't do. Classic books on evolution – Jacques Monod's *Chance and Necessity* and Richard Dawkins's *The Blind Watchmaker* come to mind – insist that our biological origins leave no room whatever for supernaturalist ideas. For writers such as these, science has discredited the idea that our existence has purpose or meaning, apart from what we create for ourselves. Neuroscience and consciousness studies treat the mind as an effect of biological functions – and nothing more. The computational approach advocated by thinkers such as Steven Pinker and Daniel Dennett is especially influential. Again, if the brain is essentially a kind of organic super-computer, it's not the sort of thing that can have psychic experiences.

But then how does one account for the fact that people occasionally seem to experience telepathic communication, or see a strikingly real-seeming apparition of a recently deceased relative, or have a brief and extraordinary sense of being located outside their body? No problem, say sceptics. These are anecdotal reports, and people are notoriously prone to error, exaggeration or simply to making things up – a point insisted on by the sceptical eighteenth century philosopher David Hume to counter claims of religious miracles. The simplest solution is always to be preferred, a principle often referred to as 'Occam's razor'. The idea that humans are fallible is uncontroversial, whereas psychic experiences – collectively referred to as 'psi' by researchers – would require enormously complex adjustments to our understanding of nature.

Unwilling to take either side's word for it, I read everything I could lay my hands on about psi. I looked closely too at the reasoning of the professional sceptics, who tend to be either university psychologists, such as Ray Hyman and Richard Wiseman, or stage magicians such as James Randi. One early discovery was that some scientists and intellectuals have taken seriously claims of telepathy and suchlike, and devoted a lot of time to its study. These people are hardly cranks: they often hold university posts as psychologists, physicists, biologists, statisticians, astronomers and philosophers (one of the best known, Princeton's Robert Jahn, is a rocket scientist). They analyze data, carry out experiments in controlled conditions and report them in their peer reviewed journals – just as one would expect with any scientific activity. They don't always accept each others' claims, and controversy among them is lively. But on one thing they seem to be more or less unanimous: there occur certain mental processes that are currently unexplained by science.

I found the controversy shrill and curiously hard to penetrate. Richard Dawkins has dismissed the paranormal as 'bunk', and those who sell it as 'fakes and charlatans',[1] while Randi, who Dawkins admires, calls it 'woo-woo' and the study of it 'farce and delusion'.[2] But at last I reached the moment that anyone will recognize who has devoted themselves single-mindedly to a subject, of feeling that I was at last starting to master it. I had read much of the academic literature of psychic research, and parts of it I pored over, closely comparing the researchers' reports with the sceptical explanations. Now I found my thinking taking certain directions.

I agreed with sceptics that psi is far from proved in any definitive sense. It emerges from the research as a complex and confusing phenomenon, an effect of consciousness, seemingly (and bizarrely) one with quasi-material properties. It's elusive and ephemeral, hard to demonstrate at will. If the laws of physics are to be rewritten, along with Darwinist accounts of the origin and development of life, and much else besides, science will not really accept anything less. But beyond this, I found much of the research material compelling, and the counter-arguments lacking in explanatory power. And I strongly disagreed that the study of anomalous mental phenomena is misguided, a waste of both time and precious funds. In fact I found it hard to grasp why anyone would not feel curious about an aspect of human experience so consistent and widely reported, however odd, and whatever its causes might turn out to be.

In an increasingly secular world this thinking invites suspicion, I have to admit. I'm resigned to being lectured by well-meaning friends about wasting time on something so dubious. But I get their point. An uncompromising rejection of superstition is widely held to be a personal standard, a sign of intelligence, education and personal integrity. People who believe weird things, as sceptic Michael

Shermer calls them, are best kept at arms length.[3] Aren't they believers at heart, trying to cloak their superstitious fantasies in the garb of empirical science?

Against this, the scientists who take up psi research seem motivated by curiosity, as one would surely expect. They show little evidence of any supernatural preoccupations and side with sceptics in many respects – as indeed I do too. There's often credulity and dishonesty where paranormal claims are concerned – how could there not be? I concur absolutely with science's rejection of creationism and have no patience with codes, cults, conspiracies, 'alien archaeology' and the endless wearisome controversy about the Turin Shroud, nor Nostradamus, Bigfoot and other favourites of the paranormal canon. Perhaps some or other of these things have value, but I'll let others argue for them.

At the very least, *Randi's Prize* will give you a good idea of what it is that could make one twenty-first century European, questioning and respectful of science, come to believe in propositions that many of his peers instinctively reject. It's a record of my journey: the authors I consulted, my reactions to their research and analysis, and the gradual development of my ideas. In comparing parapsychologists' investigations with sceptics' alternative scenarios I've tried to make my thinking as transparent as possible. Can claims of psychokinesis be accounted for in terms of trickery? Do spirit mediums deceive clients and audiences with the 'cold reading' technique? Are ESP experiments too flawed to take seriously? Should apparitions and out-of-body experiences be considered internal hallucinations, or are they something more? What about those odd statements occasionally made by very young children, which suggest they have lived a previous life? And as much to the point, if any of these things are true, why are they so ambiguous? How could mainstream science be so mistaken about them?

Still, we may say, even if some of these things do turn out to have merit, why does it matter? In a world beset by change and crisis –

global warming, nuclear proliferation, pandemics, the moral challenges created by genetic technology – isn't the paranormal a rather trivial business? My answer is this: if it seems to be trivial, it is only because we prefer it that way.

Make no mistake – there is an extraordinary anomaly here. Huge passions have been aroused in the debate about religion over the past decade, but it has become plain to me that many otherwise thoughtful people have little or no idea of the extent to which paranormal and religious experiences are reported, or the potential relevance of this to their own ideas. This is not to say that mediums are necessarily in contact with the dead – there are difficult issues here, more complex than sceptics recognize, and I will touch on them – but rather that there things going on right in front of our noses which are potentially significant but which we mentally filter out.

A difficult question, tentatively addressed in the final chapter, is how secular society could ever become reconciled to the implications of paranormal and religious experience. Given the tensions caused by the growing influence of fundamentalist religion it's hard to see such a thing ever happening. Atheist critiques such as Richard Dawkins's *The God Delusion* and Sam Harris's *The End of Faith* blame superstition for the insanity of religious fanatics: educate people about scientific realities, prove to them that an afterlife is a logical impossibility, and the suicide bombers will have nothing to die for. From this perspective, to argue the case for the paranormal might be seen as dangerously irresponsible.

But there are other ways of looking at this. First, as even some scientific commentators realize, religion is at least partly a thinking response to experience, and not always, as less well-informed critics think, an irrational belief, a mental virus of which the human race may aspire one day to be purged. Psychic and spiritual intimations are an essential feature of what we are; they aren't going to go away. Surely it's better to try to understand them than to ignore or ridicule.

Second, the content of psychic experiences, the ideals they inspire, align more closely with liberal religious and secular humanist thinking than with the authoritarian fundamentalism that both camps oppose. While mindless superstition is always a concern, it won't necessarily be fuelled by a correct understanding of psi as an aspect of consciousness. How could it, if this understanding is the outcome of a rational enquiry?

On a matter such as this, one is not – and perhaps should not be – persuaded by a single book. Until you achieve a solid foundation any conviction I leave you with will be temporary, easily undone by the next article or review you come across that blandly reaffirms the paranormal to be a lot of nonsense. As I'll suggest, orthodoxy exerts a gravitational pull in this respect, although we may not recognize it as such.

On the other hand the Internet now offers everyone the opportunity to engage with this subject and make up their own minds. Primary sources that were once hard to track down – and which for that reason are often ignored by the critics – can now be accessed online, while fuller case histories and examples can be found on the companion website to this book, along with book reviews and biographies of key individuals (see *Suggestions for Further Reading* on p. 331). If you're at all committed to understanding this strange subject, you will – slowly, to be sure, and with certain psychological traps to avoid along the way – start to get a balanced perspective. In this way you will soon become more knowledgeable than many of the authors whose work I have critiqued.

I hope that *Randi's Prize* will interest those people who, from reflecting on their own experiences or on the experiences of others, do take paranormal claims seriously – and indeed may feel there's nothing really to argue about. As well as confirming their suspicions about some debunking sceptics, it will enrich their understanding of psi's complexity, and stimulate a more informed, critical approach. But I also want to speak to open-minded secularists and agnostics, and suggest there is here an area of human experience that deserves their attention. To be sure, it will require a certain suspension of disbelief to begin with, but some readers at least will see the significance as we go along. As to what it all means, I have offered some ideas of my own, but there are large questions here which all of us will respond to in our own way. If in the future we can discuss them openly, with the best available information and without fear of ridicule, then that at least will be a beginning.

A note about terms. From a scientific point of view many of the terms used in paranormalist literature are variously imprecise, inconsistent or misleading, not least the word 'paranormal' itself. While I acknowledge their limitations, I have been content to use them here as they are popularly understood.

The term 'psychical research' was adopted by the first paranormal investigators in the 1880s and is still used to describe the field, although I prefer the more modern 'psychic research'. 'Parapsychology' only came into use in the 1930s, but can be used anachronistically to apply to the earlier work, as I have sometimes done.

'ESP', short for 'extra-sensory perception', is a well-known term for certain anomalous mental phenomena. However the later term 'psi' is more generally used by researchers (silent 'p', rhymes with 'sky').

Finally, I have used the British spelling for 'sceptic' throughout rather than the American 'skeptic', except in book titles.

ONE

NAUGHTY ADOLESCENT
SYNDROME

'I would have thought, sir, it do be fairies, but them late readers and knowledgeable men will not allow such a thing, so I cannot tell what it is. I only wish, sir, you would take it away.' *Irish farmer to investigator, 1911.*

The supernatural holds a fascination for many people. In any major bookshop you will find an enormous range of books on spiritual and New Age topics: astrology and tarot, crystal healing, spirit channelling, ghosts and angels, witchcraft and paganism – the list is endless. One unifying theme is the idea that we humans are immortal beings, and that death is not the end.

The more sceptical among us, perhaps browsing the shelves out of curiosity on our way to the science section, will wonder what to make of it. Where's the scientific evidence for all this? One might have thought that by now the Enlightenment, that shift towards rational thinking that occurred during the eighteenth century, would have emancipated the world from superstition, but instead it seems to have unleashed a range of bewildering new beliefs. As secular critics say, the decline of religion means not that people now believe in *nothing* but that they will believe in *anything*.

Does it really matter if some people think things that aren't true? Certainly it does, argued the late Carl Sagan, an astronomer and science popularizer whose polemic *The Demon-Haunted World* (1996) you might find nearby on the science shelves. Extraordinary claims require extraordinary evidence, Sagan insisted; he did not rule out the possibility that some things like telepathy or psychokinesis might one day be shown to be true, but it would be foolish to accept them without solid scientific proof. Sagan further argued that scientific thinking helps us find our way in the world, to tell what's true from what's false. Its values are in many ways indistinguishable from the values of democracy itself, and we ignore it at our peril. If we persist in following irrational beliefs, a time may come when 'clutching our crystals and nervously consulting our horoscopes, our critical faculties in decline ... we slide, almost without noticing, back into superstition and darkness'.[1] Richard Dawkins's *Unweaving the Rainbow* is a likewise passionate appeal for people to lift their eyes from the ersatz wonders of the supernatural. An 'orderly universe,' Dawkins insists, 'one indifferent to human preoccupations, in which everything has an explanation even if we still have a long way to go before we find it, is a more beautiful, more wonderful place than a universe tricked out with capricious, *ad hoc* magic'.[2]

The scientists take the media to task for its woeful lack of critical awareness in publicizing paranormal claims. Dawkins says: 'Disturbed people recount their fantasies of ghosts and poltergeists. But instead of sending them off to a good psychiatrist, television producers eagerly sign them up and then hire actors to perform dramatic reconstructions of their delusions – with predictable effects on the credulity of large audiences'.[3]

For his part, Sagan praises a hoax carried out by the stage magician and paranormal debunker, James Randi, together with the Australian documentary programme *Sixty Minutes*. In 1988 the programme ran a show by a 'channelling psychic', who was actually an actor speaking out lines fed through a radio earpiece by Randi himself. The audiences and television journalists fell for it, even though the simplest checks would have exposed the trick.[4]

2 *The sceptics' view*

For someone like myself with a foot in both camps the dissonance is hard to ignore. There's an intellectual vacancy about much New Age material: as inspirational literature it often works well within its own terms, but it's less convincing when it tries to seek validation with vague references to quantum theory, or to scientists whose ideas are viewed with suspicion by their peers. On the other hand its supernaturalist world view might seem to be supported by the anomalous experiences that people often report, and which are sometimes well documented – however odd.

In my local library I picked up a book titled *This House is Haunted* by Guy Lyon Playfair, an apparently factual description of so-called poltergeist phenomena that allegedly terrorized a London family in the late 1970s.[5] Investigators Playfair and Maurice Grosse spent fourteen months visiting this family and logged any incidents of unexplained bangs and knocks, furniture coming to life and household objects chucking themselves around. Their report was based on more than a hundred tapes recorded on the spot and verbatim statements from eyewitnesses; some of the incidents they say they saw themselves. Until then I had assumed poltergeists were a quaint old folk superstition, like elves and ogres, yet here were apparently sensible people insisting that the phenomenon was real.

So what's the true explanation? When I started to look around I discovered several debunking books, many of them issued by Prometheus, the house publisher for the Committee for the Investigation of Claims of the Paranormal, or CSICOP, recently renamed the Committee for Skeptical Inquiry (CSI). This well-funded organization was set up in 1976 by humanist philosopher Paul Kurtz and is endorsed by well-known scientists. Its aim is not to carry out research itself, but to correct the uncritical promotion of the paranormal in the media; its bi-monthly magazine *Skeptical Inquirer* is popular with scientists and sceptics.[6] One of the best-known of its books is James Randi's *Flim-Flam! Psychics, ESP, Unicorns and Other Delusions* (1982).[7] Randi takes the view that most paranormal claims are delusional, and that fraud is a safe explanation in many cases. The book is a satirical romp and makes short work of people who either think they have psychic powers or who want other people to think so. For myself, my disbelief was not so complete that I could fully appreciate Randi's sarcasm, and I was interested to see if there was another side to any of these stories.

Kurtz's *The Transcendental Temptation* (1987) avoids rhetoric, which makes it clearer and more accessible.[8] As an atheist, Kurtz offers a critique of religion that explains among other things why mediums *cannot* be in touch with the dead. He tackles the spiritualist movement that swept America and Europe in the second half of the nineteenth century, inspired by the belief that spirits of the dead could communicate by knocking on pieces of furniture and causing them to tip and turn. This movement, which became a craze, was started by events that befell a family by the name of Fox in their small farmhouse near the town of Rochester, New York in 1848. Overall, their story fitted the pattern of poltergeist claims but, as Kurtz points out, the family's two teenage daughters owned up in later life to having played a prank. The revelation fatally undermined the new religion's credibility to outsiders, although it made no impression on spiritualists themselves, who continued to believe. That, Kurtz laments, is absolutely typical of many people who seem unable to accept proofs of trickery, no matter how final they may be. Psychics and mediums are often endorsed as genuine by scientists, yet hardly one of them has not been exposed as fraudulent or strongly suspected of it.

As an example Kurtz mentions an episode that occurred in Columbus, Ohio in 1984. In March of that year stories started appearing in the local press about strange goings on in the home of the Resch family, which some speculated were caused by a poltergeist.

Eventually a press photographer snapped the spook in action, and the photo was syndicated around the world – causing a sensation. In reality, Kurtz says, the effects were being caused by the family's fourteen-year-old foster child, Tina, as James Randi discovered when he went to investigate. There are several other cases of this kind. In *Looking for a Miracle* (1993), sceptical investigator Joe Nickell relates the origin of mysterious 'poltergeist' fires that plagued an Alabama household.[9] The family's nine-year old son admitted starting the fires in an attempt to force his family to return to their previous home. In another case, an eleven-year-old girl eventually confessed she was responsible for strange disturbances in her own household, which she had caused because her mother had been in hospital and she had been feeling neglected.

Other stories that were widely believed to be true were later comprehensively debunked. In Terence Hines's *Pseudoscience and the Paranormal* (1988) I found mention of Borley Rectory in Essex, touted by ghost-hunter Harry Price in the 1930s as the most famous haunted house in England. Price had reported a variety of paranormal phenomena, such as spontaneous fires, mysterious cold spots and unexplained ringing of bells. Hines also mentions the celebrated case of Amityville in New York, in which the new occupants of a large rambling house (where a series of murders had been committed a year earlier) told of mysterious voices, green slime oozing from the walls and doors being ripped off their hinges.[10]

Both stories reached a wide public. Jay Anson's racy description of *The Amityville Horror* sold over three million copies and spawned a series of blood-curdling Hollywood films. Yet as Hines tells, the true explanation eventually came to light. One of the occupants at Amityville, a troubled twenty-eight-year-old named George Lutz, kept changing his story, and as he was suffering money problems at the time it was widely supposed that he and his wife had simply made up the story for financial gain. The Borley case too was picked apart; rival investigators showed that Price had exaggerated witness statements and the occupants had probably faked some of the goings-on.[11]

I found more details about poltergeist claims in *Anomalistic Psychology* (1982) by Warren H. Jones and Leonard Zusne, psychologists at the University of Tulsa. These authors pointed out that one William G. Roll, whom they name as the principal contemporary investigator of the poltergeist phenomenon, has counted one hundred and sixteen cases that have been witnessed by the author of the report or some other reliable informant. Of these, ninety-two centred on individuals, typically young teenagers known to have exhibited signs of repressed hostility towards their parents or employers. The psychologists reasonably concluded that they were engaging in secret destructive behaviour as a way to release pent-up feelings, adding that most of the reports could be attributed to poor observation, memory lapses, and wishful thinking.[12]

These details started to get my attention. Numerical data is always good to have, and it was surprising that at least a hundred cases existed for which there was some documentary evidence. Perhaps the reports would reveal more facts. But where could I find them? And who was this fellow Roll?

3 *A close-up look*

Here and there, as I read, I came across references to the Society for Psychical Research (SPR), an organization founded in Cambridge in 1882 and dedicated to the investigation of paranormal phenomena. It now occurred to me that it might still exist, in which case it must have at least some of the early poltergeist material.[13] I tracked it down to an address in west London, although, rather absurdly, I hesitated for a while before making a visit, for fear of getting mixed up with peculiar people who might insist I join them on ghost-hunting expeditions to Scottish castles. However, they turned out to be quite normal and, most important, to be in possession of a well-stocked specialist library.

Looking around their archives I was astonished by how much scientific work had been done on all kinds of paranormal topics. Nothing had prepared me for this; there was no hint of it in the sceptics' books or anywhere else, for that matter. To date the SPR has produced around a hundred and twenty-five volumes of proceedings and journals going back the same number of years, densely packed with scholarly reports of investigations and experiments into ghosts, mediums, telepathy and suchlike, as well as surveys, reviews and debates, and all accompanied by a very lively correspondence. I also found publications by other research organizations, such as the American *Journal of Parapsychology* and *Journal of Scientific Exploration*. In marked contrast to the popular books often found in shops and libraries, paranormal claims in these documents are picked apart in forensic detail, with a detached and often sceptical spirit.

Poltergeist incidents turned out to be among the first topics the SPR looked at. From the early 1880s, their investigators tracked down reports, travelling to the scene itself and interrogating as many eyewitnesses as they could find. They dismissed several episodes as hoaxes but considered some to be genuinely anomalous, in the sense that no conceivable trick or natural phenomenon could successfully account for them. The physicist William Barrett, a driving force in the nascent organization, claimed to have observed poltergeist activity at first hand. A number of other reports are scattered through the journals right up to the present day.[14] The society's library also contains books about individual episodes. *This House Is Haunted* describes a series of events in Enfield, North London, in 1977 and 1978.[15] Matthew Manning, now a psychic healer, tells how he was the focus of a series of poltergeist-type events at his boarding school and family home in Cambridge during the 1970s.[16] Here too

I found books and articles by William Roll, and another American researcher named David Scott Rogo; also material by British writers such as Alan Gauld, A.D. Cornell and A.R.G. Owen, and the German parapsychologist Hans Bender. All of them described cases they had personally investigated[17] and some also summarized historical cases that were first reported in books and pamphlets dating from the sixteenth century.[18]

If these writers are to be believed, the scale of the phenomenon is far greater than is generally understood, and certainly better documented. But this body of evidence is not really reflected in the sceptics' writings. Zusne and Jones get their figure of just a hundred and sixteen reports from an article by William Roll in Benjamin Wolman's *The Handbook of Parapsychology* (1986), a collection of papers by paranormal researchers, [19] and imply this number is too small to be significant. However Roll was more thorough as an investigator than as a historical researcher, and it is misleading to use him as the main source in this respect. Gauld and Cornell, joint authors of *Poltergeists*, identified five hundred cases for which there are published records, and their list would have been much longer, they say, if they had included unsubstantiated media reports.

If we assume many cases never get reported, then Terence Hines is probably nearer the mark when he talks about 'thousands' of such events having occurred. However, I'm not sure I agree when he describes them as 'mild, even humorous'.[20] Witnesses talk of cutlery, cups and plates flinging themselves off kitchen shelves; eggs and other foodstuffs floating around the kitchen and smashing into the walls; ornaments and children's toys flying across the living room, hitting people on the head; tables, chairs and stools sliding abruptly across the floor; heavy objects like armchairs, sofas and cabinets tipping onto their sides or even turning upside down; drawers sliding open; pictures falling off walls; and lights, radios and other appliances switching themselves on and off repeatedly, without warning. There are several episodes of stones being thrown from an empty space, sometimes raining down from the ceiling and others in which fires constantly break out around the house. Yet others involve unexplained floods of water and other liquids that occur despite the absence of any apparent fault in the plumbing system. The most persistent reported phenomena are strange scratching or banging sounds, often referred to as 'raps', and these come from within walls, the floor or furniture – usually presaging more serious disturbances.

The ructions caused by these incidents are much as one might expect. The family concerned are first puzzled, then alarmed. They ask neighbours to come round and reassure them that they not going mad. The visitors are just as perplexed. Their next step is usually to call the police: one or two patrol officers duly turn up and may witness the disturbances themselves, but they offer no useful suggestions and soon leave. Next at the scene, maybe a day or two later, is likely to be some interested professional person such as a local doctor or vicar, or a local reporter who has heard something about it. The resulting media report will alert parapsychologists, who hurry along to see if they can capture evidence of the phenomenon. By this time, some two or three weeks after the initial outbreak, two things will typically have happened: the disturbances will have lost some of their earlier momentum, becoming more sporadic and intermittent, and a brouhaha will have erupted, in which the parapsychologists find themselves jostling with relatives and neighbours, utility engineers and press reporters, photographers and television crews, sceptics and scoffers, spirit mediums, exorcists, teachers, psychiatrists and social workers – all energetically pushing their own explanations and agendas.

There is also a third development, and one that becomes more marked as the episode progresses – the emergence of one particular member of the family as the prime suspect. Most typically it will be a girl aged between twelve and fifteen, although boys are also often involved, and their ages generally range from eight to twenty. The child is variously accused of causing the disturbances by trickery, said to have confessed doing so or reported to have been caught in the act. In some cases the investigator who writes the subsequent report is satisfied that trickery is the main cause, while in others he or she rejects this idea – even if the child has been seen playing tricks – on the grounds that it doesn't explain events that were previously witnessed and that could not have been caused in that way, for instance because the child was not anywhere close at the time.[21]

As well as keeping a close eye on the suspected child, serious investigators test for possible natural causes. Perhaps unusually heavy traffic outside is causing enough vibration to make objects fall off shelves.[22] One theory developed in the 1930s suggested many cases can be explained by the effects of underground streams, although this never really caught on.[23] Some anomalous sounds have been traced to birds, rodents or insects,[24] and other spurious events have been founded on superstitious fancies.[25] Yet there have been many cases in which the investigators observed the phenomena themselves and were no better able to pinpoint the cause than the people who first experienced it. As I say, although they often suspected a child of trying to play tricks, they became convinced from their own repeated observations that the child could not have been wholly responsible and was just imitating certain phenomena in order to be the focus of attention.[26]

Few investigators were in a hurry to speculate on the cause of the disturbance, although some abandoned the original concept of a malign 'noisy spirit'. Since the youngsters at the centre of the disturbances were frequently discovered to be suffering from repressed emotion for some identifiable reason – family upsets, difficult relationships with step-parents, and the like – it made more sense to view the incidents in terms of an eruption of mental energy that somehow interacts with material surroundings.[27] For this reason, parapsychologists tend to refer to the phenomenon as psychokinesis (PK) or 'macro-PK' (as distinct from the small-scale 'micro-PK' that experimenters try to demonstrate in laboratory conditions). William Roll's more elaborate definition of 'recurrent spontaneous psychokinesis' (RSPK) is also sometimes applied. But the fact remains that there is no explanation of any physical mechanisms for the interaction between mind and matter, and the idea of such a thing is utterly rejected by the scientific community.

4 Outside the house

Whatever the cause, there's common agreement that humans are involved in creating these disturbances, as a means of expressing some inner turmoil. But while parapsychologists think it's involuntary, not caused by any known process, sceptics apply Occam's razor. This principle, originally attributed to the fourteenth-century logician and Franciscan friar William of Ockham, says that we should not increase, beyond what is necessary, the number of entities required to explain anything. In other words, it's simpler to assume these people are doing it deliberately. Investigators can't accept this, the critics argue, because they are always looking for something that reinforces their prior belief in the genuineness of paranormal phenomena. That makes them uncritical – easy prey for tricksters and publicity seekers.

I think it's fair to say that this view of parapsychologists is prevalent among committed sceptics, certainly those like Randi and Kurtz who campaign against paranormal belief. To me, though, Gauld, Cornell, Roll, Scott Rogo and other investigators come across as intelligent and level-headed, each of them simply concerned with getting to the bottom of a rather puzzling problem. It is of course true that their failure to pinpoint a natural cause opens up all sorts of problems for science, and can be construed as some sort of proof for the existence of ghosts and spirits. But most investigators don't seem especially interested in pushing this issue, and they don't give the impression that they are following some anti-science or occultic or religious agenda. What's more, the fact that some of them see the phenomena in terms of a psychological eruption puts some distance between them and those who consider such things to be the doings of the dead.

What chiefly puzzled me as I thought about the naughty child explanation was how these children could achieve the extraordinary effects described in the eyewitness reports. I didn't rule it out, of course, I simply couldn't visualize how it could be done, and wanted to see how the link between these two rather disparate ideas could be established in satisfying detail. So I took a closer look at what the sceptics were saying.

I started with James Randi's debunking of the Columbus episode of March 1984 about the trouble experienced by the Resch family. This affair had come to the attention of Paul Kurtz, who picked it up in the national news and contacted Randi to ask if he would join a three-man team tasked with identifying the true cause. Randi agreed and hastened to the scene, where he found a media scrum of more than forty reporters, cameramen and hangers-on. However to his chagrin the family would not let him into the house, presumably having been warned about his reputation by Roll (who had already arrived and was investigating the affair himself). This of course meant that Randi could not identify the fraud at its source. His two colleagues were allowed in but they refused to go without him, and seemed to have little further involvement in the matter.

Undeterred, Randi focused instead on the media coverage. His main target was a photograph taken by Fred Shannon from the local newspaper, the *Columbus Dispatch*, which was syndicated internationally through the Associated Press. This image showed Tina Resch, the teenager at the centre of the disturbance, sitting in an armchair and starting back with alarm at a telephone that appears to be flying across the room in front of her, from left to right. Randi talked to Fred Shannon, who said that nothing had happened when he was looking directly at Tina; the only way to capture an incident was to keep the camera trained on her and look away slightly, pressing the shutter whenever he saw something move in his peripheral vision.

Quite reasonably, Randi concluded that Tina had simply waited until no-one was looking before carrying out the actions herself. He persuaded Shannon to let him see the other thirty-five frames on the roll from which the published photograph was taken. In his subsequent report he analyzed the scene: with the help of an artist's renditions of some of the unpublished frames, he demonstrated that by grabbing the telephone cord at a spot near her right hand, and yanking it hard, Tina could have caused it to fly up into exactly the position shown – without being observed by Shannon. Randi remarked that an atmosphere of 'loose gaiety' prevailed in the house at the time, and that Tina was given a great deal of latitude, for instance holding the phone in her hand while carrying on an animated conversation with other people in the room, which would have given her the opportunity to cheat.

Randi also managed to view some videotape footage that caught Tina in the act of cheating. A television crew had been vainly trying to film the spook and finally gave up, but while they were packing away their gear they left a camera running, aimed at Tina sitting on the sofa, and only discovered what was on the tape when they looked at it later. Randi describes the scene: 'Seated at one end of the sofa, near an end-table, and believing the camera was no longer active, she watched carefully until she was unobserved, then reached up and pulled a table-lamp toward herself, simultaneously jumping away, letting out a series of bleating noises, and feigning, quite effectively, a reaction of stark terror'.[28] When confronted with this, Tina admitted faking the effect but maintained she was only fooling in order to get rid of the camera crew.

Randi then talked to some of the reporters who had been sent to cover the incidents, and having seen nothing were somewhat jaded. One said he suspected the real story was the duping of the media. Others gave damning details that tended to support the idea of fraud but which were never reported, and one complained about news editors who had altered his copy for dramatic effect.

Finally Randi turned his attention to Roll, who had spent three days in the house trying to witness the phenomena himself. On his departure Roll gave a press conference in a local hotel in which he described incidents that had convinced him that this was not a teenage hoax but a genuine case of psychokinesis. Randi points out that Roll's evidence was only acquired during half an hour right at the end of his visit, when no other witnesses were present. Further, Roll did not see the movements directly, but simply inferred that Tina could not have been responsible because of her position relative to them at the time. Randi adds: 'Roll is myopic and wears thick glasses: he is a poor observer'.[29]

All this struck me as effective debunking. It didn't demonstrate beyond doubt that the Columbus affair was a hoax, but it did weaken any sense I might have had that the incident was paranormal. Analyzing the unpublished photographs was a clever stroke; it showed resourcefulness and inspired confidence that Randi knew what he was doing. Randi also complained about the relative lack of independent corroboration of the witness's testimony. Roll's might have had some weight, but turned out to be quite limited.

5 *Another debunking magician*

Sceptical writers also draw on examples provided by the magician Milbourne Christopher in his book entitled *Seers, Psychics and ESP* (1970), a critical study of various paranormal phenomena. In a short chapter on poltergeists Christopher briefly describes nine incidents that occurred in America between 1944 and 1964. Most sound exactly like the kind of cases reported in the parapsychological literature, other than the fact that they were resolved in some way or ceased to attract any more interest. In one case the disturbances ceased when a protective cover was placed on the chimney of the house, suggesting they had been caused by a downward draught. In another, a girl admitted causing a ruckus after traces of a light powder (covertly dusted onto objects) were found on her hands. Children confessed to playing tricks in three other cases. There was also an episode in which a girl was seen by an investigating magician to drop an object she had concealed previously (although Christopher notes that this was inconclusive evidence). Yet another reports how disturbances in one family ceased when the police threatened them with lie detector tests.

Unfortunately Christopher provides no references for these sources, although the sketchiness of the details suggests they are press reports. However he does describe in more depth a particular case that occurred in 1958 in Seaford, Long Island, which he himself followed up.[30] Like the Columbus episode that followed, this received international media coverage and was subsequently investigated by Roll, accompanied then by his colleague Gaither Pratt.

The Seaford disturbances took place in February 1958 in a house occupied by a family with two children aged twelve and thirteen. Disturbances were characterized chiefly by bottles that unaccountably popped their tops and spilled their contents, sometimes falling onto their sides. When interviewed by Roll, the family members described several occasions when they had seen the objects moving on their own. In one instance the father had been standing in the doorway of the bathroom when suddenly he saw a medicine bottle slide about eighteen inches across a bathroom surface and drop into the basin, and at the same time a shampoo bottle slid in a different direction and clattered to the floor. A local police detective took up the case and warned both children that they would be in big trouble if they were found to be responsible, yet this didn't stop the disturbances from continuing. On one occasion an ornament crashed to the floor and broke while the detective was in the room with one of the boys, and he subjected him to a severe grilling; the child burst into tears and insisted he had nothing to do with it.

As a debunking conjuror, Christopher's attentions were no more welcome than Randi's had been at Columbus. Barred from the house, he worked instead with reports of what had occurred, inviting journalists to his home to show them how he could perform similar feats. The reporters would hear popping noises from the bathroom, for example, and would rush in to find shampoo bottles lying on their sides, spilling liquid – exactly the type of incident that had been reported in the Seaford house. The trick was boringly simple: seconds previously, Christopher's wife, who had been hiding in the bedroom, had slipped into the bathroom and overturned the bottles, chucking some glass marbles into an enamel bowl on her way out to make explosive sounds to replicate bottles popping their tops. Or the reporters might see ornaments leaping off a shelf on their own initiative, a feat Christopher achieved with a complex arrangement of threads. If this explanation seems far-fetched, Christopher adds, there's at least one known precedent: an eighteenth-century case in which a young woman attached long horsehairs to objects and yanked them when no-one was looking.

6 *The Fox sisters confess*

A third case, which is clearly relevant here, is the well-known story of the Fox sisters as touched on above. At least it seems relevant to me, for reasons I'll come to; interestingly few sceptics categorize it as a poltergeist incident, seeing it instead as the prototype for fake mediumship.[31] Here's a brief summary of what happened, based on contemporary statements by the girls' mother and other eyewitnesses.[32]

Sometime during November of 1848, Maggie Fox, then aged fourteen, and Kate, then aged twelve, drew their parents' attention to strange 'rapping' noises in their bedroom at night. The parents heard the noises too but were unable to identify what was causing them. The neighbours were called in and they too heard the raps, but they were likewise mystified. At a certain point one of the girls discovered that the noises would respond to her spoken commands, which led to them to develop a rudimentary code – two knocks for 'yes', one for 'no', and so on. In this way it was understood that they were in communication with the spirit of an itinerant peddler who claimed that he had been murdered in the house by a previous occupant. Subsequently other people said they would receive accurate responses to spoken questions about intimate personal matters, which made them believe that the spirits of their dead relatives were also present. The noises followed the girls when they moved to the nearby town of Rochester, where inconclusive attempts were made to find out what was going on. In subsequent years, the two girls, together with their elder sister, Leah, became in great demand as mediums, passing on messages from the dead by means of the raps – an activity that other people soon found they could carry out too.

Considering the enormous historical impact of the spiritualist movement that was launched by these events, it's interesting to see what Maggie Fox said about them four decades years later. In a theatre booked for the purpose she denounced spiritualism as a miserable subject that would do great evil unless it was suppressed, and since she had started it all off, she said, she had every right to expose it. 'My sister Katie and myself were very young children when this horrible deception began,' Maggie said. 'I was eight, and just a year and a half older than she. We were very mischievous children and we wanted to terrify our dear mother, who was a very good woman and very easily frightened'.[33] Their original method was to tie a piece of string to an apple and then covertly bump it on the floor, pretending the noise was being made by an invisible spirit. This worked well, and Maggie went on to describe how, under Leah's tutelage, the two little girls learned to make raps by cracking their fingers and the joints of their toes against any surface that would conduct sound.

> The rappings are simply the result of a perfect control of the muscles of the leg below the knee which govern the tendons of the foot and allow action of the toe and ankle bones that are not commonly known. Such perfect control is only possible when a child is taken at an early age and carefully and continually taught to practise the muscles which grow still in later years. A child at twelve is almost too old. With control of the muscles of the foot the toes may be brought down to the floor without any movement that is perceptible to the eye. The whole foot, in fact, can be made to give rappings by the use only of muscles below the knee. This, then, is the simple explanation of the whole method of the knocks and raps.[34]

A similar account was given independently only three years after the first manifestations. An aunt of the two sisters, named Mrs Culver, claimed that Kate had explained to her exactly how she caused the noises by manipulating the muscles in her toes. Culver also described how Kate used mentalist skills, for example watching out for minute muscle movements on people's faces to reveal their reactions. Kate, Culver claimed, said that to make raps sound distant on the wall she would 'make them louder and direct my own eyes earnestly to the spot where I wished them heard'.[35]

Before these revelations, the initial investigations had produced mixed results. Several times the girls were examined by committees in public, where the knockings were very much in evidence, but no trickery was discovered. Yet many professionals – doctors, professors, priests and other worthies – wrote articles, gave lectures and made public statements to the effect that they had investigated the girls and were convinced that they were making the knocks themselves. They pointed out variously that the noises were always heard on a surface that the girls' bodies or dresses were touching, that the girls' faces showed signs of effort when the noises were in progress, and that when they held the girls' legs the noises ceased. They also discovered that noises could be made by cracking the toe joints.

7 *Some eyewitness testimony*

These objections look pretty decisive. If we accept that there is no other indication of a link between mind and matter, that centuries of accumulated scientific evidence rules it out, then the most reasonable and economical course must be to reject poltergeist claims – however convincing they may sometimes appear.

Yet there was something here that didn't seem quite right to me, and it kept drawing me back. If you read the literature on the subject you'll find that poltergeist incidents tend to be extraordinarily *fraught*. The people involved are overcome with panic and confusion, not just for a few hours but for days and weeks on end. This isn't an effect one expects to result from mere children's pranks. And as I said before, I often wondered how these children managed to create such convincing illusions and remain undetected.

I'll come back to this later, but first I want to tell you about something else I found. Despite their decidedly odd character, the claims are quite uniform. When Gauld and Cornell analyzed their five hundred cases they found that nearly half began with noises that were described as raps or 'knockings' or sometimes as loud thumps or thuds or 'bangings'.[36] The descriptions suggested that they often occurred after dark, often close to someone who was sleeping, although they were sometimes also heard in daylight hours.

This is how the Fox girls' mother described them, three years after the original event:

> The first night we heard the rapping we all got up, lit a candle, and searched all over the house. The noise continued while we were hunting, and was heard near the same place all the time. It was not very loud, yet it produced a jar of the bedsteads and chairs that could be felt by placing our hands on the chairs, or while we were in bed. It was a feeling of tremulous motion, more than a sudden jar.[37]

Compare this to a 1997 report by SPR researchers Maurice Grosse and Mary Rose Barrington, who checked out incidents occurring in the vicinity of a young boy in a flat in north London, and wrote as follows:

> [The knocking] moved around the top of the bed, banging at the top and then at the foot and sometimes at both places at once. It knocked very loudly at the base of the bed where it joined the wall and when I opened the cupboard at the base of the headboard there were a number of loud bangs. I tried everything in my power to locate the noise, placing my hands under the pillow, and then under the mattress, but with no success.[38]

Another similar instance was reported by the neighbour of a Mrs Harper, the mother of two adolescent girls in the Enfield disturbances ten years earlier:

> All I could hear was this knocking, and I didn't know what it was, just a strange knock on the wall. I went up the stairs, and as I went up the knock followed me. I got three distinctive knocks on the wall. I carried on up the stairs, went into the front bedroom – three knocks on the wall again. Strange, I thought to myself. I'm beginning to shake. I go in the back bedroom – same thing again – knocks following me.[39]

The British investigator Owen reported a case he followed up in Sauchie in Scotland in 1960. He interviewed a local vicar who had gone late one night to investigate some unexplained noises occurring in the close vicinity of eleven-year-old Virginia Campbell:

> On entering at the front door he heard loud knockings in progress. Going upstairs he found Virginia awake, but not greatly excited, in the double bed... The loud knocking noise continued and appeared to emanate from the bed-head. Mr Lund moved Virginia down in to the bed so that she could not strike or push the bed-head with her head, and he also verified that her feet were well tucked in under the bed clothes, and held in by them. The knocking continued. During the knocking Mr Lund held the bed-head. He felt it vibrating in unison with the noises.[40]

I could go on for quite a while longer; these examples make up only about three per cent of Gauld and Cornell's data.[41] The point is, what the Fox family and their neighbours said they heard, and what the sisters later said was a childish prank, was broadly identical to hundreds of other documented cases, in the majority of which investigators and witnesses failed to find any cause at all for, and in which nobody confessed to playing tricks, whether by bumping apples tied to string on the floor, or by cracking their toe joints, or anything else.

What made the Fox case so sensational – and so historically significant – was the element of responsiveness, that is the fact that the source of the knockings seemed to be intelligent, capable of answering people's questions, even of divining their unspoken thoughts. Interestingly, this feature too is abundantly present in the investigative literature. Here are some examples. In a Swiss case, a person present during a disturbance asked the invisible source to knock three times, which it did, and then five times, which again it also did.[42] A nun in a French convent was followed wherever she went by strange thuds and bangings; a priest sent to investigate said it seemed as though an 'uneasy soul' was trying to communicate, and if asked to rap a certain number of times it would do so exactly.[43] A Turkish school-teacher wrote to the SPR in 1905 describing the case of a local villager in whose presence unexplained raps were continually heard; it was discovered that their source, whatever it was, could answer questions accurately.[44] William Barrett, investigating a case in Derrygonnelly in Ireland in 1877, made the same discovery:

> To avoid any error or delusion on my part, I put my hands in the side pockets of my overcoat and asked it to knock the number of fingers I had open. It correctly did so. Then with a different number of fingers open each time, the experiment was repeated four times in succession, and four times I obtained absolutely the correct number of raps.[45]

Significantly, in both of the last two examples the investigator's request was *thought*, not uttered aloud. When it comes to the anomalous movement of objects, it's striking how insistent witnesses are that no-one present was responsible. They could see no link between the disturbance and any human action – and it completely spooked them. For instance a policewoman summoned at the onset of the Enfield incidents later described how she had seen a chair rise in the air and then slide a few feet across the floor. She said, 'I'm absolutely convinced that no-one in that room touched that chair or went anywhere near it when it moved. Absolutely convinced.'[46] Similarly a reporter from the *Daily Mirror* said that while he had been in the house he had seen toy building bricks hurtling around the room:

> The [toy bricks] came from one side of the room, came up into the corner, hit it very fast, very straight. Nobody had moved their arm, nobody could have flicked or thrown or whatever that [brick], nor any of the others. There were four or five pieces thrown while I was there, and one of them struck me on the head. I had a lump on my forehead for three or four days afterwards.[47]

A commonly noted feature is the unnatural way in which the objects often move. In a case that took place in Miami, which I'll describe in more detail shortly, a witness saw a beer mug 'sort of scoot off the shelf horizontally, and then abruptly fall'.[48] In the Enfield case, marbles that hurtled around the room at great speed were seen coming to rest on the floor as though they had been gently placed there, without bouncing.[49] The phenomenon was also described by Hans Bender in a case at Nickleheim in Germany, when a stone falling from the ceiling failed to bounce but remained glued in place, as though fastened by a magnet.[50]

8 Inside the house

There is a quantity of suggestive detail in the investigators' accounts that creates a rather different picture from the one provided by sceptics. The Columbus episode is a good example.[51] According to Roll's account (which was based on interviews with the family), immediately prior to the incident Tina had been in growing conflict with her adoptive parents, particularly with her father John. On one particular day John tried to punish her with a beating, but she resisted. That night in her bedroom she was surprised to see the figures on her digital clock-radio racing forwards. Then the sound came on, and she had to unplug it to make it stop. Over the next two days there were similar problems elsewhere in the house – the baby alarm monitor and the television both switched themselves on unexpectedly, and the clocks on the walls downstairs also started racing (they ran on batteries so the problem could not have been caused by a surge in the main electricity supply). At a certain point the clothes dryer switched itself on and Tina's mother Joan opened its door to stop it. But as soon as she left the room the machine's door slammed shut and it came on again. At this stage, Joan accused

Tina of fooling and made her sit where she could see her. But even then, she opened the dryer's door to turn it off and it slammed shut and started running again. Joan later told Roll that Tina was useless at covering up mischief she had caused; she also observed that in this case Tina seemed to be genuinely puzzled.

John, by contrast, continued for some time to believe that Tina was the source of the problems. However his doubts increased after he spent much of that weekend trying to stop the lights and appliances coming on by themselves. An electrician called in to help could trace no fault, and eventually realized that the problems had nothing to do with the circuits – the switches themselves were flipping up and down. The electrician tried to stop this by taping the switches down, but as fast as he could do so the lights came on again. Sometimes the tape simply disappeared, even when Tina was fully in his view.

The following Monday morning Joan heard knocking from the front door. Before she could answer, she realized the noise was coming from a candle-holder in the hallway which was banging hard against the wall. She watched it from the kitchen until finally it broke. Then, again as she watched, a carton of apple juice that had been standing on the counter by the sink sailed into the living room and crashed into an outside door, spilling juice everywhere. Following this, a picture hanging in the hallway and another large one hanging over the couch in the living room started swinging back and forth on their hooks. Joan and Tina held them in place, but when they let go, Joan said, the pictures went back to swinging.

William Roll became involved after having been contacted by Mike Harding, a reporter on the *Columbus Dispatch* who had written an article about the Resches' child-fostering activities a few months earlier. On his first visit Harding described how he was standing in the kitchen, looking into the living room, when suddenly magazines and newspapers on the end table 'shot out' and fell two or three feet away. Tina was nowhere near them. His first thought, he told Roll, was 'What the hell was that?'. Harding then went into the living room and sat down on a large couch, across from an armchair where Tina was sitting. As he talked with the girl and her mother, a small toy cradle lying near the fireplace 'flipped into the air, perhaps two feet, and dropped to the carpeting'. Tina was about six feet away. Just as he was trying to make sense of this, a full cup of coffee on a table beside Tina flipped through the air, and landed on her lap, spilling coffee, before crashing into the fireplace. Harding said: 'She was in my line of vision when it happened. Again, I didn't see her aid its movement in any way'.[52]

If any of this is to be believed, clearly there is more going on than comes through in Randi's account. You might well disbelieve it – perhaps that would be the most sensible course to take, like the sceptical philosopher David Hume, to suppose that the witnesses are exaggerating or just making things up. If this were an isolated incident, or one of only a small number, I would be inclined to think that the claims of Tina and her mother were invented, and that outside witnesses such as Harding were in collusion with them for the purpose of creating a lucrative story. I hesitate to do so, however, because, as I said before, what the Resches and other witnesses described to Roll is reflected in hundreds of other very similar reports. You may still consider this a small number, but they are dramatic and detailed and, despite their utterly bizarre nature, they are broadly consistent. The accumulated effect of reading them was to create in my mind the sense of a very distinct natural phenomenon, one which is widely (if infrequently) reported and quite unlike any other feature of human experience, yet which can be identified by the same group of curious features.

9 Detailed investigations

It was with this thought in mind that I started to review Randi's debunking in a different light. I realized that his article didn't get to grips with the goings-on in Columbus in any depth; his approach was mostly centred on a single detail – that is the photograph of Tina seated on a chair, allegedly watching the telephone jumping across in front of her. I wasn't even sure how much his analysis proved. If you think about it, an image that claims to show psychokinesis in action is a moot object: there is nothing that it could depict that could not easily be faked. Photographs have been produced of spirits, the Loch Ness monster and countless UFOs, but such things are rarely more than curiosities except to committed believers.

So Randi was simply adding substance to what many people would suspect anyway. But by doing so, and in such detail, he created the illusion that he had penetrated the whole mystery, despite the fact that he had not observed any of the claimed effects at first hand or interviewed any of the main witnesses, and therefore could not know exactly what it was he was supposed to be exposing.

Then there's Randi's oft-repeated insistence that witnesses jump to conclusions: I did not feel this was really confirmed in the research literature. People who experience these disturbances, I found, tend to react exactly as one might expect – and probably as you or I would. They don't instantly imagine that something paranormal is occurring; on the contrary, they start by assuming that a trick is being played, and, if a child seems to have something to do with it, treat him or her as the likely culprit.

Professional investigators also do the obvious things – like taking up the floorboards to see if the noises have some concealed source, or setting traps that might reveal hoaxing by family members.[53] As I say, in some cases they decide that trickery is probably the whole cause; in others they suspect it has a genuine basis, but subsequent trickery by the child makes that conclusion difficult to insist on. In other cases, the force of repeated observations at close quarters compels them to drop the idea of trickery altogether and look for something else. In short, they show what most people would consider to be proper judiciousness, discrimination and caution.

In fact, considering how controversial the claims continue to be, it's extraordinary how unequivocal the conclusion of a paranormal process at work has sometimes been. A particularly striking example is the episode investigated by Roll in Miami in the winter of 1966–67.[54] A warehouse containing souvenir items was the centre of a series of unexplained disturbances over a period of weeks. The items were knick-knacks with a Florida theme – ashtrays, glasses, ornaments and the like – stacked on shelves arranged in a simple grid system. The problem started in mid-December when objects fell off the shelves on several separate occasions for no apparent reason. The owner, Alvin Laubheim, at first assumed his staff were being careless. Then one day he realized that this might not be the problem after all. He had just shown an employee how to arrange glasses on a shelf so that they could not fall, and was walking away, when one crashed to the floor, even though it had just been placed at least eight inches from the edge of the shelf. According to Laubheim none of the staff was nearer than fifteen feet at the moment it fell. At this point boxes started to fall down on the other side of the room, and Laubheim realized something was definitely wrong. Over the next few days ornaments fell from the shelves as fast as he and his staff could pick them up and replace them. At first they tried to keep it quiet, but then delivery men started to see it. Word got around and curiosity seekers came in, at which point Laubheim called the police.

Laubheim, quoted by Roll, was adamant that various objects, both single ornaments and boxes containing several items, fell off the shelves without any visible cause. Roll quotes similar testimony from a police officer, a reporter and an insurance agent, who examined the premises for physical explanations such as floor tremors or instability of the shelves, but failed to find anything that might have caused the disturbances.

Then others arrived. Susy Smith, a writer of popular parapsychology books, visited the premises for two weeks and kept a record of what she witnessed. Other observations of objects falling onto the floor were recorded by an airline pilot and his wife. A professional stage magician, a friend of Laubheim's named Howard Brooks, also turned up and at first made light of the reports, showing how he could duplicate the incidents by trickery. On several subsequent visits, however, he witnessed breakages that occurred when no-one was in the vicinity, and he ceased thinking that trickery was the explanation. Working with Smith and other interested observers he set up objects in places where there had just been an incident, to see if it would be repeated, often with success. This experimental process was repeated by Roll, who arrived on the scene later after being alerted by Smith, and was followed by his colleague Gaither Pratt.

It was apparent almost from the start that the disturbances occurred in the presence of one staff member in particular, a nineteen-year old Cuban refugee named Julio. Accordingly he became the focus of intense observation. Roll goes into some detail about this and about his observations of other people in the warehouse, concluding that the movements could not be put down to them. He also describes how he made constant checks on objects to see if they had been tampered with or prepared in any way. But despite the concentrated efforts of himself and many other people involved, no direct connection between the breakages and any action by Julio was ever observed.

Another workplace incident, reported by German parapsychologist Hans Bender, is also worth mentioning at this point. It occurred in 1967 in a lawyers' office in the Bavarian town of Rosenheim.[55] Investigators watched and filmed as decorative plates jumped off the walls, paintings began to swing and drawers opened by themselves. There was rogue electrical activity, too: lights and fuses kept blowing, and the telephones all rang at once, with no-one on the line. As many as forty people were said to have witnessed the events, including power technicians, police officers, doctors, journalists and the firm's clients. In this case, the disturbances were associated with a nineteen-year-old secretary named Annemarie Schneider. When she walked through the hall, the lamps behind her began to swing and light fixtures exploded, the fragments flying towards her. Scientists from the Max Planck Institute in Munich, called in to help, used monitoring equipment to systematically eliminate every physical cause, including variations in the supply of current, electrostatic charges, static magnetism, loose contacts and faulty equipment. Critically, they also ruled out manual intervention and concluded that the electrical deflections could only be due to some unknown energy that depended in some way on Schneider.

What is significant about both these cases is that anomalous, apparently psychokinetic phenomena were observed by a number of different people of the type one would not normally think credulous. Both situations were favourable for investigation: being in a work environment meant that the normal family dynamics didn't intrude, and the disturbances were not so serious that the businesses could not continue to function. The Rosenheim lawyers soon lost patience and dismissed the secretary, after which calm soon returned. However in Miami Laubheim continued to be intrigued by what was going on and was fortunately not too bothered about the breakages. In his warehouse the layout was clear, with unobstructed aisles and tiers, and this made it easy to establish which members of staff were where at any given moment – far easier than if it had been a family home. And since a conjuror was present in the Miami warehouse case, it cannot be maintained that the witnesses were altogether unqualified to make accurate observations.

Of course, the truth of all these accounts does depend on the honesty and integrity of the investigators. In cases such as Columbus, Miami and Rosenheim we are offered a variety of viewpoints from different witnesses. Yet their statements are not all on public record, signed and sealed and ready for our independent inspection; they are collected and passed on by individuals like Roll and Bender. We might hesitate to take such limited sources on trust. Perhaps I should suspend judgement on these particularly compelling cases until I have personally interviewed the key witnesses – the magician Howard Brooks, the technicians from the Max Planck Institute, Alvin Laubheim, the lawyers and other eyewitnesses – to satisfy myself that Roll and Bender have not made up their testimony. A sceptical scientist might naturally insist on that, but for those of us who are just trying to make our own minds up, it isn't practical or reasonable to dismiss such claims out of hand as unreliable hearsay, considering the scale of the testimony and the credibility of many of the sources. Interestingly, although sceptics tend to think that the individuals in such cases hoax, lie and invent, they do not on the whole argue that the parapsychologists make up their evidence.

10 *The confessions examined*

If all this points towards the phenomenon being genuine, then what about the numerous instances when the people involved confess to having caused disturbances fraudulently? What about those in which they were actually caught out? In the Amityville case, the couple who owned the so-called house of horrors was said to have simply cooked up the story to earn some easy money. Tina Resch in Columbus was caught out on film. The Fox sisters described their hoaxes in great detail. Teenage tricks were said to have been involved in many of the cases dealt with by the debunking magician Milbourne Christopher. These provide a counter-argument which, while not accounting for every aspect of the reports, weakens them to the point where it's difficult to give them credence.

So let's focus for a moment on the confessions that some people are said to have made. The parapsychologists' point of view, when they can be bothered to state it, is that the incriminating statements themselves are unbelievable and for that reason probably untrue.

This might look as though they are, as sceptics say, so doggedly set in their beliefs that they just don't want to pay attention to contrary evidence. But it's perhaps not surprising that parapsychologists should think this way: the things the children are said to have admitted doing are puzzlingly unchildlike, and any confessions they make fall so far short of explaining the more jaw-dropping effects described, that it's difficult always to take them at face value.

I noticed too that in the psychic literature, with the notable exception of the Fox sisters (which I'll come back to) a confession of trickery tends to be second-hand. Often it will remain unconfirmed by the person who it is claimed made it, and it may even be explicitly denied by that person. To illustrate this, let's look at a case raised by Milbourne Christopher with regard to the use of threads, which I briefly alluded to earlier. A 1772 pamphlet describes certain 'astonishing transactions' at Stockwell in South London concerning an elderly lady, a Mrs Golding, and her twenty-year-old maid, Ann Robinson, who had come into her employ just ten days earlier (the pamphlet was written four days after the events were over, and signed by six witnesses – Christopher refers to the place as 'Stockton' for some reason). On the morning of 6 January 1772, Mrs Golding was in her parlour when she heard the sound of china and glasses breaking in the kitchen. The maid came and told her that plates were falling from a shelf, so she went into the kitchen where she saw it happen for herself. Then:

> … a row of plates from the next shelf fell down likewise, while she was there, and nobody near them; this astonished her much, and while she was thinking about it, other things in different places began to tumble about, some of them breaking, attended with violent noises all over the house; a clock tumbled down and the case broke; a lanthorn that hung on the staircase was thrown down and glass broke to pieces; an earthen pan of salted beef broke to pieces and the beef fell about; all this increased her surprise and brought several persons around her.[56]

Golding fled with Robinson to a neighbour's house, where the destruction continued. They then went to the house of her niece and at eight o'clock that evening the disturbances started up again:

> The first thing that happened, was, a whole row of pewter dishes, except one, fell off from a shelf to the middle of the floor, rolled about a little while, and then settled, and what is almost beyond belief, as soon as they were quiet, turned upside down; they were then put on the dresser, and went through the same a second time: next fell a whole row of pewter plates from off the second shelf over the dresser to the ground, and being taken up and put on the dresser one in another, they were thrown down again... The next thing was two eggs that were upon one of the pewter shelves, one of them flew off, crossed the kitchen, struck a cat on the head, and then broke to pieces... a pestle and mortar that stood nearer the left hand end of the chimney shelf, jumped about six feet on the floor. Then went candlesticks and other brasses: scarce any thing remaining in its place. After this the glasses and china were put down on the floor for fear of undergoing the same fate, they presently began to dance and tumble about, and then broke to pieces. A tea pot that was among them flew to Mrs Golding's maid's foot and struck it.[57]

All of this was 'cleared up' when a magazine editor named William Hone published an account of a conversation he had had with a certain clergyman who had died some years earlier. According to Hone, the clergyman stated he had met the maid Robinson some years after the incident, and that she assured him she had produced the effects herself. For instance, she had covertly chucked the eggs at the cat and hung joints of ham in such a way that they would fall by themselves when their weight caused the hooks to tear through their skins. She arranged a wire behind a row of plates and pulled it to make them fall over, and she attached long horsehairs to other objects to make them appear to move on their own. One detail provided in the report was that liquids in buckets bubbled and frothed over – this effect, Robinson apparently told him, was achieved by dropping certain chemicals in them.[58]

Parapsychologists argued that the events as described would be difficult even for the best magician alive to stage when surrounded by people who were on the lookout for tricks. That would be my first reaction too, but Christopher disagrees: he thinks it would be difficult, yes, but not impossible. He points out that Robinson was not surrounded and that no-one had any reason to suspect her at that point, hence they were not looking for trickery anyway. The witnesses' attention was only on the objects as they smashed, not on what the maid was doing the second before.

At first I was persuaded by the magician's smooth assurance. He is the expert after all, and what he describes is his professional *modus operandi*. But the more I thought about it, the more I wondered. This business of attaching horsehairs to objects sounds rather difficult: Would the maid have wrapped the hairs right round and tied knots to keep them in place? Just how long were they? Or did she use glue? You'd think it would require some time and absolute privacy to prepare such things unobserved. But to create the mayhem that is here described she would have had to be Wonder Woman, repeating the process in a blink of an eye, many times over. Even if she had had the opportunity to prepare the disturbances at Mrs Golding's house, would she have had the same chance to do so at the neighbour's house? And the niece's house too?

It's risky arguing with an expert, a point that the conjuror–sceptics themselves are keen to nurture. But Christopher is trading heavily on his privileged status: his scenario is unrealistic. Whole shelves of plates falling down, being replaced and falling down again, and other objects throughout the house coming alive at the same time, causing serious damage – this suggests not conjuring but somebody running amok. And if the young maid *had* really been the cause of destruction on such a scale, would this not have been perfectly obvious?[59]

11 *Rational gravity*

In my efforts to make sense of all of this, rejecting the magician's explanation was a fateful step. I felt I had crossed some sort of Rubicon that in the sceptic's eyes marked me off forever as a credulous person, clearly bedazzled by the paranormal's destructive power. But it seemed to me that if anyone is being credulous here, it's the magician himself.

This is perhaps a provocative view to take about someone who considers himself a clear-thinking critic, and I don't mean to be disparaging. But as I gained the confidence to think for myself, I found evidence of complacency on the part of so-called sceptics stacking up. Explanations of paranormal claims don't have to be coherent, I learned, *as long as they restore normality*. The idea that a young servant girl might choose to spend her limited leisure time and meagre wages procuring a chemical that would make the liquid bubble in her employer's bucket, along with all the other curious conjuring tricks, helps resolve an awkward problem but leaves appalling new ones in its wake: What was her motive? Why go to such lengths? How did she acquire the skills to do all this without being observed? In any other circumstances it's hard to think that the girl would entertain such bizarre notions for a minute. Yet here it seems the alternative is so unthinkable that just about any idea will do, no matter how intrinsically implausible it may be in itself. How is it possible *not* be sceptical about the sceptic's view?

As I came across more cases like this I started to feel that there was something rather interesting going on here. I've touched on the idea, common in sceptical discourse, that witnesses of so-called paranormal episodes fail to spot the obvious explanation because they are biased by their 'will to believe'. They hope it's true because they want a supernatural dimension to life, one that provides interest, meaning, and perhaps the prospect of life after death. One might call this *irrational gravity*, where the gravitational force of superstitious belief pulls the mind in the direction of wonders and away from cold logic. Popular television programmes on the paranormal suggests this is a common phenomenon: some people do seem willing to believe all sorts of things for which there is no credible evidence. But my reading of the investigative literature suggests that there exists a closely analogous process which I think of as *rational gravity* – a sort of backwards rationalizing that aims to expunge the sense of confusion that a paranormal claim tends to generate. There's an almost imperceptible pull back to normality, a two-stage process whereby the mind first supplies a scenario that potentially resolves the problem, and then gradually creates the conviction that *this is in fact what happened.*

Now of course this could simply be a construction that an incorrigible paranormalist puts forward to support his belief. But, as I say, it's richly confirmed in the literature. Wherever a paranormal incident is reported, the odds are that sooner or later someone (usually a person who is only marginally involved in the case, or not involved at all) will step forward with a claim that the individual at the centre of it has confessed to trickery or has been caught red-handed. The claim superficially provides an explanation, and this is gratefully accepted by sceptics, who quote it forever after as a damning exposé of fraud and chicanery. Yet when looked at closely, the claim leaves a great deal unexplained, was never corroborated in any way, and appears to have no real substance outside the imagination of the person who proposed it.

Here are a couple of examples of this process at work. In Roll's account of the Miami case, a police sergeant told a news reporter that Julio, the young man at the centre of the disturbances, had confessed to causing them by trickery. Julio, he said, had described how he used a system of threads and also placed objects at the edges of the shelves so that vibrations from jets passing overhead caused them to fall. When this quite detailed construction appeared in the local paper, Julio told the policeman to his face that it was a total lie and that he had said no such thing. According to Julio's boss, Laubheim, who was present during this exchange, the policeman didn't deny the accusation and became red in the face.[60]

There's also an odd 1919 case that occurred in a Norfolk rectory, in which quantities of oil and water cascaded down from the walls and ceilings[61] (such cases are less common than jumping furniture, but there are quite a few of them in the literature). It could not be stopped, let alone explained, and was confirmed by witnesses, including an architect, a geologist, a chemist, and even a magician who had gone there to debunk it. It got so bad that the house had to be vacated. The mystery was 'solved' in a press account some ten days later: Oswald Williams, who described himself as an illusionist, explained how he and his wife had laid a trap for a fifteen-year-old maid who worked in the rectory. The couple had laid out glasses of water, then they concealed themselves and waited. Sure enough the girl came into the room, threw the water up onto the ceiling, and cried out that another shower had occurred. When confronted with her trickery, Williams said she 'broke down and made a clean breast of it'. Yet when the girl herself was quizzed by local reporters she vigorously denied it, insisting the couple had merely persuaded her to go the house with them and then tried to bully her into confessing. 'I was told that I would be given one minute to say I had done it, or go to prison. I said that I didn't do it.'[62]

A lot of this sort of froth is generated by media rivalry. According to the Enfield investigators, two national newspapers attempted to bribe a neighbour to obtain a confession from one of the girls. One offered her a thousand pounds to say that 'what went on in that house was a pack of lies'; the other promised to 'make it worth your while' to obtain a confession...'[63] Similarly, in the Matthew Manning case, one local newspaper got the scoop on the story while another busily published alternative 'revelations' about how the events had been discovered to be bogus (again based on the gossip of outsiders).[64]

These are not isolated examples; on the contrary, they regularly turn up in cases of this kind. And as I say, such inventions only have to be set down in print to attain a sort of official status. They become part of the sceptical canon, and anyone who disputes them identifies himself, by so doing, as a 'believer'. This dynamic is invisible to professional sceptics, because, as I will spell out in more detail in a minute, they are rarely sufficiently interested in psychic claims to investigate them directly, or to read the literature in any depth. The fact that they pass on as established truth what were never really more than inventions and allegations, I believe, is largely what makes it so difficult for the non-specialist to determine what is going on.

Good examples of this confusion are the newspaper reports described in Christopher's *Seers, Psychics and ESP*. Journalists can do no more than repeat what other people tell them, so it's perhaps only to be expected that these articles often include claims of confessions or reports of children playing tricks. Christopher implies that they are the true explanation, and this is explicitly stated by other debunkers who use him as a reference. But if you look at them with some understanding of the context, you can start to see how ambiguous they are.

One of Christopher's cases concerns a country school-house in North Dakota in 1944. In a classroom, smouldering lumps of coals flew out of the bucket in which they were stored and began bombarding the walls, setting fire to the bookcase, blinds and curtains, a wall map and papers on the pupils' desks. One parent who arrived on the scene picked up a lump, by now cold; it trembled and jumped from his hand. Also a dictionary was seen to move of its own accord.[65] Some parents thought the school-house was bewitched and kept their children at home. Baffled, the authorities administered lie detector tests on the witnesses but got negative results and therefore concluded they were all telling the truth.

A few days later, the Associated Press carried a story explaining that the mystery had been resolved. As Christopher relates, four pupils confessed, in the presence of their parents and representatives of the local authorities, that it was they who had planned and carried out this 'exercise in terror'. When their teacher was not looking they had used long rulers and blackboard pointers to stir up the coal and tip the scuttle. They had hurled the coals at the walls – with underhand tosses so that she would not see anything if she happened to glance their way. They had used matches to ignite the lumps and set fire to the blinds and other objects, and had shoved the dictionary in such a way that it appeared to move on its own.[66]

If you think about it, this makes little sense on any level. How *do* you shove a book so that it appears to move on its own? And why would children act this way? If they want to be clever conjurers why aren't they playing card tricks and pulling ribbons out of people's ears? Why are they juggling pieces of hot coal in the middle of classes? It seems a rather odd sort of performance. And who was the audience supposed to be? Perhaps they were expressing hidden resentments by trying to burn the school down. But in that case why did they draw attention to themselves by using such an exotic method? And again, how could such a high level of alarm and consternation have such a trivial cause?

If on the other hand the disturbance had been genuinely anomalous, and nothing to do with child conjurers, one can well imagine what the effect of it might have been in a rural community. The parents would be terrified about demons possessing their young, the school–heads anxious about the negative publicity, and the local authorities irritated at being powerless to stop it. Newspaper reporters would not want to be made fools of, and of course their editors would want the mystery to be cleared up. These varying fears and needs converge in an overwhelming desire for *resolution*. The way out is obvious: the children must confess to having played tricks. This is easily arranged, and behind closed doors a compromise is reached. No-one will get into trouble, but a statement will be made in which the children are said to have confessed about their hoax and apologized. The press will call off their hounds, the matter will be closed, and everyone can get on with their lives. It's a falsehood created for sensible and practical reasons, but with the wider effect of becoming part of the public record, giving it an authoritative status and misleading unwary researchers.

12 *How do the children do it?*

Now let's consider the question I raised earlier: Why are the children in such cases expressing their frustrations by carrying out complex conjuring tricks, and how do they manage to perform them without either being seen to practise beforehand, or being discovered in the act?

It was the strange case of the Fox sisters that particularly puzzled me. As I researched this topic I was haunted by the image of two little girls playing a joke on their mum. From whatever angle I looked at it, and no matter how hard I tried, I could not reconcile Maggie's confessional statements with the contemporary witness testimony. I wondered how a children's game could have caused such consternation. How could little girls bouncing apples and cracking their toe joints induce the adults around them to behave like idiots? How could people be fooled so easily and so long by something so simple?

When I visualized my own young children playing a joke like this I always imagined them eventually coming clean – 'Look Dad! It was us all along, bumping these apples on the floor!' – and collapsing in fits of giggles. The pay-off of a prank, surely, is the opportunity to laugh at the victim's expense. There's nothing funny about concealing the trick well past the point where it's distressing your parents, especially when this is likely to affect the children themselves. If you read the literature you'll quickly find that poltergeist children are only too aware of the malicious gossip that the events arouse, and they are often victims of it. Their world is turned upside down, and although some of them may enjoy the novelty, others do not: they are made to sleep on the sofa in the living room, or in the basement, or outside in the car, or are sent to stay with relatives or with neighbours who may be quite unsympathetic and suspect them of stirring up trouble. In these circumstances, if they were the cause of the disturbances, you would expect them to stop at once. But they don't. Why?

Perhaps the idea of childish pranks should be upgraded to something more serious, some kind of adolescent pathology. However if that were the case I'd expect occasionally to come across alarming articles about Naughty Adolescent Syndrome (NAdS) – a curious disorder that compels its victims to make loud banging noises and knock objects off shelves, and at the same time to go to huge lengths to pretend that it has nothing to do with them. But I never have. What's more, the idea doesn't meld with more mundane expressions of adolescent rebellion. It might strengthen the argument if, as well as magically making the furniture move by itself, the poltergeist was out joy-riding Dad's BMW or using Mum's credit card to buy music CDs but as far as I could tell there's no evidence of any such patterns in the data.

My impression is that the sceptics are not particularly concerned by all this. Nor do they seem bothered about the level of conjuring skill that their scenarios require – something which I have to say has left me more than somewhat sceptical. I don't mean just the skill needed to achieve the effects that witnesses describe, but also the fact that the children seem to acquire such skills without ever giving anything away. I could accept that an emotionally confused girl like Tina Resch might want to attract attention, but it was a stretch to imagine that a person in her state of mind could spend months clandestinely preparing for her venture by learning how to make the furniture come alive, let alone put this into effect without being detected.

I didn't necessarily expect James Randi to think about this, because he did not enter the Resches' house or have any contact with the main witnesses, and he apparently lacked any prior knowledge of the phenomenon. So he would not have known how baffling these effects can be. But I'd have thought Christopher would have something to say, because he had at least come across the china-hurling Stockwell case and had read about a number of others. Yet it doesn't enter into Christopher's analysis at all. On the contrary, he muses at length on the arduous work needed to create illusions, without realizing that it undermines his general point. Mental and physical labour plus practice are necessary before a routine is perfected, he declares. A magician's fingers must be as supple as those of a concert pianist, and the magician, like the pianist, must practise constantly or he will lose his dexterity.[67]

Quite so, but just how does this apply to adolescent children? No-one seems to be caught clandestinely practising, yet the incidents begin suddenly – and are stupefying from the outset. Do teenagers really possess the necessary coolness and mental discipline to achieve this level of success? And again, how consistent is this with their being emotionally disturbed?

13 *When was Maggie lying?*

We are still left with the fact that the grown-up Maggie Fox, supported by her sister Kate, denounced spiritualism and all its works, and described how they had carried out their tricks. As I say, I saw no reason initially to suspect anything was wrong with this, but at the same time I could recognize the logic in the counter-arguments. Both women at this time were in a bad way – ageing, penurious and alcoholic. Maggie's career as a medium had never been as successful as Kate's, and her husband and in-laws had all despised spiritualism. So she may have possessed little emotional commitment to an activity that as well as making her famous had also turned her into an object of contempt. In the circumstances she might have thought she had little to lose by denouncing it in exchange for a fee of fifteen hundred dollars – quite a significant sum at that time. But the real motivation for the two sisters seems to have been a desire to get back at their manipulative elder sister, Leah, who made a comfortable living as a medium – initially by exploiting her sisters' greater talents – and whom they suspected of being involved in the temporary removal of Kate's two sons because of Kate's drunkenness.[68]

So Maggie had particular personal reasons for making her statement, and Kate had valid reasons for supporting her. But there's yet another reason why I think there is more here than meets the eye. When I summarized the background to their case earlier you probably spotted a discrepancy: I first described Maggie and Kate as being fourteen and twelve years old, but then only two paragraphs later Maggie's statement contains the claim that at the time she had actually been eight years old and that Kate was a year-and-a-half younger. My failure to explain this at the time may have raised doubts in your mind about my competence, and it does require justification, which I'll provide in a minute. But first let me suggest what its significance might be.

The ages of fourteen and twelve are given in the statement made by the girls' mother two weeks after the onset of the disturbances in 1848.[69] There's a slight variation in other sources – sometimes they were said to be thirteen and eleven – but these sorts of figures are what one generally finds, as much in sceptics' books as anywhere else. However, where primary sources are concerned, mentions of the much younger ages are *only* found in Maggie's confession. To a child, and particularly to a girl, I think most people will agree, there's every difference in the world between being eight and being fourteen, and it's surely implausible that Maggie had *forgotten* how old she was when these dramatic, life-changing experiences took place. So what possible reason would she have had for changing this detail?

What struck me about Maggie's statement – and what I think would occur to anyone who reads the text closely – is that she took great pains to persuade her audience that she and her sister were capable of fooling their mother. Mrs Fox could not understand it, Maggie said, 'and didn't suspect us of being capable of a trick *because we were so young.*' And again: 'No-one suspected us of any trick *because we were such young children*'. Maggie also suggested that being *so young* they were supple enough to manage the necessary physical contortions: 'Such perfect control is only possible when a child is taken at an early age and carefully and continually taught to practise the muscles which grow still in later years. *A child at twelve is almost too old*'. Finally, she felt obliged to explain why she embarked on the hoax in the first place, and again used her extreme youth as a justification: 'When I began this deception *I was too young to know right from wrong*'.[70]

It seems clear from this that Maggie was concerned there were certain things her audience would have difficulty accepting: that her mother would have believed adolescent girls would play such a silly trick; that girls of that age would have thought it morally acceptable; and that her sister and herself would have been capable of the necessary muscular distortions. But of course if it *had* been a trick then all of these things would actually have happened, performed by girls of at least thirteen and eleven. In that case, why would she have cause to worry? The fact that she was anxious about it suggests to me that she had not actually experienced the scenario she was referring to. In short, she was making it all up, and changing her and her sister's ages was a ploy designed to make it sound plausible.

As for the discrepancy in my account, this is the sort of thing one comes across all the time in controversies about psychic research. Such details provide clues for careful readers, which is why

I left it uncorrected earlier – to give you a sense of what you have to look out for, and what the critics won't necessarily consider to be in their interests to draw attention to, even if they had spotted it themselves.

14 *Who should we trust?*

Perhaps I am going too far, too fast. What right do I have to insist that poltergeists are real and that the claims should be taken seriously?

Taking stock, I should say to begin with that I'm not trying to get people to believe something they would rather not. In examining the reports I have done nothing that others may not do equally well for themselves, and any certainty I have gained is based on sources that anyone can review. My aim is to share perceptions, and if, when I'm done, you agree with me that there's something rather odd occurring here, something that merits a closer look, then that's plenty to be going on with. If you don't, that's fine too: I should be interested to hear your arguments.

But I do insist that we talk on equal terms, having had full access to the relevant facts, and having spent a little time reflecting on them. I want to hear explanations that relate to the *data*, not generalizations that take little or no account of the details of what people say they experienced. This is where I part company with the professional debunkers – Kurtz, Randi, Christopher, Nickell and others who we'll meet later on. Not because they lack analytical powers (which they obviously don't) and not because they are determined to find a normal solution (which they certainly should be) but because their interest in the subject is so small as to raise doubts about their qualifications to educate the rest of us.

If that sounds counter-intuitive, and perhaps even a bit exaggerated, then consider the facts. The research literature on poltergeist claims consists of several hundred published cases, of which scores have been the subject of reports by serious investigators. I say 'serious' because they have made it their business to seek out such incidents, to interview witnesses and wherever possible to observe the phenomena themselves. Their reports are often quite detailed and correspond to the extent that a clear pattern emerges. In addition, there are a handful of cases such as the Miami warehouse and the Rosenheim office in which experts in different fields are said to concur that they have observed, on many different occasions, some force currently unknown to science.

But you would not know any of this if your only source is the debunking literature. Most of the CSI (formerly CSICOP) writers name a single contemporary investigator – William Roll. One or two refer to his article in the *Handbook of Parapsychology*, while others have merely seen his name mentioned. The incidents they refer to are few: Amityville and Borley, neither of which parapsychologists take very seriously, and which in any case are not really typical; Columbus and Seaford, which were dealt with respectively by Randi and Christopher but ineffectually, as neither of them gained access to the houses involved, or interviewed the main witnesses, or observed any of the phenomena in question; and various incidents in Christopher's clutch of press cuttings, which give too little information to draw any reliable conclusions from. A British book, *Bizarre Beliefs* by Simon Hoggart and Michael Hutchinson, mentions the Enfield case, but dismisses it with a facetious comment and some gossip from a tabloid newspaper.[71]

The sceptics say that they can't be expected to check out the truth of every claim. There will always be cases where witnesses and parapsychologists believe that something paranormal happened, and where there was no opportunity for this to be corrected by the more careful testimony of an objective investigator. Most people would consider this to be a perfectly fair argument. But they will be less impressed when they discover that debunking sceptics have made little attempt to investigate *any* such incidents. The implication the critics artfully convey is false: there is no independent body of cases that they have examined at first hand and satisfactorily explained in non-paranormal terms. In fact, if they were to read the parapsychological literature they would find quite a few instances of this kind, and could use them to strengthen their argument. But I can see why they might not wish to: it would mean acknowledging the competence of the investigators who uncovered them – investigators who also described a number of cases (a large number, when considered collectively) which they were convinced were paranormal.

Interestingly, these shortcomings are invisible to the critics' audience. Scientists accept the critics as the experts because their analyses and conclusions are precisely what they expect. For instance the late Milton A. Rothman, a nuclear physicist, wanted to know where the poltergeist gets the energy needed to toss dishes and furniture around the house. Is it a new force, he asked, or a variation of something we already know about? A vital question, obviously, but only worth asking if it has been proven that poltergeists exist, and as far as he was concerned it had not been. 'Investigations by trained observers,' he insisted, 'have invariably found these phenomena to be either natural events misunderstood by the observer, or simply tricks played on the public by professional or amateur charlatans.'[72]

As I think you will now be able to see, this conventional wisdom is not at all true. 'Trained observers' here usually means 'debunking conjurors and psychologists', but 'invariably' is hardly the word when such people have attempted to investigate so few cases and observed little that might have been even potentially significant. On the other hand if Rothman had been fully aware of the many first-hand investigations carried out by Roll, Pratt, Gauld, Cornell, Playfair, Grosse, Rogo, Barrett, Barrington, Bender and others, but considered them inferior in their execution and wrong in their conclusions, then I would really like to have heard his reasons.

Even if sceptics did get out there and start checking out the claims directly, would they be any good at it? By definition, a debunker is usually considered to possess an ability to ferret out the truth, where less critical and perceptive minds have fallen for the illusion. But it's not obvious that their skills are the ones that are actually needed here. If you think about it, it shouldn't take a master conjurer to catch out teenagers playing tricks, unless you believe – as I personally do not – that adolescent children can acquire overnight the skills of a master conjurer. Nor is it clear to me why someone who approaches a claim with the conviction that it is bogus should automatically be considered a better judge than a more open-minded person who considers that it might or might not be. What really counts, surely, is the degree of commitment, care and discrimination each exhibits in their approach – factors that the hostile critics, judging by their published work, typically score rather low on.

What the debunkers especially lack is the ability to identify promising cases and to gain the trust of the family concerned. It would be hard to imagine a less promising method than James Randi's, who came to Columbus waving a cheque for ten thousand dollars and boasting how he had exposed 'many tricky teens whose fraud was perpetuated by indulgent parents and journalists hungry for headlines'.[73] Why let such a man into your home, only to see your reputation later being trashed by the local media?

15 *Hume, Occam, Randi*

Now for a word about some of the general objections that are made to explain away claims of this kind, such as David Hume's argument against miracles. In fact this is more nuanced than one would think from the way the debunkers usually cite it.[74]

The philosopher's motivation is atheistic: he wants to deter people from using miraculous claims to support religious belief. But as he develops that theme, he acknowledges that anomalies *are* observed in nature from time to time, and that these tend to modify our thinking. They are not miracles, but unknown natural events, he recognizes, merely requiring an adjustment to the law that they seem to violate. A good example of this – occurring after Hume's time – was the growing number of claims by farmers that they had seen stones falling onto their fields from the sky. Of course scientists could not accept this: how could stones possibly fall from the sky when there are no stones in the sky? In due course the phenomenon of meteorites became understood, and it was then conceded that actually stones do sometimes fall from the sky.

This has become something of a cliché in paranormalist literature, an example of obdurate scepticism getting its come-uppance, and there have been many more instances where disbelief turned out to be perfectly justified. Nevertheless the principle is relevant here: an apparently ludicrous observation, when widely and consistently reported, may represent the first inklings of a yet-to-be-discovered aspect of nature. Anomalies in an otherwise perfect model are an indication that the model may not be perfect after all, and may one day have to be revised. The history of science offers some dramatic examples of this: for instance, the ancient view of the cosmos, in which heavenly objects all revolved around the earth, was weakened by the discovery that planets appeared to have quite different orbits, paving the way for a shift to the helio-centric model. For this reason we should perhaps not be too quick to invoke Hume as a reason to dismiss paranormal claims out of hand.

Then what about Occam's razor – the principle that entities should not be multiplied beyond need or, in plain terms, that the economical solution is generally best? Suggesting childrens' pranks is a quick and easy way to resolve the challenge posed by claims of poltergeists, and seems to be clearly sign-posted in the way the incidents are reported, while to explain them in terms of psychokinesis or invisible spirits would involve a scientific revolution. This is all true. But the relevant words here are *beyond need*: the explanation has to be the simplest one that is *consistent with the facts*. If we don't know the facts – having neither investigated the phenomenon nor read the arguments of those who have – then this principle will mislead us. (It's worth adding here that parapsychologists are applying Occam's razor to some extent when they view such episodes in terms of a psychological anomaly, rather than as the action of discarnate spirits. That's not the whole story, but we can come back to it later.)[75]

But then, if we wanted to prove the genuineness of the phenomenon, to pin it down so to speak, how would we go about it? How would the claimant convince the world that what he or she experienced, or was involuntarily capable of achieving, was the truth and not a hoax? And how stringent would such a test have to be in order to convince the most obdurate sceptic? Naturally we turn to a highly regarded professional conjuror, preferably one who is second to none in his fierce disbelief of paranormal claims. If such a person were ever to be convinced, we might think, it would be the 'extraordinary evidence' that we require and we would have no option but to accept it.

I think we can start to see that the logic of this isn't quite as clear as James Randi's supporters think. At any one time, around forty to sixty people express an interest in applying for his Million Dollar Challenge, the organizers say. The offer is genuine, they insist; the money has been provided by donors and is held by Goldman Sachs in the form of bonds and will be handed over to a successful claimant within ten days. However no-one has got past the preliminaries, and most applicants fade away when they realize the seriousness of the testing.[4] Common-or-garden psychics do feature on the list of applicants, but from the claimed supernatural powers that crop up ('detecting poisoned vegetables' and 'summoning spaceships from the sky' are two that caught my eye) one would have to agree with Randi's assessment that many of them are delusional, or even mentally ill, and one can only marvel at his willingness to put himself in their way.[5]

Clearly, Randi also includes 'an ability to make objects move at a distance' in this category. As we have seen, absurd and astonishing as it undoubtedly is, precisely this phenomenon has been witnessed and documented by responsible researchers on a strikingly large scale – but it's not one that will tamely comply with the magician's requirements.

My point is to question the reliance sceptics and scientists place on a mechanism such as The Million Dollar Challenge as a means to decide about the existence of such things – as I believe many of them do. A stage magician's skills are indispensible, as parapsychologists are the first to acknowledge, but the phenomenon appears too capricious and unpredictable to submit to simple tests, and can't always be isolated from the social context.

I'd also suggest that the Challenge only has status as a *check* to paranormal claims. The moment it admits them its authority vanishes. This odd dynamic is worth reflecting on. Scientists whom critics characterise as rank believers – some of whom we will meet in later chapters – usually insist they were sceptics themselves at one time, but were forced by their investigations of paranormal claims to change their minds. That sounds to me like a fair and natural progression, and of course the opposite is also true: one-time believers also sometimes become sceptics. But for many people, the only true sceptic is one who resists psychic claims to the bitter end: someone who gives in to them, it's later said, was always really a believer at heart … wearing sceptics' clothes.

If you doubt this, consider what would have happened if Randi had observed at first hand the events at the Resch household, and come out bewildered by what he had seen. *No question*, he might have said, *I was wrong – there really are psychic forces of which I had no conception. Tina, my child, here's the cheque. Spend it wisely.* Even if this fanciful scenario were one day to be played out, nothing would change. It would make headlines briefly but would not convert sceptics all over the world into believers. Its only lasting effect would be to end Randi's career as a debunker: he would be written off as an elderly man who has finally succumbed to the madness of paranormal belief. Exactly the same fate, in other words, that he and other scoffers hand out to scientists whose ability to think rationally was never in doubt *until* they became convinced by their personal observations of psychic phenomena.

So how could we ever arrive at a safe conclusion? The least one can say is that individual cases will always be contested, and if there is ever to be a reliable consensus one way or the other it would be around a great accumulation of incidents that are well documented and corroborated and establish a clear pattern. While I'm unconvinced that ideas such as child conjurors explain the poltergeist phenomenon, I recognize that the existing testimony doesn't reach the threshold required to overturn the enormous weight of scientific disbelief in an interaction between mind and matter. We are in a rather interesting no-man's land, confronted by field research whose claims are not easily refuted, yet whose implications are simply unacceptable to the vast majority of scientists, and as a result can continue to be derided as if they were bogus.

But what if this phenomenon were to be examined in the wider context of psychic research? Could it be studied more objectively, in controlled conditions? This was attempted on a wide scale in the late nineteenth and early twentieth centuries in the investigation of séance phenomena, to which we turn next.

TWO

EUSAPIA PALLADINO AND
THE PHANTOM NARRATIVE

'The hand afterwards came and *shook hands* with each one present. I felt it minutely. It was tolerably well and symmetrically made, though not perfect; and it was *soft* and slightly *warm*. IT ENDED AT THE WRIST.' *Frank L. Burr, editor of the Hartford Times.*

'C'est absolutement absurde, mais c'est vrai.' *Charles Richet, scientist and Nobel Prize winner.*

I t's true that no psychic has ever won James Randi's Million Dollar Challenge, or, as far as I'm aware, any of the other cash prizes that have been offered from time to time. But it's also true that some scientists have become convinced through experiments that certain psychics really *can* do the things they say they can, as have some otherwise sceptical stage magicians. The question we have to decide is: How much is their conviction worth?

Most people have heard of Uri Geller, the controversial Israeli–Hungarian performer famous for his metal-bending feats. A 1974 report written by Russell Targ and Harold Puthoff, laser physicists at the Stanford Research Institute, and published in *Nature,* claimed that when Geller was placed in an isolation booth he was consistently able to reproduce drawings that they had randomly selected outside it – at odds of a million to one. They also reported how he changed the weight of a piece of metal that they had placed on an electronic scale, and how he deflected a magnetometer right off the scale – both apparently by the power of thought.[1]

However, even this limited degree of scientific endorsement is rare nowadays, and to get a good sense of what happens when scientists investigate psychics we have to go back to the nineteenth century, when the spiritualist séance was a popular activity and professional mediums were constantly in the public eye. One of the first and best known was Daniel Dunglas Home, who, like Geller, entertained people around the world with psychic performances. An ambitious young scientist named William Crookes tested Home in his own house; he reported that the medium made an accordion play a tune merely by resting his hand on it, on the side *away* from the keys, and caused a wooden plank to oscillate strongly at one end by lightly touching the other (since there was no leverage this would normally have been impossible, even if he had leaned hard on it).[2]

These feats by Geller and Home were not especially spectacular, compared with what both were said to be capable of, but experiments by scientists carry more weight than purely anecdotal claims. Other nineteenth-century investigators were equally convinced by their close-up examinations of spirit mediums: they included Robert Hare, the American inventor of the oxy–hydrogen blow-torch; the German physicist Johann Zöllner; the French physiologist Charles Richet, who later won a Nobel Prize for his work on allergic reactions; and Alfred Russel Wallace, the co-discoverer with Charles Darwin of evolution by natural selection.[3] Some of these individuals – namely, Hare, Crookes and Wallace – concluded that spirits actually *were* involved; others – like Richet – were non-committal or rejected the idea.

However, testimony even of such distinguished scientists made little impression on their colleagues. It was taken for granted that they had let themselves be duped; the only questions of any interest were how and why. Crookes had been acclaimed for his earlier discoveries, notably that of a new element, thallium. But on this subject his claims were questioned, ridiculed or ignored; he was publicly libelled to the effect that he was not a proper scientist and should not be trusted.[4] Charles Richet had been among Crookes's mockers, but himself became a target after he carried out similar research and came to the same conclusions. Zöllner and Hare too were pilloried by their colleagues, and few took Wallace's claims seriously.[5] A similar fate befell Geller's investigators, Targ and Puthoff; in James Randi's *Flim-Flam!* a chapter about them is headed 'The Laurel and Hardy of Psi'.[6]

But how could scientists at this level have been tricked? The stock explanation is that psychics are nothing more than closet conjurors, and scientists are no better qualified to investigate them than anyone else. The point was made by John Nevil Maskelyne, the Randi of the late nineteenth century, after he watched an investigation of the famous Italian medium Eusapia Palladino. 'Try as they may,' Maskelyne said, 'they cannot bring their minds down to the level of the subject, and are as much at fault as though it were immeasurably above them'.[7] It takes a professional magician to work out how a particular effect might be performed and to know what tricks to look out for. Add the fact that the séances were often carried out in near or total darkness, and that the mediums stipulated the conditions, and you have a set-up which is anything but controlled, experimental or scientific.

As regards the mechanics of trickery, there have been some quite elaborate speculations. At the Stanford Research Institute, Geller's location within an isolation booth should have ensured there was no possibility of him seeing the drawings he claimed to see clairvoyantly. But what if he had a radio-receiver implanted in a gold tooth, and could tune it to receive clandestine messages? The investigators' report was found later to have left out possibly relevant details, such as the presence of Geller's manager and close associate, who could have found a way to signal to Geller what was in the drawings.[8] If this sounds far-fetched there are simpler explanations. For instance, when Randi visited the Institute he discovered a hole in the wall of the booth, and argued that if the drawings had been pinned up within its line of sight, Geller could have used it to sneak a peek.[9]

The same sorts of conjectures were used to explain away Crookes's observations of Home. Crookes's report is thin on detail; who knows what really went on, or how a charlatan might have exploited the set-up? Home might have had time to walk around the room and size up the opportunities while Crookes and his two invited observers were busy setting up the apparatus or writing up notes. He could have distracted them with some innocuous chatter, while slipping a hair or a black thread over the end of the wooden plank and attaching it to a hook on his clothing.[10] The scientists would never have realized that the leverage was coming not from his hands but from his body.

Deciding about this is probably not difficult either for a committed believer or for a convinced sceptic: each will accept the arguments that appeal to them. But those of us whose find truth on both sides of the argument face something of a dilemma.

I got an early sense of this from two books on the subject that I found in my local library – the only two, as it happened. One was *Natural and Supernatural* (1977) by the late Brian Inglis, a historian and former editor of the *Spectator* magazine; the other was *The Spiritualists* (1983) by Ruth Brandon, a historian and biographer.[11] Inglis presents paranormal research as a series of historical events, including a remarkable number of testimonials by scientists in different fields who experimented with paranormal claimants of various kinds and, to their astonishment and consternation, found them to be true. Aside from its fantastical subject matter, his book is not unlike those popular histories by writers such as Isaac Asimov and Bill Bryson, that describe a chronological series of facts about scientific discoveries and the controversies that followed in their wake. By contrast, Brandon approached spiritualism as a cultural phenomenon, where charlatans filled the needs of a society whose religious certainties had been shattered by Darwinism. For her, the mediums' claims were obviously bogus and the scientists were duped. The challenge is to try to reveal the truth concealed behind layers of deception and gullibility.

I remember reading these two books back to back and afterwards feeling rather bewildered, as if two friends had come back from an evening together at the theatre, one claiming to have seen *Hamlet* and the other *Spamelot*. The amount of convincing detail marshalled by each author to give entirely opposite pictures was extraordinary. Inglis sympathized with the investigating scientists and seemed to share their exasperation at being disbelieved; he took little account of the critics' objections. Brandon, by contrast, created a picture of a tiresome and shabby fraud, yet without really convincing me she knew how the tricks were done; mostly she recycled suggestions by scoffers such as the magicians John Maskelyne and Harry Houdini, adding her own suspicions and conjectures.

Logically, of these two distinct, mutually exclusive narratives, only one could be correct, with the corollary that the other must be resoundingly *wrong*. But which was which? A century later we don't talk about it much, but it interests me that there is no real consensus. Many writers continue to talk about Daniel Home as a psychic of great power, as some also do of Geller. Yet psychokinesis is supposed by science to be a chimera, a mere fairy tale, which would make Home and Geller quite different specimens of humanity and – considering the astonishment their feats generated – not just common-or-garden charlatans, but conjurors of genius. Even authors who profess to be non-committal about them, or insist on their disbelief, tend not to play down their effect on their audiences, which in any case would be hard to do without misrepresenting the primary sources.[12]

But this ambiguity didn't satisfy me at all. I felt it surely ought to be possible to be figure out what was going on. Out of curiosity

I started to immerse myself in the literature of nineteenth-century spiritualism, to see what conclusions I myself might eventually reach.

2 *The séance*

My first reaction was amazement at the fantastical nature of the claims. The spiritualist séance is a joke these days, a source of gags for sitcoms and newspaper cartoons. We're vaguely aware that long ago, in the dark evenings before television was invented, men with abundant facial hair and women in funny dresses gathered round tables in the dark and held hands, and there would be loud raps, levitating tables and spirits materializing out of cobwebby stuff called 'ectoplasm'. But if we think of it at all most of us probably regard it as just another Victorian eccentricity – fathomless and inexplicable, like those bird-nest beards and bustle skirts.

So it was strange to learn how seriously it was taken, not just by cultists or enthusiasts, but also by some quite sane-seeming people, and in all classes and in all walks of life. There's a voluminous literature based on the doings of mediums, with reports of séances in the large spiritualist press, as well as the published reports of scientists and other investigators. Especially amazing or ludicrous – depending on your point of view – are the detailed descriptions of what people said they saw.

Think of a séance as a visit by a troupe of house-trained poltergeists and you're halfway there. To start things off, the medium would go into a trance. Then the temperature might drop several degrees, causing the sitters around the table to shiver. Curtains might billow out. There could be sudden loud raps and knocks in the wall and furniture, which could be used as a medium of communication. The séance table might start to rock and rise off the floor, along with stools and chairs – sometimes with people sitting on them. As the action warmed up, objects might start to glide around the room. Musical instruments might play tunes on their own initiative. There might also be cascades of pretty lights or the scent of exotic perfumes. People might feel themselves being touched, hugged or even caressed, their beards or jewellery tweaked, or see handkerchiefs removed from their own pockets and knotted in front of their eyes.

A persistent claim was of *apports*, objects that appeared on the séance table having apparently materialized from thin air. Some mediums specialized in this; one was famous for her ability to apport large quantities of cultivated flowers, which suddenly appeared on the séance table – often covered in dew. I was especially taken with an Australian medium named Charles Bailey, who, it was said, had the power to introduce into a previously empty and locked room (in some cases having first been sewn up in a sack, with only his head protruding) such bric-a-brac as beads, coins and jewels, Arab newspapers and half-cooked chapattis, also a wide range of flora and fauna including live birds, their nests and eggs, crabs, shells, seaweed and, on one occasion, a live one-foot-long hammer-nose shark.[13]

Not all séance phenomena required the presence of a medium. From the 1850s, groups of individuals found that if they gathered round a small table, gently laid their hands on it and willed it to move, they might eventually be rewarded with a result. The table would turn or tip and slide as if it had come to life. It was assumed that spirits were moving it, and in fact this technique was used as a rudimentary form of communication in place of raps – one turn or tip for 'no' and two for 'yes', for example. This table-turning was the forerunner of the modern Ouija board, where two or more people laying the tips of their fingers on an upturned glass or pointer can watch it sliding purposefully across the board to indicate letters and spell out messages, at least some of which may contain relevant information.

To me, though, by far the most bizarre reported phenomenon was the effect known as 'materialization'. A misty foam apparently emanated from the medium – Charles Richet would later term it 'ectoplasm' – and solidified into a talking head; recognized by some of the sitters, it would converse amiably for a while, and then fade away. By the early 1870s mediums were said to be producing full forms of dead spirits in this way. William Crookes famously had several encounters with a female phantom calling itself Katie King, conjured up by the teenage medium Florence Cook. Richet had the opportunity to test one that was produced by a young girl named Marthe Beraud; he reported it had a pulse, breathed, walked and talked, and appeared in many respects like an ordinary human being, except that it departed by subsiding into the floor. Richet insisted he was not mistaken about any of this. 'C'est absolutement absurde,' he kept repeating, 'mais c'est vrai'[14]

Psychic researchers have a handy term, the 'boggle threshold', by which they mean the point at which interest and curiosity boil over into thumping incredulity. If you thought you might possibly accommodate inexplicable raps and levitations, and perhaps an apport or two, you're probably by now thinking this is all an elaborate joke. This is the huge, appalling problem, not merely that hundreds of instances of this kind were documented, but that some of them were endorsed as genuine by reputable scientists who spent a good deal of time checking them out. One's left feeling that either something happened that we should be paying serious attention to, or else that a lot of people simultaneously lost their minds on an epic scale – which is equally worthy of note.

Not that sceptics don't have plenty to work with. Many mediums were blatant frauds, and some later boasted about their cleverness in print. So there's an abundance of information about how the tricks could be carried out.[15] The fakers might levitate tables by jamming a toe underneath one leg, or by using a metal rod concealed up their sleeves, or a hook sewn into their clothing. They could whip out a telescopic rod from a sleeve once the lights had been turned out, in order to fake touches by 'invisible spirits', all the while keeping up a spiritualist patter, distracting people's attention and encouraging them to see things that weren't there. Apports were faked by filching items earlier from people's pockets or handbags, or even from their homes, and then later producing them during the séance. As for the materializations, under cover of darkness the medium could wrap herself in muslin she had concealed somewhere, and impersonate 'spirits'; or else she could get an accomplice to act the part.

There were high-profile exposures. A medium named Francis Monck was unmasked when sitters at a country house gig became suspicious and searched his luggage, finding various conjuring devices. Monck tried to escape out of a window but was caught, prosecuted and sentenced to three months' hard labour for vagrancy.

Another medium, Henry Slade, later the subject of experiments with Johan Zöllner, was tried and sentenced on the same charge, although he fled to safety in Germany before hearing the outcome of an appeal. Charles Bailey was once spotted in a street market buying the live songbirds that popped up during his sittings. And Eusapia Palladino was caught cheating by a man concealed underneath the séance table, who saw her using her bare foot blatantly to perform tricks; when he reached out and grabbed it she is said to have given a 'wild yelling scream' worthy of Sarah Bernhardt (a theatrical star of the day) – 'a scream as if a dagger had stabbed [her] right through the heart [and] indicated that she knew that at last she was trapped and her glory shattered'.[16]

Interestingly, the professional psychic researchers who appeared in the early 1880s shared the doubts about séance phenomena; their interest was more in such things as ghosts and telepathy. An energetic Australian named Richard Hodgson made his name as an investigator for the Society for Psychical Research (the SPR) by debunking the séance claims of Helena Blavatsky, the controversial founder of a new religious philosophy named Theosophy. He then worked with a young man named S.J. Davey, who he found could convincingly fake certain types of séance phenomena.[17] It turned out that sitters were as excited by Davey's performance as by those of famous mediums, indicating that witness testimony was not at all to be trusted.

The SPR's reputation for scepticism on this matter was confirmed by its treatment of Eusapia Palladino, who had been widely investigated in her native Italy, as well as by teams of science professors in Poland and France. For all their insistence that her feats were genuine, the Society's investigation in Cambridge, led by Hodgson, concluded otherwise. The debunking conjuror John Maskelyne was persuaded to attend, and was shocked to see how brazenly she cheated, for instance manhandling a table to make it 'levitate' in a way that must surely have been obvious to everyone. He said later: 'Dozens of scientific men have declared that they have seen her lift a table with only the tips of her fingers touching it. All I can say is, that when I saw her lift a table, there was a vast deal more than her fingers in contact with it'.[18]

It's also true that the spiritualists could be embarrassingly credulous. Oddly, Arthur Conan Doyle, creator of the original fictional sleuth Sherlock Holmes, led the field, insisting that a magician who replicated a medium's trick must himself be psychic – a depressingly frequent retort of committed believers.[19] Spiritualists were also often intolerant of disbelievers, apparently unable to grasp that some people might have trouble accepting their extraordinary claims.

But how do we explain those many instances when people said they achieved table levitations in small groups, without the benefit of a professional medium? The answer was provided by Michael Faraday, the celebrated discoverer of electromagnetic induction. Following a hunch, Faraday constructed a table top in three layers separated by rollers, and found that when sitters sat around it and pressed their fingers down it would slide around wildly. There was no intent to deceive, Faraday stressed, but it was obvious that the table was responding to the muscular pressure that they were unconsciously exerting, creating the impression that it was moving by itself.[20]

3 *Why take it seriously?*

No one doubts that fraud was rife. What we have to decide is whether any of it was sometimes true. But is that a fair question? After all, if *most* of it was patently bogus, it makes sense to assume that *all* of it was. Why go looking for exceptions?

Also, if a particular medium was tainted by accusations of fraud, that would surely disqualify him or her from being taken at all seriously. Since pretty much every medium with the exception of Daniel Home was caught out at some time or another, that would rule them all out; even Home was widely suspected of cheating.

This point of view has always informed sceptical responses, and there's much to be said for it. At the same time, I found many of the descriptions so detailed and unequivocal that I wanted to know more. For instance, look at this detail from notes taking during one of Eusapia Palladino's séances:

> Mandolin comes out of cabinet, passing through the air in a horizontal position, and lands on table in front of all. It moves about on table several times. No one touches it and Palladino is held well. Both her hands are held tight... The mandolin sounds several notes without anyone touching it. [Palladino] is securely held and her hands are not touching mandolin, which is lying on table in full view. Mandolin plays again, [Palladino's] hands are two and a half inches from strings. She moves her fingers and mandolin sounds. Her fingers do not touch strings. Everyone sees this.[21]

Witness testimony is commonly said to be unreliable, but this description is clear, unequivocal and businesslike, and shows that the people involved are striving to make accurate observations. The fact that Palladino is not touching the instrument is repeatedly confirmed. In a séance with Daniel Home, participants sat around a mahogany table with a smooth polished top on which were some loose papers, two candles, a glass and a pencil. The table tipped up by thirty degrees – the objects should all have slid off onto the floor. *But they remained fixed to the top.* Obviously, you'd think, Home had set up the trick with glue, or something of the kind. But then the table tilted again, and this time, on the sitters' specific request, the pencil slid off while the other objects remained static.[22]

I recognize that none of this would present much difficulty for a professional conjuror. At least I guess that's what a professional conjuror would maintain. One can do all sorts of clever things with magnets and other devices, and distract the audience so that they don't see the trick. But it's also true that conjuring is a highly mechanical business, particularly where complex illusions are concerned; they have to be set up beforehand, and are usually performed at a distance from the audience. That would be challenging for mediums like Daniel Home who performed impromptu séances in other people's houses, and who would have had little opportunity to do much preparation. And it would surely be out of the question for those like Eusapia Palladino, subjected as they were to close and repeated scrutiny by teams of people whose first assumption was that she was trying to trick them.

Here I disagreed with sceptics, who tend to argue that mediums always dictated the conditions (such as the level of light, and so on) and that the investigators meekly submitted. That's fair enough in relation to mediums' professional work with the public, although spiritualists themselves did not care to be tricked, and often imposed some degree of control. But it's much less true of the scientific investigations, where visibility and physical controls were insisted on.

The point here is that, to *truly* match the mediums' level of ability, debunking conjurors like Maskelyne and Houdini would have needed to repeat successfully the same performance while members of the audience, some of whom were themselves amateur conjurers, swarmed all over the stage looking for hidden apparatus and watched their every move. If under these circumstances they still managed to create the effect without the trick being understood, they would have to come back the next day, and the next and the next, to give the audience another chance. It's fair to say that this does not form part of most magicians' repertoire – in fact a rule is never to carry out the same trick more than once in front of the same audience. I also wondered about the motives of fakers who willingly offered opportunities to be exposed, virtually without limit, and about the fact that the investigators were sufficiently intrigued by what they observed to want to carry on.

With poltergeist claims it's surprising to find children skilled at conjuring tricks. Here it's odd to find convincing magic tricks being done by *women*. Conjuring is one of the few professions where women are under-represented compared with men: they were only recently admitted to the Magic Circle where they are still in a small minority. I can just about imagine that performers like Home and Geller might entertain people with close-up magic. But it was intriguing to find women like Eusapia Palladino doing similar things, and some of them apparently with the same degree of dexterity. Other women, like Florence Cook, Kathleen Goligher, Marthe Beraud and Mina Crandon, seem to have been good at convincing researchers who were constantly trying to catch them out, which suggests that if they really were playing tricks, they were extremely skilful.

4 *Table-turning*

We also need to be aware of an issue concerning Michael Faraday's explanation for table-turning. We may agree with Faraday that unconscious muscular pressure by the people sitting round a table with their hands placed on top might cause it to tip and slide. But this would not by itself explain why it would do so in such a way as to indicate letters that spelled coherent messages. Perhaps we could come up with some psychologically plausible formula. However what Faraday does not explain at all is how the table might levitate completely off the floor on all four legs, sometimes to the point of seeming to come alive.[23] Look at this description:

> The 'rising' was generally preceded by a continuous fusillade of 'knocks' in the substance of the table ...; when the knocks had, as it were, reached a climax, the table slowly swayed from side to side like a pendulum, stopped completely, and then, as if imbued with life, and quite *suddenly*, rose completely off the floor to a height of a foot or 14 inches at least, and nearly always came down with immense force ... This table, I may add, was a round, rather heavy, walnut one, with a central column, standing on three claw legs, and it would have been impossible for us unaided to have developed the force (by muscular energy) required to produce this manifestation.[24]

Sometimes, one report stated, the table would be outrageous in its behaviour – hopping on one leg, getting on chairs and performing other curious antics.[25] Note, too, the ubiquitous rapping noises that are so often reported in connection with this sort of psychokinetic phenomena. Another frequent element is the immense force of the levitations, also their variability and response to verbal requests, as though some intelligence was involved. The characteristic of behaving like a person was also often cited. Once, a table:

> ... seemed to act as an excited person would, and proceeded to execute all manner of very lively movements – rocking, swaying, jumping, dancing, tilting, oscillating bodily both slowly and rapidly: it shook like a live thing even when totally levitated, almost shaking our hands off. Because the levitations were not very high, I said: 'Come on – higher!' at which the table rose up chest high and remained there for eight seconds.[26]

This description comes not from Victorian times but from the relatively recent 1960s, when a series of experiments was carried out by psychologist Kenneth Bacheldor working with a small group of trusted friends. Bacheldor attached the table legs to sensors that would indicate if one of them lost contact with the floor by causing a lamp to light, and was able to measure the force by using strain gauges. He started with Faraday's explanation of unconscious muscular action very much in mind, but realized that with this sort of occurrence it could no longer apply: you can't push a table into the air when your hands are laid on top of it – either unconsciously or in full awareness.

If you think the passages I've just quoted are exceptional, and can be treated as anomalies amid a mass of quite unremarkable testimony, that's not the case at all: the research literature contains scores of descriptions of this kind.

Here's a particularly interesting piece of testimony from a man who experimented successfully with friends and was satisfied there was no trickery; equally, that the scientific explanation given by Faraday did not in the slightest account for the phenomenon. 'I believe in my own mind,' he concluded, 'that it must have been some psychic force which passed from our own bodies and neutralized the laws of gravitation.'[27] Coming from a confirmed believer this would be unremarkable, but it was actually stated by John Maskelyne, which raises an interesting question. When a debunking conjuror, supposedly that most qualified of experts, says he has himself experienced a widely claimed paranormal phenomenon, one that he concedes is not caused by trickery, and starts talking about psychic forces neutralizing the laws of gravitation – what are we supposed to think?

Few people took much notice of Maskelyne's experience, and sceptics rarely mention it, which reinforces my point that debunkers are credible only in their natural condition of disbelief: when they change their minds they possess no more authority than anyone else. But more obviously, it dilutes the idea, implied – if not actually stated by campaigning sceptics like Maskelyne and Randi – that conjurers can duplicate any psychic feat.

In fact, there are many other cases on record of conjurors having interacted with psychics and confessed themselves to be stumped. Take, for instance, the case of Jean Eugène Robert-Houdin, today considered the original and archetypal stage magician. In 1847 Robert-Houdin was commissioned to attend a sitting with the clairvoyant Alexis Didier. The conjuror was happy to accept, having earlier exposed a faker and being in no doubt that he would do so again. He blindfolded Didier, then laid out ten playing cards face down upon the table, each of which Didier correctly identified. He carried out this test a second and third time, and each time Didier again correctly named every card. Didier was equally successful with a number of other tests, for instance identifying a hair that Robert-Houdin produced as belonging to his son, and producing the words 'after this sad ceremony' when asked to reveal any phrase on page eight of a book Robert-Houdin had brought with him (the phrase was actually on page nine).

Endorsing a description of these events, Robert-Houdin wrote: 'I am bound to state that the facts reported above are absolutely correct and that, the more I think about it, the more impossible is it for me to class them among the activities that comprise my art and works.' After a later, equally stupefying sitting with Didier, the conjuror wrote as follows: 'I came away … as amazed as it is possible to be, and convinced that it is absolutely impossible that either chance or superior skill could ever produce such wonderful effects'.[28]

Magicians have also endorsed séance phenomena. A German conjuror by the name of Samuel Bellachini said he had investigated the medium Henry Slade's performance 'with the minutest observation' and dismissed any idea that they could be carried out by conjuring tricks or the use of mechanical apparatus.[29] And here is the illusionist Harry Kellar, who had debunked plenty of spiritualist mediums in his time, describing a levitation by William Eglinton:

A circle having been formed, I was placed on Mr Eglinton's left and seized his left hand firmly in my right. Immediately on the extinction of the lights I felt him rise slowly in the air and as I retained firm hold of his hand, I was pulled to my feet, and subsequently compelled to jump on a chair and then on the table, in order to retain my hold of him. That his body did ascend into the air on that occasion with an apparently utter disregard to the law of gravity, there can be no doubt. What most excited my wonder was the fact, for I may speak of it as a fact without qualification, that Mr Eglinton rose from my side, and, by the hold he had on my right hand, pulled me up after him, my own body appeared for the time being to have been rendered nonsusceptible to gravity.[30]

Far from being embarrassed to make such admissions, the conjurers in fact seemed open-minded and curious. So although some in the conjuring fraternity are aggressively vocal against psychics they don't necessarily speak for all of their colleagues. And again, it's interesting to compare these informal encounters with the requirements posed by James Randi's Million Dollar Challenge. Must we suppose that expert, sceptical conjurors such as Robert-Houdin, Maskelyn and Kellar were all fooled, while Randi's testing would have been too rigorous to allow him to be taken in?

5 *Eusapia Palladino*

At the time I was pondering these things, a controversy about Eusapia Palladino blew up in the quarterly journal of the Society for Psychical Research.

It was started by Richard Wiseman, then a lecturer, now a professor of psychology at the University of Hertfordshire, who has since become well known for his sceptical critiques of the paranormal on radio and television.[31] Having himself once practised conjuring professionally, Wiseman brought his expertise to bear on the report of a second SPR investigation of Palladino, whose authors, on having a closer look, unequivocally considered her ability to be paranormal.

Going into some detail Wiseman described a method that Palladino might have used to fool the investigators, involving a hidden accomplice, which they seemed not to have been aware of. Wiseman's paper drew heated responses from other SPR members who insisted this could not possibly be the case. Far from backing down Wiseman then accused his critics of making major mistakes in their analysis, drawing yet more furious responses.

I was impressed by the passions the case roused, but at the same time did not know who to believe. I just didn't know enough about the background. If Wiseman's arguments were sound, and Palladino really could have cheated in this way, then one of the strongest pieces of evidence in favour of paranormal séance phenomena would be pretty much dead. On the other hand, if he was wrong, then the episode might have real significance. The only way to find out which was the case was to roll up my sleeves and get to grips with the primary sources.[32]

A poor child growing up in the slums of Naples, Palladino is said to have been at the centre of poltergeist-type activity herself, and in her teenage years was pressed into giving séances. Spiritualists were hugely impressed by her abilities and urged scientists to take a look. The first to take up the challenge was Cesaré Lombroso, an Italian professor of criminology. Lombroso hesitated for some time – as a convinced materialist it was not the sort of thing he would normally dream of getting involved with – but in the end his curiosity got the better of him.

In 1890 he investigated her, together with three psychiatrist colleagues, and declared that it was just as he had been told: among other things this strange woman could cause articles of furniture to levitate at a distance, produce raps on walls, and bring forth sounds from musical instruments without touching them.

Lombroso's report led a group of professors of various disciplines, whose materialist convictions had likewise been hitherto unchallenged, to conduct a thorough investigation in Milan in 1892. A total of seventeen sittings were held in a private apartment. The reports issued later described repeated sightings of phantom hands, and as objects bumped and glided round the room, apparently of their own volition, there was much scholarly amazement and cries of '*Eh! il uomo invisibile!*' (H.G. Wells's novel *The Invisible Man* had recently come out). 'It is impossible to count the number of times that a hand appeared and was touched by one of us,' the professors said. 'Suffice it to say that doubt was no longer possible. It was indeed a living, human hand which we saw and touched, while at the same time the bust and arms of the medium remained visible, and her hands were held by those on either side of her'.[33]

The only dissenting voice was that of the physiologist Charles Richet. He was astonished by what he had seen but, as he later said, he lacked the nerve to contradict the beliefs of a lifetime.

Two years later Richet decided to have another look, getting together with a Polish scientist and two stalwarts of the SPR. One of these was Frederic Myers, a classical scholar from Cambridge who had helped found the Society and was to be one of its most active members. The other was Oliver Lodge, a physicist who among other things invented the spark plug and was one of the first people to transmit a radio signal. The four men held sittings with Palladino in Richet's holiday home in the south of France, where they were convinced they witnessed psychokinetic effects. Besides the usual table levitations, a large melon and other objects glided through the air, and there were frequent billowings of the curtain. They often also felt touches by an invisible hand, and Myers at one point felt himself being hugged from behind while Palladino was sitting opposite him.[34]

Parapsychologists are often the strongest critics of each others' work, and this is a typical instance. The report that Myers and Lodge wrote up was torn to shreds by their SPR colleague Hodgson, whose earlier experiences had left him decidedly sceptical.[35] Hodgson argued that the report did not definitely rule out the possibility of Palladino getting a hand free, after which she could have performed all sorts of tricks using concealed hooks and other apparatus.

Myers politely agreed that he was at fault for not describing the precautions they took in more detail. But he insisted that he and the others were convinced that 'on no single occasion during the occurrence of an event recorded by us was a hand of Eusapia's free to execute any trick whatever', adding that they were well familiar with the dodges Hodgson had described.[36]

It was decided to resolve the issue by bringing her to Cambridge. Alas for Lodge and Myers, during this investigation Palladino cheated openly, completely erasing their positive endorsements.

What the investigators observed on this occasion was that Palladino exploited any inattention on their part to get a hand or a foot free.[37] By this time her use of the 'substitution' trick was notorious: if her hands were lightly held by a person on each side of her she could gradually bring both of them together and then slowly pull one away, so that the controllers were left unknowingly holding the same hand. In fact, none of Hodgson's elaborate theories were borne out in Cambridge: she was not discovered using telescopic rods or concealed hooks or anything else of the kind; having got a hand free she merely used it to rap the table or push an object to make it move. Similarly with her feet – as long as the controllers' shoes were laid over her own they might feel confident that all was well. But, the critics argued, they wouldn't necessarily know if the boots actually contained her feet; she might have wriggled one free without them realizing.

6 *Hypnosis?*

By now I was more confused than ever. I could not begin to understand why it was so difficult to agree what was going on, or why some saw Palladino as a sort of sorceress, while others considered her a wily faker. There was nothing for it but to press on and hope that somewhere along the way the muddle would sort itself out.

At this stage I started to pay more attention to the idea that mediums might induce a sort of hypnotic illusion in their audience.[38] I didn't really think they were made to 'see' things by the medium's artful suggestions – 'Look, look, the table is rising, watch it rise!' – as although this might have worked for ordinary charlatans it could not realistically account for the level of detail reported in Palladino's case. But what if it was not she who was in a trance, as the investigators thought, but *they themselves*, unwittingly brought into that condition by Palladino? If that were the case she would be able to cause them to see just about anything she wanted, just as stage hypnotists manage in some extraordinary way to do with members of their audience. There's no agreement about the mental process involved, but it obviously happens, and would comfortably explain why some sitters reported things that are just flat out impossible.

The problem with this is that some people are more susceptible to hypnosis than others, and putting several individuals into a trance can't normally be done collectively, let alone covertly and in a short space of time. But then, I reflected, perhaps the ones who were convinced by her were those she had managed to cast her spell over, and those who remained entirely unimpressed were the ones who were not susceptible. That would nicely explain why some people saw the actions of invisible spirits and others saw clumsy tricks. Problem solved! However I had to abandon the idea of hypnosis altogether when I learned that the phenomena she caused were on occasion registered by measuring instruments, establishing their objective existence.

This was demonstrated during a series of forty-three sittings held with Palladino between 1905 and 1908 in Paris, attended by eminent scientists and intellectuals including Richet, Pierre and Marie Curie (the pioneers of radiation), and the philosopher Henri Bergson. Palladino's chair was suspended on a weighing machine and sensors were attached to the table to register its movements by means of a recording device, one for each leg, which wouldn't however work if the table was being lifted from below. The instruments proved that the table levitated, sometimes with all four feet off the floor, when Palladino's feet and hands were restrained. The machines also demonstrated that the force of the motion was coming from *her*, and that there was no physical connection between her body and the object.[39]

This investigation did not settle matters because although the subsequent report listed many such incidents it also noted Palladino's attempts to cheat, and it stopped short of committing the group to the certainty that she had psychokinetic powers. But privately at least some of the investigators seem to have believed that she did. Pierre Curie wrote to a colleague in 1905: 'It was very interesting and really the phenomena that we saw appeared inexplicable as trickery – tables raised from all four legs, movement of objects from a distance, hands that pinch or caress you, luminous apparitions, all in a locale prepared by us with a small number of spectators all known to us and without a possible accomplice'.[40]

The following year he wrote: '…these phenomena really exist and it is no longer possible for me to doubt it. It's improbable, but it is so, and it is impossible to deny it after the séances we have had in perfectly controlled conditions …There is here in my opinion a whole domain of entirely new facts and physical states in space of which we have no conception'.[41]

7 *Palladino in Naples*

In 1908 the SPR carried out its second investigation, commissioning a series of sittings in Palladino's home town of Naples. As I mentioned, the subsequent report not only reversed its earlier negative verdict, but did so with a new emphasis and clarity, as a result of which it is considered to be one of the strongest endorsements of this kind of psychic claim.

One reason for its influence is the collective experience of the three investigators. Everard Feilding, a minor British aristocrat, had in the past exposed fraudulent mediums and considered himself a sceptic. Hereward Carrington, an American psychic researcher, had written at length about phoney mediums and described a great many of their dodges, having investigated them for years. Both he and the third team member, Wortley Baggally, were amateur conjurors, and Baggally claimed he could perform many séance tricks himself.[42] On the face of it, these people were well enough equipped and motivated to discover any deception that Palladino might try.

It's also clear that the three planned the investigation very thoroughly. They chose a large hotel on the sea-front in Naples, and hired a suite of three rooms that they checked and secured to exclude the possibility of an accomplice entering unnoticed. They gave a lot of thought to the arrangement of the furniture and the lighting, to make it as easy as possible to observe any phenomena and at the same time to control the medium. The set-up was the usual one, with Palladino seated at the head of a small table, one person on either side of her, each controlling a hand and a leg. Immediately behind her was the 'cabinet', a concealed recess created by placing a thin black curtain from wall to wall, in which was placed a stool and other objects such as musical instruments.

In some cases other people were also present, but most of the sittings were attended by just two or three of the investigators together with a stenographer. To keep as close a grip on the proceedings as possible each of them called out what they were seeing and the stenographer noted their comments verbatim, as well as the exact time they were made. This detail in the reporting was crucial if the investigation was to advance matters. All three understood that success depended on how well Palladino was shown to have been controlled, and they were careful to describe exactly what they experienced from one moment to the next, as this example shows:

10:26 PM   The table is going up again.

Feilding: Both medium's hands are off the table. As I am speaking I am looking under them, between them and the table. Her left foot was absolutely motionless against mine. My right hand on her left knee.

Baggally: My control the same as before, I could see under both hands.

Carrington: I saw a clear space under both wrists.

10:27 PM   The table went up again in the air on the two legs furthest from her.

Feilding: I put my left hand between her wrist and the table. Her left hand did not touch the table. Her left foot is firmly on my right. My other hand was on her knee. The right hand was also off the table while the table was going up.

Baggally: And during this levitation, my left hand was on her right knee and her right foot was on my left foot. I could feel it clearly.[43]

The level of electric light could be varied and, interestingly, Feilding said afterwards that the darkest sessions were often the least successful ones. At the start of the sitting Palladino would give some yawns, followed by enormous hiccoughs that signalled the start of her trance. There would then follow levitations of the table, which were frequent and easily visible in a level of light that was good enough to read small print by. None of the precautions they took hindered them in the slightest, Feilding reported.

> Eusapia had no hooks, either at her wrists or under the front of her bodice, and we could never discern the slightest movement of her knees or feet. We very often had our free hands on her knees, while her feet were controlled either by our feet or by one of us under the table, and were generally away from the table legs, an absolutely clear space being sometimes discernible between her and any part of the table.[44]

The most frequent phenomenon, and the easiest to control, Feilding said, were the billowings of the curtain behind her.

> The medium sat well in front of the curtain: her feet and hands were absolutely controlled. She would approach one of her hands, held by one of ours, to within about a foot of it, and the curtain would bulge out, sometimes gently, but sometimes with considerable force. The bulge was a round one, as though blown from within, and not in the least appearing as if any string or attachment were made to the outside. The coming out of the curtain happened generally as she approached her hand towards it, not as she withdrew it, as would be the case if there was an invisible attachment.[45]

There were constant noises behind the curtain, apparently caused by the small table shaking violently and the various small objects which had been placed there falling off it. On three or four occasions, Feilding said, this table appeared over the medium's shoulder, as though lifted by someone through the parting of the curtains behind her head and placed against the larger table in the séance room. It would then try to climb up on the table, although it never fully succeeded in doing so, and would eventually fall back, as if tired. Eventually they tied it down in the cabinet. After doing this the objects, which included a bell, a tambourine, a stringed instrument and a toy piano, at a certain stage glided out on their own and placed themselves on the table outside.

Especially startling were the frequent touches of an invisible hand, of which the fingernails could clearly be felt, when they were certain that Palladino's hands were restrained. During the later stages, hands could actually be seen through the parting of the curtains. Their appearance varied: sometimes they were as white as paper, at others a natural colour. Occasionally they carried objects. Once a grasp by a hand was seen as well as felt.

All this aroused in me rather queasy feelings of astonishment, but it also at last gave me a sense of why there are two contrary views of Palladino. Up until then I had tended to attribute the inconsistency of results to the varying skills and temperaments of the investigators. I felt, as sceptics do, that bias must be involved, although I was less inclined to attribute it exclusively to those like Myers, Lodge, Richet and Feilding who endorsed her, and not to those like Hodgson who never did. It had not occurred to me that, at least in this case, there might be a much simpler explanation: that the inconsistency lay in Palladino herself. Yet it was starting to become clear that this might be the case. What if she was not exclusively either real or fake, but could be one or the other at different times?

A point to mention here is that Palladino was tiresomely temperamental, which made her a difficult subject to deal with. In Naples, Feilding said, her behaviour varied considerably: when she was in a good mood she would let herself be properly controlled, even to the extent of letting her hands be tied up. But if she was tired and irritable she wouldn't allow this. At such times she would behave deviously, demand the light be turned down, and take every opportunity to produce the effects manually. It was also unquestionable that for long periods she brazenly played the hand substitution trick. The third, fourth and tenth sittings were all of this nature, Feilding said, and if these had been the only ones they had carried out they would have concluded she was merely a cheat. But interestingly, it was when she was in an ebullient mood, the light was good, and the control was strong, that they started to get strong and convincing effects.

Palladino herself seemed aware of this. She explained – and it seemed to be confirmed by observation – that psychokinetic effects occurred during her trance state by a process of will. The initial channel for the will would be physical: if you or I want to lift something we grasp it with our hands and raise it up, and this was a natural impulse in her also. It was by checking this impulse, allegedly, that the psychokinesis could be unlocked. For this reason she is recorded shouting '*Controllo!*' at moments when she felt the energy building, to ensure that she was properly held and did not release it by reaching out to perform an action manually.

Experienced investigators also learned that they needed to create the right balance. She needed to be restrained, but not too tightly as this would inhibit any effects. This was what Feilding and his colleagues did at Naples. But it had not been the case at Cambridge thirteen years earlier, where Hodgson went to the opposite extreme, relaxing the control for the specific purpose of seeing what she would do. Since she found it easy to get her hands and feet free, she used them. The natural result was that the investigators, as well as invited guests such as the conjuror Maskelyne, went away thinking that that was all she was capable of.

8 *Palladino in New York*

This was not the end of the story. The Naples series was negated by a series of exposures made during Palladino's trip to New York and other American cities over the following year. The visit was organ-

ized by Feilding's colleague Carrington, who having at last found
someone he considered to be a genuine medium was keen to show
her off to American scientists. There were two particularly damaging setbacks: the magazine article in which the Harvard professor
Hugo Münsterberg claimed to have revealed her chicanery, and
an investigation carried out by the psychologist Joseph Jastrow, in
which she was seen to do nothing but cheat.

The Münsterberg exposé gets a lot of attention from sceptics, and
I'll come to that in a moment, but it is Jastrow's intervention that
probably carries the most weight. Jastrow did something similar to
Münsterberg – he got a conjuror to hide under the table and see what
Palladino did with her feet. It was observed that she fished around
behind her to try to kick the stool with her foot; she made the table
'levitate' by getting a toe under one leg and lifting it with her hands;
and she caused the billowings of the curtain either by kicking it or
blowing out of the side of her mouth.[46]. Halfway through the second séance they did restrain her tightly, and from then on no effects
whatever occurred.

Inevitably, this account tended to weaken in my own mind the
positive view that Feilding's report had created earlier. It's as definite
in its conclusions as his is, and has the enormous advantage of not requiring the acceptance of a paranormal process. But I did rather wonder how Jastrow and his colleagues could so effortlessly have resolved
a problem that other investigators had missed throughout hundreds
of sessions over a period of two decades. It seemed to present no difficulty to them at all, and in fact Jastrow himself remarked on this, as
Maskelyne had done at Cambridge, that it was incredible that people could not see the tricks. Then I considered that this is consistent with Palladino operating on two quite different levels, and, just
as significantly, it's consistent with Jastrow and his team failing to understand that possibility. What they saw would have been the 'level
one' Palladino, the grumpy one who was in a bad mood and whom
they lacked the experience to control, not the 'level two' Palladino that

Feilding and his colleagues were able over a longer period to catch extended glimpses of.

You can see this clearly in the discrepancies between Jastrow's remarks and the observations reported by other investigators. Take for instance his description of the billowing curtain. Jastrow said he saw her making movements – kicking with her feet and puffing hard – that would cause the curtain to 'bulge'. Yet neither of these dodges would begin to account for what was observed by Feilding, Baggally and Carrington at Naples, and by Richet, the Curies and others at the Sorbonne. In the extract I quoted a moment ago, you will recall Feilding's description of how Palladino sat well in front of the curtain and gradually held out one of her hands, which was held by one of theirs, to within a foot of it, and as she did so it bulged out *towards* them. It was a rounded bulge that could only be achieved if it had been blown from the other side. Feilding was very explicit about this:

> If we made a sudden grab at the bulge, no resistance was encountered, and the bulge subsided as though one had pricked the surface of a balloon. There was no attachment to her hand, as we constantly verified by passing our hands between her and the curtain. Nor would any attachment produce the same effect, as the curtain was so thin that the point of attachment of any string would at once have been seen. Besides these bulges in response to her or our gestures, there were spontaneous movements of the curtain, often very violent, and frequently the whole curtain would be flung out with so much force that the bottom of it came right over to the further end of the table.[47]

Feilding adds that sometimes, at her request, one of those present could hold out their own hand and the same thing would occur. If that is the case, the likelihood of her achieving it by trickery is yet more remote.

In the last chapter I attached significance to the fact that investigators who tracked down and directly witnessed poltergeist-type phenomena were more thorough and methodical than the debunkers. I suggest that is also the case here. If Feilding's report could be judged in comparison with Jastrow's in a neutral way, unbiased by concerns about the outcome, Feilding's would surely be judged the more impressive, in terms of procedures, scope and attention to detail. To recap: Feilding and his colleagues had considerable first-hand experience of fraudulent mediums. They carried out eleven séances, and after the first three they were still uncertain; if there had been no others besides these their verdict would have been negative. Jastrow, by contrast, carried out only two sittings, and his conclusion never seems to have been in doubt; as a vocal debunker of paranormal claims it would have been surprising if they had been. At Naples the investigators sometimes had visitors, but mainly worked alone, the optimum conditions for concentration. In Jastrow's, by contrast, as many as fifteen people seem to have been present, which surely must have been distracting. Finally, Jastrow published no verbatim records, and took it for granted that he would be believed, which was perhaps fair from his point of view, but was an attitude he would surely have criticized in his opponents.[48]

Here, too, it was a growing sense of the shallowness of the critics' responses that shaped my thinking. The investigators seemed to want to get to the bottom of the mystery, and didn't mind how long it took. By contrast, sceptics seemed more concerned to subvert their conclusions than to create substantive foundations for an alternative view. Some were transparently motivated to manipulate perceptions. A good example is the article by Münsterberg that described the exposé during which Palladino gave her 'thrilling Sarah Bernhard' scream, indicating that she knew 'her glory was shattered'. Among the verbatim records of her American séances, in a volume later published by Carrington, I was interested to come across that particular séance described in detail. Here is the relevant extract:

A black object comes out of curtain and is seen by all. It touches Professor [Münsterberg]. Curtain blows out. Various sounds heard in cabinet.

Right controller's hand rests across medium's knees. Her feet resting on right controller's. Left controller, Professor [Münsterberg] is holding both hands. Curtain continues to blow out. [Palladino] screams sharply. Reason not known. Right controller says one knee and foot rest against his. His hand across both knees.

Left controller holding both hands. Controllers say that control is all right. Slight sound of tambourine. Table tilts on two legs furthest from medium. Controllers discuss control of feet and finally decide they are controlling both. Table tips at an angle of forty-five degrees on two legs farthest from the medium. Controllers say that [Palladino] did not touch the table. She places one leg across Professor [Münsterberg's] knee. Complete levitation. Professor [Münsterberg] touched again on elbow. Right hand perfectly visible. Left hand held by Professor [Münsterberg]. Professor [Münsterberg] touched again distinctly.[49]

In case you missed it, 'screams sharply. Reason not known' is all that was noted at the time. Now when I first came across Münsterberg's statement – and indeed every subsequent occasion I encountered it in the sceptical literature – I assumed that this was a rip-roaring exposé, that the sitting broke up in confusion, and that Palladino was sent home in disgrace. Those are the images his words create.

But it turns out nothing like that happened at all. According to Carrington, she grumbled afterwards that someone had grabbed her foot, but no one at the time knew what she was talking about. It doesn't mean that she wasn't trying to cheat, but it does contradict the impression created by the professor that this had been laid bare for the whole world to see.

9 *More rational gravity*

I'd argue, too, that Münsterberg's behaviour indicates the presence of rational gravity, the mental process that restores order by manufacturing alternative normal scenarios. He describes the touches as 'uncanny', and says he plainly felt the thumb and the fingers. 'Her achievement was splendid,' he adds. 'She had lifted her unshod foot to the height of my arm when she touched me under cover of the curtain concealing the table behind them without changing in the least the position of her body'.[50] But did she really? In any other context this would be hard to believe. Try squeezing your upper arm lightly, and then imagine a short, stout, middle-aged woman dressed in an ankle-length dress sitting by your side, both of whose hands you are holding out in front of you, having created that sensation by covertly using her foot. It's just not a reasonable proposition. On the other hand, if the idea of being manhandled by an invisible entity made you queasy – and Münsterberg was obviously disgusted and horrified by this sort of thing – is this not how you might respond, by manufacturing an alternative that you could live with?

Again – and this is the really interesting part – once a Harvard professor has stated in print that a fraud has been uncovered, a mental manoeuvre has achieved the status of historical fact. What was really never any more than conjecture is represented as certainty, entering into the public domain as part of the case against psi. Münsterberg's description is so detailed, colourful and emphatic that one naturally assumes it's a report of what actually happened. And I began to feel that this is characteristic of sceptical literature as a whole. Much of it consists of just this kind of speculation, the mentation of minds writhing to escape from an uncomfortable dilemma, and the joshing, often sarcastic tone not entirely concealing an underlying anxiety.

Here, too, a sceptic could insist that this is just one of the ways in which paranormal believers persuade themselves that there is such a thing as psychokinesis. Surely they are the ones whose reasoning is being subverted. Yet just as with poltergeists, there's plenty of evidence that rational gravity in relation to spirit mediums is a real psychological process. One of the first to comment on it was Charles Richet, who eventually realized that it was the reason why he had felt unable to agree with the positive endorsement of Palladino after the Milan investigation:

> At the moment when these facts take place they seem to us certain, and we are willing to proclaim them openly; but when we return to ourselves, when we feel the irresistible influence of our environment, when our friends all laugh at our credulity – then we are almost disarmed, and we begin to doubt. May it not all have been an illusion? May I not have been grossly deceived? … And then, as the moment of the experiment becomes more remote, that experiment which once seemed so conclusive gets to seem more and more uncertain, and we end by letting ourselves be persuaded that we have been the victims of a trick.[51]

Feilding makes a similar point in his report on Palladino. He explains that he had approached this investigation seriously doubting that she could have created so much impact with the petty tricks she was observed to use. But at the same time he was unable to credit the reports himself, especially as all his previous investigations of physical mediums had revealed nothing but 'childish frauds'. The first séance, therefore, produced feelings of surprise; the second, feelings of irritation at being presented with an insoluble problem; and it was almost a relief in the third session when they caught her cheating. By the fifth, he had seen abundant evidence of her ability under tight control, and the struggle of trying to come to terms with its manifest absurdity had produced a kind of intellectual fatigue.

It was in the sixth session that a breakthrough occurred. Now he found his mind starting to absorb ideas that he had previously repelled, like raindrops streaming off a waterproof coat. For the first time, he says in a much quoted passage:

> … I have the absolute conviction that our observation is not mistaken. I realize, as an appreciable fact in life, that from an empty cabinet I have seen hands and heads come forth, that from behind the curtain of that empty cabinet I have been seized by living fingers, the existence and position of the very nails of which could be felt. I have seen this extraordinary woman sitting visible outside the curtain, held hand and foot by my colleagues, immobile, except for the occasional straining of a limb, while some entity within the curtain has over and over again pressed my hand in a position clearly beyond her reach.

Notice too what Feilding says next:

> I refuse to entertain the possibility of a doubt that we were the victims of a hallucination. I appreciate exactly the fact that ninety-nine people out of a hundred will refuse to entertain the possibility of a doubt that it could be anything else. And, remembering my own belief of a very short time ago, I shall not be able to complain, though I shall unquestionably be annoyed, when I find that to be the case. I shall be told that this sudden declaration of conviction is absurdly hasty, highly unphilosophical and unworthy of a student of psychic science. Perhaps it is; but the precise moment at which conviction is reached differs in individuals not, I think, according to the cogency of the facts presented to them, but according to their willingness to abandon a position which they feel to have become untenable.[52]

These underlying psychological processes seem to me to be a very natural response to a paranormal phenomenon. It's surely what we should predict. To witness something that contradicts all knowledge and experience would surely require a good deal of getting used to. But of course there is no mention of it in the sceptical literature:

debunking psychologists and magicians assume that paranormal effects are illusory, so they would see no reason for any such mental distortion to occur. And as they seldom engage with the primary sources they rarely come across any evidence of it.

10 *Wiseman vs Palladino*

This psychological response also affects you and me as third-party observers. How we react depends on our temperament, education and experience, of course, as well as any prior conviction. But it's true to say that many of us will fight to retain our sense of normality. Struggling to keep a balance, we will pick up on some detail and our imaginations will work on it.

This has been my own experience, and it may well be yours here, scanning what I have been saying for anything that seems to offer an opening, and perhaps sometimes feeling you have found it. 'Ah ha!' you may have thought, '*that's* how she did it. This McLuhan fellow just hasn't spotted it.' Because I haven't specifically ruled out this loophole – possibly for no other reason than for lack of space – it gives you something around which to create an alternative construction. Having effortlessly identified the key to the problem that also eluded the investigators who were actually present, you will then proceed to marvel at their credulity and blindness to the truth.

As I say, this is a natural mental process, and one that I think anyone who wants to understand this episode – or the investigation of any paranormal claim for that matter – needs to recognize. In effect, we have to extend our critical faculty so that it encompasses *itself*: the detective watching the detective, so to speak. For we can't always assume that it will work in a perfectly neutral way, or that it's immune to distortions created by the object of its attention.

We should also remember that we lack the advantage these investigators had of being able to examine the phenomenon at close quarters and over a period of time. We are interrogating a deposition by someone who is probably long dead, and coming up with all sorts of alternatives. We don't have the original experience to work with; all we have are words on a page, and what we see in our mind's eye is whatever our imaginations have managed to reconstruct. The writer is not there to answer our questions and provide the necessary reassurances. Naturally it's easier to trust our doubts than to start making awkward readjustments to our worldview.

To gain some insight into how this happens let's go back to the controversy about Palladino that was started by Richard Wiseman. Writing in the SPR journal, Wiseman suggested that all the incidents witnessed by Feilding, Carrington and Baggally in Naples were explicable on the basis that Palladino had an accomplice. Rather handily for his argument, her husband was a circus conjuror by profession and would have been an obvious candidate. Perhaps he gained access to the adjoining room through the door to the hallway, or even through a trapdoor in the ceiling. He could then have removed a fake panel that he or someone else had constructed earlier in the door leading to the séance room (a photograph shows that the door was partly obscured by the curtain concealing the cabinet recess). Once hidden behind the curtain, the accomplice could have staged all of the effects.

At first I could not judge the strength of Wiseman's arguments, or of the rebuttals of his SPR critics, or of his rebuttals of their rebuttals, all of which left me mightily confused. What did strike me was Wiseman's forceful tone in castigating the original investigators for failures and inconsistencies. Their report is 'badly flawed', he says, and the diagram of the furniture layout they provided is 'grossly misleading'.[53] This robust language made me doubt their judgements; they can't have been such good investigators after all. Wiseman was equally scathing towards those SPR members who rushed to their defence, and this made me think that they too were being insufficiently rigorous.

Much later, when I had spent some time reading and thinking about Palladino, I returned for another look, and it was only then that I grasped just how cheeky Wiseman was being. As his critics pointed out, Palladino was tested many times in many different situations and this *modus operandi* could not apply in all of them (in the south of France she was tested successfully in the open air). One would think that a method that involves clambering through a hole in the wall a few feet away from three investigators on the look-out for tricks, concealed merely by a flimsy curtain, is hard to sustain. In any case, the report mentions three occasions when the investigators looked behind the curtain, which would at once have given the game away. The nature of the effects is often directly at odds with the offered mechanism: as we have seen, the curtain often blew out with great force, lifting up as high as the table – if an accomplice was doing this he or she would be uncovered. On one occasion the phenomenon continued after the sitting had ended, when they had turned up the lights and pulled back the curtain. Feilding notes too that the most impressive effects were the swelling of the medium's dress and the complete levitations of the table, which could not have been performed by a hidden accomplice.

In an energetic comeback to all this, Wiseman pointed out that he was merely suggesting how it *could* have been achieved in this way, rather than dogmatically insisting it was. This disarms his critics but does not weaken the attack, as it's not a distinction his audience would care about. In short, it seemed to me that Wiseman's achievement here is less to provide a realistic alternative than to change perceptions. By challenging the report in a robust way he has got the opposition on the defensive. Hypothetically, a fellow sceptic could now write something like: 'Believers insist that the Naples investigation of Eusapia Palladino is firm proof that she had magical powers. However, more critical observers have found serious flaws in the report that suggest her feats were actually carried out by a concealed accomplice' (followed by a reference to Wiseman's paper). That wouldn't have been established, but readers of such comments wouldn't know that unless they were to go into it in some depth.

11 *Séance sex*

I accept that I seem to be on the wrong side of this argument, defending something most of us know in our bones just ain't so. Perhaps what Richard Wiseman and other sceptics are doing is entirely legitimate – never mind how they go about it. The claims have to be dealt with somehow. Normality has to be restored.

I can see the logic of this, yet, as I read, something troubled me. For amid all the confusion and controversy, another thing became increasingly clear: the debunking sceptics haven't provided a coherent alternative. In fact it's hard to feel that anyone has seriously tried to do this. It's a matter of a few weeks' work to skim the literature, identify the major exposés, scandals and confessions, and then string them together in a sceptical narrative. The mix can be leavened with a bit of humorous banter and creative speculation to build a picture of mundane trickery. The 'wonders' are put down to petty villainy by the con artists, and stupidity on the part of their dupes. The debunkers chip away at witnesses' credibility by questioning their personal motives, finding fault in circumstances that in any other context would be unremarkable, and creating a murky atmosphere of conspiracy that in a straightforward reading is entirely absent.[54] For me, none of this rang true.

I noticed also that sex plays a big part in the debunking books, although that's perhaps to be expected, with sitters holding hands in the dark and young girls being tied up by excited professors. It's tempting to indulge in innuendo: if it can be suggested that an investigator and a medium are a secret couple then a motive has been uncovered for them to have partnered in collusion.[55] Ruth Brandon goes in for this approach: her book *The Spiritualists* is heavily suffused with psychological gamesmanship, where investigators are seduced by duplicitous young women, and lies, jealousy and fornication are obscurely present. As so often is the case, I found her constructions vaguely persuasive, in the sense of discouraging me from taking the mediums seriously, and it took an effort of will to realize that they don't really resolve anything.

There's a small but pertinent example where Brandon tries to explain away Palladino, whose career, she thinks, was flavoured by a 'taint, or titillation, of slightly unsavoury sex'. The extent to which the relationship between medium and sitters was sexual is made clear, she reports, in the comments of Lombroso and another professor after the Milan sessions in 1893:

> They gave it as their opinion that Palladino's phenomena were due to a redirection of fundamental sex-energy. They reported that her menstrual secretions increased at the start of her trances, that she had a particular zone of hyperaesthesia near her ovaries, and that when phenomena were about to occur they were sometimes accompanied by voluptuous erotic sensations followed by orgasm.

This is peculiar, certainly, but surely carries no sense that the relationship was any more sexual than that between gynacologist and patient. When Brandon goes on to comment, 'Whatever may have been the conditions under which these facts were ascertained, it is hard to believe that they were either wholly detached or entirely scientific,' [56] it's hard to know what she means. That the medium distracted the investigators by letting them look up her skirts? That they were helping to create the erotic sensations? Or what? The insinuation doesn't clarify anything; the effect is purely rhetorical.

Brandon is in her element when dealing with the posthumous sex scandal concerning William Crookes. Following his work with Daniel Home, he investigated Florence Cook, then a nubile sixteen-year-old. Crookes reported that on several occasions as Cook lay trussed up in a curtained recess – a fact that he insisted he monitored and verified – the female ectoplasmic spirit calling herself Katie King emerged briefly to converse with him, and once even let him kiss her.[57] The erotic frisson in this extraordinary account lent a certain degree of plausibility to a claim that surfaced in 1949, according to which Cook herself stated there had been no spirits, and that the investigation was merely a cover for an affair between the two of them.[58]

And indeed, how else are we going to explain something so seriously surreal? Brandon thinks it feels right and explains all the facts: Crookes's wife was pregnant at the time and he might have been on the lookout for a bit of rumple tumple on the side. It does deal with a nagging problem: given the circumstances, it is hard to imagine that a man of Crookes's intelligence could not have known, if this was the case, that the spook was Florence acting the part. And there's no question that it has saved the critics a good deal of trouble.[59]

But if Crookes really was looking for sex he might have found it in much easier ways. For this would have been an extraordinarily elaborate and time-consuming deception. The experiments in his home involved some of his scientific associates, one of whom helped to rig the girl up in an electrical circuit that would have been hard for her to escape from undetected.[60] As for the evidence upon which the story is based, critics tend not to realize how common these third-party and posthumous 'confessions' are, or appreciate the possible motivations that cause them. In her lonely middle age, Cook might well have made these comments as a means to distance herself from what she now viewed as a dubious past.

Even if we could make the love affair theory stick, we still have to deal with the similar, equally astounding observations made by

Richet and other professional investigators. Or for that matter, statements such as this, which described what happened when the lights were turned up on the ectoplasmic Katie King.

> Her features faded and became blotted out, appearing to turn one into another. The eyes sank in their sockets, the nose disappeared, the frontal bone caved in. Her limbs appeared to give way under her, she sank lower and lower on to the carpet like a falling building. At last nothing but her head remained above the ground, then one or two light masses of drapery, which disappeared with extreme rapidity, and we were left standing under the light of the three gas burners, our eyes fixed on the spot which Katie King had occupied.[61]

Is this fiction, or what? We can disregard it, or mentally file it under 'weird and unsubstantiated'. But that doesn't help us get to the bottom of it.

12 *The will to believe*

When all else fails, the critics fall back on the 'will to believe'. It doesn't matter how complex the effect is; the idea that the witnesses were biased by their emotional needs is imbued with the power to account for everything, a sort of über-explanation, a trump card that carries all before it.

Brandon deploys it for instance when tackling the astounding effects that Richet, Lodge and Myers observed with Eusapia Palladino in the south of France. She describes these in detail, agrees that they were extraordinary, and concedes it would have taken considerable skill to dupe such distinguished people. She's so relaxed about it that it almost seems she is about to reverse her position and admit that they must have happened as described. But no, it turns out there's an explanation, and it's simply this: all three men were clearly *enthusiasts* who were 'very much disposed to believe in the medium if they possibly could.'[62]

I'm guessing that Brandon here has been influenced by Donovan Rawcliffe, a British psychologist whose 1952 debunking of paranormal claims, *The Psychology of the Occult,* she appears to have relied on to a large extent, as have many other sceptics. Rawcliffe's book is saturated with the notion that the supernatural casts a malign spell, crippling people's critical faculties. He doesn't bother to even speculate about what Palladino was doing during the Naples sessions, but simply says she was conjuring, as should have been obvious to anyone whose mind had not been subjected to the 'insidious propaganda of superstition.' Indeed, he goes on, only the most prejudiced or those afflicted by the 'insidious will to believe' could arrive at any other conclusion.[63]

Didn't the views of the people who investigated her count for anything? No, because they weren't objective, Rawcliffe explains. Psychic researchers seldom are. Richet, Myers and Lodge all believed in the unseen world and died steadfast in their belief, with their 'will to believe' continually in conflict with their 'will to know'. He singles out Richet as an excellent example of 'a great scientist succumbing to the insidious yearning for mysticism', a story repeated over and over again in the annals of psychic research.[64]

In reality none of these men talked or behaved like religious enthusiasts, any more than most academic parapsychologists do today. It's true that Myers, probably more than most of his colleagues, was strongly interested in the idea of survival of consciousness after death, and hoped that his researches would confirm it. But he was not at all like the dogmatic spiritualist who, having seen tables levitate and heard voices from beyond the grave, is angrily dismissive of those who refuse to believe – there are plenty of people like that, and very tiresome they are too.[65] Myers's motive, by contrast, was to see if he could establish empirically a rational justification for the belief in survival, any evidence that might persuade scientists and academics of it, and he devoted the later part of his life to collecting and examining this in forensic detail.[66] He would hardly have bothered with that if he had faith. In fact scientists in all sorts of fields are fired by a hope that the object of their search will turn out to be true, and are willing to let their peers make a judgement based on the quality of their findings and arguments, as Myers was.

In the case of Lodge, it was constant exposure to the phenomena of psychic research that led to his conviction that consciousness survives death, although as we shall see, this was less on the basis of mediums like Palladino than the clairvoyant type we are more familiar with today. But the case of Richet is the most interesting because, despite everything the Frenchman personally witnessed with Beraud, Palladino and others, he flatly rejected the idea of survival and insisted there must be a purely materialist explanation. This view is articulated in his memoir, which Rawcliffe cites in his bibliography.[67] Possibly Rawcliffe knew this and didn't think it relevant, in which case I would have been intrigued to hear his reasons, or else – which I suspect is more likely – he had not read Richet's book.

As is true with so many sceptics, Rawcliffe's hyperbolic exasperation rather precludes the crisp factual description and critical comment one would prefer, which is certainly typical of Myers, Lodge and Richet, and for that matter the majority of academic parapsychologists. And if we're talking about prejudice it's hard to absolve the critics of a share in it. They tend to see themselves as possessing an absolute commitment to free enquiry, truth and reason. Yet to me the excitability of some of their declarations casts doubt on that – in fact, the emoting is often so intense I have wondered what on earth is going on in their heads. Parapsychologists have often noted – and many of them are psychologists, who might be expected to know – that the discomfort implicit in sceptics' reactions hints at personal insecurity. It's as though the claims must be resisted to the last gasp because they threaten disorder and insanity.

You can sense this emotional undercurrent in Rawcliffe's over-egged denunciation of the paranormal as a 'dim underworld of psychological automatism, suggestion, hypnosis, hallucination, neurosis, hysteria, functional malady, sensory hyperacuity, delusion, fraud, prestidigitation, and limitless credulity'.[68] It's strongly present in the debunking studies by Hugo Münsterberg, whose nervous constitution seemed permanently in danger of buckling under the threat of other people's superstitious beliefs.[69] Houdini's books too contain heated denunciations of mediums as 'human leeches' sucking every bit of sense from their victims, and references to mental asylums bursting with insane spiritualists.[70]

Debunkers in more recent times are just as prone to this sort of overstatement. James Randi's *Flim-Flam!*, like much of his subsequent work, boils over with angry indignation: readers who share his disbelief can enjoy seeing their frustrations being given full expression. But to less-committed readers Randi's judgements are so extreme as to raise suspicions about his reliability, for instance when he describes parapsychologists as 'psi nuts' and 'wide-eyed nincompoops', 'not rowing with both oars in the water', or when he approves someone else's comment that they have 'thinking defects and decayed relations with reality' – all surely belied by their university positions, their scientific reputations, and the scholarly, reasonable tone of their work.[71]

13 The phantom narrative

There is a convention, observed by some writers who tackle a paranormal subject in depth – and who develop a certain sympathy with it – to withhold any final conclusion about its veracity. Given its deeply controversial nature, this is an absolutely natural thing to do. But it does throw up some rather odd anomalies. Personally, I'm sceptical – just to take one example – that Barbara Weisberg, author of a useful recent biography of Kate and Maggie Fox, having presumably lived with her subjects for years and entered fully into their inner lives, their loves and relationships, dilemmas and struggles, could really remain undecided – as she finally implies – about whether or not the girls were congenital life-long cheats and liars. I am also unpersuaded by her suggestion that it doesn't matter – that knowing the truth is not what's important.[72]

This tension is surely the inevitable product of a tectonic clash between twenty-first century worldviews – one in which séance phenomena are an odd effect of nature, or visitations by spirits, or whatever, and one in which they are not merely distasteful but could not conceivably occur. We can't ignore the events altogether, but we can neutralize them in an inclusive post-modernist embrace, just as anthropologists do when they talk about the supernatural beliefs of pre-modern peoples.

Yet once we fully acknowledge the part played by historical pressures in shaping our ideas we should surely become less squeamish about overcoming them. For, in my view, a dispassionate analysis of this subject does yield an answer, and for one essential reason: the alternative narrative provided by sceptical writers, their idea of what *really* happened in those darkened parlours – an alternative truth that their imaginations can cope with – is manifestly incoherent. It doesn't make sense: it's misty and insubstantial, a ghostly shadow of the real thing – a *phantom* narrative. Interestingly, when this insight eventually took shape in my mind, the head-scratching stopped. The dissonance that had long held me in its grip melted away, having been caused, I now realized, by listening to clever people confidently explaining something they understand nothing about at all.

But what then? If the phantom narrative is an artefact of the doubting imagination, it at least shields us from ideas which are wildly difficult to accept. Our late nineteenth-century forebears, we would have to conclude, stumbled upon something so challenging, so hard to assimilate, so *irrational*, that they managed to suppress it, and in our yet more sophisticated age we see no reason to act any differently. The unthinking masses can amuse themselves with it, if they must, but Academia has better things to concern itself with. In fact it has largely airbrushed the subject out of history. Remarkably, there are biographies of famous scientists that barely refer to the passion for psychic research that occupied much of their time, and there are cultural histories of the Victorian period that don't once mention spiritualism, one of its biggest obsessions.[73] If we notice the subject at all, we can't grasp its true meaning, buried as it is under layers of funny anecdotes and absurdities, allegations and misunderstandings. We treat it as a joke.

Why would we want to excavate something that is so potentially awkward? I believe we have no choice, being the inquisitive creatures we are. It's because mysteries challenge our imaginations that we have science and technology. It does not surprise me that professional historians and biographers are starting to show interest in these early psychic investigations; in fact considering how relatively untrodden this ground is – and the fascinating subjects it offers for in-depth examination – their restraint up until now has been heroic. When they start to have more faith in their own judgements, they will reveal to the thinking world something extraordinary, for they cannot fail to notice the phantom narrative or be motivated to expose it.[74]

At the same time, this is not purely a historical matter. Séance activity may not get the same sort of attention as it did before, but it still sometimes goes on, arousing the same bitter controversies.[75] If it was more common during the late nineteenth century, that may have been because people had fewer activities to occupy their spare time than we do, and used it to experiment. These days it's not something we think of doing; we have quite different interests. But the implication is that focusing mental energy to make raps sound, tables levitate, or even create some of the other weird effects, are things that ordinary people – you, or some member of your family even – may be able to achieve with a bit of practice. That's not an argument for doing it, but it's something to think about.

Pursuing this idea a bit further, it's interesting to speculate what the results would be. What if the sceptics' nightmare were to take place, and a new craze for table-turning, say, were to sweep the world? Would we be any more prepared to accept its reality this second time around? I don't think it's likely: it's hard to bridge that psychological gulf between seeing a small table jerking and jumping on its own, beyond any shadow of a doubt, and convincing other people that that's what really happened. It's worth noting the influence of Uri Geller in stimulating public interest in the idea of mind interacting with matter, yet along with it, since his feats can to a large extent be duplicated by sleight of hand, the parallel conviction that such claims are bogus.

Perhaps new kinds of technology not available in the nineteenth century might be employed that would settle the matter once and for all. Infra-red photography could be used to see what was happening in the dark, for instance. But again, I doubt that it would: questions would still be raised about the operators' competence and honesty. This is the essential point: it's not just a question of creating watertight controls; it's about our ability to reconcile ourselves to the *idea* of psychokinesis.

There's a curious phenomenon I have found often in the literature, that some investigators could never quite bring themselves to accept the evidence of their eyes. They doubted the rigour of their work, and kept going back to repeat it with ever tighter controls. Nagging at the back of their minds must always have been the worry about what would happen when they stepped over the line and became *believers,* seduced by the supernatural's strange spell. How would they adjust to this strange new reality? Would they have to start believing in the spirits of dead people? Or, heaven forbid, in *God?*

That's a question I've dodged until now, whether the scientific validation of séance phenomena, if we can accept it, amounts to an endorsement of the genuineness of spirits – of the survival of consciousness after death, in other words. Some investigators themselves were unconvinced, which continues to be the case today. I'll come back to this, but in the meantime, mediums have not gone away, their approach has merely changed. Where séance effects can be equated with mechanical tricks, claims of telepathy and clairvoyance pose different, more subtle challenges. This is what we will be looking at in the following chapters.

THREE

COMMUNICATORS

'I have a gift, a capacity – a delusion, if you will – which is called 'psychic'. I do not care what it may be called, for living with and utilizing this psychic capacity long ago inured me to a variety of epithets – ranging from expressions almost of reverence, through doubt and pity, to open vituperation.'
Eileen Garrett, medium.

These days, mediums don't bother with funny goings on in darkened rooms. Instead they hear the dead speaking to them directly, and see the images they create in their mind's eye. Or so they say...

Chances are that if we ever start seriously wondering about this, it will be because of a bereavement – the loss of someone we were close to. Let's imagine the case of Glenda, a middle-aged woman grieving for a husband who died suddenly of a heart attack. To try to console her, a well-meaning friend suggests she watch the television programme *Crossing Over*, in which an American medium named John Edward passes on messages he claims to receive from deceased family members of people in the audience.[1] If she can believe her husband lives on in a spirit world, it may help her to recover.

There's nothing at all dramatic about what Edward does, Glenda finds. He stands still on the stage and passes on 'messages' from the invisible dead, cocking his head as though trying to catch what they are murmuring in his ear. Or else he seems to see them gesturing and holding up symbolic objects – like a game of charades. Interviewed afterwards, the audience members he had singled out seem impressed. Most are convinced he genuinely was in contact with their deceased loved ones, and some are overcome with emotion.

Glenda excitedly mentions this to her brother. But he tells her to have a closer look. She'll see that Edward is constantly asking questions of the people in the audience he is addressing, and their life stage, gender and social class give him a pretty good idea of the kind of person they are hoping to contact – husband, father or child, and so on. By throwing out names and ideas and asking for validation as he goes along he can build an accurate picture based entirely on what he or she is telling him. This is the technique known as 'cold reading' and its victims don't even understand the role they play in providing information.[2]

Of course, Glenda's brother goes on, sometimes Edward will be spot on. He might correctly tell an audience member she has a bad back, or is carrying her husband's wedding ring in her purse. But these are quite common situations and not hard to guess. In fact it's likely he gets things wrong at least as often, and instead of admitting so he will chide the person for having apparently 'forgotten'. In any case this is television, he reminds her – the failures have simply been edited out.

There are even worse ways of cheating. Mediums have been known to keep an eye on newspaper reports and obituaries for details that may prove useful in the future.[3] Or their assistants can mingle with the audience before the show and eavesdrop on their conversations.[4] By this means they can pick up all sorts of information: that the tall blonde woman in blue is the step-daughter of the grey-haired woman in black, and that they hope to contact the latter's husband who died recently in a work-related accident. By producing these details during the show, the mediums can elicit gasps of astonishment at their supernatural powers.

If this *is* what mediums do, it's not merely a very common deception but also a pretty cynical one. Those nice, spiritual, *caring* people would be confidence tricksters of the worst kind. It's all the more repulsive because the people they are apparently trying to help are so vulnerable. And for a committed secularist it's hard to see what else to think. If you take it as given that the mind is the brain, that there's no soul to survive death, and there are no spirits of the dead, and never could be, then you'll most likely share one reviewer's opinion of *Crossing Over*, that it's 'sheer, unadulterated, transparent nonsense which preys upon the gullibility of some extremely sad people.'[5]

It also needs to be said that professional psychics can make a lamentable impression. It's common to hear that this or that clairvoyant has predicted the death of a famous person or some natural disaster – but only ever said so after the event! And the proofs that are offered are less than convincing. Scandals often come to light about psychics bilking gullible clients out of huge sums, for instance by persuading them that they have some malady that only they can cure. And psychics who in rare cases have submitted to public tests have performed poorly, reinforcing sceptics' perception that their powers are illusory.[6]

2 *Piper and Leonard*

Where spirit mediums are concerned, some sceptics recognize that they may genuinely think they're in touch with the dead and consider themselves to be performing a useful service. Perhaps on some level they really are hearing voices and seeing images, but can't accept that it's just their imagination. Mediums themselves say the difference between erroneous intuition and the real thing is not always easy to determine.

You might think the best way to decide what's really going on would be to carry out rigorous large-scale experiments in controlled conditions. You would need to ensure that the medium can't acquire information covertly, and eliminate any opportunity for picking up clues from body language. The medium's responses would then be examined as objectively as possible, by means of an independent scoring system, to determine whether the information provided actually is relevant, or just seems so.

Yet as I discovered, there's nothing really like this in early investigative literature about clairvoyant mediums. The reason seems to have been that researchers quite quickly became convinced that, in stark contrast to séance phenomena, this was *unambiguously* genuine. The private information that mental mediums were able spontaneously to give about people who they had just met, and could not know anything about, was far too detailed and accurate to be anything other than supernormal, which in their opinion made the imposition of physical controls superfluous. It's a view that can and must be questioned, but at first sight we do seem here to be in different territory. We are analyzing statements, not looking for trapdoors and hidden apparatus. That suited scientific investigators like the Harvard psychology professor William James, who were frustrated by the difficulties of monitoring séance mediums and found these purely intellectual challenges far more congenial.

It was James who discovered Leonora Piper, a young housewife from Boston, who had given some surprisingly accurate readings to members of his family. She was subsequently investigated by Richard Hodgson, the British psychic researcher who, as we have seen, was decidedly sceptical about séance mediums, but with Piper became convinced he had found the real thing. The work with Piper spanned the two and a half decades between 1887 and 1911, and involved other researchers besides Hodgson, on both sides of the Atlantic. Shortly afterwards, in 1915, the SPR started working with a medium in London named Gladys Leonard (who I shall talk about more later), and this activity continued into the 1930s.

Leonard and Piper were by no means the only such mediums to be investigated, but they were the most prolific: their sittings were written up in more than a hundred separate papers, some of them of book length.[7] Typically a detailed analysis is followed by appendices containing verbatim records of sittings upon which the papers' conclusions are based. Most of this material deals with the small change of daily life: the doings of the sitters and their relations, friends and work colleagues; their personalities, relationships, behaviour and attitudes; mishaps and illnesses; meetings, journeys, undertakings and quarrels. Unlike clairvoyants, who claim to have a direct perception of these things, the medium appears to be acting as a sort of go-between with the spirit world, conveying comments from an individual, now dead but once known to the sitter, of the kind that will hopefully convince the sitter of that person's continued existence. Unsurprisingly, given the context, the messages are often couched in the language of psychotherapeutic counselling, touching matters of great emotional significance to the sitter.

A significant feature is that, like nineteenth-century séance mediums, but in contrast to mediums today, Piper and Leonard mostly appeared to work in a state of trance. A brief period of meditation would be followed by some convulsive movements; their facial features might become contorted and they might start to groan, seeming to change into a different personality that was quite distinct in its manner of speaking, attitudes and behaviour. To spectators it really appeared that a disembodied spirit had come, from who-knows-where, to possess the medium's body as a means to communicate with the living.

Piper was 'controlled' in this way by several such personalities throughout her career. During the early stages she took on the persona of an elderly Frenchman, speaking with a gruff masculine voice and a stagy French accent (a sitter named Rogers Rich heard himself addressed as 'Rowghearce Reach').[8] She – or we might say 'he', since the personality was so lifelike – said his name was Phinuit, which he pronounced 'Finee', and he claimed to have been a doctor living in Marseilles. Phinuit diagnosed sitters' physical ills and prescribed simple remedies; he also gave advice on their private affairs, about which he unaccountably knew a great deal, and sometimes gave forecasts of future events, some of which turned out to be accurate. At the end of the session he would seem to become tired, his voice weak and confused, and he would fall silent, at which point Piper gradually returned to her waking state, apparently knowing nothing of what had been going on.

Now this sounds like play acting, although to pretend to be in a trance, *and* to talk like an old man with a foreign accent, at the same time as performing a cold reading, seems unnecessarily ambitious. On the other hand it might act as a distraction, and it would also reinforce the conviction that something paranormal was taking place. In that sense, it could simply be a sort of convention, one that perhaps was adopted by one or two mediums, and found to be successful was imitated by all the rest. But I think the point still stands that, as well as being a competent mentalist, the medium would also need to be a talented mimic; these skills don't necessarily go together and are rarely seen being deployed at the same time.

There's also the fact that during her trance Piper seemed immune to normal sense impressions and did not respond when she was pinched or slapped. It's not impossible that she could have faked indifference to unexpected pain, but she also did not react when a spoonful of salt was placed in her mouth, nor when ammonia smelling-salts were suddenly thrust beneath her nose.[9] These salts give a powerful kick to the system, as I once discovered, and feigning indifference would be difficult, especially if she hadn't been expecting it to happen.

Piper's investigators had practical experience of trance states from their dealings with séance mediums. But the phenomenon had been known since the discovery of hypnotism in the late eighteenth century, and there had been many reports of entranced patients sometimes showing clairvoyant capabilities. For instance the individual might casually mention that a particular person known to both doctor and patient was on his way, although no appointment had been made, and half an hour later this person would knock on the door. Some practitioners set tests, and discovered that the patient, blindfolded and sitting in a chair, could identify what objects the doctor had in his right pocket, or identify the tastes of substances the doctor, unseen by him, put in his own mouth. There were patients who could 'read' with their fingertips, detect colours by touch, or divine the contents of opaque sealed envelopes. One woman was said to be able to read a book placed on her stomach while her head was covered in a cloth and turned in another direction.[10]

3 *Some Piper examples*

What really impressed the researchers about Piper was the 'veridical' quality of the information, that is, its level of correspondence to the facts. An example is the case of Harlow Gale, one of several sittings described by Frederic Myers, Oliver Lodge and others in the SPR's first report on Piper, published in 1892. Like almost all the new sitters, Gale had been introduced to Piper without being named or identified, and his visit had not even been planned in advance, which made it highly unlikely that she could have acquired the information clandestinely beforehand. At one point during the sitting Piper, as Phinuit, remarked:

> What is that thing your father wears over his shoulders? He looks quite important in it. He wears it because of his throat. He is in a different place from here.

This was correct: Gale's father lived in Minnesota and customarily wore a white silk handkerchief to protect his throat from the cold air.

Phinuit then said:

> William, a brother. He is small, a bright little fellow, dark
> eyes, clear complexion, a pretty fellow, smart as a cricket.

This was a broadly accurate allusion to Gale's brother William, a boy
of sixteen, although the size was wrong. Next:

> You have got a sister. She sings, and plays two different
> instruments; one with keys and one with strings –
> particularly the one with keys. She is a little younger than
> you, probably; but her age is difficult to tell from her
> appearance. She is older than William.

This too was largely accurate: Gale had a sister younger than himself
and older than his brother William. She sang and played the piano
well, although no stringed instrument. Phinuit continued:

> There is a minister in your family, an uncle, in the spirit.
> Tall, fine physique; wears spectacles; with a high forehead;
> something like you. He is your father's brother. He died
> some little time ago – away from you, across the water. He
> died suddenly… He used to wear a cape – a long coat thing.
> He was not Episcopal, but like a Methodist – that sort of
> doctrine.[11]

Almost all of this was accurate: Gale's uncle was a Baptist mission-
ary, and the physical description was correct, again apart from the
height. He had died suddenly fifteen years earlier while travelling in
the Middle East. He never wore a cape at home, but had one made
before leaving for his trip to wear over his overcoat.

These passages contain the usual mix of general items that might
apply to anyone, and specific ones that make the business notewor-
thy. What is surprising is that almost all of them are accurate, although typically there were some wrong items. There was no verbal assistance, thus providing little for a cold reader to work with.

Against this, however, the transcripts give no indication of what clues the medium might have picked up from the sitter's appearance and body language. It also needs to be pointed out that Piper often had some tactile connection, holding her hand up to the sitter's forehead or holding the sitter's hand, which, as the sceptics point out, is a method used by mentalists to pick up minute muscular reactions to their statements. On the other hand – and this especially impressed the researchers – the information was produced quickly, volubly, and with little appearance of effort, which counts against the idea of an interactive process.

As I say, some of the items are general; for instance, a sister who plays the piano would not have been uncommon for an educated man. To mention a dead uncle who wore spectacles, died some time ago and bore a facial resemblance to the sitter is also a safe gambit for a cold reader, since these details are likely to apply to anyone over a certain age. But for a faker to identify the uncle as a clergyman, without any prior hints to work with, would have been reckless, since the man could have been a lawyer, an accountant, a businessman, or just about anything else. One might perhaps argue that Gale had unwittingly provided some clue, but however much we advertise information about ourselves in our demeanour and body language, we surely don't do so for our relatives. Similarly, 'died suddenly' and 'overseas' are too particular to be worth attempting without some guidance, as they have at least an equal chance of being wrong – most people die in their own country. The same also applies to his cape, and I would suggest that attempting to identify the minister's denomination would be unnecessarily rash.

Sceptics point out correctly that mediums often throw out names until the sitter picks one up and runs with it – 'I'm getting a Mary. No, a Martha. Or something beginning with an M. Is it Min... Mel...? Mandy! Thank you'. Piper did sometimes do this, but on many occasions she would give a name and stick to it, even if it was not at first recognized. Here's an example described by a sitter afterwards:

[Piper] broke off very abruptly once and said, 'Who is Sadie?' 'I do not know.' 'Yes, you do. She says she did not know you, but knew Lettie. She had a cancer in her cheek – Now you know?' 'Yes.' 'She says, give her love to Lettie.' This was a young girl whom I had never seen, who died as described, and of whom I had heard much from 'Lettie'.[12]

If 'Sadie' had been a shot in the dark in a cold reading it would surely have been abandoned in favour of other names beginning with an S. In fact it's quite common for mediums to stick to a name and insist that they have got the right one, and that is a sensible strategy for a cold reader, as it transfers the blame for any mistake onto the sitter for lapse of memory. But here Piper not only persevered with the original name – instead of trying to find one that would be more acceptable – but also went on to offer highly specific information that led the sitter to recognize someone who was not part of his immediate family and for whom the facts closely fitted. One could reasonably object that once vague facts are extended to a sitter's relatives, friends and acquaintances the odds of their being relevant are vastly increased. Lots of people get cancer. But 'cancer of the cheek' is very specific, and the individual is also identified by name.

Piper's statements were often far more detailed and confidently given than, as I understand it, is possible with cold reading. Look at this example:

Phinuit mentioned the name 'Fred'. I said that it might be my cousin. 'He says you went to school together. He goes on jumping-frogs, and laughs. He says he used to get the better of you. He had convulsive movements before his death, struggles. He went off in a sort of spasm. You were not there.' My cousin Fred far excelled any other person that I have seen in the games of leap-frog, fly the garter, etc. He took very long flying jumps, and whenever he played, the game was lined by crowds of school-mates to watch him. He injured his spine in a gymnasium in Melbourne, Australia, in 1871, and was carried to the hospital, where he lingered for a fortnight, with occasional spasmodic convulsions, in one of which he died.[13]

As Phinuit, Piper also often described events that the sitter did not recognize, but later discovered to be true. One person returned for a second sitting complaining that the herbal infusion Phinuit had recommended as a cure for an ailment had failed to work. Phinuit commented, rather brusquely, that the servant who had prepared it had used the wrong measurements, had forgotten to watch it while it was being cooked, and was a fool anyway. The sitter later found that her cook had in fact used a quart where she should have used a pint and had let the mixture boil right down, wrongly thinking it would make no difference.[14] In another case he mentioned that a relative, whom he did not specify, was suffering from a sore thumb. This meant nothing to the sitter, who failed to discover anyone in his family with that particular problem. However a little later an aunt mentioned she had received a letter from some cousins, and having been asked if there was any news stated casually that a little girl in the family had had an accident: she had injured her thumb in a machine.[15]

4 *Cold reading?*

It struck me, looking at this material for the first time, that it does offer some possibilities for a sceptic. Some of the Phinuit sittings involved people who had already been to one or more session – as many in seven in one case. One can't be sure that information which appears spontaneous, detailed and accurate might not have been gained during an earlier session in a much more laborious way by a process of cold reading. Also if there was a likelihood of the individual returning for another session, there's less likely to be complete anonymity, and the medium could make enquiries about that person in the interval.

There are cases where sittings that produced reams of correct information were given for individuals who were closely related to subjects of earlier sittings. If none of the sitters were identified to the medium she would have had no obvious way of knowing the relationship, but it's difficult to feel confident about that. One can also find passages that look like classic cold readings, where the medium fumbled and made wrong statements. A few of the sitters were quite sceptical, were determined to give nothing away, and thought the whole thing was fraudulent.

It puzzled me that debunkers rarely make these points, and in fact seldom go into any detail at all about Piper.[16] I eventually realized that most of them have not read any of the material at first hand – this certainly applies to most of the CSI (CSICOP) writers – and the few criticisms they do make tend to be lifted from a single source, usually another critic.

For me, considering the quantity of striking successes, the overall impression is not one of faking. If cold reading is the true explanation, I'd expect to see the medium starting with general statements, then gradually firming up as she watches the sitter's body language and receives feedback to the questions she is artfully posing. But the successful transcripts don't show that: they show the information pouring out while the sitter says little or nothing. They do show Phinuit sometimes asking for validation of his statements, which is what a cold reader does. But a cold reader would surely then follow this lead, and here that does not necessarily happen; instead Phinuit goes on to produce new details which may also be quite accurate. At times Phinuit was curiously unreceptive to hints thrown out by undisciplined sitters, and indeed seemed to be quite uninterested in them.[17] For a cold reader that would be a wasted opportunity.

I noticed too that Piper sometimes impressed people who approached her in a determinedly sceptical frame of mind. A man named Brown, describing a private sitting that Hodgson had arranged for him, began by giving his opinion that she faked the trance and simply proceeded by guesswork and questioning. He attempted to thwart this by giving nothing away. He also thought she was able to add information that she had gathered previously. However, despite this apparent failure, Brown was interested enough to go for a second sitting, and this time the medium did get some details right. In answer to his question, 'Who is Horace Brown?' she correctly identified his uncle. Of course this wouldn't have been too difficult if she had known the sitter's own surname, but precautions had been taken to ensure she did not. When Brown went on to ask about this person's son, his cousin, the medium correctly identified him and his activities. Brown considered this 'interesting and remarkable':

> My question would afford a professional guesser the opportunity to get in some pretty good work, but there was no appearance of guesswork. Nothing was said to draw me out in the slightest degree – unless it was to make me ask questions. The replies were not given in a hesitating and half-questioning tone, so that I could deny or correct, or the speaker readily change them if occasion required; they were plumped out in the most positive and decided manner, and, so far as my knowledge extends, with but one partial exception, were exactly right.[18]

Brown had stated earlier that he did not think this process was paranormal, but the way he expressed himself suggests that he was at a loss for an explanation. He could have remarked how easy it would have been for the woman to have spied on him, or to have had an accomplice break into his house and rifle through his drawers, but he did not; nor did he come up with any other hypothesis. In my experience this is quite a common response when people discuss the paranormal – to deny vigorously that they take it seriously, and insist they know how the tricks are done, and then to implicitly con-

tradict themselves by going on to describe experiences of their own
that they found impressive and that they don't even attempt to explain away.

5 *Fraud*

I'd argue the Piper material supports the researchers' conclusion
that ordinary cold reading, at least as it's described by sceptics today, is not a sufficient explanation for her successful sittings. If the
mechanism of suggestion and feedback, apparent to some extent in
the minority of failed sittings, is not visible in the majority of successful ones, the notion would need to be reinforced in some way.

For instance one might propose that the mechanism is invisible
because Piper was highly skilled, and was taking advantage of body
language in a way that of course cannot be apparent from the transcripts. But, as I say, the sheer speed and accuracy with which the
information was provided, with names, places and details often delivered correctly, and without revision, tends to rebut that. As a last
resort one might maintain that the transcripts were made incorrect-
ly or doctored afterwards to give a misleading impression. While
it's true, as we will see, that there have been instances of this kind of
fraud in parapsychology, they are quite rare, and a conspiracy on the
scale required to create the Piper material would be hard to imagine.

To me as I read the research, the explanation that fairly shouts out
loud is that Piper managed to snoop around other people's houses,
or obtained inside information in some other way, perhaps talking
to people who were connected with the sitter. But we come back to
the same problem: Piper was not dealing with ordinary members of
the public, who might easily give away their interest by being members of a local spiritualist association, or book appointments in their
own name. This was a scientific investigation in which people were

sent to her anonymously and instructed not to identify themselves, severely restricting any opportunities for intelligence-gathering. The investigators took the possibility seriously enough to find out if she was in fact doing anything of the kind, having her and members of her family trailed by private detectives for several weeks, but failed to turn up any sign that she was trying to get information about potential sitters.

Just to be clear about the researchers' conclusions, here is what William James said about Richard Hodgson's reports:

> Dr Hodgson considers that the hypothesis of fraud cannot be seriously maintained. I agree with him absolutely. The medium has been under observation, much of the time under close observation, as to most of the conditions of her life, by a large number of persons, eager, many of them, to pounce upon any suspicious circumstance for (nearly) fifteen years. During that time not only has there not been one single suspicious circumstance remarked, but not one suggestion has ever been made from any quarter which might tend positively to explain how the medium, living the apparent life she leads, could possibly collect information about so many sitters by natural means.[19]

This was also the view of Frank Podmore, and anyone who is familiar with the work of the early SPR knows how significant this is. Having joined the society as an enthusiastic researcher, Podmore soon became its most rigorous sceptic, tireless in his efforts to find natural causes for the seemingly paranormal events uncovered by his colleagues, and ingenious in coming up with alternative explanations. He is more formidable than most sceptics writing today, because – unlike them – he was aware of the extent and nature of the investigative material, and the challenges it poses. Yet Piper seems to have defeated him. He calculated that the number of sittings written off as failures numbered barely ten per cent, and it was difficult to suppose that she could have been that lucky that consistently.

Against the possibility that Piper collected information via some spiritualist network, he pointed out that only a small portion of the sitters had visited other mediums, and in any case her performance was vastly superior to that of most others. Like me, he thought the most obvious explanation must be that she employed detectives in some sort of intelligence-gathering network. But to get the detailed and intimate information she came up with by these means would be costly and time-consuming. It would also need other people's help, which would make her vulnerable to blackmail.

Podmore also noted 'the consummate skill which has enabled her to portray hundreds of different characters without ever confusing the role, to utilize the stores of information so laboriously acquired without ever betraying the secret of their origin.' In short, he concluded:

> If Mrs Piper's trance-utterances are entirely founded on knowledge acquired by normal means, Mrs Piper must be admitted to have inaugurated a new departure in fraud. Nothing to approach this has ever been done before. On the assumption that all so-called clairvoyance is fraudulent, we have seen the utmost which fraud has been able to accomplish in the past, and at its best it falls immeasurably short of Mrs Piper's achievements. Now, that in itself requires explanation.[20]

Having abandoned any serious idea that Piper was faking, the researchers dedicated their efforts to answering what to them seemed by far the more baffling and urgent question: Where was she getting the information from? Were spirits of the dead really communicating through her, or was she simply tapping into the minds of the sitters by some telepathic process? This is something I will touch on later; at this stage we should just note that they were convinced they were dealing with a paranormal event, and that telepathy was the minimum that was needed to account for what she was able to do.

6 *The sceptics' views of Piper*

I was interested to know how sceptics deal with conclusions which are so unequivocal and seemingly based on thorough investigation. Unsurprisingly they feel under no obligation to accept them.

The case against Piper is briefly described by psychologists Leonard Zusne and Warren H. Jones, who point out that 'Phinuit', supposedly the spirit of a French doctor, knew as little French as she herself, and not much at all about medicine. They go on to say that much of the information about deceased persons conveyed to Piper, and claimed by William James and others to be accurate or impossible to obtain by normal means, turned out, on closer examination, to be 'highly erroneous'. On at least one occasion, they continue, she conveyed messages from the spirit of a non-existent person who had been invented just to catch her out. Finally, they say, she lost her mediumistic ability and admitted that her performance must have been 'an unconscious expression of my subliminal self' and that it offered no scientific evidence in favor of the survival hypothesis.[21]

Of these statements, three are misleading when taken out of context and one is not really true at all. The psychologists don't know this because they seem not to have read any of Piper's material themselves – they are just getting the dirt from other sceptics, in particular Joseph Rinn, a contemporary of hers and a friend of Harry Houdini, a fellow debunker. Rinn's method, crude although common, was to chuck everything he could think of at the problem without worrying about how plausible or convincing it was, or what it actually meant.

For instance, Rinn mentions the gossip that Hodgson was falsifying details in the Piper material, because he wanted to build up the reputation of the American Society for Psychical Research and thereby ensure his continued employment.[22] Left to ourselves it's the sort of construction that we might have naturally come up with. It could never work here though, not least because Piper was endorsed by many other investigators besides Hodgson. Zusne and Jones probably realize this, as they don't mention it. But they might also recognize that when Rinn talks about Piper's information turning out to be grossly inaccurate, he can only cite two instances. It's true that he discusses them at some length, but that's pointless, as no-one is claiming that Piper *never* made a mistake. The challenge that the psychologists seem not to have understood is that many of the facts she came up with checked out *exactly*, even where it concerned matters which the sitters themselves were not aware of at the time.

On the other hand, the doubts about Phinuit are true – and are one of the big puzzles of the material. This trance-ego of Piper's claimed to be independent of her, although manifesting through her body, but was never able to give a satisfactory account of his identity. For a Frenchman he appeared to know little French; his knowledge of medicine was slight for a trained doctor; and investigations yielded no trace of a person of that name. Other personalities that subsequently communicated through Piper seemed similarly to be products of her imagination: they included the novelist George Eliot, who described meeting a character from one of her novels in heaven, and an obviously phony Julius Caesar.

These inconsistencies have a major bearing on whether or not the Piper material is evidence of survival of death. In fact the SPR researcher Eleanor Sidgwick and some other researchers concluded that Phinuit was what they called a dream creation, an artificial construct in the medium's mind.[23] This alone was not conclusive proof against Piper being in touch with genuine spirits; other communicators could give good evidence of once having lived. But the researchers became increasingly aware that what they were observing was a creative process, akin to what happens in hypnosis. There was a high level of suggestibility; they noticed that Piper seemed to pick up information that was in the sitters' minds and weave it into the drama as if it came from a dead person. It was even discovered that communicators who had provided convincing evidence of having survived death vouched for the genuineness of deceased people who were completely fictitious, and had been invented purely for the purpose of catching them out.[24]

As I started to become aware of this, my first thought was, well in that case the medium must simply be making all of it up. From there it was a jump and a hop to assume there must be something wrong with the investigators, who were so desperate to believe in an afterlife that they just didn't notice.

But by now I was starting to recognize this sort of rationalizing as an automatic mental process, and to take it into account. I reflected that the researchers showed themselves to be cool and analytical: the moral and religious issues that preoccupied spiritualists rarely concerned them. Then again, doubts about the identity of the communicators and about the nature of the process have no bearing on the accuracy of the information that Piper produced. This is the essential point. Unless you can come up with plausible normal mechanisms for how she could have achieved this, telepathy is the absolute minimum that can explain what Piper did. One might add, if you are a phony medium it's hard to see how you can make your illusion more convincing by inventing a 'spirit control' who claims to have been a French doctor, when you neither speak French nor know anything about medicine.

I thought at first that the debunking psychologists must have understood all this perfectly well and were fudging the data to mislead their readers. It looked as though they were treating the researchers' doubts about Phinuit being a real spirit, which was well founded, as a reason for doubting that the process was in any way paranormal, which does not at all follow. There may in fact be an element of this, as debunking tends to be opportunistic. But I have also come to think that they may really be confused here. They are used to thinking in either/or terms, and the idea of a genuine paranormal process working to create an illusion is just too paradoxical for them to follow.

Look, for instance, at how Zusne and Jones treat the episode of Piper's 'confession', the last of their four points. It's the case, as they say, that Piper once publicly expressed doubts that she was actually in touch with spirits (although it was not at the end of her mediumistic career but ten years earlier in 1901). At this time she temporarily withdrew her services from the American SPR, apparently rebelling at Hodgson's brusque treatment of her. In a press interview she insisted she had always believed that the mediumistic phenomena she generated could be explained 'in other ways than by the intervention of disembodied spirit forces' and that telepathy strongly appealed to her as 'the most plausible and genuinely scientific solution of the problem.'[25]

Piper and Hodgson soon made up, but in the meantime her statement – itself unexceptional, since it was what some researchers themselves thought – was treated as a sort of confession: that is the word Rinn uses, and most of the sceptics who describe the incident follow him in that respect. But this was surely no true confession. To qualify as such, Piper would have to have explained how exactly she faked her clever feats – and this she notably failed to do. What we actually see is the subject of a research programme opting for the simpler paranormal explanation in preference to the more complex paranormal one, and it's hard to see how that really helps the sceptics' case.[26]

7 *Some Leonard examples*

Shortly after Piper's retirement in 1911, British researchers discovered Gladys Leonard, whose capabilities were at least as rich as Piper's, and whose work I will now briefly describe. Leonard too had a trance personality, in this case a lisping young girl who called her-self Feda. The material is quite similar to Piper's in other respects as well, consisting of sittings' transcripts, and is of similar quality, with a large amount of highly detailed and accurate information that would be hard to account for in any normal way.[27] As with Piper, the investigators had Leonard trailed by detectives, who reported she made no apparent effort to gather information on potential sitters.[28] Yet again, they fairly soon abandoned any idea that she might be faking; their concern was to demonstrate the process and determine to what extent, if at all, it pointed to survival of death rather than telepathy between medium and sitter.

By now researchers had started to develop other experimental ap-proaches. 'Feda' proved willing to co-operate and became involved in a long-running series of book tests. In these tests, the experi-menter would place some books on a shelf in an unoccupied room in his house, ensuring that no-one else knew what the titles were or in what order they were placed. A colleague with no knowledge of the location, or anything that could provide clues, would go to sit with Leonard in her home, and she would direct them to take down, say, the third book along from the left, and would then identify a phrase or idea that would be found on a specified page and line. In one particular case, she said, about a quarter of an inch above a line drawn half-way down page fifteen, the words 'a long pole' would be found. The book she indicated turned out to be Henry James's *Daisy Miller*; it was taken down and the passage was found to be 'I should like to know where you got that pole'.[29] The pole referred to here is elsewhere in the book described as 'a long alpenstock' and the sense was entirely accurate, although the words slightly at variance.

Many of the tests were unsuccessful, however, and those that did check out might theoretically be explained in terms of chance. This possibility was examined by comparing over five hundred of Leon-ard's book tests with a control series of eighteen hundred that did not involve a medium. Of the genuine tests seventeen per cent were classed as successful and nineteen per cent as approximately successful, while the control yielded only two per cent successful and three per cent as partially successful, reinforcing the suggestion that some unidentified process was involved.[30]

Another innovation was the 'proxy' sitting, in which Leonard was found to be capable of providing accurate information about people who were not actually present. The link would be provided by the sitter, who would have been given the name and one or two details of a deceased person whom she had not met and knew nothing about. Feda would establish contact with this person, who would then provide a number of details about him or herself as evidence of having survived death.

In one case, an investigator who was working with Leonard was asked by E.R. Dodds, an Oxford professor who was sceptical about survival, to try to contact a deceased individual named Frederic William Macaulay, the father-in-law of a scientist friend of Dodds. Subsequently Leonard, alone apart from the investigator, went into her trance state and speaking as Feda appeared to contact Macaulay, who passed on various items of information as evidence of his continued existence. She correctly described his occupation as an engineer, the details of the rooms where he worked, and his final illness. Of a total of one hundred and twenty-four items of information, his daughter later classed fifty-one as completely accurate and forty-four as good or fair – there were only twenty-nine that were doubtful or that she knew to be wrong. Here's an extract:

> *Feda*: I get a funny word now … could he be interested in … baths of some kind? Ah, he says I have got the right word, baths. He spells it, B-A-T-H-S. His daughter will understand, he says. It is not something quite ordinary, but feels something special.

> *Daughter*: This is, to me, the most interesting thing that has yet emerged. Baths were always a matter of joke in our family – my father being very emphatic that water must

not be wasted by our having too big baths or by leaving taps dripping. It is difficult to explain how intimate a detail this seems … The mention of baths here also seems to me an indication of my father's quaint humour, a characteristic which has hitherto been missing …

Feda: … Godfrey. Will you ask the daughter if she remembers someone called Godfrey. That name is a great link with old times.

Daughter: My father's most trusted clerk, one who specially helped in the hydraulic research, was called William Godfrey. He was with my father for years and I remember him from almost my earliest childhood.

Feda: What is that? … Peggy … Peggy … Puggy … He is giving me a little name like Puggy or Peggy. Sounds like a special name, a little special nickname, and I think it is something his daughter would know …

Daughter: My father sometimes called me 'pug-nose' or 'Puggy'.

'Macaulay' also referred to 'a special cup that he drank from and that he could show to people or people might ask to see … not an ordinary thing'. Feda did not understand this, but it too was recognized as a silver tankard that he had won as a prize for shooting.[31]

Critics argue, with some justification, that one should not rely on validations made by sitters, since for all sorts of reasons they may accept information given about themselves that actually could apply to anyone. This has been tested in recent experiments, which I will come to shortly. But it was beginning to be understood in the 1930s, when efforts were made to establish just how much of the information could be independently confirmed. In one experiment, mediumistic communications appearing to come from a pilot killed in action were sent to families for whom this might be relevant, to see if the information given could apply to them also. As it turned out, the material matched the people for whom it was specifically intended four to five times over chance levels.[32]

8 Hansel vs Leonard

Leonard is little mentioned by British critics, and hardly at all by their American counterparts. I think the reason for this is that the original literature offers them fewer ready-made opportunities than for Piper, and vastly fewer than for Eusapia Palladino, which means there's relatively little of a controversial nature that they can work with. An exception is the 'Raymond' episode of 1916, which attracted a good deal of public comment at the time. It concerns the scientist Oliver Lodge, who in that year published a book called *Raymond, or Life and Death* in which he described his apparently successful attempts to contact, through Leonard, the spirit of his soldier son, recently killed in battle. Passages in the book that dealt with Raymond's supposed experiences in the afterlife caused a sensation, in particular because they told how the dead could continue to enjoy worldly experiences, to the extent, if they wished, of putting their feet up with a whisky and a cigar – a fanciful notion which was mocked in the press.

Lodge described at length a particular episode that began when 'Raymond' told him to look out for some regimental photographs taken shortly before his death, and which his family would shortly receive. The pictures duly arrived, and they helped convince Lodge that the words being spoken to him through Leonard were genuinely coming from the surviving spirit of his son. This was picked up by C.E.M. Hansel, a British psychologist, in his influential 1980 debunking book *ESP and Parapsychology: A Critical Re-Evaluation*. Hansel draws attention to the fact that many of the people Leonard appeared to get in touch with were dead young soldiers, so she could draw on a sort of stock description. It's a good point, and one that researchers themselves raised, although neither they nor Hansel really develop it.[33] With regard to the information given by Leonard to Lodge about the photos, he goes on to say: 'This was a fairly safe bet, as it must be exceptional for a British officer to avoid regimental and mess photographs. But Sir Oliver Lodge was very impressed when "Raymond" mentioned such a portrait, which only subsequently turned up at the Lodges' home.[34]

The implication here is that Lodge had succumbed to wishful thinking, and of course if he actually had based his conviction on something so flimsy then one would be bound to think so too. It would be quite surprising in a man of his intellectual standing, but this in turn would reinforce the argument that a scientist is not necessarily the best judge of such matters.

However, having previously read Lodge's account I knew that the matter was a lot more complex than this. Lodge was indeed impressed – not by the prediction that he would receive a regimental photograph (which was initially made by a different medium), but by further details which he obtained in a sitting with Leonard. The most striking of these was that an officer standing behind Raymond tried to lean on his shoulder. When the photograph was subsequently delivered this was found to be the case, and Raymond looked annoyed by it.[35] It did not apply to any of the others officers in the group, and is not a common characteristic of group photographs, so cannot therefore fairly be viewed as a lucky guess by the medium. This was Lodge's judgement, and to my mind a reasonable one. My point is not that it's a clinching argument in favour of Raymond having survived death, but rather that the critic is misrepresenting the evidence. He has omitted the detail that gives the incident its meaning, in the process making the scientist look like a fool and the medium like a lucky chancer.[36]

Sceptic literature is full of this sort of casual misrepresentation, and as I mentioned earlier I used to think it was deliberate, a quick and easy way of denigrating parapsychologists and persuading readers that the explanation is easily found. I no longer think this. What it really demonstrates, I believe, is the coping mechanism employed by the convinced sceptic. Some people really do seem to find it more difficult than others to engage with the material, and to recognize what the paranormality consists of. It's as though they mentally filter out the key elements that pose the challenge, that puzzle other people so greatly. They literally *can't* see it, so they can't understand what the fuss is about.

A happy side-effect of this mental process is that it puts their opponents' judgement in doubt. It's a natural response, perhaps, but as we have already seen in the interaction between Hugo Münsterberg and Eusapia Palladino, it is fatally damaging in the context of a scholarly enterprise. The adulterated version enters the sceptic literature, where it tends to be treated as the authoritative one. And for once, I should emphasize, we are not comparing subjective interpretations, but rather two published versions – the original description and the sceptic's mutant copy – which you can verify by laying the two texts side by side. I'd suggest that is why the arguments of committed sceptics like Hansel should be treated with caution, because they can't seem to deal with the material at all objectively.

In this particular case it gets much worse. Hansel has so far shown no interest in mediumship nor grasp of the detail. But he nevertheless feels qualified to provide a psychological explanation, and embarks on a construction formulated by Joseph Jastrow, involving the 'sensorial' and 'memorial' components of memory. In the dim-lit séance room conditions, he thinks, the sensorial component is reduced, making the messages the medium transmits 'garbled, ambiguous, and difficult to interpret exactly'. The sitter is being given what psychologists call a projection test.

> Vague, ambiguous, or meaningless material that can be interpreted in various ways is presented to the subject, thus providing full scope for the memorial component. Conclusions about the subject are then drawn from the manner in which he responds.[37]

This is the outline of cold reading, but in describing it Hansel seems quite confused. He apparently doesn't realize that Piper and Leonard did not require dimly lit séance conditions – just as mediums today do their stuff under the glare of lights on stage and in television studios. Nor do the reports show the material to be at all vague or meaningless; as I say, it was precisely because it was so surprisingly detailed and accurate – from the outset, before any interaction took place – that researchers like James and Hodgson were impressed.

Hansel's most extraordinary idea is that the medium is both producing information in a genuine trance *and* shaping it opportunistically. During the trance, he says, the medium may hear 'imaginary voices' and have 'visual and kinesthetic delusions,' afterwards displaying loss of memory about the events that took place during the seizure.[38] If the medium was unhappy about this, a psychiatrist would doubtless diagnose her as mentally ill, he adds. But if the medium is experiencing a seizure *and* hearing voices, how can she be simultaneously studying the sitter's responses? Also, knowing that the symptoms of mediumship are similar to the symptoms of the mentally ill does not help much, if mediums do not at all consider themselves to be ill.

Hansel can rely on his readers knowing nothing about Leonard, and caring less; most will already assume that mediumship is bogus and his assertions will confirm it. But to anyone who knows about the subject his critique gives off a sort of desperation. It's as though he is himself projecting vague, ambiguous or meaningless material and expecting his readers to somehow shape it into a satisfying explanation. 'Don't worry if you don't understand it,' he seems to be saying, 'trust me – I'm a psychologist.' The analysis lacks seriousness: there are no quotes from the records, no references to the detail, no attempts to understand the challenges. It's an *ad hoc* defensive construct, a pot pourri of incompatible ideas aimed at reassuring like-minded sceptics that there's nothing paranormal in mental mediumship, and so nothing to worry about.

9 *Oldfield vs Vandy*

The Piper and Leonard material had a considerable impact on my thinking, and I wondered why it's so little known. Neither of these mediums were caught in fraud, or even plausibly accused of it. The research is voluminous and consistent, and there has been no serious challenge to its paranormality within the parapsychological community, which as we have seen is not the case with other categories of phenomena. William James famously called Piper his 'white crow', a fatal negation (or 'falsification', as the science philosopher Karl Popper, using a similar image, would later call it) of previous assumptions.[39]

I can absolutely see why James felt like this. The research can't be wished away: human beings have lived who have been observed repeatedly to break the rule that information is only transmitted by means of the physical senses, in conditions in which fraud would be difficult or impossible, and to an extent that far exceeds what can reasonably be held to be achievable by methods of cold reading. Yet these findings have had no impact at all within the scientific community. Scientists, academics and sceptics among the general public continue to believe that mediums, if not deceiving other people, must at least be deceiving themselves, and so are fair game for abuse.

Of course, critics will say, the material is a product of parapsychology, which as every right-thinking person knows is a pseudoscience, not to be taken seriously. But what if a piece of this research were to break out of its ghetto and present itself in its original form, rather than the garbled version offered by professional debunkers? How would the academic mind respond? I got a glimpse of the answer to this in an article entitled 'Philosophers and Psychics: The Vandy episode' by a Dr Kenneth Oldfield, published in the *Skeptical Inquirer*.[40] Oldfield was challenging a paper he had seen in a philosophy journal, that argued the case for telepathy based on a 1930's case from the Society for Psychical Research. It centred on a young man named Edgar Vandy, who had drowned and subsequently appeared to convey the fact of his survival through several different mediums. Vandy, it appeared, was able to give detailed and consistent information about his life and the circumstances of his passing, which his family considered good evidence of his having survived death.

On the principle that these aberrations have to be quickly put right, Oldfield rolled up his sleeves and set out to demolish the paper. A reputable peer-reviewed journal had no business publishing this sort of thing, he insisted. It wasn't serious science, and the magazine's referees were failing in their duty by not having blocked it. It should surely be obvious that mediums are not genuine, he added, otherwise someone by now would have won Randi's prize.

Oldfield pointed out a number of flaws in the SPR's original report. Far from being accurate, he revealed, the mediums made numerous mistakes about Vandy and the events surrounding his death. These included the time that had elapsed since the drowning, which they got wrong, and the suggestion that he drowned in the sea, when in fact the accident took place in a swimming pool. The mediums also failed to name a new type of printing machine that Vandy was working on, called a Lectroline, even though this was a big part of his life and something they should surely have been able to divine. There were some hits, he acknowledged, but he concluded that these could all be explained in terms of cold reading, luck, preparatory research, and common tricks.

The article that Oldfield was critiquing drew from an analysis of the Vandy case by Charlie Dunbar Broad, a professor of moral philosophy at Cambridge, who used it as an example in his 1962 book *Lectures in Psychical Research*.[41] Several philosophers have been intrigued by parapsychology's riddles and have made an important contribution to psychic research: Broad's is considerable. He devoted a chapter to the Vandy case because it seemed to him to be convincing evidence of psi, although not necessarily of survival. So it was interesting to see a sceptic set it apart so effortlessly, especially one who seems to have read at least some of the original material.

10 *The Vandy sittings*

Briefly, the incident took place as follows. Edgar Vandy was an engineer and inventor aged thirty-eight. On the morning of Sunday 6 August, 1933, a friend called at his home in London and they drove together to a private estate in Sussex, where they were joined by his friend's sister. Since it was hot, the two men decided to bathe in the swimming pool near the house. According to the friend's account, Vandy went into the pool first and when his friend got there two or three minutes later he was face down in the water, apparently having difficulties. He struggled to get Vandy out, but failed, and then went to fetch help; however, he was dead when they returned. The medical evidence subsequently showed less fluid in his lungs than would have been normal if drowning had been the sole cause and bruises that suggested he had fallen and been stunned, having possibly dived in or slipped and banged his head.

Vandy's two brothers were concerned that the coroner's report did not explain exactly how he died. They also wanted to know why his companions did not help him to safety in time. One of the brothers had an interest in parapsychology and, although not a believer in survival of death, he thought that a psychic might gain some paranormal cognition of the event. Having heard a parapsychologist named Charles Drayton Thomas lecture on Gladys Leonard some weeks earlier the brothers approached him to see if he would carry out a proxy sitting with her on their behalf, and whether he could recommend other mediums that they might visit themselves.

About three weeks later Drayton Thomas was having a session with Leonard, talking as usual with Leonard's trance personality

Feda. He had not mentioned Vandy, and had no plans to raise his case at this sitting. However Leonard, as Feda, suddenly said: 'Do you know a man who passed just lately; it was quite sudden?' This person had been well and vigorous until quite recently, she went on. 'I seem to get a thought from someone, as if they thought of you. Keep a look out. This may be a proxy-case about someone who went out through falling.'[42] It now occurred to Drayton Thomas that all this might have to do with the letter about Vandy which he had received three weeks earlier, although this had said nothing about 'falling'. Leonard continued that her vision concerned a young man, and repeated that she was getting the sense of a tragic accident involving a fall. Drayton Thomas now told her what he knew, and that if it was the person he was thinking of he had two living brothers. He added that there was something mysterious about the circumstances of his death. Leonard, as Feda, continued in a rambling way:

> It was not his fault, he says... There was a funny feeling in his head... Stepping out unconsciously... thinking of other things... I was holding, grasping something. Think I let go... Then it seemed as if my mind became curiously blank... I can't remember exactly what happened – though I was falling down and through something, as one does in sleep... It has nothing to do with them at all, and they could not have helped me in any way at all... I'm so deeply sorry about all the trouble...[43]

Drayton Thomas sent a record of these statements to Vandy's brothers. Subsequently, one of the brothers visited three different mediums and the other independently visited two of them, making a total of six sittings (including Leonard's) with four different mediums. The brothers did not identify themselves, or disclose the purpose of the sitting. They also took care not to give information by asking leading questions or making unnecessary comments. To ensure they did not misremember the details of what was being said they took someone else along to take shorthand notes.

Their records show that the mediums each made several accurate, or almost accurate, statements. For instance, one mentioned a brother who had died in an accident, describing a gap caused by a broken tooth, and stating that he was ten years younger than the sitter (eight years in fact). She gave a correct description of the brothers' father's business losses, incurred through others' dishonesty, and added that he 'seems very interested in wireless and keeps using wireless terms...' (he was a wireless expert and had run a small manufacturing business). She also said he played the violin and another instrument (he was a competent violinist and also played the banjo).

What is especially striking about the case is the high level of agreement between the different mediums' statements. In three of the six sessions an old scar on Vandy's face was mentioned; in five, the sense of drowning; in all six, a fall on his head; and in four, that it was not suicide. To get the full impact of this, here are some relevant statements numbered by session:

1. Something hit him... He had some blow to the head.

2. Did he get hit on the head, as if his head had touched something? ... Now he illustrates that he seemed to double up and fall. I think a fall on the head.

3. I get the idea of a fall, an accident... I was falling down through something, as one does in sleep.

4. I get the blow. I get it he was knocked unconscious... I get falling, a feeling of falling.

5. He gives me such a frightful pain. I don't know what happened – I seem to get a grasping sensation of some sort, as though I cannot hold on to the earth and had to let go.

6. As he stood near me I felt a distinct blow or crack on the head... I seem as if I had fallen forward.[44]

So in all six sessions the presence of one of Vandy's two brothers – or in Leonard's case, the previous contact with the investigating sitter – induced in four different mediums *almost identical sensations*. This concordance would not surprise supporters of the cold reading hypothesis, since the mediums would all be working from the same material – the statements and body language of the sitter. But neither of the brothers was present in Leonard's case, and in the case of the other five sittings they both insisted on keeping silent, which, if true, surely makes this explanation unlikely.

Similarly five out of six of the mediums grappled with the sense that the communicator was trying to shield his companions from blame:

> 1. He does not want you to enquire too deeply into the cause of the death... there was somebody else.
>
> 2. One point he insists on, and that is that he was talking to someone, and he deliberately does not give the name. There is someone on this side – it gives me a feeling he is trying to protect.
>
> 3. It has nothing to do with them at all, and they could not have helped me in any way...
>
> 4. I feel that he could tell me more than he will tell me, but he might implicate someone else.
>
> 5. It's as if there were someone else... He is telling me that he was not alone. There was somebody near him who swam away or got out and did not wait to help him...[45]

References to drowning and water were also frequent:

> 1. He shows me water. Was there water in connection with his death? He shows me his arms and legs, he was dressed in a short swimming-suit...
>
> 2. He shows me water... He dived naturally and was killed.
>
> 3. He is ... showing me a scene as if he could have been near water – not the sea, a little amount of water.
>
> 4. I am getting a sensation of floating out on water ... as

though something happened, but I am in water…

5. I don't know whether he was a strong swimmer – there is sea at the back of him.[46]

Most of the mediums also made detailed references to Vandy's inventions, including his new printing machine as well as the wireless and other contraptions. Much of this information was garbled but nevertheless consistent with the different projects he was working on. For instance:

> Does he know a man called 'Mac'. He is saying something that sounds like: 'Mac understands some work that I am doing.' This man would understand for he is saying: 'Press has not yet quite the right weight behind it'… Something heavy… He holds on to a thing like – Has he got something where two sides come together? Where you insert something in between, and two things come together? … He shows me a red and a green light…[47]

'Mac' was a familiar name for MacNamara, the lithographic expert who was helping Vandy to build an accessory for the Lectroline machine, which would rule parallel lines for reproduction by lithography. The description of two sides coming together was appropriate for a printing device, and the mention of the red and green pilot lights was accurate.

11 Questionable logic and circular reasoning

To sum up, there are four people, none of whom the two brothers had ever met previously, or who could know anything about either them or their deceased brother and his rather unusual interests, all of whom accurately identified significant circumstances of his death that cross-referenced to a high degree. Broad and other commentators found this to be remarkable, and worthy of investigation. So did I, but this is not Oldfield's reaction at all: what weighs with him are the *inaccuracies* and *omissions*. The discovery that the mediums had made several mistakes confirms for him that they are failing to show any psychic knowledge at all.

Now you might think that is a reasonable line to take, and it's true we might have a discussion about it. We would weigh up the relative proportion of accurate to inaccurate material, and the opportunities for cold reading, all of which involves making arbitrary and subjective judgments. Parapsychologists recognize this, which is why they started to shift to experimental methods that include the use of control groups. But in this particular case two things stand out: firstly, the truly remarkable preponderance of accurate material, which surely goes far beyond what most people would think possible by cold reading; and secondly, the complete absence of any indication by Oldfield in his article that he is either aware of it or considers it requires any explanation.

For instance, as I mentioned, Oldfield criticizes the mediums for not being able to name the machine Vandy was working on, the Lectroline. But he fails to say that most of them referred to Vandy's mechanical interests, and some identified his work with wireless and printing, which is pretty specific. Again, he lists 'drowning in the sea' as a mistake. But in context, it's a minor inaccuracy. It would only have been a mistake if Vandy had fallen down the stairs or been run over or got himself electrocuted, or had a heart attack, or something else. 'Drowning' is actually correct: it's 'in the sea' that is wrong, and that error is counteracted by the fact that in four of the six sittings the mediums spoke merely of 'water' and one specifically stated that it was not the sea.

I have to say I don't at all understand Oldfield's logic. Suppose as a journalist I fly to Ethiopia to cover a famine story, which involves hiring a taxi and driving to a rural village in a distant region. Interview-

ing potential informants I strike up a conversation with a talkative
market stall holder, in which he casually refers by name to several
of my friends and family members back home, mentions particular
incidents in my life, and gives an excellent appearance of knowing
all about me. I am certain we have never met and am utterly dumb-
founded. But wait! Now that I consider the matter, at the end of the
day and in the tranquillity of my hotel room, I recall that the fellow
seemed to think I live in West London, when actually I live in *South*
London. Ah ha! Impostor! Not so clever after all. And to think he
almost had me fooled.

What fascinates me is the ease with which the critic – hitherto,
as far as I can tell, a complete novice in parapsychological matters
– assumes that his insights are superior to those of experts in the
field. He knows almost nothing about it, yet has deigned to cast an
eye over their work and pronounced it wanting. Parapsychologists
can complain, but no-one will listen, because they are regarded as
pseudo-scientists, the lumpens and marginals of academic society.

It's an example of the circular reasoning that is endemic in sceptical discourse. 'Unfortunately we can't believe parapsychologists when
they claim to have observed paranormal phenomena, because they are
unreliable observers. How do we know they are unreliable? Why, because they claim to have observed paranormal phenomena.' It makes
no difference how eminent they may be, or how many scientific or
intellectual achievements they have to their name – on this matter the
object of their interest automatically disqualifies them from serious
consideration.

12 *Schwartz tests star mediums*

I believe that anyone with the patience to get to grips with the Piper
and Leonard material, and who approaches it with an open mind,

will understand the point. But it will always be meaningless to people who are committed to the scientific consensus that such things can't happen. If they are ever to be convinced they would need proof that addresses their doubts directly. At the very least this would mean testing mediums under robustly controlled conditions that preclude the slightest possibility of acquiring information about sitters by normal means.

The fact that this has only been attempted recently is partly, as I mentioned, because it wasn't felt to be necessary – the investigators believing the quality of the information ruled out fraud – but also because by the time parapsychologists started turning to experimental approaches in the 1930s they had lost interest in what they called gifted psychics, and instead were trying to uncover statistical evidence of psi experiences among ordinary people. So the work of Gary Schwartz and his colleagues represents something of a departure. Schwartz, a professor of psychology at the University of Arizona, performed experiments involving John Edward and other well-known American mediums, and later published the results both in parapsychological journals and in a book for general readers called *The Afterlife Experiments* (Schwartz and Simon, 2002). This work raised a new set of issues. In what follows I'm going to briefly describe the experiments and analyze the sceptical reaction.

Two of Schwartz's first experiments were 'single-blind', whereby the sitter knew the identity of the medium but the medium had no prior knowledge about the sitter. More significantly, they were separated by an opaque screen so that the medium could not pick up visual clues from the sitter's body language. The medium was further restricted by having questions answered merely by 'yes' or 'no' answers, which limited any possibility of picking up clues from the sitter's answers. A third experiment was 'double-blind', whereby the sitter and medium were both unknown to each other; they were also in entirely separate locations and communicated only by telephone. To make things even more interesting, in part of this experiment the telephone's mute button was activated by the experimenter so that they could neither see nor hear each other.

The first experiment was held during a single day at the University of Arizona in February 1999.[48] The plan was that five mediums, including Edward, would each give a separate reading for two women, both of whom had experienced the death of at least six family members during the previous ten years. Both women signed statements confirming they had had no previous contact with any of the mediums or had given them any information about themselves. The schedule of all ten readings was not quite completed by the end of the day, but one sitter had been given a reading by all five mediums and the other had readings by Edward and one other. Subsequently a group of university students was asked to make guesses about the women to act as a control group against which the observations could be compared.

The issue at stake was whether under circumstances that largely precluded cold reading the mediums could nevertheless come up with accurate statements about people they had not met and had no knowledge of. Later the two sitters were asked to score transcripts of the readings, placing each item of information in one of six categories, such as 'name', 'initial', 'historical fact', and so on, and rated on a six-point scale in which a score of -3 was 'definitely an error' and $+3$ was 'definitely correct'. The average accuracy rate was eighty-three per cent for the first sitter and seventy-seven per cent for the second. This was well above the student control group, whose guesses were rated at an average accuracy rate of thirty-six per cent.

Both sitters were impressed by the relevance of the medium's statements to their private affairs. One reported that all of the six deceased individuals who she had earlier listed as possible contacts had in fact come through and had been observed by all five mediums independently. Chief among these was her teenage son who had shot himself; the mediums all reported information about a deceased son, and two appeared to know how he had died.

In the later experiment, a medium sitting in Schwartz's Arizona office gave a telephone reading for a sitter in Los Angeles.[49] In the first phase of the experiment, she attempted to get information during a half-hour period of meditation before the sitter was even called up on the telephone. In the second phase, the phone connection was made and the mute button was activated at the sitter's end for the first ten minutes so that the medium could not hear anything the sitter said. The sitter was called George Dalzell, and he subsequently rated the accuracy at around ninety per cent. This session showed particularly high accuracy rate as regards names. Before the session Dalzell had mentally invited four deceased individuals to communicate: a close friend named Michael, an aunt named Alice, his father Bob, and another friend named Jerry. During the first two phases the medium reported that she was being told the reading was for someone named George and that there was a deceased friend who wanted to communicate named Michael (the one George was most interested in). She named another deceased person as Bob, and a deceased friend as Jerry. She also heard an unfamiliar name which she said sounded like Talya, Tiya or Tilya, which George recognized as his living friend Tallia. The medium went on to mention a deceased person named Alice, whom she identified as an aunt. She produced another five names corresponding to friends, and three other names which were unknown to George – but they all had high significance for the two experimenters who were present with the medium.

In the third phase of the experiment, the medium finally made verbal contact with George. She collected four pieces of information which were unknown to him at the time, but which he was later able to confirm as accurate. The medium then correctly described Jerry as being often intoxicated and sitting on bar stools. He had been an alcoholic. A particularly interesting instance occurred when she said Michael showed her an old stone building that he described as a monastery on the edge of the river on the way to his parents' home in Germany. After the reading George phoned Michael's parents in

Germany to ask them about this; they revealed there was an old abbey on the river's edge near their house, where they had held a service for him a few weeks earlier.

13 *Randi vs Schwartz*

Schwartz's experiments attracted a good deal of media interest. This was because the first of them had been sponsored by a television company, which later broadcast a documentary about it, and because this was a rare attempt by a senior scientist in modern times to publicly validate spirit mediums. Professional sceptics of course were keen to counter the perception that he had succeeded, and it's worth looking at their observations in a bit of detail, as it gives the opportunity to see how these controversies develop.

We can start with James Randi, who seems to have been a little slow off the mark and was prodded by his supporters into making a response. He obliged by posting a short critique on his website in his familiar rumbustious style. Claims that Schwartz believed in the Tooth Fairy might be going too far, Randi said, but he was clearly adored by the media as a real scientist 'who embraces bump-in-the-night ideas without a trace of shame'. The experiments were merely 'a series of games and amateur probes', lacking any scientific value. All his technical attachments were just 'bells and whistles', and for Schwartz to apply statistics to his data was like 'measuring chimneys with a laser beam to determine whether a fat man in a red suit can get down them, and to thereby explore the reality of Santa Claus'.

> If Schwartz were less interested in bragging — endlessly! — about his academic background, and would become more involved in doing *real* science rather than just doing the cosmetics, I think he might begin to be taken seriously. He is the perfect example of the Ivory Tower resident.[50]

Randi added that Schwartz's reports were not published in *Nature* or *Science*, but in an obscure parapsychological journal, implying that they therefore did not qualify as real science. Schwartz had not implemented the protocol that Randi had suggested prior to the experiments, bringing his judgement in question, and had demanded unreasonable restrictions that prevented Randi from being involved, contradicting his aspirations to honesty and openness. A stills frame from the videotape showed there was a gap in the screen through which the mediums could have peeked at the sitter, so clearly the sitter was not properly isolated, as Schwartz had claimed. In addition, Schwartz refused to send the transcripts to Randi, so the magician could not fully expose the way the cold reading was carried out.

Randi also argued that Schwartz was 'rooting around in the database' and coming up with names, numbers, initials, and anything that he could point to as being highly likely to connect with the reality of the subject. He dismissed this as 'blatant data-searching, one of the most pervasive and destructive aspects of bad science.' And why did Schwartz dare not apply for his prize? Could it possibly be that the scientist did not really trust his medium, or was too wealthy to need the money, or did not care about giving it to hungry children or to further AIDS research?

In reply, Schwartz pointed out that the reports were not published in science journals because their editors almost never give space to parapsychological articles. He went on to say that he had been quite willing to share data with Randi, as he had done with other visiting magicians and scientists, but was not prepared to hand the full transcripts over just so that Randi could prepare a hatchet job. Yes, there had been a gap in the screen, although this was not two inches as Randi claimed elsewhere, but less than a quarter of an inch, and had been quickly sealed up when it was discovered, as Randi well knew. Far from engaging in blatant data-searching, Schwartz continued, every item of information provided by the mediums was scored in a complete analysis. That had been done precisely to rule out any possibility that sitters merely remember the hits and forget the misses, and to explore the phenomenon in as much detail as possible. He added that a claim by Randi that he had received 'millions of dollars' to do his research was false – he was actually given thirty thousand dollars.[51]

My own feeling was that Randi's arguments didn't relate to Schwartz's work in any substantive way and in fact amounted to little more than invective. I wondered if perhaps the magician hadn't bothered to read the reports of the experiments and was simply rehashing old clichés. Then I remembered – it doesn't matter. Randi isn't trying to help people like me who want to understand the issues, but merely to reassure his audience of sceptics, while discouraging potentially open-minded members of academia, the media and the general public from taking Schwartz's results seriously.

14 Wiseman and Hyman vs Schwartz

Better-targeted criticisms were made by Richard Wiseman and Ray Hyman, a professor of psychology at the University of Oregon, who both took the line that the experiments were too flawed to sustain the claims that Schwartz was making for them. As we will shortly see, this is probably more effective in counteracting the claims of experimental parapsychologists than the blunderbuss approach of polemicists like Randi, which it has largely replaced.

Wiseman, responding with his University of Hertfordshire colleague Ciaran O'Keeffe to the report of Schwartz's first experiment, argued that possibilities for cold reading by the mediums had by no means been eliminated.[52] Although the mediums were separated from the sitters by a screen, they might still have been able to obtain clues from their voices when they gave their yes-and-no answers. This interaction would have given away their gender, age, and socio-economic group, and the mediums could adjust their patter accordingly; an older person would be more likely to have experienced the death of a parent, for instance, so offering an item of information appropriate to such a person would be a safe bet. The mediums might even have been able to pick up other clues unwittingly provided by the sitters from the sounds they made when they moved, their breathing, or their odour.

They then criticized the judging procedure: the mediums' statements might actually have been ambiguous, they suggested, and the sitters merely confirmed them because they had a need to believe, or because they were eager to please the television people and the scientists.

The critics also objected to Schwartz's control methods, which involved presenting students with questions generated from the medium's accurate statements, and getting them to guess at the answers. This was not a real comparison, they argued, because the sitter might be influenced by selective remembering, whereas the students would be making a pure guess. They argued that a much better control is a blind reading, in which the sitter is asked to evaluate both his or her own reading and the readings made for other sitters.

Ray Hyman responded at length in a review of *The Afterlife Experiments* in the *Skeptical Inquirer*, in which he dealt with the broad range of Schwartz's work. If one wanted proof that the dead still live, Hyman insisted, this was not it. He rejected Schwartz's challenges to sceptics to accept or explain away the data, insisting that it was not up to them to disprove his results, but for him to provide incontrovertible proof. He added: 'Probably no other extended program in psychic research deviates so much from accepted norms of scientific methodology as this one does'.[53]

Hyman, himself a former amateur magician, revealed that he had been a member of a panel of seven professional mentalists and

cold readers that Schwartz had consulted. Although many of them
had been sympathetic, he said, they agreed that what his mediums
did was no different from what they would expect from any cold
reader. He insisted on the subjectivity of the mediums' statements
and said that the specific items of information were much fuzzier
than Schwartz believed. 'His examples are selected just because they
appeared to contain such specifics,' Hyman said. 'This raises the difficult question of how to actually assess how much of this is just
coincidence'.[54] Getting the sitters themselves to rate the accuracy
scores in their own readings introduced a serious bias, he argued,
as they had been carefully chosen for their belief in survival, and
naturally hoped to find confirmation of their loved one's continued
existence. The agreement by the sitter that a certain statement was
true could not be taken on trust; it had to be independently verified
by the experimenters to have any value.

Replying to Hyman, Schwartz first tackled the point about cold
reading. He pointed out that one of the mediums in the first experiment asked only five questions of the sitter, yet was able to generate a hundred and thirty pieces of information, including people's
initials, names, causes of death, historical facts, and descriptions of
their personal appearances. The sitter gave these an accuracy rating
of over eighty per cent, a level of success that Schwartz insisted is not
a characteristic of cold reading.

Schwartz also claimed that all of the seven professional magicians
had agreed that they could not apply their conventional mentalist
tricks under Schwartz's experimental conditions, where they had no
knowledge of the sitter's identity, and no verbal or non-verbal visual
or auditory cues or feedback. Hyman and two others claimed that if
they had a year or two to practise, they might be able to figure out
how the mediums were faking it. But none of the magicians, he said,
was willing to demonstrate how they could do it, or submit to experimental testing themselves. Against the notion that sitters might
have felt pressured to accept incorrect statements as true, Schwartz

agreed that this might happen in real life but not in experimental situations where they had to defend their ratings to scientists and the media. If anything, in such circumstances they would be conservative, he suggested.[55]

15 My view of Schwartz's experiments

My own first reaction to Schwartz's work was that it has as much in common with the investigation of Eusapia Palladino and other séance mediums as with the work on Piper and Leonard. Perhaps more to the point, it raises similar issues to more recent laboratory experiments aimed at demonstrating the existence of ESP (which have been going on since the 1930s, and which we'll look at shortly). The problem in both cases has been to create a protocol that is sufficiently rigorous to exclude even the minutest possibility of information being transmitted by some conventional means, or at least to convince critics that this has been achieved.

So I understood what Hyman and Wiseman were doing. I agreed with them that the experiments were flawed in important ways, in the sense that loopholes and grey areas existed that could not conclusively rule out manipulation by the medium, or where inferences were drawn that perhaps were not fully justified. For instance getting students to act as a control group was worth doing but it was never going to be sufficiently rigorous to satisfy a sceptic.

Then there's the question of accuracy. I agreed with the critics that an acceptable protocol would have to include some mechanism for independent verification. Schwartz argues that it's unreasonable to have to check on details like the sitter's father's name, and one might add that many of the evidential items that mediums come up with refer to intimate facts and incidents known only to the sitters – which is precisely why they are evidential. But when it comes to potentially significant items of information that the sitter does not recognize, for instance the business with the German abbey, it's surely worth the experimenter attempting to verify it independently.

In an ideal world Schwartz might have acted differently in some respects. First, he wouldn't have gone so noisily public with single-blind studies when double-blind is the gold standard. His claims might have been more credible had he revealed his work only through academic journals, and let others hype his findings to the media. He would have taken greater care to avoid slips like leaving a gap in the screen, because even if they can't plausibly be held to affect the experiment they can be exploited by critics to make it seem sloppy. He would have established a reliable protocol, perhaps with just one or two star mediums, then worked to perfect it, and then repeated it; and waited for other experimenters elsewhere to confirm that it worked.

On the other hand, given that no-one has attempted an experiment of this kind and on this scale before, Schwartz's achievement is by no means negligible. Critics can no longer argue that mediums can't perform under controlled conditions, as he has shown that even where they are not permitted to engage with the sitter in order to get feedback they can still perform to the same standards. The transcripts do show the mediums asking for validation of their statements, but they don't on the whole show the trial-and-error approach described by Hyman and others in the cold-reading process. This would seem to suggest that reading body language and getting the sitter to unwittingly provide snippets of real information is not, after all, an integral element of mediums' methods.

Schwartz has also clouded the sceptics' view that the mediums' information is endorsed by the sitters only because it's very general. This tack is taken, for instance, by Wiseman and O'Keeffe, who cite a study in which a quarter of respondents agreed that they had someone in their family called Jack, and a third agreed they had a scar on their left knee. In other words, seemingly specific items of information that might impress a sitter could apply to many people. But there's plenty in Schwartz's experiments that contradicts that. For instance all five mediums obtained information about a deceased son; three heard the initial M for the son; and one said the name Michael. None gave a false initial or wrong name for the son. Also none claimed to have received information about a deceased daughter, which would have been wrong.

Hyman's discussion of this point is particularly interesting. He cites the instance in which one medium mentioned getting the name of someone associated with the sitter 'that sounds like Talya, Tily, or Tilya'. A sitter with a strict criterion, he suggests, might not accept this as referring to a friend whose name is Tallia, while one applying much looser criterion might accept it as referring to a Tony or even a Natalie. Schwartz replied – with justification, in my view – that a name as unusual as that was surely specific enough: a poll he carried out showed that only about two per cent of the people he asked knew someone with a name 'that sounds like Talya'. Hyman concedes that he does not seriously think the sitter would misremember or misreport having a friend with a name like this. But if the outcome is so earth-shaking and scientifically revolutionary as he claims it is, he goes on, then Schwartz should at least make the effort to independently check on some of these facts.

It seems that what we are arguing about here is not whether the mediums are genuine, but whether or not the experiment has demonstrated that beyond all doubt. It's not their honesty that's in question, but the experimenter's competence. Interestingly, Hyman says he has no hesitation in rejecting fraud as an explanation. In reply to Schwartz's rebuttal he even denies he ever claimed that he could with training duplicate what the mediums had accomplished, or that the mediums were using cold reading. He merely observed – and he specifically emphasized that this was a subjective opinion – that he could see little difference between his mediums' statements and those of the typical psychic reader.

> I want to emphasize again, it is not for me, or other critics,
> to show that his mediums are using cold reading or some
> other ploys. The burden of proof is on Schwartz to show
> that he has convincingly eliminated such possibilities.[56]

While Hyman is not directly insisting that mediums are fakers, he wants to protect scientists from having to take the business at all seriously. He provides the rationale for continuing to reject it. It looks suspicious, it's unsupported by known science, and until flawless positive experiments are carried out, there's no reason for anyone to stop thinking otherwise.

I don't necessarily disagree with this reasoning. At the same time it doesn't seem to me to be adequate to the situation. If there are any indications at all that some humans can divine – for want of a better word – information by channels other than the five senses, that's of huge importance for understanding the true nature of consciousness. These experiments offer a strong suggestion of that, although not necessarily any more than the work with Piper, Leonard and other mediums, not to mention the enormous amount of work carried out with clairvoyants of various kinds in the past century, and all the other indications of this gathered by researchers in many different contexts. If their minds were capable of such feats, then who is to say that the minds of many other people might not also be, or indeed that in some sense *all* of us are implicated to some degree. This is the underlying assumption in experimental parapsychology, which we will be looking at next.

FOUR

UNCERTAIN SCIENCE

'Positive evidence keeps coming from a tiny group of enthusiasts, while negative evidence keeps coming from a much larger group of skeptics.' *Martin Gardner, writer and sceptic.*

'Gardner does not attempt to document this assertion, nor could he. It is pure fiction. Look for the skeptics' experiments and see what you find.' *Charles Honorton, parapsychologist.*

'These disturbing phenomena seem to deny all our usual scientific ideas. How we should like to discredit them! Unfortunately the statistical evidence, at least for telepathy, is overwhelming. It is very difficult to rearrange one's ideas so as to fit these new facts in.' *Alan Turing, computer scientist.*

Here's a spooky story from the late nineteenth century. A man (let's call him John) is woken up in the middle of the night by his next-door neighbour, whose wife has just had a terrible nightmare – can he come and help? It appears the woman has dreamed about her brother, a local farmer, seeing him return to his farm in his carriage, take the horses to the barn, climb up a ladder to the hay-loft, lift a gun to his head and shoot himself. His body then rolled over in the hay. At this woman's urgent insistence, the husband and John ride to the brother's home nine miles away. The two men walk across to the barn, where they find the horses tethered, and climb up to the loft. There they see the brother's dead body in the place and position as described by his sister in her dream, and the pistol lying beside it.[1]

'John' was the father of an American science professor, who in later life related this compelling event to a young student named Joseph Banks Rhine. Rhine himself had often heard such anecdotes as a boy growing up in the mountains of Pennsylvania, and they aroused his curiosity. Having trained as a botanist he switched to psychology, and in 1930 established an experimental parapsychology department at Duke University in North Carolina, the first of its kind. Rhine's aim was to investigate the closely linked phenomena of telepathy, clairvoyance and precognition, which he termed 'extrasensory perception' or ESP.[2] The term most commonly used now in parapsychology is 'psi', which also includes psychokinesis. Rhine's early results with card-guessing experiments caused a stir, and at the time some scientists were impressed.[3]

In recent decades parapsychologists have been exploring other new areas. For instance, Charles Tart has looked at altered states of consciousness, Stanley Krippner at ESP in dreams, and Dean Radin at precognition and presentiment. Russell Targ, Hal Puthoff and Edwin May have all done extensive work in remote viewing, while another experimental protocol, named 'ganzfeld', has been adopted by William Braud, Adrian Parker and Carl Sargent, among others. Random-number generators have been used in an attempt to demonstrate psychokinesis, notably by Helmut Schmidt and by Robert Jahn and Brenda Dunne at Princeton. The biologist Rupert Sheldrake has come up with new experimental approaches to test, among other things, the sense of being stared at and telepathy in people and animals. Psi experiments have been carried out at the universities of Northampton and Edinburgh, of Freiberg in Germany, of Shanghai Jiao Tong in China, and many others around the world.[4] Psi exists, the researchers insist, and the scientific establishment should respect their findings.

Alas for them, as far as most scientists are concerned, ESP has no more substance than UFOs or astrology or, if they want to labour the point, unicorns and the Easter Bunny; they regard it as a childish belief that amuses the masses but that serious people should steer clear of. Parapsychology is a pseudo-science, the critics insist, that apes science but without truly following its methods. Some go so far as to stigmatize it as 'pathological science' – the search for an entity so elusive that it can barely be discerned, and whose supporters let themselves be misled by wishful thinking.[5] A storm of protest ensued a few years ago when the organizers of a science festival invited Sheldrake to speak on telepathy, a subject that one critic irritably complained was nothing more than 'a charlatan's fantasy'.[6] If parapsychologists were ever to come up with compelling evidence, the cliché goes, they would be elbowed aside by real scientists stampeding to the laboratory to work on this strange new phenomenon for themselves.

Are parapsychologists justified in claiming to have demonstrated a robust and reliable effect in laboratory conditions? Or are sceptics right to insist that this is not the case, and that the search was misguided from the start? Here again we could simply pick the view that best matches our feelings and preconceptions, and I guess that is what many people actually do. But if we want to feel that the choice we make is the one that is best evidenced we will have to get to grips with the arguments.

2 *Coincidence*

From a psychological perspective, there are all sorts of reasons why someone might think they have experienced something psychic. I'll be looking at these more closely in the next chap-

ter. But one likely explanation is that most of us seriously underestimate the extent to which extraordinary coincidences do
occur.

Considering how many millions of dreams are dreamed all
over the world each night, it is only to be expected that from time
to time one of them will coincide with a real event. Unsurprisingly, it will be taken to be a kind of prophecy, remembered and
remarked upon because it seems to have come true, when in reality the pairing is no more than a normal chance occurrence. It's
a fact that people commonly underestimate the frequency with
which close matches occur. A popular example is the birthday
paradox: students in a class are often spooked to find they share a
birthday with someone else. But they shouldn't be, as the chance
of any two people in a class of twenty-three sharing a birthday is
around one in two – in other words, not at all unlikely.

Richard Dawkins expands on this reasoning in his book *Unweaving the Rainbow*. People are wrong to gasp at the extraordinary coincidences or the claims of psychics, he argues, or to
think that something mysterious and providential has been going
on behind the scenes. What we need, he suggests, is 'less gasping
and more thinking'. The sting can be taken out of coincidence by
'quietly sitting down and calculating the likelihood that it would
have happened anyway'.[7]

In practice, not many people are equipped to work out the
odds, but the argument is fair enough. Here's a small example.
One autumn I bought tulip bulbs in three lots of ten, intending
to plant them in window boxes: one with whites, one with yellows and the third with reds. Unfortunately at some point the
bulbs all got put in one bag and since they looked exactly alike I
had to plant them all mixed up. Despite this, somehow they managed to sort themselves according to my original plan: when they
bloomed six months later the whites all came up in one box, the
yellows in another and the reds all in the third.

I suppose one could argue this wasn't a coincidence at all; perhaps there actually *were* discernible differences between the three different types of bulbs – in terms of their shape, size and colouration – which I picked up on unconsciously. In fact, as I recall, I didn't look at them, I just stuck my hand in the bag and planted them as they came. On the other hand there's no reason why such things shouldn't very occasionally happen by chance. Just because the odds against it are quite high it doesn't mean that it couldn't happen at all. As sceptics say, there are zillions of opportunities for extraordinary coincidences to occur in the world, and we have no right to maintain there is anything special about those that do occur.

It's still quite a subjective argument, though. Here's another instance. A small boy gets a black eye in a playground accident, and back at his home, an hour or two later, his mother is amazed to notice that his twin brother is also sporting a black eye. For her, this is beyond weird, and she may recall having heard anecdotes of a person feeling intense pain in his leg, and later learning that his twin sibling, who lives in another part of the country, has just that moment fallen down a drain. If she is a philosophical type, she might think there is some connecting principle, some meaning behind the appearances. Not at all, says the sceptic, there is a much more obvious explanation. What probably happened was this: while the first child was involved in an accident, his twin might have got into a fight with another child, unseen by her, and resolved not to tell her for fear of being punished. This chap clearly has no experience of small children, the mum retorts: no five-year-old gets into a scrap right in front of her without her noticing, or bravely holds back his tears after being thumped. The usual sort of acrimonious exchange starts up, with each side baffled by the other's obtuseness.[8]

3 *Card-guessing and other psi experiments*

What's needed is some way of getting past the subjectivity, a method of establishing whether or not such apparently uncanny matches and coincidences actually *are* purely fortuitous, or whether this is so obviously unlikely that some other explanation has to be looked for.

Parapsychologists believe they can do this by exploiting the law of averages. They seek to create, under controlled conditions, the same kind of extraordinary matches that people report in real life: the sense that individuals are telepathically in touch with other people at a distance, for instance, or clairvoyantly receiving information about distant events, or even in some cases precognitively – before the event has taken place. But as well as trying to impress us with the quality of these matches they aim to demonstrate the presence of psi quantitatively, by showing that they are occurring more frequently than chance will allow. Their earliest method was card-guessing: this was successfully tried by the first SPR researchers, notably with the five young girls of the Creery family (although this particular episode ended in controversy, as I'll describe in a bit more detail later). Charles Richet was the first to adopt a systematic statistical approach.[9] But Joseph Rhine took it to a new level, establishing an experimental protocol that could be adopted by other researchers.

Rhine's method involved a twenty-five-card deck designed by his Duke University colleague Karl Zener, containing five each of five symbols: star, circle, square, cross and wavy lines. If you try to guess the cards as someone turns them up one by one, unseen by you, you should expect to get an average of five right each time you work through the deck, the total number divided by the number of symbols. This is the mean chance expectation (if you were rolling dice, you would expect to call a number correctly an average of once in every six throws). Of course the individual results will vary wildly:

the first time you run through the deck you might correctly guess eight, ten or even fifteen cards, and your luck might hold for two or more consecutive runs. But under normal circumstances, luck is all it would be. If you carry out ten or twenty such runs the chances are you will also get bad scores, and your final average should always come out at around five per run.

It's the consistency of this mean distribution that makes experimental parapsychology possible. A significant deviation from the mean would indicate that some influence is at work. If in controlled conditions you get high scores over a long period – for instance if you end up with an average of eight correct in each run over many scores of runs – a parapsychologist might consider you have some psychic ability.

In Rhine's first tests with these Zener cards, published in the early 1930s, students scored a total of two hundred and seven hits in eight hundred trials, or single card guesses, where a score of one hundred and sixty would have been the mean expectation; the odds of that happening by chance are fewer than one in a million. Some of Rhine's subjects proved to be particularly high scorers. A theology student named Hubert Pearce was the subject of four experiments involving a total of seventy-four runs; where a score of 5 was the mean he scored averages of 9.9, 6.7, 7.3, and 9.3 – the odds against this are a hundred thousand billion *billion* to one (that's a 10 followed by 22 zeros). In one of the experiments Pearce was guessing cards at pre-arranged intervals while the experimenter Gaither Pratt was turning over the cards in another part of the building. This meant Rhine could argue there was no realistic possibility that Pearce could have been getting the information by any means other than ESP.[10]

Card-guessing is simple to carry out and to quantify statistically. But this 'forced choice' method – so-called because it involves a limited pool of possibilities – quickly gets boring for the people doing the guessing, and by the 1960s parapsychologists were shifting to more open, 'free response' approaches, where one person holds an image in his or her mind and the other attempts to guess what it is. The early SPR research contains a good many successful experiments of this kind.[11] There's also a famous example from the 1930s described by the American novelist Upton Sinclair in his book *Mental Radio*: he found that his wife was able, after getting herself into a suitably relaxed state, to accurately reproduce simple sketches that he had drawn earlier in a separate room.[12]

The thinking here is that ESP impressions get crowded out by normal mental activity, and that the subjects of such experiments have a greater chance of success if they can first get into a semi-hypnotic or meditative state. Following this reasoning, in 1969 Stanley Krippner and Montagu Ullman carried out a series of experiments on sleeping subjects in a laboratory in New York's Maimonides Centre. Their subjects were periodically woken and asked to describe their dreams, which were found frequently to match images that a person in another room – termed the 'agent' – had been trying to project to them. In one case, an agent concentrated on a flamboyant painting that depicted marching Mexican revolutionaries. Woken a few minutes later the subject described a dream of what seemed like a Hollywood film epic, apparently set in New Mexico against a backdrop of mountains and Indian villages, and involving large crowds of extras.[13]

The Maimonides experiments were a landmark in parapsychology and produced a large number of striking matches. But they were costly to carry out, and so experimenters came up with a method that was both simpler and lent itself to statistical assessment. This is the ganzfeld approach, in which the subject, or 'receiver', uses meditative techniques to get into a relaxed state, aided by being isolated in a soundproof room. The eyes are covered by halved ping-pong balls onto which a red light is directed, in order to create a uniform visual field. To complete the sensory isolation a sort of whooshing sound like radio static is piped through headphones.[14] All this encourages

a state of relaxed mental disassociation to develop, potentially opening the receiver's mind to extra-sensory influences. At this point
the 'sender', sitting out of sight and out of earshot in another room,
starts to watch a short video clip, selected randomly from a group of
four, and attempts to make and hold strong mental images of what
it contains. This process is repeated at intervals for half an hour or
so, during which the receiver is encouraged to describe any imagery
seen in his or her mind's eye.

Never myself having experienced anything like this it was hard
to imagine it working. Yet parapsychologists report that certain people not only perceive an abundance of images in these set-ups, but
also that the shapes, forms and intuitions often closely match scenes
and events that the sender has been watching on film. Occasionally they are spot on. In one instance a receiver, her eyes and ears
covered, states that she is getting the sense of a black-and-white film
about a concentration camp, while the sender, supposedly out of
earshot in another room, is watching scenes from a black-and-white
film about a concentration camp.[15] Close matches of this kind in
fact are not the norm, but there's often enough detail in the subject's
responses to single out the correct video clip from the three 'decoys'
(those which were selected as part of the original group but which
the sender did not watch). This is determined afterwards in the
judging stage, when either the receiver or independent judges not
otherwise involved in the experiment view all four clips and select
the best match. If chance alone is operating over an extended period
a correct match will be made one time in four, a level of twenty-five
per cent. But parapsychologists say that in fact ganzfeld subjects often score at levels of fifty per cent or more, and over a long period
have been scoring consistently around thirty-three per cent.[16]

Striking results have also been claimed in tests of remote viewing. In one form of such a test, a person acting as the sender goes to
a pre-selected location, while the receiver, who is under supervision
in an isolated room some distance away, describes any images that

come into his or her mind. Experiments carried out by physicists Harold Puthoff and Russell Targ at the Stanford Research Institute in the 1970s sometimes produced startling results. An example: the sender walked up and down a yachting marina while the receiver, who was in an office building several miles away, described seeing a 'little jetty or little dock' where there were 'little boats, some motor launches, some little sailing ships, sails all furled'.[17] This work developed into the well-known Stargate programme run by the US military for intelligence purposes during the 1980s. Among other feats, the programme's subjects were said variously to have correctly identified a Soviet airfield, located a Soviet Tu-95 bomber that had crashed in Africa, and discovered the location of kidnapped personnel in Italy and Lebanon.[18]

Surprisingly, parapsychologists found that the receiver's impressions sometimes matched those of the target location, even if they were recorded *before* this was chosen, suggesting the operation of some precognitive function. Other experiments were performed with a virtual disregard for distance. Both precognition and distance were present in experiments carried out by Robert Jahn and Brenda Dunne. In one case the receiver sensed a strange yet persistent image of the sender inside a large bowl: if it was full of soup the sender would be the size of a large dumpling. Some hours later the sender arrived at the intended target – the radio telescope at Kitt Peak, Arizona, some two thousand two hundred miles away, which is indeed shaped like a large dish.[19]

In the course of all this, parapsychologists claimed to have uncovered some general characteristics. They say psi is encouraged by an optimistic, almost playful attitude – in other words, not one of intense concentration but, on the contrary, of letting go and relaxing. As the novelty wears off it becomes more like work, and that is when scores start to fall to chance levels. This became strongly apparent in 1942, when psychokinesis experimenters at Duke started to notice unexpected patterns in their dice-throwing data. It always seemed that the first trials were best and then there was a falling off. They re-examined earlier experiments and found that this 'decline effect' was general, and so visible as to be significant in the order of a hundred million to one. It was also found in ESP tests. The protocol was checked for possible flaws in the test conditions, recording errors or other explanations, but nothing was found that could reproduce this pattern artefactually.[20]

Parapsychologists also came to suspect that experimental outcomes can be influenced by the beliefs and feelings of participants. The tendency of paranormal believers to score better than sceptics was confirmed in the so-called 'sheep–goats syndrome' experiments in the 1950s.[21] Curiously, the non-believing 'goats' tended to score at rates *below* what chance would predict, the so-called 'psi-missing' effect. To the enormous confusion of sceptics, parapsychologists argue that *this too* is evidence of psi, and that, by their attitude, committed disbelievers can unconsciously affect the outcome in the opposite direction.

This particular characteristic emerged in some rather striking psychokinesis experiments by Jahn and Dunne.[22] The researchers used a random-number generator with a front panel that displayed the numbers being produced in the form of a graph line. While the machine chugged along unattended, the numbers fell within a band that represented chance levels, and subjects were tasked with mentally forcing it to produce numbers outside these limits. Only a few subjects succeeded, and the significance in most cases was small, but curiously each seemed to do so in specific ways. One individual might consistently push the graph line above the average, yet be unable to push it below; another might achieve the opposite. Also, a particular subject's graph lines might form consistent patterns that were quite unlike anyone else's, as the print-outs clearly reveal. But this is not all: when subjects were asked *not* to try to influence the machine the numbers adhered more strictly to the baseline than they would have done if left themselves.

Rhine noticed a psi-missing effect with Pearce, who he claimed was so reliable that he never went below chance unless he was specifically asked to, in which case he could produce very low scores. This 'voluntary' scoring is the very opposite of chance, Rhine commented:

> This man can get a score of 9 or 10 if I ask him for a high score; if I ask him to run low, he can get a 1 or a 0; he can go back up on the next run if I say 'high' and down on the run succeeding that if I say 'low'. If this is a matter of chance performance, then the rise and fall of that steam shovel I see out of the window is a chance performance.[23]

But parapsychologists go further to suggest that experimenters themselves can unconsciously influence the outcomes. They believe there is significance in the fact that some experimenters consistently get successful results and some consistently do not, and surmise that this has something to do with the individual's own attitude and expectations. It does not surprise them that sceptics don't get positive results. Psychologist Susan Blackmore says she failed to find experimental evidence of psi, which reinforced her conviction that it doesn't exist,[24] and Paul Kurtz claims likewise, although he gives few details.[25] In the crazy world of psi, if it exists, this 'experimenter effect' paradoxically might make sense.[26] But of course on an evidential level it greatly complicates matters, since it encourages a perception that parapsychologists just aren't being sufficiently critical.

4 *What sceptics say*

Let's turn now to the critics' arguments. First, as we saw, they have objections regarding parapsychology's claim to be a science at all. A commonly cited shortcoming is an absence of replicability. A reliable experimental protocol would mean that psi's existence would not depend on the say-so of a handful of enthusiasts but could be demonstrated by any suitably qualified scientist anywhere and at any time. But this quality is manifestly lacking. Some experiments yield high effect sizes, while others are only marginally significant or come out at chance levels. So there's no guarantee that what Smith and Johnson report in Los Angeles one year can be repeated and verified by Suzuki and Hujimoto in Tokyo the next. Instead, parapsychologists are said to select, or 'cherry-pick', the data that supports their case, and to disregard any that does not.

The critics also complain that, unlike other sciences, parapsychologists define the subject of their search by what it is *not*. They can't point to a tangible entity: all they can do is assume it must be operating if any involvement of the five senses has been eliminated. Nor is their database cumulative, the sceptics say. Unlike other sciences they are not building on an established base; they are always trying to demonstrate that the thing they are looking at actually exists.

What especially bothers sceptics is that psi can't be reconciled with established scientific principles. Telepathy seems to mean that two people's brains are resonating with each other, one sending out some kind of radiation and the other receiving it. But there are big problems here. Not the least is the question of selection – how does a brain distinguish which brain to resonate with from all the thousands of other brains in its neighbourhood? Some pre-established link seems to be involved: a remote viewer doesn't randomly pick up the thoughts going on around her but those in the head of the person she is concentrating on, even if they are in different countries. That is a second difficulty, in as much as there's no sign at all of attenuation with increasing distance; it seems to make no difference whether the receiver is in the next room or on the other side of the world. All this makes it seem altogether unlikely that we are dealing with a physical energy or a force, as these terms are usually understood – it might be explicable in terms of Jungian synchronicity, but that's not an acknowledged scientific concept.

It would help if parapsychologists had something to offer here, but theorizing has not been the main focus of their activity. Some fit psi into an evolutionary framework: telepathic and clairvoyant episodes frequently look like a call for help or an alert to imminent danger, so perhaps they provide survival advantage.[27] Viewed in this way, telepathy might be seen as the remnant of some faculty that preceded the development of speech and language. But arguably this approach creates as many problems as it solves, because there's no plausible mechanism and it only partly explains the data.

Attempts have been made to seek a theoretical basis for psi in quantum mechanics. For instance telepathy might be explained in terms of the non-locality paradox, where under certain circumstances particles widely separated in space appear to be connected – through no discernible medium. But although the parallel is striking, there's a big difference between sub-atomic particles on the one hand and the biological system of the brain, the 'macro' level where psi is allegedly occurring, which tends to weaken its value as an explanation.[28] And the way that New Age writers routinely use quantum theory in support of their mystical metaphysics enrages the sceptics, who insist this is quite unwarranted.

So how could the parapsychologists' results be explained? Rhine's initial claims caused a good deal of head-scratching. Perhaps his statistics were skewed, and he was just making calculations in a way that would support his claims. But this was contested by professional statisticians, who checked the maths and found no error.[29] The numbers themselves indicated significance, which would then have to be explained away on some other grounds. In fact some statisticians have been impressed by the size of the anomalies claimed by parapsychologists and have been among their strongest defenders.[30] While the critics continue to raise questions about statistical methods, I sense they recognize this is not their strongest argument.

Another solution was to invoke the sceptical philosopher David Hume: perhaps the parapsychologists were being deceived by their subjects. It seems this was generally suspected, but it was a while before anyone spelled out how it might have happened in practice. In 1960 C.E.M. Hansel investigated the Pratt–Pearce series and later revealed what he claimed were loopholes that a dishonest participant could take advantage of.[31] He located the library on the ground floor where Pearce had sat alone and guessed the cards, also the third floor office where Pratt had turned them over at one-minute intervals. Hansel discovered that the office had a glass window that opened onto the corridor, and proposed that, unknown to Pratt, Pearce had simply nipped upstairs and peeked through. When a different office was used, Hansel noted a trapdoor immediately above the table where the experimenter had sat; obviously Pearce had got above the ceiling somehow and looked through it to catch a glimpse of the cards.

Unsurprisingly parapsychologists were disgusted by these allegations. To claim fraud and gullibility on such a scale was indecent, and surely also implausible: shouldn't somebody have spotted Pearce lurking in the corridor?[32] But creating an atmosphere of doubt and suspicion works, as we've seen in other contexts, and you can't blame sceptics for doing it. They only have to come up with a potential alternative scenario, however far-fetched it might seem, to undermine the claim that psi has been demonstrated.

Moreover, critics can point to several cases of fraud in parapsychology experiments, both by the subjects and the experimenters themselves. One of the earliest, as I mentioned, involved the Creery sisters, whose clergyman father brought their uncanny success at card-guessing games to the attention of SPR researchers. In the initial experiments the girls' scoring was very high, but it subsequently tailed off, and the work was totally discredited when two of them were later found to have developed a code as a means to signal to each other.[33] Another apparently successful display of telepathic cognition, between two young men named Smith and Blackburn, was written off thirty years later when Blackburn revealed it had been a hoax, despite the indignant protestations of Smith, who continued to insist it had been completely genuine.[34]

Just as serious are two relatively recent cases of fraud by parapsychologists, which were both uncovered by their colleagues. One concerns Walter J. Levy, who in 1974 was a twenty-six-year-old medical student appointed by Rhine to run the laboratory at Duke. Levy was testing the psi abilities of rodents, and seemed for a while to be having considerable success. However some of his co-workers became suspicious about his behaviour and eventually caught him faking his results.[35] The other scandal concerns G.R. Soal, a British researcher whose dazzling results with one particular subject in the 1940s aroused admiration, but also growing suspicion among his colleagues, and were conclusively shown in a computer analysis carried out after his death to have been achieved by surreptitious tweaking.[36]

There's no question that these cases have seriously damaged the discipline's credibility. But I think even most sceptics realize how hard it is to sustain the idea that several thousand positive results in many different parts of the world are uniformly caused by people cheating. Since the whole thrust of experimental parapsychology is to find evidence of psi as a general human capability, the ambience is rather different from the set-up of the faking charlatan: the participants in the experiments are drawn from the community, often with psychology students volunteering to take part. They are not paid, honoured or even identified, so have no obvious incentive to fake their results. As for the scandals, it can be argued that scientific fraud exists in many disciplines, and there's no reason why parapsychology should have been spared in this regard.

On the other hand, parapsychologists arguably invite criticism by continuing to show interest in high-profile psychics. There's much less of this now than in the 1960s and 1970s, partly because there seem to be fewer people like Uri Geller around, but also because parapsychologists are wary of being burned by scandals. A notorious case was James Randi's 'Project Alpha' hoax, which was targeted at the McDonnell Laboratory for Psychical Research, a new foundation set up in 1979 at Washington University in St Louis, Missouri. One of the experimenters' first projects was to study the so-called 'Geller children' who seemed able to emulate Geller's metal-bending feats. Randi wrote with some sensible suggestions, which the experimenters ignored. They were shamed when it was publicly revealed that the only two subjects who were consistently successful had been conjurors planted by Randi, thus exposing them as incompetent.[37]

However, the experimental ganzfeld work was a more obviously scientific approach, and by the 1980s it was becoming clear that its apparent success called for a more thoughtful response. Accordingly, psychologist Ray Hyman argued that sceptics needed to change their thinking. When confronted with extraordinary claims, he suggested, instead of accusing parapsychologists of fraud and charlatanism it would surely be better to respond with 'rationality, objectivity, fair play, integrity – in short, with accepted scientific principles'. Unfortunately, Hyman stated, scientists are not trained about how to behave under such circumstances, and their reactions tend to be erratic and emotional.

> If there is truly 'pathology' in these cases, the pathology seems to be exhibited as much in the reaction of the scientific community as in the claims of the offending scientist. The gut reaction of the scientific orthodoxy is to discredit the offending claim by any means possible – *ad hominem* attacks, censorship, innuendo, misrepresentation, etc.[38]

This 'panic reaction', Hyman argued, usually does succeed in discrediting the bizarre claim, but doesn't disprove it. Worse than this, the ineptness of the criticism stifles debate, and helps to confirm other people in their belief. Nor do scientists learn why people made such gross errors, which means they just go on making the same mistakes. If they were allowed to fully debate the claims, instead of automatically rejecting them or remaining ignorant of them, they would not fall into the trap of endorsing Uri Geller and other follies.

As this last bit suggests, Hyman is actually no more sympathetic to parapsychology than Randi or Hansel. Nor are workers in the field especially grateful for his condescension – as one commentator remarked, it's the difference between politely asking a beggar to go away and kicking him into the gutter.[39] In 1988 Hyman chaired a US National Academy of Sciences investigation that concluded there was 'no scientific justification from research conducted over a period of a hundred and thirty years for the existence of parapsychological phenomena.'[40] Stunned parapsychologists pointed out the implicit bias involved in asking a professional sceptic to guide the proceedings, since it was his prejudices which were being listened to; the other principal evaluator on the panel was also a convinced sceptic and CSI (CSICOP) member. They revealed that the review covered barely a tenth of the systematic scientific effort in parapsychology, and contradictory conclusions in a study that Hyman himself had commissioned had been ignored.[41]

5 *Methodological flaws*

Hyman's new approach did not mean that bias had been removed. Still, as an observer I was relieved to find that at least some critics resist the temptation to hiss and spit; it makes the arguments clearer, and one is not always having to distinguish fact from rhetoric. Of course ordinary decency is not the motivation here. The reason why the critics felt they no longer needed to abuse parapsychologists was that they had discovered a much more effective way to sideline them – by finding fault with their methods.

And indeed, there turned out to be all sorts of potential means by which psi experiments might result in false-positive outcomes. One of the most common is poor security, giving rise to 'sensory leakage'. We came across a crude example of this in the previous chapter, the gap in the curtain screen that could have given an illicit advantage to the mediums in Gary Schwartz's experiment. One of the earliest claims in an ESP context was the discovery that some Zener cards were not completely opaque, which meant the symbol might conceivably be visible to the subject when the sender held it up. The subject might also see the hidden side of the cards reflected in a glass surface such as a clock or picture, a technique used by card sharps, unless measures were specifically taken to rule this out. Similarly, if subjects are given an opportunity to handle envelopes that contain drawings they might gain clues as to which is the correct target, for instance surreptitiously holding them up to the light to see if they can discern an outline.

Another possibility in experiments on remote viewing is that subliminal clues are unwittingly provided that give away the nature of the intended target location. For instance when criticising experiments by Targ and Puthoff at the SRI, psychologists David Marks and Richard Kamman found fault with the judging procedure, the stage at which transcripts of the receiver's impressions were matched up with descriptions of what they were trying to guess.[42] They pointed out that the presence of particular remarks in the transcripts might give clues that would help them make an accurate fit. So for instance, in one set of ten trials a pool of only ten target locations was used, and some of the subjects' impressions, it was later discovered, contained references to previous sessions. The judges would therefore know in certain cases which locations to ignore. The judges might also be guided by certain clues: if photographs that had been taken of the target location included trees without their leaves, they could safely ignore any sessions that had been taken in the summer months, increasing the odds of making a correct selection.

Clues can also be picked up, it's suggested, if proper randomization procedures are not carried out. It has been shown that humans gravitate strongly towards patterns and are notoriously poor at producing truly random selections. If an experiment involves matching numbered items, a subject might score above chance simply by having learned which numbers the experimenter tends to favour. Only the use of a published table of random numbers or randomization machinery can eliminate these biases. Then there are questions of inadequate documentation, where the experimenter fails to give evidence of proper safeguards in key areas. It can also be argued that the experiment may be biased by 'optional stopping', giving a positive result only because it ended when the receivers were scoring strongly. Had it gone on longer, the receivers' scores might have fallen off, and the average would have been at the expected chance levels.

In 1981 Hyman asked for a database of ganzfeld results that he could independently scrutinize.[43] He was given thirty-four separate reports that described a total of forty-two separate studies carried out during the previous seven years. Of these more than half had been classified as achieving overall significance and the average hit rate of all the senders was about thirty-five per cent. Hyman went through all the records and pointed out the potential for various procedural flaws.

Once these were taken into account, he argued, the claim that psi had been demonstrated was greatly diminished. He also raised the possibility that parapsychologists were only reporting successful studies; he surmised that studies that had failed to produce positive results might be lying unpublished in file drawers, and when these were added into the analysis the significance would disappear (the so-called 'file-drawer' problem). Taking these and other issues into account, Hyman recalculated the results, finding that the overall scores had diminished to chance levels, and concluding that the database was too weak to support any assertions about the existence of psi.

6 *Creating doubt*

These criticisms have had a lethal effect on the credibility of experimental parapsychology within the scientific community. They certainly had an impact on my own thinking. I did not seriously suppose that the successful experiments had been faked, and found Hansel's alternative scenario for the Pratt–Pearce series rather unconvincing. But I started to feel that a positive result might indeed come about through a combination of loose controls and unacknowledged bias on the part of parapsychologists. The potential problems diminished in my mind the sense that some degree of paranormality had been demonstrated.

At the same time I wasn't certain how this worked in practice. How could an experimental flaw, or a combination of flaws, create the appearance of a paranormal effect? I soon discovered that parapsychologists were having the same difficulty; in fact they rejected the criticisms as nitpicking that couldn't have affected the final outcome.[44] Experiments in which senders had handled the target location material did not turn out more significant results than those in which the target was not touched, so this could not reasonably be considered a flaw. Statisticians criticized Hyman's statistical analysis: one called it 'meaningless', while another who was commissioned by Hyman himself found no evidence that ganzfeld results could be attributed to flaws.[45] Nor could the file-drawer problem be the solution: to annul the significance, the number of unsuccessful and unpublished studies would have had to have been far greater than was possible, given the limited resources of such a tiny discipline.[46]

Nevertheless, as I say, Hyman and other critics had created enough uncertainty to save scientists the bother of having to take it seriously. Their intervention confirmed just how water-tight experiments have to be if claims regarding the existence of psi are to carry conviction. It's the same problem we found with Eusapia Palladino and Gary Schwartz's experiments with mediums – in such complex set-ups it's practically impossible to rule out each and every loophole that might occur to a doubting critic. I get the impression that parapsychologists often don't provide the necessary safeguards until they are forced to by the critics' long lists of complaints, since they can't imagine that anyone would seriously raise such unlikely possibilities. At this point a bitter dispute starts up. Observers like ourselves are in the same position as before – jurors trying to decide between the highly charged claim and counter-claim of opposing counsel.

This is especially hard when the subject is so emotionally charged. Despite Hyman's strictures some critics still take a confrontational approach. For instance, in his critique of Targ and Puthoff's remote-viewing experiments, David Marks excoriates the scientists as responsible for either *'gross incompetence'* or a *'cynical exercise in deception and fraud'* (his italics).[47] It's startling when you realize these are not dodgy psychics he's talking about, but university research physicists carrying out scientific experiments.

In general, Marks considers that parapsychologists are 'medicine men' or 'shamans'; their experiments are 'sloppy,' 'a catalogue of errors' or 'poorly done', with details that are 'deeply troubling' or 'disturbing'. The ganzfeld approach has been 'put on a pedestal', he says, but thanks to the critics' vigilance it now lies 'in tatters'.[48] All this emoting makes his arguments hard to judge dispassionately: it will quickly convince people that parapsychologists are superstitious cretins who should not be allowed near a laboratory.

This isn't to say that the critics didn't make valid points about Targ and Puthoff's early experiments. Considering the enormity of the conclusions, the experimental protocols clearly need to be faultless. Here too, it might have been wiser if the pair had been less forthright initially, and had worked to build up as much confirmation as possible before making such provoking claims.

But there's a point here which I think has not really been recognized. Psi – as it is conceived, and whether real or imagined – is a product of mentation, yet also one that apparently has the abnormal property of bringing about effects in the material world, most dramatically by causing objects to move at a distance. In that sense, it is essentially a *hybrid;* it consists of two entities so different from each other that they sit at opposite ends of the scientific spectrum. Within psychology, experiments usually aim to show how people think and behave in certain defined situations. That typically doesn't require a high level of security: subjects are not expected to cheat, and sensory leakage is seldom an issue. Psi experimenters, by contrast, are required to provide the kind of certainty expected in a physics or chemistry lab. But you can't do that with *people*; mental activity can't be isolated like a physical entity such as a gas or metal. Even if the experimenters always use the same person as a subject there's no guarantee that his or her mood will not vary, and that the conditions that enabled him or her to produce evidence of psi in abundance one week will not have vanished the next.

When I eventually grasped this I started to feel that the sceptics' complaints about 'sloppy' methodology are somewhat bogus. They labour to give the impression that parapsychologists are inferior scientists, and imply that they personally could never commit such gross derelictions. A more nuanced view would be that psi experimenters are early explorers in a new field of discovery, whose inevitable mistakes can be avoided by those who follow – as has been happening. In fact, as we will see in a minute, sceptics make exactly the same sorts of blunders in their attempts to create failed replications. There's nothing wrong with that: as I say, it's to be expected in a new science that is feeling its way. It learns by its mistakes. But it reminds us not be let ourselves be too easily swayed by the hostile rhetoric.

7 *The sense of being stared at*

Ganzfeld and remote viewing are the two types of experiment that have attracted the most attention, and I'll have a bit more to say about them later. But other approaches have provided results that on the face of it seem just as significant, for instance looking at telepathic links between bonded pairs of individuals. In a 1997 televised experiment with a pair of identical twins, a polygraph monitoring one of them showed large fluctuations occurring at the moment when the other twin, well out of earshot, was exposed to a loud and unexpected disturbance.[49] Similarly, a twin monitored by a functional magnetic resonance imaging (fMRI) scanner showed a highly significant increase in electrical activity of the visual cortex when the sibling viewed a flickering light. This very precise correlation has odds against chance of fourteen thousand to one, and there have been several apparently successful replications.[50]

Similar approaches have been followed by Rupert Sheldrake, a Cambridge-trained biologist well known for his proposal that an information field may underlie all physical organisms. His idea is that organisms are shaped by 'morphic resonance', a process whereby forms and behaviours that have developed in one place can encourage the emergence of similar ones to develop elsewhere.[51] As a potential rival to Darwinist theory it's easy to see how this would raise hackles among mainstream scientists, and indeed his book on the subject was famously denounced by the science journal *Nature* as 'the best candidate for burning there has been for many years'.[52]

Pursuing his belief in psychic connectivity, Sheldrake identified interactions that might be worthy of investigation, such as the idea that some people sometimes have a sense of being stared at intently by another person. To find out if this has any basis in fact, Sheldrake proposed a simple experiment. Person A, the equivalent of the receiver in a ganzfeld set-up, sits with his or her back turned, in front of person B, the equivalent of the sender, at a distance of two or more metres. At a given signal, B either looks at the back of A's head, or looks away and thinks about something else. Person A then states an intimation of what B is doing, whether looking or not looking, and B records this response by ticking the appropriate column on a test sheet. Person B then makes a signal, for instance by activating a mechanical clicker, and the process starts again. At the end, the number of right and wrong guesses is totted up for the looking and not-looking trials separately.

This experiment is so simple that a child of eight can do it, and many have. In 1998 Sheldrake published the results of experiments carried out by classes in primary schools, five in the US and three in Germany.[53] The combined results showed a clear preponderance of correct guesses in cases in which the subjects were being looked at: seventy per cent of the subjects were right more often than they were wrong, with odds against of thirty million to one. Some children showed a particular gift and were tested individually; two were found to be right nearly eighty-eight and ninety-four per cent of the time, respectively, which is a staggering departure from chance expectation.

Interestingly, the children showed no special ability to call correctly when they were *not* being looked at: such instances were at chance levels. Sheldrake suggests this is significant for two reasons. First, it's what one would predict; the claim is that one can guess when one is being stared at, a very specific sense and not at all comparable to *not* being stared at, which is not something we would have any reason to intuit. And second, it largely disposes of the idea that the children were cheating, either by peeking or by picking up subtle cues; if they had been doing this they would have shown an equal ability to guess correctly in both categories.

Sheldrake considered the possibility that the subjects could have seen what the looker was doing by means of peripheral vision. Since this doesn't extend to having eyes in the back of their head one might think it implausible, but to rule it out he carried out equally successful experiments in which the subjects were blindfolded, or communicated through windows, eliminating such sensory cues.[54] He also considered the more serious possibility that individual lookers might communicate their intentions unconsciously in the way that they signalled the start of a new trial with the mechanical clicker. However he discounted this, since trials in which a single signal was given to the whole class by the teacher actually showed more positive scores.

8 Sceptics vs Sheldrake

Precisely because the experiment is so easy to carry out, sceptics were confident they could get a negative result by doing it themselves and by tightening up the method. The first to try were Richard Wiseman and Matthew Smith, who aimed to eliminate any possible cueing by situating the subject and the looker in different locations and putting them in contact by means of closed-circuit television (although this method had previously been adopted by parapsychologist Marilyn Schlitz and others with significant results).[55] Instead of asking the subjects to decide whether or not they were being observed, they recorded their reaction by monitoring their galvanic skin resistance, an accurate way of measuring emotional arousal. The psychologists also used randomization tables to ensure that the lookers did not start to alternate between looking and not looking in ways that the looker could predict.

Surprisingly, from their point of view, the subjects turned out to have significantly more positive responses in the looking than in the not-looking trials, suggesting the existence of a psychic sense. But Wiseman and Smith explained the apparent success as an effect of the way they had carried out the randomization, in which more looking trials preceded not-looking trials than vice versa. They argued that a positive result could occur if the subjects' skin resistance declined throughout the session as they became more relaxed. They concluded the result was almost certainly artefactual, and recommended that rather than use truly random sequences, future research should aim to avoid such possible artefacts.

In reply to this, Sheldrake pointed out that Wiseman and Smith had apparently not looked at their own data to see if it bore out their claim. He asked for the data and was given about half of it. He claimed that actually it did not support their contention: in seven out of seventeen cases the skin resistance actually increased and there was no artefactual effect in the opposite direction, as one would expect.[56]

In a later experiment, Wiseman acted as the looker himself and here there were no significant effects.[57] However, that finding in itself was rather remarkable, and for this reason – he was collaborating with Marilyn Schlitz, a parapsychologist who had achieved significant findings in remote-viewing experiments, and whose results on this occasion were positive, even though she was using the same closed-circuit television set-up and the students acting as subjects were drawn from the same pool. The only variation was the experimenter. Since Wiseman conceded he found the business of acting as a looker 'enormously boring' Sheldrake could argue that he had not been very good at it: the students did not sense they were being stared at because Wiseman was not psychically involved.[58]

Other staring experiments were carried out by Robert A. Baker, a former psychology professor at Kentucky University and a CSI (CSICOP) fellow.[59] Interestingly, Baker carried out his first attempt in public places, in the kinds of real-life situations where people actually sometimes do get the feeling that someone is staring at them. He tried this a total of forty times, staring at an individual in a public location such as a cafe for between five and fifteen minutes, then approaching the person to describe what he had done and ask them to fill in a response sheet. He claimed to have obtained negative results, as he did in a second, more conventional experiment. In reply, Sheldrake pointed out that in the first experiment five of the thirty-five people actually had, according to Baker's own description, noticed something unusual: two said they were aware they were being stared at and three reported they felt something was 'wrong'. However Baker had dismissed this by retrospectively introducing a new criterion, that they had not been able to pinpoint the source of the staring. A sensitivity to being stared at, Sheldrake argued, did not necessarily imply an awareness of the position of the starer. In two cases, Baker said, the individuals were obviously paranoid; again, even if this was true, it would not mean they were not psychically aware of what he was doing.[60]

Baker's experiment must have required considerable commitment to carry out and it turned up some interesting issues. However since it was quite unlike Sheldrake's, it can't really be said to have refuted his results. Baker's second effort *was* based on Sheldrake's protocol but still departed from it in significant ways. For instance he allowed subjects as long as sixty seconds to make up their minds, which Sheldrake argued makes it a much more deliberative process, as well as encouraging distractions.

A more serious challenge was mounted by David Marks and John Colwell. Like Wiseman, they took the line that Sheldrake's procedures were not properly randomized. They also objected to the subjects being given feedback, whereby they were told after each attempt whether or not they had succeeded, which could quickly enable them to sense a natural pattern that they could then exploit. For instance they might learn from experience that if they had guessed correctly that they were being looked at on two consecutive occasions, then the next occasion was more likely to be negative.[61]

These possibilities seemed to be confirmed by an experiment carried out by John Colwell, who first tested to see if feedback made any difference to the outcome. Sure enough without feedback, he found, the results were not significant; however there was a definite significance where there was feedback, with odds against of more than a thousand to one. An analysis then showed that the data was not in fact completely random, which seemed to confirm that the subjects were probably learning to read the patterns. Colwell then repeated the experiment, but with sequences taken from random-number tables. As he and Marks predicted, no ability to detect staring was observed, and also no learning. They concluded that the effect vanished when trials were properly randomized.

This looked to me like a pretty effective criticism, but Sheldrake had an interesting response. He pointed out, first, that Colwell's original results were in remarkable agreement with his own and those of other investigators – significance in the looking trials at the thousand-to-one level and no significance in the not-looking trials. He agreed that feedback seemed to improve the results, enabling participants to improve their performance with practice, and that the experiment provided clear evidence of a learning effect. But whatever the true cause of this, he doubted that it had anything to do with the randomization procedures he had been using, which ironically were precisely those that Richard Wiseman had recommended as a means to get rid of the significant effects he too had unexpectedly achieved.[62] The fact that Colwell's second experiment failed to produce significant effects, he suggested, might have more to do with the fact that the starer in this case was a different person, a sceptic whose negative expectations might have influenced the way he looked at the subjects.

Sheldrake went on to point out that in more than five thousand of his own successful trials the randomization had in fact been absolutely structureless, as the critics demanded, since it consisted of nothing more than the starer tossing a coin before each trial. The same was also true of more than three thousand equally successful trials in German and American schools. These significant results could therefore not be an artefact of pseudo-randomization, as the critics argued. He added that he had also carried out more than ten thousand trials in which no feedback was given, which would make it impossible to achieve implicit learning, yet here too the results were still highly significant.

For me, the clincher was this: if an ability to learn from feedback and patterns were indeed a factor, it would be as visible in the not-looking trials as in the looking trials. But it wasn't. Colwell's subjects scored at chance levels in these, just as Sheldrake's had. Significant improvements occurred only in the looking trials. Colwell suggested this might have happened if the subjects had focused more on the detection of staring than non-staring episodes. But this is a pretty big 'if'; they must have been able to selectively detect when staring trials were happening, otherwise their scores would not have been above chance levels and shown such an improvement in successive sessions.

My judgement is that Sheldrake's results are significant and deserve to be taken seriously. The findings are based on large-scale research and have been repeated by other investigators, apparently by some of the critics themselves. Further, the naysayers have not convinced me that that the results are the consequence of ineffective randomization or any other artefact.

It's true that as long as sceptics are putting up resistance, nothing is resolved. But notice how inconsistent they are. In their own experiments they get positive results, but either do not acknowledge them or else retrospectively change the criteria in order to eliminate them. They carry out a 'failed replication', but vary the method to the point that it's not really a replication at all. They try to improve the procedure in the expectation of eliminating significance, and when, despite all their precautions, they end up achieving significance, they criticize their own improvements. This type of behaviour seems truly to deserve the kind of ridicule that they commonly dish out to parapsychologists.

So it would be wrong to take at face value the critics' claims to have definitively debunked anything. Experimental parapsychology is a work in progress; mistakes have to be made and sceptics are no more infallible than parapsychologists. Perhaps out of this confrontation can come co-operation; that has happened in some cases as we shall see later. But in the meantime, I want to show you an even more dramatic example of critical confusion.

9 *A psychic dog*

As a biologist Sheldrake has devoted much of his career to investigating animal behaviour. During his childhood he was especially fascinated by the abilities of homing pigeons, and the behaviour of domestic pets also caught his attention. One day a neighbour told him she always knew when her son, a merchant seaman, was on his way home by the way her cat took to waiting on the doormat from about the time his ship was docking at Southampton.[63] This and other observations led him to think seriously about the possibility of telepathy in animals.

In 1999 Sheldrake published a survey of pet owners in and around the Manchester area in which around half of dog owners, and a third of cat owners, said they believed they had some sort of telepathic connection with their animals.[64] This was particularly noticeable in the case of dogs: around forty-five per cent of respondents said the pet appeared to other family members to behave in ways that suggested it knew when its owner was about to return home. Of course this could have been because dogs can recognize the approach of a familiar car or familiar footsteps or sense a familiar odour. However in sixteen per cent of cases described by the owners, the dog reacted more than ten minutes in advance of the return, which would make any of these ordinary explanations less likely. (Similar results were obtained in a survey in California.)

Sheldrake then tested Jaytee, a terrier cross owned by young woman named Pam Smart in the north of England.[65] Smart usually left the dog with her parents when she went out, and over the years they noticed that it seemed to anticipate her arrival by going to wait at the window by the front door, sometimes as much as half an hour beforehand. At first they assumed this was a matter of routine: the dog went to the window almost every weekday at about 4:30 PM, the time that Smart normally left work in Manchester, and remained there for most of her journey. But then Smart lost her job and started going out and returning at different times. Even with this irregular pattern Jaytee would still go and wait by the window for several minutes before she came through the front door.

At Sheldrake's suggestion, Smart and her parents kept a written record of the dog's behaviour over a period of nine months. In a series of journeys recorded between May and July 1994, the dog reacted in this way ten minutes or more in advance of Smart's return on twenty-seven occasions, over eighty per cent of the time. On most occasions Jaytee reacted between ten and forty-five minutes in advance of her arrival. However it was hard to estimate how closely the reactions corresponded to the time she set off at, so from July to the following February Smart also recorded her journey times. On fifty-five out of sixty-three occasions the dog showed an anticipatory response at least six minutes before she arrived home, nearly ninety per cent of the time. In twenty cases, Jaytee reacted exactly when she set off, or within two minutes of this time, and there was a clear tendency for the dog to react earlier when the journey was longer. In other words, his reactions suggested that Jaytee could sense not just when she was about to arrive but also when she was setting off on her journey.

Jaytee did not always react, however. Sheldrake speculated that this might be because of distractions, by a neighbour's bitch being on heat or a sore paw, for example. Sheldrake also tried to eliminate the possibility that the dog recognized the sound of Smart's car by getting her to return in a taxi – a different vehicle each time – or by bicycle; but this did not seem to have any negative effect. And to test the possibility that Smart might unwittingly have communicated her return times to her parents in some way, experiments were held in which she began her journey home at times selected at random after she had left. Again, this did not seem to change the outcome.

Sheldrake's publicity about his work with Jaytee attracted the attention of some Austrian television film makers. To see if they could capture the effect visually, a film crew followed Smart around the shops while another team filmed the dog. At a certain moment Smart was asked to return home. Subsequently a Channel 4 documentary showed the two films side by side on a split screen, with a timing counter on each to demonstrate that they were synchronized. At more or less the same moment that Smart was told they were leaving, the dog pricked up its ears and went to wait by the window.

The publicity about this apparent success led Richard Wiseman to provide comment. The psychologist speculated along the conventional lines, that Jaytee might be hearing Smart's return in some way away, or might be showing knowledge of an established routine.[66] Sheldrake then invited Wiseman to look over his data, and explained that he had eliminated these conventional explanations. By this time Sheldrake was using a video camera to tape the dog's behaviour, and offered Wiseman the use of it so that he could verify the effect for himself.

About a year later Sheldrake was shocked to hear that Wiseman had been speaking at sceptics' conferences about how he had investigated the dog himself and found that it was not psychic after all. According to Wiseman, his filming had shown no correlations whatsoever between Smart's movements and the dog's behaviour, implying that the events shown in the television documentary were at best a fluke. In 1998 an article authored by Wiseman and two colleagues in the *British Journal of Psychology* described his experiments in detail. This article was publicized by a press release from the British Psychological Society, which led to spate of newspaper headlines like 'Psychic pets are exposed as a myth' and 'Pets have no sixth sense, say scientists'.[67]

In a tetchy note in the SPR's journal, Sheldrake argued that Wiseman's data, which Wiseman had agreed to share with him, actually revealed the same correlations that he believed he himself had established.[68] He wanted to know why Wiseman was putting a different spin on them. In his reply, also published in the journal, Wiseman argued his objective was to deal with the claim made by the television documentary, that he was not concerned with Sheldrake's research, and indeed was under no obligation to consider it.[69]

Sheldrake clearly did not accept this response. However by this time, as was often the case, I had become so confused that I could not understand what was going on. I more or less grasped what Sheldrake was doing, but I was less clear about Wiseman's approach, and I could not see who was right. Eventually I did what I should have done in the first place; I rang the British Psychological Society and got them to send me a copy of Wiseman's article.[70] As I read this through everything started to become clear.

10 *What Wiseman did*

The first thing I noticed was that Wiseman was concerned to establish reliable criteria for success, criteria that could be objectively verified, rather than interpret past events. Sheldrake had not done anything like this, so it straight away made me think that Wiseman was being more methodical. Wiseman decided that going to wait by the porch window for no apparent reason would be the signal that Jaytee had telepathically intuited the beginning of Smart's return journey, apparently because this was what she and her parents themselves thought. To establish a correlation point he divided up Smart's absence into ten-minute segments, and required the dog's signal to occur in the precise segment in which Smart started her return journey. Wiseman would remain with the dog and videotape its movements. Meanwhile his colleague Matthew Smith drove Smart to a distant location and the two would hang around until Smith, at a pre-arranged, randomly chosen time, informed Smart that it was time to return. Wiseman's tapes were sent to the third team member, a psychologist at the University of Edinburgh, to assess independently for any correlation between the dog's movements and Smart's return journey.

Wiseman and Smith carried out a total of four experiments, all of which seemingly failed to show any correlation. I'm going to summarize their results briefly, and again this should provide an insight into how these sorts of controversies develop.

In the first experiment, Smart's absence was recorded between 7:10 PM and 10:10 PM. During this time, Jaytee made a total of thirteen trips to the porch. The first time the dog visited the porch for no particular reason was at 7:57 PM. Smart and Smith did not leave for home until 9:00 PM so this was considered a failure. However, Smart later pointed out that the dog only stayed there for a fairly brief period of time and that a better indicator of a possibly psychic reaction might be when it remained there for a longer period. Reviewing the tape they noted three occasions on which Jaytee stayed there for more than two minutes, at 8:09 PM, 8:58 PM, and 9:04 PM, and the last two of these were in fact both close to the departure time. So Wiseman decided in future not to look for the first time the dog went to the porch for no apparent reason, but the first time it went for no apparent reason *and* waited there for more than two minutes.

An unexpected issue that emerged was that there were lots of distractions outside: cats, people and cars all coming and going. So it was hard to know whether the dog was going to the window to see what was going on, or because it had intuited Smart's return. To minimize such background noise they decided to run the second experiment in the afternoon rather than the early evening. This time the dog visited the porch at 1:59 PM, when it should have responded between 2:18 PM and 2:27 PM, so this too was considered unsuccessful. However, changing the time of day had not cut out the background activity: Smart pointed out that the local fish van had arrived at a crucial moment and that there were many other distractions.

Wiseman and Smith carried out their third experiment in the winter, in the hope that the cold weather would limit the amount of activity going on outside. This time the dog went to the porch at 9:31 PM when it should have responded between 9:36 PM and 9:42 PM, so Wiseman classed this too as a failure. However, as Smart pointed out, the dog did wait there throughout her return journey. In the fourth trial, the dog achieved its first 'hit', visiting the porch at 10:44 PM, at the start of the segment it needed to coincide with. However, it only stayed there for a few seconds, and since Smart had earlier persuaded Wiseman to include the length of time it spent there as a distinguishing characteristic of the signal, this too had to be discounted. Wiseman does note, however, that the reason the dog may have left the porch so quickly was because it felt ill, as he went straight into the garden and vomited.

To sum up, on the first two occasions the dog's first visit to the porch 'for no obvious reason' occurred before Smart set off on her return journey, when a successful outcome required the two events to more or less coincide. On the third occasion the two almost coincided, but not quite. On the fourth, they did coincide, but the dog did not remain there for the stipulated two minutes. Wiseman concludes from this that '…in all four experiments Jaytee failed to detect accurately when Smart set off to return home.' He adds: 'Although four experiments would be too few to rule out a small psychic effect, they are sufficient to contradict the claim made by the media that the effect is strong and completely reliable'.[71] He also suggests that Jaytee exhibited the target behaviour so frequently that selective memory, multiple guesses and selective matching could often have provided sufficient scope to give an owner the impression of a paranormal effect.

As I say, I was initially impressed with the methodical way that Wiseman set the parameters for the experiment. But as I started to grasp what he was doing this feeling evaporated, and I experienced that growing sense of incredulity that sceptics themselves sometimes complain about when critiquing the work of parapsychologists. I sympathised with the scientists' difficulty in trying to interpret the animal's behaviour; the dog could not simply put up its paw and say, 'She's on her way, guys', so they had to judge by how it was acting. But then I started to question not only the specific methods they were using to achieve this, but why they were doing it all.

Let's start with the criterion they used to judge the dog's signal, not only that it should be seen to be going to the window for no reason at the right time, but also that it should be *the first time* that it did so. This made no sense to me. If the dog goes to the window at 6:00 PM when there's nothing going on outside, and therefore no obvious reason for it to do so, it doesn't follow that when it goes again at 7:00 PM, again for no discernible reason, this is not because on this occasion it has telepathic intuition of its owner setting off home at this time. The first doesn't rule out the second; indeed, there's no logical connection between the two events at all. Yet this was the reason Wiseman gave for classing the first experiment as a failure.

Furthermore, Wiseman's method is vulnerable to the possibility that even on those occasions when the dog went to the window for no obvious reason, it actually might have heard something outside that it wanted to check out. The superior senses of animals, and particularly dogs, is a major element of the sceptic's case: if one can argue that a dog's ability to sense its owner's arrival comes not from innate psi but from hearing the owner's vehicle at a much greater distance than many people would consider credible – which on this topic sceptics routinely do[72] – then one can reasonably argue the dog could also pick up the sound of a squirrel rustling the leaves in a nearby tree, or a cat crossing the road, or just about anything else (my Staffordshire terrier is always barking at noises outside that I haven't noticed). Here, the occasions when Jaytee went to the porch window might be classed as 'for no obvious reason' only because the scientists did not observe the distraction that caused it. This is exactly this sort of oversight that critics like Hyman and Marks deride as fatal flaws, as indeed Wiseman himself might have done had he been reviewing the experiment rather than carrying it out.

Now look at the effect of Wiseman's other requirement that the dog should wait by the window for at least two minutes. This was sufficient to judge the fourth experiment a failure. Although it was the only time Jaytee's first visit 'for no obvious reason' did coincide with Smart's departure, he quickly left again. But if he left because he felt sick, as Wiseman implies, then Wiseman is surely unjustified in claiming that the dog failed to show a telepathic response: the only reasonable conclusion is that the experiment was spoiled and that it failed to prove anything one way or the other.

Here's something else that Wiseman made no allowance for. If the dog was telepathically in touch with Smart one could argue this wouldn't necessarily show as a reaction to what she *did*, but what she *thought*. In theory at least, this could apply in the third experiment when the dog responded five minutes before Smith actually announced their departure. Since they were simply killing time in a pub and it was getting late, it would have been natural for her to think that their departure must be imminent. Smart could also have picked up from Smith the fact that they were about to leave from barely perceptible clues he might have given, such as signs of nervousness, a surreptitious glance at his watch, or drinking more quickly. Of course Smith would have guarded against this, but there's no guarantee he would have succeeded, as sceptics in other similar contexts are at pains to point out.

My conclusion from all of this is that the approach was so ill-conceived it had no chance of demonstrating anything one way or the other. Sheldrake, by contrast, avoided these pitfalls because his approach was statistical, showing that a correlation between the dog's behaviour and its owner's movements is visible over a long period. He did not try to distinguish between causes of the dog's behaviour on a few occasions in order to determine what it was or was not aware of at a given moment. He just confirmed that on repeated occasions over many months the dog spent significantly more time waiting by the window in the period when his owner was on her way home than at other times. His graphs show this quite clearly: where the vertical axis represents the dog's waiting time in minutes, and the horizontal represents hours of the day, a more or less horizontal line bumps along the bottom, where the dog is spending hardly any time at the window, then abruptly shoots up to a high level which is more or less maintained.[73] The significance lies in the fact that these spikes correlate more or less exactly with all or part of Smart's journey home. (We can still object that a telepathic link is merely assumed from the correlation, and could in fact have quite different causes, but if no obvious naturalistic explanations can be offered it's arguably a fair assumption to make.)

In 2000, Sheldrake published a fuller paper based on his and Smart's continued research with Jaytee, this time using the video-taping methods that Wiseman had used. Where Wiseman carried out four experiments, Sheldrake and Smart carried out a hundred and seventeen. These confirmed Sheldrake's earlier data, and when tabulated showed the dog spending an average of four per cent of its time by the window during the main period of Smart's absence compared with seventy-eight per cent while she was returning. This tended to confirm Sheldrake's own conclusions: he was able to demonstrate that Wiseman's data also fitted this pattern closely.[74]

Compare this with Wiseman's own comment in an interview that 'the dog was constantly going to the window'. In fact the dog was at the window so much, he said, 'it would be more surprising if it wasn't at the window when the owner was returning home'. His conclusion was that pet owners are 'kidding themselves'.[75] Since his four experiments did not measure this point, and since they are refuted by Sheldrake's far more extensive statistical study, it can only have been Wiseman's subjective impression. In that case, who is kidding who?

11 *Science or propaganda?*

It remains to ask why Wiseman would have adopted such a clumsy approach. No serious parapsychologist would try to determine whether a particular individual was psychic on the basis of such limited data, or expect any claim of psi arising from it to be taken seriously. So, conversely, how would such an experiment demonstrate the lack of it? The short answer is that Wiseman was not trying to establish the existence of psi in this particular context so much as its non-existence, which meant any shortcomings in the experiment wouldn't matter. But that is only part of the explanation.

As Sheldrake noted, Wiseman had embarked on this project after picking up on the comments of two television presenters discussing the Austrian documentary film. The presenters accurately stated that the film showed the dog going to sit by the window at precisely the same moment his owner set off home. However they then went on to give the impression that this *always* happened, which was not the case at all: the correlation was not between the dog's movement and the owner getting up to go, which could be timed in a few seconds, but between the dog's waiting and the owners' journey, which might be a matter of ten or twenty minutes. Wiseman was quick to exploit this unwarranted exaggeration: all he needed to do, in order to prove the claim as false, was show was that it did not happen on a few occasions, and indeed Sheldrake himself wouldn't have been able to confirm it. If Wiseman had told Sheldrake exactly what he planned to do, Sheldrake would surely have tried to talk him out of it, pointing out that the media claim was wrong and that disproving it wouldn't achieve anything useful: only a statistical investigation would be worth doing.

This brings us to what, to me, is the most interesting aspect of this affair: the interaction between the two scientists – or rather the lack of it. Wiseman did not argue that there were flaws in Sheldrake's monitoring or that his statistical analysis was wrong; for that matter he did not comment on any of his judgements. Instead he ignored Sheldrake altogether, and responded to his protests with chilly indifference. He was not obliged to take account of Sheldrake's unpublished findings, he argued. He was only interested in the media claims.[76] Since critics are normally eager to attack parapsychologists' work, this looked to me as if he knew he couldn't confront Sheldrake on his own ground, especially after Sheldrake had eliminated his initial speculations. Yet that did not stop him implying in public that he had directly debunked Sheldrake's work.[77]

If Wiseman had been interested in taking this field of study further he would have co-operated with the scientist who had laid the basis for it. That is certainly what I would like to have seen, and what I think would have advanced our understanding about an area that many people are legitimately interested in. But as a professional sceptic Wiseman saw a chance to stop it in its tracks, and it's interesting how well he has succeeded. As is so often the case, a poorly thought-out, misinformed, and opportunistic enterprise yields a result that becomes part of the critical literature and can be referred to as if it was the last word.

Let me show how an incident like this contaminates an entire category of research. Sheldrake has done other work with pets, notably an investigation of an African Grey parrot called N'kisi.[78] The bird, owned by New York artist Aimée Morgana, can utter English words, sometimes in the form of full sentences, and has a vocabulary that is seven hundred words strong. Morgana contacted Sheldrake to describe how N'kisi often says phrases that correspond to what she is doing or thinking, even if they are in separate rooms. Sheldrake investigated this by means of a controlled videotaped experiment, in which owner and parrot were placed in different parts of the apartment as Morgana looked at numbered photographs at intervals and N'kisi made his usual comments. The result was highly significant statistically, and Sheldrake's report gives an abundant number of examples where the parrot's comments exactly matched her thoughts.

A story about Sheldrake's experiment with N'Kisi appeared in *USA Today*, and in this way came to the attention of the CSI (CSICOP). The organisation's PR person then wrote to the magazine to express his indignation. He found the article 'disappointing, even disturbing'. Interestingly, he had nothing at all to say about the parrot. However he complained about the lack of any mention of Sheldrake's previous pet research with Jaytee, and the fact that Richard Wiseman 'failed to find any evidence that the dog had an extrasensory ability to predict its owner's return'. Sheldrake's findings about the parrot therefore carried no credibility, he implied. He concluded:

> Contrary to the rhetoric floating around, the field of parapsychology is getting a fair hearing from psychologists like Richard Wiseman and Susan Blackmore in England, and Ray Hyman in the United States. The fact is that despite the hype this field of research continually fails to produce reliable, repeatable results.[79]

As you may by now be able to see, this sort of statement is quite misleading. Behind the spin and the simplification is a complex story, but not one that the casual observer is likely to understand, or that professional sceptics have the smallest interest in helping you with, even if they had grasped it themselves.

12 *What's the score?*

Let's go back now to the experiments that have most claimed the sceptics' attention – remote viewing and ganzfeld. What are the latest results, and where does the debate now stand?

Once sceptics started to get involved one would expect the parapsychologists to take account of their criticisms, and this is effectively what happened. They persuaded Hyman, as the most articulate critic, to commit to a protocol that he would consider flaw-proof. On the basis of this, Charles Honorton, a parapsychologist based at the University of Edinburgh and a driving force behind the ganzfeld approach, came up with method called 'autoganzfeld', which computerized the processes in order to reduce the security loopholes and other potential sources of artefactual results. By 1994 he and Daryl Bem, a psychologist at Cornell University, were able to report a combined hit rate of thirty-two per cent for ten autoganzfeld studies carried out between 1983 and 1989, significantly higher than the twenty-five per cent mean level. That was only slightly lower than the thirty-five per cent recorded for twenty-eight ganzfeld studies carried out between 1974 and 1981.[80] In other words, even after eliminating the supposed flaws, subjects were still getting about one in three right, when if chance alone was operating they should have been getting only one in four.

This 'meta-analysis' appeared in the prestigious academic journal *Psychological Bulletin,* one of those landmark events where parapsychologists break through to the mainstream. However, the success was qualified a few years later when Richard Wiseman and Julie Milton carried out a meta-analysis of thirty studies that had been conducted between 1987 and 1997 and found no overall statistical significance.[81] Milton later noted that when subsequent replications were taken into account the accumulated studies did achieve a significant effect, although smaller than for the earlier ones. On their own, the ten new studies that she added had a highly significant combined hit rate of around thirty-six per cent and when added to the previous thirty the overall hit rate was more marginally significant at about thirty per cent.[82]

Parapsychologists blamed the decline in significance in the later meta-analyses on the fact that several of the studies they covered departed from Honorton's standard protocol.[83] For instance one had subjects trying to identify snatches of music instead of video clips. If this had worked it would have extended knowledge about psi, but it turned out that the subjects had no special ability in this regard, and since it was a large study it merely diluted the database.[84] On the other hand one large and highly successful study, which used subjects with creative temperaments, had been excluded by Wiseman and Milton (it is common practice in meta-analysis to exclude studies with atypical data) and this meant the results were skewed towards non-significance.[85]

A later meta-analysis by parapsychologists surveyed the literature to update all known trials from 1974 to 2004, and found an overall hit rate of thirty-two per cent in more than 3000 sessions, an effect associated with odds against chance of twenty-nine quintillion to one (that's 29 followed by 18 zeros).[86]

The size of this effect over such a long period looks pretty definitive to me. Critics might counter that it would be neutralized if *all* the data were included, on the assumption that studies with negative results were never published. But Dean Radin calculates that for this to happen there would have to be twenty-three such studies for every known one, requiring continuous activity for thirty-six years – an utterly implausible idea. And sceptics who still believe that experimental flaws are to blame may be disappointed, as their champions are themselves starting to have second thoughts about this.

Not that critics have completely given up. Wiseman for instance has raised the possibility of weaknesses in the acoustic separation between the rooms in which the receiver and sender are sitting during ganzfeld experiments. The sender watching a film clip might bang the chair or stamp on the floor in excitement, sending sounds or vibrations through to the other room where the receiver might hear them and be appropriately influenced.[87] This approach is curiously similar to his assault on the Feilding Report of Eusapia Palladino described in Chapter Two – a far-fetched hypothesis which nevertheless commands attention for the self-belief of its author and the cogency and detail of its presentation. It underscores the difficulty of providing a completely reliable protocol and in so doing keeps the doubts alive.

Yet it says a lot that critics have to fall back on such speculative theories. And in fact one gets the sense that they are starting to make concessions on this point. Wiseman himself has said that the studies and results in recent ganzfeld work represent an impressive achievement; he praises their 'very high level of methodological sophistication,' and concludes that parapsychologists 'may indeed be starting to corner their elusive quarry', as long as improvements continue to be made in the way that this type of experiment is designed, reported and criticized.[88]

13 *Psychic spying—Hyman vs Utts*

Interestingly, Ray Hyman has talked in similar terms in the context of Stargate, the US government's remote-viewing programme. The background to this project is as follows. In the 1970s the Pentagon became alarmed by reports that the Soviet Union was involved in 'psychic spying' and decided to set up its own unit. It commissioned the physicists Targ and Puthoff at the SRI to provide the theoretical background and training, and recruited military personnel and some civilians as remote viewers. As we saw, this early work was strongly criticized. However other scientists subsequently joined the programme and the protocols were substantially tightened. In 1995 parts of the programme were declassified and reports of it have been made in the press and on television. In addition, books by participants have been published that contain detailed descriptions of how viewers located and described distant targets with surprising accuracy.[89]

Throughout the programme the remote viewers were in demand by the army and the CIA for a variety of intelligence operations. However in 1995 the programme was terminated: apparently it had been concluded that statistically significant laboratory effects had been demonstrated, but more replications were needed. To inform this decision a scientific assessment was commissioned that brought together Hyman with Jessica Utts, a professor of statistics at the University of California and a supporter of parapsychology. The pair, who had clashed before over the ganzfeld results, were given a small amount of data from the past three years. From this, Utts argued that psychic functioning had been 'well established' and that the statistical results were 'far beyond what is expected by chance'. Arguments that the results could have been artefacts of methodological flaws were 'soundly refuted', she asserted. Referring to existing work on remote viewing, Utts pointed out that effects of similar magnitude have been found in parapsychological laboratories around the world, a consistency that is not readily explained by claims of experimental flaws or fraud. Utts also argued that qualitative results should not be dismissed just because they can't be assessed statistically, citing as an example a case where a viewer had not only described a distant installation accurately but was also able to identify its purpose.[90]

Hyman did not agree with Utts's conclusions, but he did seem to have softened his stance somewhat:

> I admit the latest findings should make parapsychologists optimistic. The case for psychic functioning seems better than it ever has been. The contemporary findings … do seem to indicate that something beyond odd statistical hiccups is taking place. I also have to admit that I do not have a ready explanation for these observed effects.[91]

However Hyman then went on to explain at length why this should not instantly convert scientists to a belief in the validity of parapsychological claims. This was not the first time that the discipline had come up with seemingly incontrovertible results, he said, only to see them later dashed by revelations of fraud or methodological flaws. It still remains a fact that parapsychology lacks repeatability. And its data is not cumulative: parapsychologists do not build on their earlier discoveries but are always in a position of having to prove that psi exists. No other science, Hyman argued, depends on an entity that can't be demonstrated, but can only be inferred to exist by the claimed absence of normal mechanisms.

Taking the last point first, Utts pointed out that parapsychology is not alone in this regard: many interactions in physics and in the social and medical sciences can be observed but not explained.[92] Take the effect of electromagnetic fields on health, which has been long suspected but never convincingly demonstrated. A recent report concluded that some links to diseases such as cancer and immune deficiencies appear real and warrant steps to reduce exposure to electrical fields, adding that biologists have failed to pinpoint a convincing mechanism. In other words, Utts insisted, a statistical effect has been convincingly established, and it is now the responsibility of science to try to explain it.

Utts went on to criticize Hyman's argument that parapsychology is the only field of scientific enquiry that lacks a single exemplar that can be assigned to students with the expectation that they will observe the original results. Many demonstrated effects are statistical in nature, she points out, such as the connection between taking aspirin and preventing heart attacks, or between smoking and getting lung cancer. Not everyone who takes aspirin will be safe from heart attack, nor will all smokers get cancer. But the research means one can accurately predict the proportion who will. This is a statistical science, she emphasizes, and repeatability requires thousands of experiments.

Utts also roundly rejected Hyman's general criticisms of parapsychology. She argued against his claims that the discipline lacks a cumulative database, maintaining that, on the contrary, it is truly impressive for a science that has benefited from so few resources.[93] This last point is worth reflecting on: it has been calculated that the total amount spent by parapsychology over several decades is roughly what American psychology departments spend in *two months*.[94]

I noticed a distinct difference in style between the two. Utts is crisp, clear and to the point: this is what the data says, and in her view as a professional statistician this is what it means; the statistical significance has been demonstrated so widely and so often that there is obviously something going on. The alternatives having been examined and discarded, this something must be psi. Hyman by contrast tends to rely on abstract speculations, which he spins out at length; where Randi uses invective to get the blood boiling, Hyman smothers you with a blanket of negative generalisation.

In essence, the psychologist's conclusion is rather similar to his argument about Gary Schwartz's work with mediums. It's not that the results themselves might not sometimes be interesting or significant, just that parapsychology lacks the credibility as a discipline to make them stick. In practical terms he is probably right. Not because, as he claims, positive results have been dashed by revelations of fraud and incompetence – which I've suggested that sceptics greatly exaggerate[95] – but because of inertia. Average significance levels in ganzfeld experiments of around thirty to thirty-five per cent compared with a mean level of twenty-five per cent – apart from one or two blips in the record – may not seem interesting to the non-specialist, but in scientific terms they are astonishing. And when you learn that even those critics who take the trouble to analyze the work are running out of objections, one might argue that parapsychologists are starting to carry their case.

At the same time, it would take a lot to convince scientists that something as dramatic as psi has been definitively proved. The database of parapsychology is too fragile to bear the crushing weight of its implications. We might legitimately conclude that the problem is not exactly that psi has not been demonstrated, but that the phenomenon is not strong enough, or clear enough, or the demonstrations of it sufficiently decisive, to convert the scientific community and persuade it to undertake the huge shift of perspective that psi would seem to demand.

For me, all this exposes the oddly flimsy philosophical basis upon which our idea of reality is based – and incidentally, again, that applies whether or not psi actually exists. I understand the frustrations that scientists feel about parapsychology, and can see why they consider it to be a pseudo-science. But really, who or what is to blame here?

We have got into the habit of assuming that reality is that which is revealed by science, forgetting that science is an instrument created by human minds, based on rules and assumptions we can all agree on, and is necessarily focused on the objective and the material. It's the reality that is true for all of us – biological beings living in the terrestrial environment – and can be reliably demonstrated. The scientific method's extraordinarily successful and fecund results have by now convinced us of its infallibility, but we can't legitimately insist that nothing can escape its gaze, especially when that something is immaterial, yet – inconveniently and jarringly – seems to have material effects, and when there is abundant and striking evidence of it.

If that argument seems contrived or self-serving, look at it from a different perspective. If psi actually *is* a genuine entity, and the wide public experience of it is not illusory, *how would we know?* What sort of science would it be that could verify such an odd hybrid? And, to acknowledge the sceptics' concerns, would it be a science we could rely on?

None of this is necessarily to argue that scientists *ought* to accept parapsychology's findings, on the basis of the evidence it has so far come up with, but rather to suggest that the matter is more complex than they recognize. I'll come back to this later; however now I want to go on and look at how people experience psi in their daily lives, and how psychologists account for it.

FIVE

EXPERIENCE AND IMAGINATION (I)

'I have noticed that if a small group of intelligent people, not supposed to be impressed by psychic research, get together and such matters are mentioned, and all feel that they are in safe and sane company, usually from a third to a half of them begin to relate exceptions. That is to say, each opens a little residual closet and takes out some incident which happened to them or to some member of their family, or to some friend whom they trust and which they think odd and extremely puzzling.' *Walter Prince, psychic researcher.*

'My skepticism caused me to reject many of the studies I read, easy fodder for the voice in me that refused. I can't go there, I told myself. That stuff's not possible and I won't be taken in.' *Elizabeth Lloyd Mayer, clinical psychologist.*

Coming home from work one evening I'm surprised to see a stranger sitting in my living room. Then I realize it's someone I know, a friend from university named Alex Harrison who I haven't seen for years. I say 'Hi' and dump my bag in the corner, but when I look up again the chair is empty. That's odd. I look around but I can't see him anywhere. I check to see if he's gone into the kitchen or bathroom, but he's nowhere to be found. Only my wife could have let him in, but she's at work, and when I mention it to her later she claims not to know what I'm talking about.

For a while I tussle with the obvious explanation, that it was some kind of weird hallucination. But I just can't accept that: it just seemed so real. It really was Alex sitting there, fatter and with less hair than I remembered, but with the same impish grin. It didn't feel like I was conjuring up a memory. It had the quality of an *experience.*

However by the following morning I am starting to become resigned to the fact that it actually *was* a hallucination. That's obviously what hallucinations are like – spookily convincing. And it's true, I have been rather overdoing things recently. I vaguely think of emailing Alex. We were quite close friends at one time, but we lost touch years ago, and I don't have his address.

Months pass, and the post brings a new issue of the university magazine. Browsing through to the obituaries page I read that Alexander Radcliff Harrison, of the 1971 intake, has drowned in a tragic yachting accident. Checking the dates I'm shocked to find that it precisely coincided with the moment I saw him in my living room.

I've made the details up, but not the substance. People in surprising numbers say something like this really did once happen to them, and with just this sense of clarity. Yet I only found out about it from reading the literature of psychic research, and as far as I'm aware it's not widely known that such things occur. Children tell stories about haunted inns, and the hitch-hiker who turns out to be someone that died twenty years ago. But this particular variant, of unexpectedly seeing a person one knows, and this person suddenly vanishing into thin air – and being later found to have been somewhere else, either dead, dying or in danger – is not only one of the most common ghost stories reported in real life, it is surprisingly absent from popular culture.

My point is that some things only get discovered when people start asking questions. In this case it was the founders of the Society for Psychical Research, Frederic Myers, Edmund Gurney and others, who in the 1880s began a formal enquiry into ghosts as part of their general research into paranormal claims. Through press advertisements they collected a large number of anecdotes, and the more striking ones they published and analyzed. There were quite a few of the traditional haunted-house types, but these were actually a minority; by far the largest sub-category was this 'crisis apparition', as they called it, and that has been confirmed by later surveys in Britain, America and other countries.

One might say the mere fact of people making such claims isn't surprising, given the widespread belief in afterlife and the supernatural. As before, what makes them worthy of notice is that information conveyed in a purely mental event should seem to correspond with facts in the real world, like the story I described in the last chapter, of the woman who dreamed of her brother shooting himself. Other details are sometimes also discovered to match with what happened in reality, like the way that the apparitions look (unfamiliar clothes, or an injury perhaps), or actions they appear to be performing, or the details of their environment. Another reason for considering an apparition to be paranormal is where it is seen simultaneously by two or more people, which, in the absence of any obviously natural stimulus, would make it less likely to be a simple hallucination. Similarly suggestive are those instances where a witness does not recognize an apparition, but can later identify the person concerned from a photograph.

2 *The psychology of the believer*

I was interested to see how sceptics tackle this sort of thing, and they do indeed have a variety of arguments. But before I get onto specifics, I want to take a brief look at their general views about the origins of paranormal belief, now considered so obviously unfounded that it is routinely included in psychological studies about the fallibility of human reasoning.

The thrust of the psychologists' argument is that we humans are hopelessly compromised by our genetic inheritance. We live in complex societies and are capable of subtle reasoning. But our drives, instincts and thinking patterns developed far back in our hunter–gatherer past, adapted to the demands of the natural environment. This means we can be easily led astray. Even those of us who are not obviously unintelligent or gullible may misapply the powerful perceptual tools that evolution has provided us with, so that we end up with false ideas about the world and our experience of it.

So for instance, in *How We Know What Isn't So*, Thomas Gilovich points out the fallacy of basketball players when they think, as apparently they often do, that a player who has been scoring well is 'hot' and is due for more success. This sounds logical, but has been roundly contradicted by the author's examination of the available data: players who have just scored once or twice are *not* more likely to succeed on their next shot. Similarly, people who gamble rationalize their losses in an illogical way that encourages them to keep on going.[2] Psychologists also point to the human tendency to find significant connections between events, even where none exists. A craving for meaning leads us always to look for patterns and inclines us towards 'magical thinking'; we see the hand of God or Fate in what are actually random events that just happen to group together in apparently significant ways.[3]

One of the fullest studies of this erroneous thinking is *Parapsychology: Science or Magic?* (1981) by James Alcock, a psychologist at the University of Toronto and a leading member of CSI (CSICOP). Alcock starts by emphasizing that we are hard-wired to have what we wrongly interpret as psychic experiences. We can't help it – it's an abnormal side-effect of brain functions such as visual perception and memory. 'If we are not aware,' he says, 'that because of the way our brains are structured we should expect to have moving and seemingly inexplicable experiences from time to time, then we may fall prey to our transcendental expectations and conclude that we have had a paranormal experience whenever rational explanation seems to fail.'[4]

The unreliability of testimony plays a big part here. Psychological studies show that people who are exposed to the same experience will describe it in all sorts of different ways. In one famous experiment a group of subjects were shown a film of a road accident. Asked to recall it one week later, those participants who had heard it described with the word 'smash' made higher estimates of the speed at which the vehicles had been travelling than those who had heard it described more mildly with the word 'hit'. More people in the former group also recalled seeing broken glass, when actually there had been none.[5] So we should be on our guard when we hear anecdotes about apparitions and near-death visions. In most cases, Alcock suggests, the person telling the story will be recalling something that happened in the past, and his or her memory will have been corrupted to include elements that in fact didn't occur. Over time this unconscious creative process will shape the memory into something that fulfils the individual's need for meaning, but which does not correspond to what actually took place.

What some people take to be telepathic communication can also have mundane causes. I might be standing in a cinema queue with my wife when she suddenly starts talking about a mutual acquaintance about whom I had at that very moment been thinking. Amazing! She must have read my mind. But a more likely explanation is that someone who looked rather like this individual passed by and started an unconscious train of thought in both of us simultaneously; we simply responded to the same stimulus.

Alcock has a rather interesting idea concerning subliminal perception in the context of dreams. Suppose I dream that a particular individual is dying, and the following day I hear that this person died at more or less exactly the same time I was dreaming. This may seem astonishing, Alcock says, but consider this: I may have picked up the information unconsciously in some way, for instance by perceiving that the person looked extremely ill, and the dream brought that fact to my conscious mind, appropriately embroidered. The result is that a mysterious connection is established and wondered at.[6] Or let's suppose a woman is sleeping within earshot of a television that happens to be broadcasting details of a train crash live, and the details become part of a dream – reading the news next day, she may be stunned at the apparent coincidence between her dream and the disaster and may be certain that she has experienced precognition.[7]

Dreams can even bring about their own fulfilment, Alcock also suggests. For instance, a man suffering with anxiety might dream that he will have an accident, and this might make him so tense that he does in fact fall over or crash his car. Or perhaps precognition is part of a process of simple anticipation of the day to come. Occasionally, the fiction of dreams mixes with the anticipation of reality to provide an unexpected combination of events, which then actually occur. 'It is all too easy', Alcock says, 'to be struck by some small correspondence between the vague memory of a dream and some subsequent event, and then come to believe that significant features of the event were also part of the dream'.[8]

Some psychologists consider that ghostly experiences may be caused by a combination of expectation and circumstance. For instance a person who spends a night in a supposedly haunted hotel is more likely to interpret strange sounds as being ghost-like than if they were heard in his or her own home. It is also the case that many people experience remarkably life-like imagery during hypnagogic and hypnopompic sleep – the periods when one is drifting off to sleep or just waking up – and this could explain why some people report seeing apparitions.[9] In the same way, the experience that some people report of sensing an invisible presence is a purely psychological phenomenon, and does not mean that a spirit is hovering nearby.[10]

Then there's the inherent ambiguity found with visual information. This point can be illustrated with a line-drawing that changes meaning if viewed from a different mental perspective. Common examples are the head of a duck which when facing the other way looks like the head of a rabbit, and a profile of a face that can be perceived either as a young girl or a toothless old crone.[11] Unless we have trained ourselves to look out for this kind of perceptual ambiguity we may jump to the conclusion that we have experienced something paranormal when we have not.

Psychologists are also concerned – as too are parapsychologists – to uncover any pattern or characteristic that distinguishes someone who is a typical believer. The stereotype of a ditzy female who will believe anything was widely prevalent in the nineteenth and early twentieth centuries, but has been long redundant, they note.[12] And credulity is not linked to the lack of an education; many university students and senior academics take at least some aspects of the paranormal seriously.[13] However, recent studies do suggest that the people who think they experience paranormal incidents tend to have a higher facility for mental imagery, and are good at imagining and visualizing.[14] This makes it likely that people who see ghosts or experience visions in near-death situations are fantasizing in some way.

The critics take psychic investigators to task for failing to take all of this into account. Zusne and Jones complain that they do not treat the material within the framework of psychology, or relate their findings to psychological knowledge in any systematic way. Rather, they say:

> … the research is to prove a particular ideological point: that humans have souls, that these souls survive the death of the body, that telepathy, and so forth, are a fact, and therefore, science's view of human beings and the world is invalid.[15]

Sceptics also argue that researchers are wrong to attach so much significance to anecdotal reports, as these may well be unreliable.

In the early days of parapsychology, Alcock states, considerable effort was put into the investigation of such anecdotes. But, he continues:

> ... time after time, whenever details of the story could be checked against objective records, such glaring discrepancies were found as to cast serious doubt upon the accuracy of any part of the report. Even the reports of individuals whose integrity and intelligence were beyond question were found to have fallen victim to the distortions of memory.[16]

3 Ghostly encounters

Most of this is theoretical, however. The psychologists don't talk much about actual claims. To be sure, they do discuss subjects that at one time or another have interested psychic researchers, but not the type that I was mainly concerned with. Take stigmata for instance, the curious way in which wounds or bruises sometimes appear on the hands or feet of religious devotees, apparently mimicking the wounds of Christ's crucifixion. It is reasonable to suppose that this has some nervous or psychosomatic origin, and it raises important questions about how the mind can affect the physical organism, but it is not actually paranormal.[17] Similarly with fire-walking; the ability to walk across red-hot coals is remarkable, but physiological explanations readily offer themselves.[18]

It was the startlingly anomalous experiences that I have just been describing that I wanted to get to the bottom of. Let's start with apparitions. In 1886 the SPR published its monumental *Phantasms of the Living*, a thirteen-hundred-page anthology of individual cases collected by Edmund Gurney, Frederic Myers and Frank Podmore;

its two volumes contain more than seven hundred narratives, sifted from around three thousand letters, of which most were sent in response to advertised appeals for individual experiences.[19] The published anecdotes were accompanied in many cases by some form of corroborating testimony, from one or more persons who could independently verify who said what, and what happened when. They came either in the form of letters, sent in response to follow-up enquiries, or interviews carried out by the researchers who, with commendable persistence, made rail journeys all over the country to get people's stories face-to-face. The book also contains a substantial amount of discussion and analysis by Gurney.

Phantasms was followed in 1894 by the SPR's massive Census of Hallucinations, a poll of seventeen thousand people, of whom ten per cent said they had at least once had the experience of seeing or hearing something that was not there.[20] This is perhaps the fullest survey of its kind but it is by no means the only one. In the following decades reports continued to appear, both individually and in discussion articles in the journals of the SPR and other parapsychological societies.[21] A collection by Joseph Rhine's partner, Louisa, of several hundred American narratives appeared in 1956, and there is also a large German collection from this period.[22]

Typically the narrators describe having a dream or a waking hallucination of someone well-known to them, often apparently in a situation of stress or danger. Sometimes the vision includes specific surroundings, such as a ship or a train, which the percipient can later describe. These experiences are vivid, quite unlike a normal dream, and often leave the percipient with a sense of alarm or dread; they are also startling enough to be shared with friends and family members, immediately or very soon afterwards.

In cases of visual hallucinations the researchers noted particular characteristics. Apparitions were seen in bedrooms at night, in lighted rooms and outside in daylight, also in reflecting surfaces such as mirrors and dark windows. If the room was dark, the form might appear to shine or shimmer in a golden, bluish or grey haze. Far from being a vague or wispy impression, it would appear to be quite substantial and remain in direct view for several seconds before abruptly vanishing, causing the witness to wander around confusedly looking for a secret door. Or else it might become transparent and fade slowly. If the apparition was recognized by the percipient, the form would sometimes seem younger and healthier than he or she remembered, but it might also appear pale or distressed or suffering from a physical injury. Sometimes it might try to communicate by gesturing, smiling or frowning, and in other cases the percipient might intuitively sense what it wanted to say.[23]

To repeat, what makes these experiences memorable is the fact that the details of the hallucination closely match real events, as is later discovered. In one case described in *Phantasms* a woman woke with a start, feeling she had had a hard blow on her mouth, and with a distinct sense that she was bleeding under her upper lip. She grabbed a handkerchief and held it to her face, but after a few seconds was astonished to see there was no blood. It was only then that she realized that nothing could have struck her, as she had been lying asleep in bed. She looked at her watch and saw that it was seven o'clock. Her husband was not there, and she assumed that he must have gone out on the nearby lake for an early morning sail, as he often did. When he returned he was nursing a wound in his mouth – a sudden squall had thrown the boat round and the tiller had struck him, causing a bad cut to the upper lip. Asked what time this had occurred, he said it would have been around seven o'clock.[24]

In another case, a ten-year old girl was walking outside when she experienced a strong waking vision of her mother lying on the floor at home. Her mother had been in good health, but in the vision she appeared to be lifeless, and, curiously, in a room which was seldom used. The impression was so real that before going back to the house the girl first went to fetch the local doctor. Her father was surprised to see them, not suspecting that anything was amiss. However when they went together to the unused room, they found her mother lying on the floor, having suffered a heart attack..[25]

Phantasms includes a large number of cases such as the one I made up at the start of this chapter, where a person who appears and disappears suddenly is subsequently found to have suffered an accident or illness – often fatal and in a distant location. Here's an actual example: An army officer, stationed in Maulmain in India, was getting out of bed one morning when he saw an old friend who he had not seen for some years entering the room. He greeted the visitor and told him to get a cup of tea on the balcony while he got dressed. Going out onto the balcony some moments later he found no one there. He asked the servants and the sentry outside, but they had not seen anyone of that description either entering or leaving. Two weeks later he received the news that his friend had died some six hundred miles away, at roughly the same time this incident occurred.[26]

Early cases such as these are redolent of a bygone era of governesses, servants and the Indian Raj, and encourages the perception that interest in ghosts, like séances, was a peculiarly Victorian preoccupation, and not really something that we in our more enlightened times should be bothering with. But as I mentioned, similar reports have been made in more recent years. In one American case from the 1950s an eighteen-year-old schoolteacher described getting an unexpected visit from a former pupil, a fourteen-year-old boy who seemed to have developed an emotional attachment to her:

> I was seated at my desk shortly after our afternoon studies began when a voice said, 'Hello, Miss Long'. Glancing up, there he stood, smiling at me, hat in hand, holding on to the door. 'I told you that no matter where you taught I was going to your school and here I am.' Pleased as well as startled, I smiled back, exclaiming, 'Truman, how did you get here?' He replied, 'Oh, I just came. Where can I sit?' I was aware of the dead silence in the room and every pupil

seemed frozen in their places, mingled emotions stamped
on their faces, all eyes watching me. Ready to reply I noticed
that instead of a solid substance, as he had first appeared,
the figure was fading out and I could see the details of the
room through him. Shaken, I, who hadn't thought of him
before, couldn't get this out of my mind. A few days later
a letter from my mother telling of Truman's sudden death
really made me have the creeps. He had been only slightly
ill for a few days and his mother was planning on sending
him to school the next day. He had been downstairs eating
his noon lunch. At 1:30, the time I saw his apparition, as he
started to go back upstairs he collapsed and died, hanging
on to the stair post.[27]

The time of death is hard to establish: the person whose apparition is
seen might indeed be dead at the time, but it makes more sense from
the researchers' point of view to suppose that she was still conscious
at the time she was seen by the percipient, even if she only had minutes or seconds to live. For that reason – not that it would make
much difference to a sceptic – the researchers viewed these not as
classic ghost stories but as indications of a telepathic interaction between two living people at a moment of crisis for one of them: hence
the title *Phantasms of the Living*. This concept is reinforced by the
fact that crisis apparitions also involve people who are in danger of
death from an illness or accident, but subsequently recover. There
are other similar cases in which the incident was traumatic but not
necessarily life-threatening.

For Gurney and his colleagues this material reinforced the indications of telepathy and clairvoyance that they believed they had independently uncovered from their experiments. In the main, what
they saw was a purely mental process, an involuntary transfer of information from the agent to the percipient at a time of emotional
crisis; there was no actual ghost in the sense of a form that was objectively present. It was indeed a hallucination, a term that the researchers used freely in its conventional sense, of seeing something

that is not there, but one that they considered to be paranormal in that its content was acquired telepathically.

An argument frequently made by sceptics is that hallucinations are much more common than is usually supposed. This allows them to suggest that the content may also from time to time coincide with some actual event, and such cases are the ones that are remembered and wondered at. Interestingly, one of the main authorities for the frequency of apparitions comes from the SPR researchers themselves, with their Census of Hallucinations, in which ten percent of respondents stated they had at least once had the impression of seeing, hearing or being touched by something that appeared to have no external cause. But the survey also underscored the frequency of coincidental matches that occurred between the content of the hallucination and a crisis in the affairs of a friend or relative at a distant location. One would of course want to argue that such coincidences could occur in the normal course of things. However this was not borne out by the researchers' detailed analysis After they had weeded out all but the most reliable of the narratives, and measured the small fraction that remained against the known death rate in Britain, they concluded that one in forty-three apparitional hallucinations coincided with the death of the person whose apparition was seen. This figure was four hundred and forty times more than could be expected by chance – a highly significant margin.[28]

4 *Some other types of encounter*

Although crisis apparitions turn out to be the largest category of encounters, other types also exist that seem to stretch beyond the boundaries of the possible. For instance there is occasional evidence of collective percipience, whereby two or more people simultaneously see the same apparition. Take for example the woman who looks out of a window in her large country house and is astonished to see, strolling through the garden, her pet Persian cat who had died a few weeks earlier from an injury. She rushes outside and chases after it, but it pays her no attention and disappears into some bushes. Ten minutes later she sees the cat again and goes after it. In both instances both she and the cat are observed simultaneously by another person. The animal is seen independently half an hour later by the woman's maid, this time inside the house. The girl fetches it a saucer of milk and follows it down a corridor, but it does not respond to her calls and then vanishes completely. The witnesses' conviction that they saw the cat in reality is so strong that they think they must somehow be wrong about it having died: their doubts are only put to rest when the gardener digs up the cat's carcass.[29]

Surprisingly, considering the persistence of interest in the idea of ghosts, hauntings in which an apparition is seen in the *same* location by different people turn out to be a much smaller category in the SPR research. However there are a few outstanding examples of this kind of encounter. A well-authenticated report from 1892 described the ghost of a woman in a Cheltenham house which, over a period of eight years, was seen by at least seventeen people, in many cases more than once, and by some on repeated occasions. The figure was tall, wore a long black widow's dress and held a handkerchief to her face that masked her features, and she often seemed to be crying. She would suddenly appear in different parts of the house, even outside on the lawn in broad daylight, and could be followed, usually to her favourite position behind a couch by the living room window. If spoken to, she would appear to be about to speak but would then move away suddenly, often passing through a wall. She looked to be three-dimensional but was non-material, like a hologram – she did not displace thin threads placed across her path and if someone tried to touch her their arms passed right through her.[30]

In other cases the percipient did not recognize the apparition, but was later able to identify who they'd seen in a photograph, or someone else identified the individual from hearing the percipient's description. These scenarios typically occur when the percipient is a guest at a hotel or staying with acquaintances. One such case involved an English guest in a hotel in Madeira, who awoke one night to see a young man of about twenty-five, dressed in white cricket flannels, standing at the side of his bed. He lay still for some seconds to convince himself that someone was really there, then sat up and looked more closely. He spoke to his visitor, asking what he wanted. The young man did not speak, but struck out at him with his fist, which however did not reach him; he then slowly vanished through the door. In the morning the man described what had happened to another English guest, a long-term resident at the hotel, and she recognized from his account a previous occupant of the room who had died unexpectedly some months earlier. She mentioned nothing about this at the time, but a few days later she showed him a photograph: he immediately recognized the young man. He was not dressed in cricket flannels in the picture, but apparently he had sometimes worn these.[31]

Particularly intriguing are those experiences in which a piece of information is conveyed that is unknown to the percipient but is later discovered to be accurate. One instance of this kind concerned a travelling salesman, who was writing at a table in a hotel room one day when he suddenly looked up to see his sister, who had died of cholera nine years previously, sitting on a chair beside him. He distinctly noticed a long red scratch on her right cheek, a detail he mentioned when he described the incident to his parents later. Hearing this, his mother was overcome with emotion: while dressing her daughter's dead body, she said, she had accidentally scratched her cheek, and told no one about it, but simply covered it up with powder.[32]

A much smaller category of experience, but one that is rather a suggestive of a paranormal process, is that in which people have a sense of leaving their own body and travelling to another location, where they then appear as an apparition to someone else. One day in December 1935 a farmer living near Indian Springs, Indiana, was worrying about his father, who he feared might be ill. Shortly after going to bed that night he found himself looking down on his own body lying in the bed, then travelling through the air to his father's house, where he passed through the walls and came to stand at the foot of his father's bed. His father was surprised to see him and spoke to him, although he didn't hear what he said. The knowledge came to him that his father was in fact quite well, at which point he found himself travelling back to his bedroom and entering his physical body once more. He then immediately got up and wrote down the time and details of what had happened; his father did the same.[33]

5 *Analyzing the reports*

As with other categories of paranormal experience, the effect of reading hundreds of these accounts was to make me feel as the researchers felt: here is a phenomenon that cannot be easily ascribed either to ordinary psychological or social processes, or to superstitious impulses. Many of the witnesses come across as educated and articulate people; some hold senior positions in professional life and academia. They tend to point out that they wouldn't have taken anything like this seriously before they experienced it themselves, and they remain generally sceptical about the paranormal. The incidents come out of the blue, and there is rarely any sense that people are fitting them to some preconceived idea.

Yet I often found myself latching onto some detail that might suggest a normal explanation. For instance in the case of the girl with the scratched cheek, you could argue that her brother had unwittingly seen the scar when her body was being dressed or when it was on view before the funeral, even if he was not consciously aware of it at the time; the detail perhaps emerged in the hallucination many years later as an unconscious strategy to convince himself that she had survived death. Similarly, on reading the narrative about the cat it occurred to me straight away, as I'm sure it did to you, that it must be a case of mistaken identity – perhaps the witnesses simply saw a cat that looked like their's, or even a wild animal like a small fox.

At the same time, it's a mistake to suppose that the first explanation that pops into our heads didn't also occur to the researchers, or to think that they failed to take account of it in their follow-up interrogations and analysis. The case of the cat does seem trivial at first, but it becomes a bit less so when we learn that there were no other cats in the neighbourhood; that the garden was securely walled to keep out foxes and rabbits; and that all the witnesses were convinced it was the pet Persian they saw and no other. We would then have to argue that these circumstances were not as they were reported to be – which is like saying we just don't believe it.

I'd also suggest that a five-line summary can't really convey the sense of certainty that people feel when they experience such incidents at first hand. Returning to the case of the girl with the scratched cheek, the brother says he was sitting smoking a cigar and filling out sales orders when he suddenly became conscious of someone sitting on his left side, with one arm resting on the table:

> Quick as a flash I turned and distinctly saw the form of my dead sister, and for a brief second or so looked her squarely in the face; and so sure was I that it was she, that I sprang forward in delight, calling her by name, and, as I did so, the apparition instantly vanished. Naturally I was startled and dumbfounded, almost doubting my senses; but the cigar in my mouth, and pen in hand, with the ink still moist on my letter, I satisfied myself I had not been dreaming and was wide awake. I was near enough to touch her, had it been a physical possibility, and noted her features, expression, and details of dress, etc. She appeared as if alive. Her eyes

> looked kindly and perfectly natural into mine. Her skin
> was so life-like that I could see the glow or moisture on
> its surface, and, on the whole, there was no change in her
> appearance, otherwise than when alive.[34]

One could argue that the impression the incident made on the percipient is actually irrelevant, and it is only the surprising coincidence that we should be concerned with. But to my mind, the sense of dramatic impact, combined with the veridical details, militates against the idea that these episodes have a commonplace origin and are being worked on by imagination to make them more than they are. On the contrary, as we'll see in a moment, there's evidence that the opposite process is at work, that the episode loses its impact in the telling so that to others it seems easily explicable.

The researchers did not seem to me to have been remiss in looking for normal explanations themselves. Gurney was well aware of the potential relevance of hypnagogia, for instance, but argued that it could not be more than a partial explanation at best.[35] Many reported apparitions occur during the day when the percipient is fully awake and the conditions for hypnagogia are not obviously present. Also, apparitions are often seen in isolation and they are fairly stable and can last for several seconds, none of which is characteristic of hypnagogia which tends to be a sweep of jumbled images flowing rapidly in front of one's vision. Even if an apparitional hallucination could be ascribed to hypnagogia this wouldn't explain cases in which it coincided with the death of the appearing individual, or was regularly seen by different people in a particular location, or was observed by more than one person at the same time.

Gurney devotes a substantial chapter in *Phantasms* to discussing the standards of evidence and the various problems that one is likely to encounter. He says a lot about error and exaggeration, agreeing that people who are interested in the paranormal will be looking out for anything that seems to provide evidence of it, seeing elements that are not there or rushing to misinterpret occurrences that might have an alternative explanation. Where this tendency exists, he goes on, it is inevitable that the reported memories will be elaborated over time until inconvenient details drop out and the rest 'stands out in a deceptively significant and harmonious form'.[36] Yet Gurney insists that the instances he describes show no evidence of this. Only a very small number appear to attach any religious or philosophical significance to what they experienced: for most it is just a rather remarkable family occurrence.

The point about fallible memory was by no means lost on Gurney: he discussed its ramifications at some length. But he argued it was vitiated in his study by the large degree of corroboration that he and his colleagues were able to procure. It is true that very few striking dreams or apparitional hallucinations were noted down *before* it was realized they matched a real event that occurred at the same time – a shortcoming that critics often complain of. But there are many cases in which the event was mentioned immediately or very soon afterwards to one or more people, and some time *before* knowing it matched a real event. If the incident had in fact been spurious, the idea of a coincidence would have had to be moulded in the minds of these confidants, as well as the mind of the original percipient. Corroboration regarding the time and date of the dream or hallucination also comes in letters and diary entries, and where a coincidental death is concerned this could easily be checked in public records.

Gurney adds a small but potentially significant detail: there is nothing particularly *creative* about these testimonies. They always stop at a certain point. If this is an imaginative process, he asks, why is it so restrained? Why do the apparitions not speak to the people they appear to, or hold conversations, or produce physical effects such as opening a door and leaving it open – actions that would leave a trace of their presence? If people were starting with the *idea* of the apparition, rather than just describing something that had happened to them, they would surely embroider it in these obvious ways. Yet this doesn't happen: not a single first-hand narrative was rejected because it was inconsistent with the norm. This reinforces the sense that there exists some objective phenomenon which the percipients are more or less faithfully describing. Where stories had in fact degraded, Gurney found, was where they *were* described second hand, as having happened to someone else. In such cases it was indeed very likely that they had been embroidered or misremembered, or that facts had been changed for dramatic effect.

6 *The critics critiqued*

Reflecting on all of this, it seemed to me that both sides were making important points. Until I read the psychologists' books I had not fully realized how vulnerable humans naturally are to faulty reasoning. I've noticed in myself a lamentable tendency to wishful thinking in such things as my personal finances and, as far as I can tell, most people share this to a least some degree. In fact it's apparent in just about every area of daily life; we all betray self-interest about things that concern us closely. But I hadn't grasped how unreliable memory can be. When I started to pay attention to this I was shocked to discover how often my recall – of images, places and people's faces, events, scenes in films and so on – turned out on review to have been partly or wholly inaccurate.

Since memory and perception are involved in paranormal claims it's likely that normal mental malfunctions we know little about might be the cause of mistaken impressions. For whatever reason, many people do take the possibility of the paranormal seriously and may find meaning in what are actually random occurrences. Subliminal perception and the effects of suggestion are demonstrated phenomena; so too is 'cryptomnesia', the emergence of long-forgotten memories of information a person may have read about or been exposed to, not always consciously registering it. Such things may well be implicated in certain types of seemingly paranormal experience, as parapsychologists themselves acknowledge.[37] And in general it is reasonable to suppose that people are often uncritical when it comes to assessing their own experience.

If I'm unconvinced that the psychologists' analysis provides the whole answer it is because it doesn't connect in any obvious way with the experiences that interest psychic researchers. I expected the critics to apply their insights to specific cases in order to show that their analysis is superior, and that there are alternatives that the researchers hadn't sufficiently taken into account. If they could do this consistently in a specific category of experience, they might neutralize the paranormal element and there would then be no reason to pay it any special attention. But this doesn't really happen. Rather than dissect specific cases to show how parapsychologists' judgements are unwarranted, the critics simply repeat claims about exposés and cheating and experimental flaws that they have skimmed from the literature. So what one gets is a lot of quite insightful psychological material about faulty reasoning, with episodes from the debunking literature tacked on afterwards, but with no clear indication of what the two have to do with each other.

For instance when I read Gilovich, in *How We Know What Isn't So,* discussing the way in which people jump to erroneous conclusions in daily life, I hoped he might provide concrete examples of how this leads to false paranormal claims. I'm sure it occurs, and it would be instructive to see a convincing documented apparitional case, for instance, persuasively explained in conventional psychological terms. But although Gilovich devotes a chapter to erroneous belief in ESP, much of it is taken up with experimenter fraud by Soal and Levy and the flaws revealed in remote-viewing experiments. In other words, he focuses on deception and methodological error, in order to convince us that we are wrong to base our belief in ESP on unreliable scientific data, and then follows with a few conventional sceptic nostrums, for instance the tendency to attach meaning to plain coincidences.[38] Similarly, Neher, Hines, and Zusne and Jones all repeat the potted debunkings written by others such as Brandon, Rawcliffe, and contributors in Kurtz's *A Skeptic's Handbook of Parapsychology*, apparently without looking at the primary sources. And they don't really attempt to demonstrate how the psychological patterns and mechanisms they describe underlie the paranormal perceptions in such cases. As for James Alcock, he purposely avoids discussing specific claims, which means his explanations never have to do any real work.

The critics do draw heavily on psychological studies to confirm their generalizations. But I found myself wondering how relevant these really are in the context of paranormal-seeming experiences. Take the issue of unreliable memory: it would be hard to exaggerate the importance of this in the psychologists' analysis, an all-purpose explanation that can be used to cast doubt on any disputed event that happened earlier than last week. I did not at all question the validity of studies that showed the vagaries of memory, but something is rather obviously missing: the element of *emotion*. Here, by contrast, we are often dealing with a shocking anomaly, one that makes the incident unique and stamps it on the memory. An apparition is a once-in-a-lifetime event that the witness vividly remembers, not just for its personal relevance but because it matches nothing in his or her previous experience.

It strikes me that sceptics take very little account of this. One writer claims to be surprised at how little people remember about actions that he carried out in their presence as little as ten minutes earlier.[39] His point is that if people are so unobservant in daily life why should their testimony about anything be taken seriously? But surely this is comparing apples with pears: such a test contains none of the emotional impact that makes paranormal-seeming incidents so memorable. Let's suppose the experimenter picks up his pen and puts it in his pocket, then takes a sip from his coffee, taps his computer keyboard, and so on. Questioned later, people who were with him at the time may not recall such trivial actions, and there may well be variations in what they say did or didn't take place. But if they had seen him pour his coffee on the carpet, cut off his tie and set his hair on fire, it would be another matter; these actions would be so discordant as to become an *experience,* something they might accurately recall for long afterwards.

It's a similar story with the matter of visual illusions. It is true that we can respond in more than one way to an ambiguous stimulus. A line-drawing that can be 'seen' in two different ways offers equal choices: you can automatically recognize one perspective and be unaware that there is another one until it is pointed out to you. One can argue from this that a nervous or superstitious person might see a ghost, whereas someone who is more down-to- earth would see merely an interesting play of light. But it wouldn't be a very good argument, because it does not explain incidents that are remark- able precisely because they are so *unambiguous.* If you unexpectedly see someone you know well standing in front of you, and hear him greet you, and you look again a split second later and he is no longer there, yet there is no question that he could have left the room or that it was not the person you think it was, and a short while later you learn he was killed in an accident at the time you saw him, then you are confronted with an utterly bewildering set of circumstances in which no alternative perspective is readily available.

The insight we are offered is always that flighty people jump to a paranormal conclusion while those with their feet on the ground prefer the equally accessible normal one. But I'm not convinced that the gulf of understanding between the so-called sceptics and the so-called believers is anything like as dramatic as the critics would like us to think. People who describe such experiences are by no means always keen to be thought credulous, nor are the things they say easily explicable in terms of cognitive errors, which in many cases is precisely why they get reported. I'm suspicious, too, of the psychologists' habitual tone of reassurance; they are always telling us that it is 'all too easy' to make a simple misinterpretation, and that it is 'hardly surprising' that such and such a mistake should come about. The aim is to close the perceived gap between the uncanny and the ordinary, and the effect is suggestively soothing. But if an uncanny incident really is so easy to explain surely the person it happens to can mentally adjust to it. The reason why some incidents seem paranormal is because they defy all kinds of explanation, both the obvious and the not so obvious ones.

Although critics try to avoid explaining actual reports, they quite often make up examples to illustrate their points. In so doing, they work backwards, as a crime fiction writer does, constructing a scenario that they can explain, since it originates in their own imagination, but which they think other people who lack their training and insights would be unable to spot.

Here's an example of one such story described by a sceptic. A doctor comes down to breakfast one morning to find his elderly aunt crying about a dream she has had during the night. In her dream she saw her brother and there were a lot of flames. She is sure something has happened to him. The doctor dismisses the idea, but on opening his mail he finds a letter telling him of the death of the brother and of plans to have him cremated, and advising him not to tell his aunt until it is all over. Now this doctor is a very sceptical person, but is struck by the coincidence and is therefore inclined to consider it evidence of something paranormal. Later the truth dawns on him. His aunt must have looked through the mail and seen a letter addressed to him that she thought might contain news of her brother, so she opened it and discovered the details. Being ashamed of what she had done, she must have gummed the letter back up, but to make her nephew aware that she knew what had happened she invented the story of the dream.

The sceptic calls this a case that was 'nipped in the bud'. One can imagine how easily it might have been mistaken for a psychic incident, he comments, if the doctor had been less observant and had failed to notice the old lady's prior contact with his correspondence.[40] But that was not my response at all: I couldn't imagine any serious person mistaking this for a psychic incident; the possibility that the aunt had read the letter would have been the first thing any alert researcher would have thought of. In any case, the point of having other people's testimony and follow-up interviews was to weed out this sort of thing, which is why stories like this aren't typical of those discussed in the research. In the end, the point that the sceptics actually convey is the implausible degree of gullibility in other people required for their thesis to work.

7 *Fallible memory*

It was the critics' idea of memory corruption – a supposedly creative process that morphs an ordinary incident into a paranormal one – that perplexed me most. But I needed to understand it because it is so fundamental to their analysis. Zusne and Jones dismiss all the narratives described in *Phantasms of the Living*, insisting they are 'useless as scientific evidence' because none had been written down immediately after the events happened, and some were only recorded only years later. 'Memory is fallible', they argue, 'and it is much more fallible when it involves matters that affect the individual personally and emotionally, as matters pertaining to the occult do.'[41] They go on to insist that there is no such thing as a reliable, objective informant, regardless of how upright, socially eminent, or educated he or she might be. Retrospective falsification, the mixing of imagination and memory, is the rule in these stories rather than the exception, they say. The dreams that are described were remembered later as having been actual physical events; one that follows a significant event is remembered as having come before it and, therefore, as being prophetic of it, and the story itself gets better and better in the retelling, with significant but inconvenient details being omitted and other details added.

All this is very categorical, and I did try to keep the precept 'useless as scientific evidence' responsibly in view while reading *Phantasms*. But I didn't think that the conditions required for a transformation from normal to paranormal were present in these accounts to the degree that the critics imply. It's true that a vivid and suggestive dream, one that coincides in detail with an event taking place at that time in a distant location, may be described to researchers years after it took place. However as I mentioned before, other people remember the person describing the dream the following morning, a few hours after it occurred. This was the whole point of getting corroboration from other witnesses. If they are all reporting the same thing it would mean that two, three or even more people are not just misremembering the details, but are doing so in exactly the same way to convert a normal set of circumstances into one that is supernormal – an idea I don't consider realistic.

Interestingly, Gurney says that where the memories of his informants did show signs of degrading the result was quite the opposite – it made the incident *less* paranormal rather than *more* so. This seemed to suggest that their memories had not exaggerated the details but smoothed them over. If true, this would be more evidence of rational gravity, the tendency of the mind to deal with an anomalous experience by subtly altering it to conform to daily norms.

I'd argue that the critics are missing an important point here, and one which, as cognitive psychologists, they should be better equipped than most people to identify. I can illustrate it by describing one of their main sources, a paper by John E. Coover, written in 1927 and reprinted in *A Skeptic's Handbook of Parapsychology*.[42] Coover, a sceptical American psychologist, gives three examples to illustrate the supposed corruption of memory in the recall of paranormal incidents, all from the parapsychological literature.

The first example concerns discrepancies in descriptions given by William Crookes at two different times about certain experiments that he carried out with mediums. Since the results in both versions were claimed to be paranormal – and by any standard utterly extraordinary – I'm not sure why Coover thinks this illustrates his argument; it proves that memory is fallible but it does not show a normal incident degrading into a paranormal one.

Coover's second example is potentially more relevant. A respected science historian named Sir David Brewster attended a sitting with Daniel Home in a London hotel in 1855. Shortly afterwards he wrote in a private letter that a small hand-bell was laid on the carpet and, after sitting there for a while, rang out when nothing could have touched it. It then 'came over to me and placed itself in my hand,' he noted.[43] Brewster wrote that he could give no explanation. Yet four months later he was recorded as having told friends it was a trick that Home had managed to carry out using his feet. The discrepancy between his initial reaction and his subsequent observation was only discovered when Brewster's letter was published following his death.

This example does indeed confirm that memory is corruptible, but in *exactly the opposite sense* to that which Coover intends. Brewster's original perception was that he had seen something paranormal; after the passing of a few months the experience had become reorganized in his mind with the paranormal element now removed. This implies that the memory of an incident can degrade to *blank out* any perception of anything paranormal having occurred – *not to create it*. Coover acknowledges that the logic goes in the opposite direction to that he is claiming, but argues that it doesn't matter, as it still demonstrates how memory corruption impairs the reliability of testimony. I'd say it matters a good deal. Far from showing that people 'misremember' normal incidents into paranormal ones, under the insidious pressure of their superstitious longings, he has actually drawn attention to the reverse process, whereby people misremember anomalous experiences in a way that minimizes the uncomfortable dissonance. The failure here is to recognize that this dissonance exists, and furthermore that it may be fatally implicated in the way the sceptic himself reasons. I will come back to this in a moment.

A different set of issues is raised by Coover's third example, which at first sight does seem resoundingly to prove his point. It concerns an experience that happened in 1875 to a Sir Edmund Hornby, chief justice in the city of Shanghai, which at the time was being run by an international colonial administration. Hornby was visited one night by Hugh Nivens, the editor of the *Shanghai Courier* newspaper, who wanted some details about a judgement Hornby was to give the following morning. Apparently this was a routine event, but in this case it was twenty past one in the morning and Nivens had inexplicably appeared in Hornby's bedroom. Confused, Hornby told him he had already written out the judgement and Nivens could get it from his butler. However, Nivens pulled out a notebook and insisted on getting the information there and then. This exchange followed:

> *Hornby*: 'Who let you in?'
>
> *Nivens*: 'No one.'
>
> *Hornby*: 'Confound it! What the devil do you mean? Are you drunk?
>
> *Nivens*: No, and never shall be again. But I pray your lordship give me your decision, for my time is short. This is the last time I shall ever see you anywhere.'[44]

Worried that the argument would wake his wife Hornby eventually relented and gave Nivens the details he wanted. Nivens appeared to write them down in his notebook, then got up and walked out. Hornby looked at the clock: it was half past one. His wife now awoke, thinking she had heard people talking, and the judge told her what had happened. The next day he learned that Nivens had never left his home that night, and had died of a heart attack around the time

Hornby thought he was talking to him. There was no question that Nivens could have left his own bed, and the judge's servants denied that they had let anyone in at that late hour.

Gurney and Myers related this story in an article for *The Nineteenth Century*, a monthly current affairs magazine. It was seen there by a Shanghai resident who had known both Hornby and Nivens, and claimed to have found discrepancies between the facts and Hornby's description. The most notable was that Hornby could not have discussed his vision with his wife, as he was not married at the time. He had been widowed two years previously, and did not marry again until three months after the journalist's death.[45] Confronted with this, Hornby admitted his memory must have deceived him, and that his vision must have occurred at least three months after Nivens's death rather than synchronizing with it. This was a big embarrassment to the researchers, who published an apology and retracted the case.

Sceptics love all this; it seems completely to vindicate their suspicions. Quite how Hornby's mind had played this trick on him is not terribly clear, and few of the psychologists have much to offer in this regard. Perhaps the fullest attempt comes from Neher, who suggests that Hornby might have overheard a conversation concerning Nivens's death some months earlier, and this registered in his mind subliminally, only emerging into his consciousness in the form of a vivid dream that night. Or he might have had a dream of the sort, and only the next day learned of Nivens's death some months earlier, giving it the appearance of a precognitive vision. Whatever subjective hallucination or vision Hornby experienced, Neher says, over time he modified it to 'fit his notion that it was paranormal.'[46]

I puzzled over the incident, and found it hard to let go. It tends to discredit many of the stories in *Phantasms* which it so clearly resembles, but without a better understanding of the psychological processes involved it was difficult to see where the errors lay in specific cases. It does not illuminate or explain anything. One is just extracting a generalization and then applying it in an equally general way.

If you read Hornby's narrative you will see that it is very detailed, and does not at all suggest a vague or forgetful person. It was astonishing to me that a senior judge, *of all people*, would display confusion on such an epic scale while giving testimony. His behaviour in other respects shows the conscientiousness and attention to detail that one would expect, as he goes to interview the man's wife and closely quizzes his own servants. I could not grasp how such a man could have dreamed or creatively misremembered a series of events as complex as this. The notion seemed to mystify him too. He commented:

> As I said then, so I say now – I was not asleep, but wide awake. After a lapse of nine years my memory is quite clear on the subject. I have not the least doubt I saw the man – have not the least doubt that the conversation took place between us.[47]

Then there was that gap of at least three months that subsequently appeared to have elapsed between the event and his 'dream'. It struck me as surprisingly long. It is one thing to say that memory is unreliable, but surely something else to argue that a person could retrospectively consider events that took place at such a wide interval to have occurred at the same time. For some reason Hornby had experienced a shock, which had helped lodge the incident in his memory. That would help to explain why, in his own words, he could recall it perfectly nine years later. But without the coincidence the shock effect would have been greatly reduced, if there had been any at all. Pondering all of this, I started to wonder whether there might not be some significance in the detail of Hornby *not being married*. The fact that he immediately discussed his experience with his wife, and that she was able subsequently to corroborate this, would have reassured the researchers. Being unmarried, as it turned out, there could be no wife. But it wouldn't necessarily mean he wasn't sleeping with a woman, or indeed that this woman was not the one who he married three months later.

Looked at in this way, an explanation presents itself rather readily, one that has more to do with the social mores of the time than with fallible memory. Ladies who slept with men they were not married to had to be discreet if they cared about their reputation, especially if they belonged to the upper classes. When the discrepancy was publicly aired Hornby faced a difficult choice: to withdraw his statement at the cost of appearing a fool, or to stand by it and hear his wife being called a whore. Of course he chose to protect his wife. The researchers seem to have understood this perfectly well, but were bound by discretion; they dropped hints that the true explanation didn't in the least reduce the story's paranormality, but that they were not at liberty to reveal it.[48].

I suppose that to a sceptic this must seem like yet another example of the credulous believer insisting on a paranormal scenario even after a normal one has been handed to him on a plate. But it's one of the many occasions when one finds oneself having to choose between two different kinds of implausibility. This is the central axis on which the whole believer–sceptic dynamic turns. The critics can't accept the apparent unlawfulness in paranormal claims, but they accept without demur a scenario that makes no sense at all, and which a little thought rapidly clears up. Indeed, the explanation is surely so obvious that if our positions were reversed, and the critics depended on this interpretation to make their case, they themselves would be vocally pressing it.

If we take the Hornby example out of the equation, as I believe we must, the critics are left with practically nothing to substantiate their case that fallible memory discredits narratives about apparitions. In fact it's hard to see that they have any real argument against the paranormality of apparitional incidents at all. Much of what they say is just bluff and misinformation.

For instance Hansel comments confidently that none of the stories in *Phantasms* 'has withstood critical examination'.[49] It sounds authoritative but is actually nonsense: sceptics have hardly exam-

ined any of them, let alone all of them, and most seem to be barely
aware that the research exists. Or consider Alcock's remark, which
I quoted earlier, that 'time after time, whenever details of the story
could be checked against objective records, such glaring discrepancies were found as to cast serious doubt upon the accuracy of any
part of the report'. I'm sure that when you read that the first time you
attached a certain credence to it, as I did. It's what one expects, and
it's the way professional sceptics always talk. But Alcock's source is
merely Rawcliffe, and when I looked it up I found, as I expected, that
Rawcliffe offers no evidence to back the idea at all: it's just part of his
slightly mad harangue.

This needs to be stressed: what the debunkers are claiming here
is a straightforward reversal of the facts. When the investigators
checked against objective records they often found a very close correspondence between what happened in someone's head and the
events that took place at a distance, and of which that person could
have had no conceivable knowledge. That's why they took it seriously and, in their minds, that's what justified continuing research of
this kind. Without this confirmed correspondence it's unlikely that
academic researchers would have become interested in the topic,
and then it really would be of purely psychological interest.

8 The psychology of the sceptic

It would be difficult to exaggerate the hold that the psychologists
had over me as I tried to reconcile the two different versions. Their
analysis is so authoritative, and so responsibly rooted in the science
of actual studies, I was convinced it must provide the answer. But
it didn't, and I couldn't understand why. Few of their ideas seemed
to fit in any useful way with the experiences that people reported.
Yet my failure to imaginatively grasp the justice of their arguments

seemed to me for some time to be just that, a failure, and one for which I alone was responsible, an effect of my intellectual shortcomings, and perhaps, who knows, of insidious superstitious longings.

Here as elsewhere, what swung the matter was the growing realization that the critics aren't really talking about the parapsychological research at all, but only their *idea* of it. It should have been obvious from the start, but I just didn't see it. Eventually it dawned on me: the reason I couldn't attach sense to what they were saying was because they had hardly read any of the material and had little idea what its challenges were.

I started to feel that the psychologists might one day turn a spotlight on their own thinking processes in discussions of this kind. For there's plenty of evidence that the idea of psi can have a deeply unsettling effect. This topic was explored by the late Elizabeth Lloyd Mayer, a Californian psychoanalyst whose orthodox thinking suffered a rude upset when a psychic helped her recover a valued stolen possession. Months of conventional searching produced no result, so she rang up a dowser, who gave her the address in her home town where he believed the item then to be – without stirring from his own home two thousand miles away. The item was then soon recovered.[50]

Mayer struggled to come to terms with this 'extraordinary knowing', as she termed it, and found she was not the only one who found it difficult to accept. People's ability to tolerate ambiguity varies; they react in different ways. Some are capable of nuanced responses, recognizing that they are dealing with two quite incompatible modes of thought and managing to switch between them. Others find the dissonance impossible to accommodate and become angry or dismissive, even at the expense of logic. Mayer cites the case of an individual who peer-reviewed an article on remote viewing that had been submitted to an engineering journal, stating that it was methodologically impeccable and that he could find no reason to reject it, but still recommending that it not be

published, as it was the kind of thing he would personally not believe in *even if it existed*.[51]

It's rare for this aversion to be stated so openly, although there
are similar statements on record. But the underlying attitude is arguably implicit in a lot of the responses we've looked at so far, and
it's something that parapsychologists have long speculated about.
Walter Prince, an early twentieth-century paranormal researcher,
wrote a book, *The Enchanted Boundary,* that mocked the tendency
of otherwise intelligent people to spout excitable nonsense whenever confronted with evidence of psi – as if it had cast a strange
spell over them.[52] And from time to time the critics draw attention
to their own anxieties. Towards the end of Alcock's *Parapsychology:
Science or Magic?* I was startled to find him musing about the kind of
world this might be if psi was genuine:

> There would, of course, be no privacy, since by extrasensory
> perception one could see even into people's minds. Dictators
> would no longer have to trust the words of their followers;
> they could 'know' their feelings. How would people react if
> they could catch glimpses of the future?

How could the stock market function if traders could use precognition, Alcock pondered.

> If most people could foresee the future, how would life be
> with millions of people all attempting to change present
> circumstances so as to optimize their personal futures?
> What would happen when two adversaries each tried to
> harm the other via PK? The gunfights of the Old American
> West would probably pale by comparison.[53]

It's perhaps worth pointing out that this nightmare hardly matches
with what people actually experience. Psi interactions are typically
involuntary – unbidden intuitions concerning close friends or family members; they often arise as a result of some strongly emotive

incident. To be sure, professional psychics who believe they possess this intuition in abundance may give the impression they can switch it on at will, but few (if any) produce results that are at all reliable. Perhaps because sceptics' ideas are largely formed by these people's exaggerated claims, they tend to see psi as a kind of super-hero power, and are baffled that clairvoyants have to tout for business at psychic fayres when they could be earning fortunes in the stock market. But there's little in the literature that suggests psi lends itself to that sort of thing.

Worries about the implications of psi are also expressed by Cambridge psychologist Nicholas Humphrey in *Soul Searching* (1995), an attack on paranormal belief. Religion and the paranormal, Humphrey says,

> ... by blurring the distinction between life and death, destroying the grounding of one mind in one body, confusing the issues of personal responsibility, and undermining privacy, would rob the world of the oxygen of individuality on which all things bright and beautiful – natural and cultural – have relied for their creative energy.[54]

What other people see as a curious but essentially natural phenomenon here takes on a sort of moral malignancy. If Humphrey's idea of psi were true then perhaps we really should be alarmed. But to acknowledge that psychic interactions occur on rare occasions is not to say that they make us less physical, individual or creative. What's so interesting is that, like Alcock, Humphrey slips into the conditional tense. The thing the critics want us not to take seriously ought not to be true, because it would be calamitous.

As it happens, I think there really are issues to be faced in this regard, although in a serious enquiry we can't afford to be misled by our fears and preferences. I'll have more to say about that later. My point here is that sceptics are right to implicate psychological processes in thinking about the paranormal, but entirely wrong to suppose that it doesn't affect them too. Their complaints about the superstitious masses – that they don't think critically, that they are biased by their beliefs, that their claims don't stand up to scrutiny – can often be quite justly said of them as well. And indeed why should they be any different? I don't accept that a rigid and pitiless logic separates them from their more open-minded fellows, as some of them seem to believe. Temperament and experience must surely shape their thinking, as happens with everyone else.[55]

We may not know it, but I suspect many of us are equipped with a psychological gag reflex. If we can't swallow a claim, we sick it up. And when, rejecting this or that spooky story, we congratulate ourselves for our healthy scepticism, we *may* be thinking with cold clinical detachment, but it is equally possible that we are just signal-ling our sanity, to ourselves and our peers, affirming our right to be considered a member of the club of right-minded people. So if reports of the paranormal 'turn out to be untrue' when subjected to careful scrutiny, or 'crumble into nothing in front of our gaze', or 'disappear into thin air' – as debunking writers tend to insist[56] – it's perhaps not always because they *are* that insubstantial, but because they can't withstand the withering force of our disbelief. We ration-alize them out of existence. Just as the immune system mobilises the body's defences against infection, so our minds hedge the distur-bance around with objections, and, if the emergency is really dire, with invented 'exposures' and 'confessions'.

Finally, as I say, I'd feel more confident about the psychologists' analysis if I sensed they were connecting with what people say actu-ally happened to them. In the next chapter I want to go a bit deeper into that, looking at the profound impact some types of experiences can have on a person's life, and starting to engage with the religious implications.

SIX

EXPERIENCE AND IMAGINATION (II)

'Mysticism is a rational enterprise. Religion is not. The mystic has recognized something about the nature of consciousness prior to thought, and this recognition is susceptible to rational discussion. The mystic has reasons for what he believes, and these reasons are empirical.' *Sam Harris, The End of Faith.*

D o campaigning sceptics ever have paranormal experiences? Perhaps they do, and unlike other people manage to see them for the illusions they really are.

James Randi tells of waking up one night alarmed to find himself apparently spread-eagled against the ceiling. Looking down, he saw himself lying in his bed with its familiar chartreuse bedspread, on which his pet cat was sleeping peacefully. The experience ended there, and when he woke later his first impression was that he must have been observing the scene from outside his body. But then a family member pointed out that the bedspread was at the laundry and the cat had been locked outside, in deference to a house guest with an allergy. Randi realized that he had experienced a vivid dream or hallucination; what he saw was a mental reconstruction based on memory.[1]

Something similar is described by Susan Blackmore, a psychologist and widely-quoted commentator on paranormal claims. In her 1982 book *Beyond the Body* Blackmore mentions an incident when, as a university student, she was smoking cannabis with some friends and suddenly had the sense that she was situated outside her body. The experience lasted for two hours and while it was going on she was able to describe her light-headed feeling of roaming large distances at will. But she later understood that what she had seen didn't match the reality. She had observed a particular roof as having chimneys and red tiles, but when she checked later she found it was actually grey, and had no chimneys. Like Randi, she concluded that no part of her had left her body at all, and that her imagination had constructed the experience from memory.[2]

If this is right, it's an insight that has escaped most people who have reported having an out-of-body experience. There are also books by alleged adepts at 'astral travelling' who claim to know how to trigger the experience at will.[3] In recent years the phenomenon has been widely reported by accident victims and hospital patients who come close to death – the well-known 'near-death experience'. All these reports have added weight to the popular notion that there's a soul that will separate from the body at death and fly off to some other dimension to continue a different kind of life. That's supported by other typical features of near-death visions: a sense of interacting with deceased relatives, perhaps also – in what Kenneth Ring has called the 'core' experience – of flying at speed up a tunnel towards a bright light, being engulfed by ineffable feelings of joy, and undergoing a kind of moral judgement.

These are very powerful images, and they seem to be convincing to the people who experience them, instilling the firm belief that death is not the end; many subsequently go through a major life transformation. Yet although the phenomenon has reinforced a certain kind of religious belief, it has barely dented the scientific and secular consensus that there is no soul and that therefore there can be no kind of afterlife.

So what *is* the explanation? No one who reports the experience has actually died, it can be argued, and from that perspective it's not a literal description of what happens after death. Psychologists have suggested that 'out of body' awareness may be an effect of 'depersonalization', a mechanism by which the ego-consciousness copes with the threat of annihilation by manufacturing peaceful feelings. Sceptics also note that it is inconsistent across different cultures and historical periods: Asians do not on the whole see deceased relatives (a common feature of Western descriptions), while medieval reports, although clearly referring to the same psychological phenomena, are more likely to involve a tour of Hell or to treat the incident as a case of mistaken identity where someone else was scheduled to die – both, as it happens, literary motifs of the period.

All this strongly suggests the experiencer's imagination is responding to expectations. It's hardly surprising, says James Alcock:

> … that a patient recovering from cardiac arrest being told (erroneously) that he had been clinically dead, and having no schema in which to place such an hallucinatory experience (if that is what it was), treats it as an 'after-life' experience. Assigning that label then makes it even more wondrous to the individual.[4]

Here too, 'misremembering' plays a role, psychologists argue. Many such reports are of incidents that occurred years or decades in the past, which makes it likely that events have been unconsciously layered with new details. Chris French, editor of the British *Skeptic* magazine, has noted that in a large study carried out by Dutch cardiologist Pim Van Lommel, four out of thirty-seven patients in a control group who had suffered a cardiac arrest (but who at the time reported no near-death experience) changed their minds on a follow-up interview two years later – evidence, French believes, that these 'memories' can in fact be manufactured.[5]

If one accepts that *something* is causing these episodes it makes sense to look for a common biological origin. It's often proposed that they are triggered by 'cerebral anoxia', which occurs when the supply of oxygen to the brain is interrupted, and 'hypercarbia', the corresponding build-up of carbon dioxide. Both conditions are known to cause hallucinations, so this might make sense. Some types of anaesthetics and medication are known to have hallucinatory properties. Also implicated are endorphins, the natural opiates released in situations of physical stress; these would account for feelings of tranquillity and euphoria.[6]

Sceptics point out that many of the elements are associated with non life-threatening conditions. Religious feelings and visions can occur spontaneously as a result of stress, drugs or illness. So-called 'mystical' or 'peak' experiences – a sudden powerful up-rush of religious feeling – are as widely reported by healthy people as by those undergoing a medical trauma. Hallucinations with a quasi-religious content are an occasional effect of epilepsy and schizophrenia, as well as ingestion of psychotropic substances such as LSD (lysergic acid) and mescaline, which can in addition give a sense of interacting with supernatural entities or of having lived past lives.[7] All this points clearly to some alteration in the temporal and parietal lobes, the areas of the brain mainly associated with emotion and the sense of time and space. Brain scans of meditating monks have been found to exhibit consistent patterns at the moment of maximum quietness, and University of Toronto psychologist Michael Persinger has demonstrated that light stimulation of the temporal lobe area can induce mystical and religious feelings, including a sense of psychic communication, of being out of the body, and of invisible presences.[8]

The conclusion reached by sceptics is that the source of these feelings, ideas and images is the workings of the brain, not any kind of interaction with an unseen world. In her 1994 study published in *Dying to Live,* Blackmore attempted to create a scientific model of the near-death experience, for which she selected some of the better existing ideas and added some of her own. One of her most striking suggestions is that the tunnel is an optical illusion caused by neurons firing randomly in the visual system. The density would be strongest at the centre and fade out towards the margins, she argues, creating the appearance of a tube or tunnel. The reason why people say the light never hurts the eyes is because it's a purely cerebral event, in which the retina and the nerves are not involved.[9]

2 The challenge for science

These sceptical ideas are strongly resisted by scientists and medical professionals who research the phenomenon. The initial data was purely anecdotal – a collection of stories told to Raymond Moody, a psychiatrist, whose slim volume titled *Life After Life* (1975) was the first that most people had ever come across about the near-death experience.[10] But more serious studies followed. A statistical analysis by University of Connecticut psychologist Kenneth Ring confirmed that the experience was not obviously determined by any recognizable feature, such as the subjects' religious beliefs, cultural background or physiognomy, or the manner of their nearly dying. Among similar studies based on interviews, paediatrician Melvin Morse has revealed that children have almost identical experiences, and cardiologist Michael Sabom has discussed cases reported by some of his hospital patients.[11]

The information provided by hospital studies is more extensive and immediate. In Pim Van Lommel's 2001 prospective investigation, three hundred and forty-four survivors of cardiac arrest were interviewed shortly after the event and sixty-two reported a near-death experience, yielding a wealth of scientific data.[12] This will be dwarfed by a study currently being carried out in a number of medical centres in Europe and America, co-ordinated by Sam Parnia at the University of Southampton, whose results are expected in 1212–13.

With so much data to work with, researchers argue that enough is now known about the phenomenon to cast doubt on the sceptics' explanations. Anaesthetics and medication could not explain near-death experiences reported by people who have come close to death by drowning or road accidents, or by heart attacks outside the hospital, they point out.[13] There's also the fact that anoxia is associated with loss of consciousness, whereas the near-death experience is a state of hyper-alertness and visual clarity, opposites that are hard to reconcile.[14] It's true that any stimulation of the temporal lobe caused by anoxia might lead to a hallucination, but anoxia is known to knock out the memory centres quite rapidly, which would make the recall of events supposedly taking place after its onset rather surprising. Pilots who experience sudden oxygen cut-off at high altitudes or in training do not generally report near-death experiences: interestingly, one pilot who underwent an oxygen shortage *and* a near-death experience on separate occasions said there was no similarity between them.[15]

A question for both sides is why, since these brain events presumably occur to most people in near-death situations, is it that only a minority have the experience? It's more obviously a problem for sceptics, though; if endogenous endorphins are triggered in the traumatic state of nearly dying, why is the near-death experience the exception rather than the rule? [16]

Here's another mystery: how does an individual lay down coherent and vivid new memories at a time when the conditions for consciousness are resoundingly absent? The research by now includes more than one hundred cardiac arrest cases, where life functions had for a significant period totally ceased. Cardiac arrest, the authors of *Irreducible Mind* point out that this is a 'physiologically brutal event':

> Cerebral functioning shuts down within a few seconds. Whether the heart actually stops beating entirely or goes into ventricular fibrillation, the result is essentially

instantaneous circulatory arrest, with blood flow and oxygen uptake in the brain plunging swiftly to near-zero levels. EEG signs of cerebral ischemia typically with global slowing and loss of fast activity, are visually detectable within 6–10 seconds, and progress to isoelectricity (flat-line EEGs) within 10–20 seconds of the onset of arrest. In sum, full arrest leads rapidly to establishment of three major clinical signs of death – absence of cardiac output, absence of respiration, and absence of brainstem reflexes – and provides the best model we have of the dying process.[17]

On the face of it, then, it is remarkable that someone in this condition can be having any kind of conscious experience. In one well-known case a woman called Pam Reynolds was operated on to remove a massive aneurysm: her heart was stopped to achieve a state of total brain shutdown, the blood was removed from her brain, her ears were blocked and her eyes taped shut. Yet she later reported a full near-death experience during this time. She seemed first to leave her body, hearing comments being made by members of the surgical team and watching as an electric saw cut into her skull. She then felt herself being pulled along a 'tunnel vortex' towards a light and saw several deceased relatives, all permeated by an 'incredibly bright' light. As she said afterwards, she was not merely *aware* during this state of seeming unconsciousness, but was 'the most aware that I think I have ever been in my life'.[18]

Sceptics counter that it is over-hasty to suppose that *nothing* is occurring in the brain during these states. Instruments that measure electrical activity from the scalp may not be able to detect what is going on in the deep centres; we can't insist that someone is 'clinically dead' as long as we lack the means to rule this out completely. In response, researchers question whether, even if some activity *were* still going on in the depths of the tissue, beyond the reach of instruments, it could conceivably be sufficient to create any kind of conscious experience. Considering that normal consciousness is entirely absent in these clinical conditions, they consider the answer must surely be 'no'. Another idea is that these experiences may occur in the period either before or after the crisis of clinical death, when some cerebral activity is still occurring. But even then, people in this state are normally amnesic and confused, a state of mind that is quite unlike that found with the near-death experience – and they never experience any life-changing impact as a result.

3 Could out-of-body perception be an illusion?

It was the veridical claims of 'out of body' perception that I was concerned with most, because, if true, they would be hard to reconcile with scientifically verified norms. As with clairvoyant mediums and extra-sensory perception, the claim that people obtain information they could not have acquired by any known means presents a logical conundrum, and ought to provide clues about whether this is a real or an imagined experience. So I want to look closely here at what individuals say about this, and how the sceptics explain it away.

Susan Blackmore suggests that what we perceive in the 'out of body' state is actually just a model of reality constructed from what our senses tell us is 'out there'. Normally our brains have no trouble distinguishing reality from imagination. But in certain situations, such as before sleep or during a trauma, perhaps as a result of stress or oxygen deprivation, this model becomes confused and unstable. In such a situation, she suggests, to restore a sense of normality the mind will switch to a memory model of what it *thinks* is happening. However vivid and life-like it seems, this model is actually artificial, merely a product of mental processes. (Other parapsychologists agree that the sense of being outside the body is indeed an illusion, but think that experiencers are in some way employing psychic perception to discover what is going on around them.[19])

None of this would remotely impress the people who experience these episodes themselves. Typically they insist that their bird's-eye vantage point was where they were physically located, and that what they saw and heard from it was what actually happened. It was no dream, no hallucination. True, in some cases the details are no more than the patients might have expected: people were gathered round their bed crying or hospital staff resuscitated them by means of cardiac defibrillation, and so on. But to me the level of specific detail in these statements can be rather surprising. The individual may claim to have watched exactly what people were doing in the laundry room in another part of the hospital, or repeat the banter of the medics in the operating theatre, or recount the exact sequence of events at the scene of the accident they were involved in – much of which they claim subsequently to have verified.

Here would seem to be a difficulty for sceptics. How can an internal construction based on memory exactly correspond to an actual event? It might do so by chance, but where there exists an exact correspondence in a number of details this would be hard to insist on.

Having previously read Blackmore's work on out-of-body experiences, where on the whole no medical trauma is present, I was interested to see how she would tackle veridical claims in the context of the near-death experience. One approach is to suggest that the images that the mind creates are informed by 'residual sense.' That is, the patient may *seem* to be unconscious, but he is still exposed to the sounds of what is going on around him, and his brain may be able to make sense of them.

Studies have established that anaesthetics do not always knock the patient out completely, she points out, and there have been cases of people enduring the nightmare of being operated on while still partially conscious. In some cases they report hearing sounds around them during an operation.[20] If the brain is getting a feed of information it can construct images of what is going on, in the way that a person listening to a radio drama creates a mental picture of a scene which she can't actually see.

However in general Blackmore doubts there is anything that really needs explaining. She downplays the phenomenon and implies that it's not significant. We ought to be careful before accepting people's testimony, she says, because they might be exaggerating in order to attract attention. Or perhaps they want to convince themselves that something important happened – their very enthusiasm ought to put us on our guard. If they retained a degree of sensory perception during an apparent state of unconsciousness, what they perceived could have been filled out later from reading books or watching television. It's not really surprising that a person's vision might seem to be restored, because the imagination can be extraordinarily vivid. The claims seem so dramatic because there's a temptation to make a big deal out of them, based on the distortion of memory, wild newspaper claims and the 'tendency to make a big story out of a very weak case'.[21]

This is not at all what most researchers think. For example, Michael Sabom interviewed twenty-five patients under his care, all of whom described a near-death experience: as a control group he found another twenty-five people who had gone through a medical crisis with reporting an experience. A few of the near-death experiencers, he found, could give highly specific accounts of the particular circumstances of their resuscitation, describing the equipment used and other features that closely matched the medical records. What's more, these details would not have been accurate if applied to another case, he stated. The control group were also able to give details about the procedures they underwent but were much less specific, and most made at least one major error in their account. Sabom concluded that the information that the near-death experiencers came by could not have been based solely on their prior knowledge of the medical techniques.

I found the surprise shown by Sabom's patients at specific aspects of their operations particularly telling. One male patient reports watching the surgeon pull his heart out, examine it closely and snip pieces off. 'It's not shaped like I thought it would be,' he commented later. 'My heart was shaped something like the continent of Africa, with it being larger up here and tapered down. Bean-shaped is another way you could describe it.'[22] A female patient reports how she watched closely as her back was operated on: 'I came right down to the operation and I was amazed how deep my spine was in my back … It was really incredible how deep my spine was. I had thought it was right on the surface. Then I saw them reach in and pull the disk out. it seemed like they had a long pair of tweezers but angled at the end, with which they actually removed the disk.' [23] This patient watched as complications developed and the surgical opening had to be sewn up in a hurry. She saw the surgeon pulling the skin too roughly at the top, leaving a gap; later she examined the scar in a mirror and the gap was plainly visible.

It wasn't clear to me how unconscious patients could register surprise of this kind through the processes that the psychologists describe. To have imagined it would require some prior memory, which apparently in these cases would have been inaccurate. It's surely unlikely that they were helped by a residual sense of hearing, since the doctors and nurses would not be surprised by the shape of the heart or the depth of the spine, and would have no reason to draw attention to these things among themselves.

To me these looked like eye-witness accounts; if I had not known the context it wouldn't have occurred to me to doubt that they came from a conscious observer at the scene. In sum, the idea that unconscious patients could come up with such vivid and detailed descriptions through the normal processes of imagination and remaining sensory awareness began to seem quite fantastic.

4 Some questions about Blackmore's analysis

This last idea led me to take another look at the critics' arguments. To begin with, I had problems with the idea of partial consciousness arising from an incomplete anaesthetic. Blackmore almost makes it sound as though this is a regular occurrence, but the evidence she provides to support her contention is necessarily flimsy: awakening during surgery is known to occur on a minor scale – in only 0.1–0.3 per cent of all general surgical procedures, which is a tiny level of incidence when compared to the number of near-death experience reports among cardiology patients, for instance. Furthermore, there isn't the slightest overlap between this and the emotional aspects of the experiences themselves. Patients who remained conscious during their surgical procedure reported feeling deep distress and pain, while those who claim to have near-death experiences felt detached, calm and comfortable, even while they were watching their bodies being sliced open and their internal organs pulled out.[24]

In Blackmore's analysis, sensory awareness is not the only thing going on here; the effect also requires an imaginative process that is backed up by prior knowledge, fantasy, lucky guesses and faulty memory. I accept that a person might imaginatively reconstruct the event, even to the extent of producing uncanny correspondences with reality. What I don't understand is *why* someone would do this. Clearly some motivation is involved: the brain is apparently striving to create a particular effect, using every available resource to restore the sense of normality. Yet it does have a more simple and effective way of dealing with extreme situations, which is to shut off consciousness altogether. Why does it need to go to such extraordinary lengths to create a convincing illusion?

Look at what we're saying here. Suppose a motorcyclist skids into the path of an oncoming truck and ends up in a bloody heap on the tarmac. His nervous system is signalling a maximum degree of alarm: the pain and shock overwhelms him and he blacks out. Yet in the midst of all of this his brain apparently finds the resources to create a picture of what is going on around him. Why does he need this? The information can be of no use for as long as he is unconscious; he is helpless and utterly dependent on the goodwill of others. There can be no compelling survival advantage and so no obvious reason for this faculty to have evolved. Or do we think we need this ringside seat that nature thoughtfully provides, because it helps in some way to watch the worst thing that has ever happened to us – gory mutilation possibly followed by death?

What especially interests me is the way the critic deals with the most compelling aspect of this phenomenon, the fact that the details of the scene and the events, as experienced by the individual, closely correspond to the reality. As sceptics do, Blackmore reconstructs the events in a way that leads to her desired conclusion; people get confused, they forget things, they exaggerate. Here she imagines a scenario in which someone is talking about their recollections of another patient after being resuscitated in hospital:

> I could see you there, down the hall, you were wearing that green coat and skirt and your favourite pearl necklace. You were talking to George and he was waving a newspaper about. You looked terribly pale.[25]

But what if, Blackmore goes on, some of these details were actually wrong. Suppose the woman being observed was wearing the coat, but not the skirt and necklace, and she, not George, had a grip on the newspaper? No one in this situation would be that bothered about accuracy. In this way a myth is born and corroboration apparently provided, all through a combination of fragmented normal perception and apparent, but erroneous, corroboration.

This did not convince me at all. I could imagine occasional isolated claims being tackled in this way, but to apply such an ephemeral construction to such a large, consistent and dramatic category of experience as near-death reports stretches credibility to breaking point. The conclusion I was left with is that the psychologist is inventing obvious discrepancies and assuming, unreasonably in my view, that people lack the will or ability to spot them.

It helps the sceptics' take on things that any verification of an individual's out-of-body perception that is made later – by a relative or hospital staff - is not often corroborated independently. Of course this might just mean that the concerns of people involved in a near-death trauma – either their own or that of a loved one – do not remotely coincide with those of the scientific researcher. On the other hand, it does allow sceptics make inferences in support of their thesis – that anomalous perception can't be corroborated because it doesn't happen.

5 *A doctor debunked*

But what of cases where claims of anomalous perception are made by a trained professional rather than a member of the public? The cardiologist Michael Sabom presents a problem here, because his scientific data were gathered in controlled conditions but still, from the sceptic's point of view, give the wrong result. Paranormal perception in claimed out-of-body states, he insists, is occasionally accurate and can be verified.

Again, it's interesting to see how sceptical academics deal with this. A study of the near-death experience by two American psychiatrists, Glen Gabbard and Stuart Twemlow, focus on the psychological aspects. They challenge Sabom, pointing out that 'only' thirty-two of his one hundred and sixteen subjects reported that they could observe what was going on around them while they were unconscious. Most of these perceptions, moreover, weren't particularly specific and couldn't be verified after the event. In fact, only six cases had enough detail to be validated, which the sceptics regards as a weak result.

But his findings were still compelling enough, and I wasn't surprised to find the psychiatrists trying to demolish them completely. They start by finding fault with Sabom's methods, criticizing his control group on the grounds that it consisted of patients who merely had similar symptoms and who had not been involved in the type of crisis that gives rise to near-death experiences. They go further in suggesting that the methodology was generally unsound on several counts, and imply that the findings should be set aside.[26]

However they still seem unconvinced that they have got to the core of the matter, and feel the implications of mind–body dualism – which they believe any sane person will reject – are still uncomfortably present. They themselves are not experts in the paranormal, they concede, but they know someone who is. Step forward Terence Hines, whose textbook provides them with some standard arguments about magical thinking, misunderstanding coincidence, and so on. Having mentioned these aspects, the authors then invite us to consider that the detailed awareness claimed by Sabom's patients can be put down to *chance*. Or else, they go on to say, people who make extraordinary claims may have been duped or could be lying; even some scientists have been taken in by Uri Geller, and perhaps this cardiologist is being equally credulous. They also raise the possibility of dishonesty, although in such a vague way I wasn't sure if it's the doctor or his patients we're supposed to suspect, nor do they even attempt to speculate about the methods or motives in either case.

I was left with no idea which, if any, of these abundant possibilities might be involved here, or how they relate to Sabom's data. I doubt whether the psychiatrists know either; they seem not to accept that anti-paranormal arguments have to mean *something* if they are to work at all, and be applied in a relevant way. It's as though they hope they can make a troublesome anomaly vanish just by waving a debunkers' book at it, much the same way as a Bible might be used to ward off vampires. And to put a cardiologist and his critically ill patients in the same category as a supposedly fake psychic surely reveals the weakness of their strategy.

6 *A determined sceptic*

Blackmore, meanwhile, is not at all impressed with Sabom and she briskly disposes of his findings. Yes, she concedes, his patients give unexpectedly plausible accounts. But, she goes on, 'without access to complete details of what happened (and these can never be obtained) we can't know just how closely it really did fit the facts at the time'.[27] In other words, we should not just take his word for what he is claiming.

To make quite sure we have got the point, Blackmore raises an episode which at first sight seems to cause her position some difficulty. This is a much-discussed case of a patient who went 'out of body' during a cardiac arrest while in hospital, who, during her roamings, observed a tennis shoe stuck on a ledge outside the building.[28] She established later that she couldn't have seen the shoe from the position her body was in at the time, even if she had been fully conscious, or indeed from anywhere else within the building. To try to verify this, a health-worker visited the hospital later and with some difficulty located the shoe in the place the patient described. This is often cited as hard evidence of paranormal perception. However Blackmore characteristically swats it away, saying that near-death experiences should not need such legitimization for they are valid in themselves, as experiences. But this case, she continues:

> … underlines all too clearly how people use claims of the paranormal to convince themselves and others that what

they experienced was real and that they are not going crazy. And if the need is so strong there's always the suspicion that the claims may be exaggerated or even invented.[29]

By this time Blackmore had given up trying to demolish the claim's veridical challenge and has switched instead to undermining its legitimacy. She reinterprets it in the light of her own ideas, and in so doing makes the experiencer look foolish. It seems unfair to blame the patient for taking the incident as confirmation that her experience actually happened, when she was probably surrounded by family members, nurses and doctors, all of whom (like Blackmore) were trying to convince her that she only imagined it. Why shouldn't she be excited to find that her strange vision corresponded to reality, and is therefore unlikely to be a symptom of incipient craziness? But to the critic, apparently, it's suspicious behaviour, and merits a ticking-off.

So who's doing the inventing? Not the patient surely, since there was independent corroboration. Or is Blackmore saying the health-worker might have made it all up? The trail goes dead. 'This is, sadly,' she continues, 'one of those cases for which I have been unable to get any further information'. She continues:

> Perhaps it may yet be possible but until then I can only consider it as fascinating but unsubstantiated. … The suspicion must be, rightly, or wrongly, that there may be no properly corroborated cases that cannot be accounted for by the perfectly normal processes of imagination, memory, chance and the use of the remaining senses.[30]

Considering the illusory, non-veridical nature of her own out-of-body experience, it's legitimate for Blackmore to question the claim of other such episodes to be described as paranormal, and understandable that she should use any means available. But I think even she realizes that the weight of the evidence is against her. Having run out of arguments she resorts to bluffing, like a courtroom lawyer with a patently guilty client and nothing to lose. It's the process of seeding doubt: 'The claim can't be *proved*, and so, ladies and gentle-men of the jury, you must dismiss it as spurious'. That might be fair enough in a murder trial – one can't afford to jail an innocent person without hard evidence – but in a scientific context it leaves awkward questions unanswered.

Actually, I doubt whether this phenomenon *can* be proved to the satisfaction of science. There are too many loopholes. Suppose someone who has been blind from birth has an out-of-body experi-ence and is able to describe objects and events that correspond with reality.[31] She couldn't be said to have constructed an image from residual awareness, because, being blind, she would have no visual memory to draw on. Ah yes, but unfortunately we have only the woman's word for it that she was blind from birth; there's no docu-mentary evidence and, sadly, the doctor who delivered her cannot be traced, so we can never know for sure.

But what if the subject is young and there's ample documentary verification that she had been born without sight? Would this con-vince? Unhappily, no. You see, there's no guarantee that a blind per-son hasn't got some residual sensory ability; it's more than likely that she has developed ways of getting information through the senses of hearing and touch. We really know very little about what the brain can do. Also we have to remember the time that lapsed between the time she came round from her operation and the point at which she spoke of her experience. Perhaps she overheard some nurses talking and pieced together the details of what went on. And after all, we are dealing with only one person – a sample of one. We have to keep on looking and researching.

Nothing can stop the counter-arguments. The person involved *might* have been mistaken, *might* have had residual sensory percep-tions, *might* have read about it in books, *might* simply have made it all up. None of these 'mights' have to be demonstrated, as long as the burden of proof is still considered to lie with the person making the extraordinary claim.

But in the meantime, for their part, those scientists, psychologists and humanists who deny that there is anything paranormal going on here must surely recognize *why* this is widely believed to be the case. And they need to understand that the sorts of confused and frankly implausible arguments they often end up using are viewed with incredulity by the wider public, among whom, it should not be forgotten, these claims originate in the first place.

7 *Listening to the experiencers*

Let's focus on this word 'subjective' for a moment. What is true for me – and perhaps also for other like-minded folk – may be in direct opposition with what other people believe.

I touched earlier on the objective status of science, how it concerns itself with what is true for all of us, as biological beings, and about which there can be no disagreement. The tangible and material can be verified by any qualified person at any time, while subjective impressions, on the contrary, are not open to this kind of universal validation. The role this distinction has played in the Enlightenment is clear, enabling an essentially unifying process which, in an optimistic analysis, can be held to have furthered the development of political and social stability.

Late nineteenth-century scientists by and large considered themselves to be 'positivists', subscribing to the philosophical argument that the only real experience is that which is derived from the senses. In the first half of the twentieth century this current of thought culminated in 'logical positivism', which broadly holds that nothing that cannot be verified experimentally is meaningful at all. Its most literal expression in science was the behaviourist school of psychology, which treated thoughts as meaningless ephemera, and instead looked for insights about humans in the behaviour of rats, dogs and pigeons in experimental situations. This historical development is attributed at least partly to 'physics envy' among psychologists, a need to demonstrate their scientific credentials by focusing on demonstrable entities rather than intangible thoughts. Now, at a time when human consciousness is being intensively discussed and investigated, it's sobering to reflect that for much of the last century *it was not even acknowledged by science to exist.*

Yet while subjective feelings are of little interest to science, they are everything in the social sphere. Those of us who are not members of ethnic minorities, who are not gay or poor or disabled or sick, can find it hard to put ourselves in their shoes, to understand the challenges they face. For that matter, being in one particular minority does not necessarily make us more sympathetic to those who belong to others. Our separateness, as Nicolas Humphrey rightly notes, is what makes us human; it's also the source of many of our problems. Our task, as friends, neighbours, service staff, therapists, doctors, scientists, politicians – or as fellow humans, for that matter – is to be aware of what other people are telling us, to try to grasp what they feel and experience, and to take that into account in our own reactions. That's what drives social progress.

But when it comes to paranormal claims there are limits to our broad-mindedness, especially in developed, secular-minded countries. It's true that polls show belief in such things as ghosts and ESP to be quite high, and that might seem to be supported by the proliferation of television programmes about the paranormal. But is it really the case? In a fictional or documentary setting the paranormal is perceived to be entertaining, but when it turns up in real life it can be threatening. People who describe having had a near-death experience often say that doctors, nurses and family members got angry and agitated when they first tried to share their experience, and there are those who for years never even dared mention it.

This is now perhaps less true than it used to be, however a reluctance to listen continues to be characteristic of professional sceptics. Their defensive posture leads them to talk about *claims* as opposed to *experiences,* too preoccupied by the challenge to their imaginations to think at all closely about what is actually being said. From their perspective, people who report paranormal-seeming incidents are creating problems, if not actually setting out to cause mischief, and this point of view is bound to create a distortion in their readers' minds. Their insistence that these are mere anecdotes – and for that reason unscientific, undeserving of serious attention – means they lack exposure to first-hand testimony. Blackmore's *Dying to Live*, rather tellingly, is sparsely illustrated with direct speech: a comparatively bland extract from an individual's reported experience at the beginning is followed here and there by a few short quotes, none of which begin to convey the intensity of the experience as it appears elsewhere.

By contrast near-death experience researchers' studies are laced with copious quotations from individuals who are only too happy to describe something they may have kept locked up for years. This brings the phenomenon alive for the reader; it's more than just a concept, an idea. There's a palpable sense of awe in the first-hand accounts, of euphoria, exultation and mystery. Experiencers struggle to find superlatives to convey the colour, the beauty, the forms, the music – much of which, they insist, is ineffable, utterly beyond description. Those who write it down are able to seek out the most apt word, or turn of phrase, to express the memory. But in a way you get an even greater impact from transcripts of taped interviews, as people who relive the event in their imaginations choke up, grasping for words that will convey the enormity of it.

Listen to these little excerpts, taken at random from extended quotes in Kenneth Ring's *Heading Towards Omega:*

> '…if you took the one thousand best things that ever happened to you in your life and multiplied by a million, maybe you could get close to this feeling…'

'…this wonderful, wonderful feeling of this light…'

'There was the warmest, most wonderful love. Love all around me … I felt light-good-happy-joy-at-ease.'

'I can't begin to describe in human terms the feeling I had at what I saw. It was a giant infinite world of calm, and love, and energy and beauty.'

'As I absorbed the energy, I sensed what I can only describe as bliss. That is such a little word, but the feeling was dynamic, rolling, magnificent, expanding, ecstatic – *Bliss*.' [32]

How many people can say that anything – *anything* – they have experienced in this world matches up to these descriptions? My point is that, without such live comments, readers may be left with the impression that what people experience can be described as 'euphoria' or 'a tremendous sense of well-being', a linguistic down-sizing which makes it comparable to the effects of a stiff whisky or a good workout at the gym. It's then all the easier for a sceptic to argue that it's explicable in neuroscientific terms, a release of endorphins perhaps.

It's natural to look for matches: 'that's the claim – this is the explanation'. But if the original claim is not accurately represented, the explanation can't be fully trusted.

8 *The transcendent element*

This is especially relevant with regard to other elements that attract comment from experiencers and researchers, but which are relatively absent from critical analysis. Two in particular interest me: the sudden recall of a person's life, and the religious response to the 'being of light'. Both are briefly described here:

It proceeded to show me every single event of my 22 years of life, in a kind of instant 3-D panoramic review… The brightness showed me every second of all those years, in exquisite detail, in what seemed only an instant of time. Watching and re-experiencing all those events of my life changed everything. It was an opportunity to see and feel all the love I had shared, and more importantly, all the pain I had caused. I was able to simultaneously re-experience not only my own feelings and thoughts, but those of all the other people I had ever interacted with. Seeing myself through their eyes was a humbling experience.[33]

That sense of seeing how one's actions have affected other people is particularly strong:

…it was like I was seeing it through eyes with … omnipotent knowledge, guiding me and helping me to see. That's the part that stuck with me, because it showed me not only what I had done, but even how what I had done had affected other people… [34]

There doesn't seem to be anything accidental about this – in fact it's hard to view many of these episodes as being anything other than deliberately didactic. It's remarkable enough that a person's inner consciousness seems to persist when all life functions have apparently ceased, but there's more: the individual also experiences a mega-powerful attack of *conscience*. This intrigued me. I found myself wondering: why, if this is simply a hallucination, does it so consistently involve an intense personal examination, and one based on a powerful sense of the effect their own words and actions have had on other people?

The word 'sense' here is literally accurate but doesn't begin to do justice to what near-death experiencers report. Describing the stage when they are interacting with the 'light', they don't say they gained a sudden insight into how other people felt; they say they experienced the other person's feelings – *as if they were their own*. A woman sees the younger sister she bullied when she was young, and for the first time feels what the little girl felt, understanding the full extent of her anguish. A hit-man becomes aware of families of the people he murdered and is swamped by their feelings of devastation. The feedback is physical as well: a truck driver who once beat up a pedestrian in a fit of road rage feels his *own* fist crashing into his *own* face.

> And I felt the indignation, the rage, the embarrassment, the frustration, the physical pain. I felt my teeth going through my lower lip – in other words, I was in that man's eyes. I was in that man's body. I experienced everything of that interrelationship between [myself] and that man that day.[35]

These are powerful images, and they are too widely reported in the research material to be dismissed as spurious; they form a clear pattern. Here too, I found it hard to resist the idea that the process is in some way *intended* to impact on attitudes and behaviour: people who experience it are often profoundly changed and may go through personal and professional upheavals as a result. How do we account for such a thing? I'd love to hear a scientific theory that could explain how one shares other people's feelings, not in the conventional way of being able to sense them, or name or describe them, but to experience them *exactly as if they were their own,* and moreover at a time when all life functions appear to have ceased. I don't mean some formula couldn't be worked out, but it's yet one more feature to load onto a framework already tottering under the burden of sceptical speculation.

9 *Belief and experience are not the same*

Of course, the ideas of selfless love and of being judged for one's sins are the essence of the Christian Gospels. So how we respond to the near-death experience is likely to depend as much on how we feel about religion as on the scientific data. For a conscientious but secular-minded person the choices are not ideal: accept explanations that are at best incomplete, if not obviously flawed, or be prepared to modify strongly held beliefs.

In practice it seems there's no real difficulty here for convinced sceptics. The founding publisher of the American *Skeptic* magazine, Michael Shermer, for instance, thinks it's obvious that near-death experiences are 'hallucinatory wishful-thinking experiences' and that paranormal researchers go out of their way to verify them in order to support their religious leanings. The visions may be reported by people who are not overtly religious, he adds, but researchers fail to point out that they are nevertheless exposed to the Judeo–Christian worldview. 'Whether or not we consciously believe, we have all heard similar ideas about God and the afterlife, heaven and hell.' The fact that people of different religions see different religious figures he takes to be 'an indication that the phenomenon occurs within the mind, not without.'[36]

Agnostics can explore a possible third way, shunning any literal interpretation of a paradisial afterlife inhabited by Gods and angels, while acknowledging that the appearance of such a thing fulfils some useful purpose. That's the route taken by Carol Zaleski, a Harvard religious historian who drew attention to the inconsistencies between modern and medieval reports in her 1987 comparative study *Otherworld Journeys*. Zaleski infers from this disparity that such descriptions can't be telling of something that objectively exists, but she nevertheless considers them important, not as a 'direct transcript of the truth', but as a 'lure toward truth', by leading people out of anxious, mechanical, or vicious patterns of thought and behaviour. Perhaps the chief virtue of our tendency to conceive of another world, she suggests, may be that it provides a sense of orientation in this world, through which we would otherwise wander without direction.[37]

This pragmatic stance avoids the twin perils of dogmatic scepticism and naive superstition. It also opens the door to a naturalistic explanation of religion, that humans have a predisposition to value universal co-operation, expressed as the Golden Rule – that is, to treat others as one would want to be treated oneself. In other words the central drive is real, while the religious imagery is the illusory setting in which it is dressed. But how easily we forget that this near-death experience is *involuntary*. Patients and accident victims who are unconscious, and in some cases clinically dead, surely can't have a tendency to conceive of *anything*.

It's important to keep in mind that what we are talking about here is religious *experience*, also to note that this is a category that science has not yet learned consistently to distinguish from religious *belief* – a shortcoming which in my view fatally undermines much scientific discourse on religion. The near-death experience, in its fullest manifestation, is not a voluntary identification with certain ideas and doctrines – it's *experience*. If we cavil that actually experience is something that only happens when we are conscious, then we might prefer to think of it as a kind of dream, always remembering, however, that to dream *is to experience* – it is only when we wake that we recognize what occurred as an illusion created by the brain during sleep. But if we feel that we can now relax, and that the matter has been appropriately pigeonholed, that is absolutely not the case, for experiencers insist, unanimously and passionately, that what they experienced *was not a dream*.

Nor can I accept the suggestion that these experiences – impactful, clear and consistent – are essentially formless, and that they are shaped and given meaning by the individual after the event. Sceptics like Shermer and Alcock rather imply that if they experienced it themselves they would not be misled, or at least not for long – rather they would recognize it to be hallucinatory. But is that credible? The literature on near-death experience is now very large, and I can't recall ever seeing a secular version described anywhere: that is, a hospital patient who reported going up a tunnel to a bright light, being flooded with ineffable feelings of bliss in the presence of an angelic being, yet far from being overwhelmed and changed by the experience, dismissed it as the effects of anaesthetics, no big deal. On the other hand, it does happen the other way round: a person who claims to have been agnostic or atheist at the time of the experience is just as likely to be affected by it as a religious devotee, if in slightly different terms.[38]

It's the same with those 'mystical' experiences described in collections by William James, Alister Hardy and Raynor Johnson, among others – brief but life-changing moments of enlightenment.[39] People who have had them don't afterwards say they suddenly felt marvellous for no reason, still less that they experienced an inexplicable mental aberration. On the contrary, even those who insist they aren't religious consistently employ a spiritual and religious vocabulary. They say that for one ineffable and never-to-be-forgotten moment the heavens opened and they saw into the very nature of things. They speak of an effulgent light and – repeatedly – of *the peace that passes all understanding*. They experience the new insight that *all things and all people are connected*, fragments of a single whole, that the human spirit is immortal, and that love is all that matters. They say things like 'I can remember feeling exultantly "This is God", and God, after all, was both personal and immense.'[40] For contemplatives in all the religions it's a state of mind that can be accessed at will, as the reward of committed spiritual endeavour; their writings include detailed descriptions of it and how it is to be achieved.[41]

It's true we can also talk about this in secular terms. Neuroscientific research has reinforced the sense that the brain has some religious centre; while ideas of a 'god gene' or a 'god module' are probably misleading, they highlight the existence of a class of mental events, some neurological patterning which, when suitably stimulated, has the potential to generate that kind of sensibility which we term 'religious'.[42]

We see it in certain types of epilepsy, known in ancient times as 'the divine madness', which some believe to have had a critical influ-

ence on the founders of Christianity and Islam, St Paul and Moham-
med. It's also implicated in the quasi-religious delusions suffered by
some schizophrenics. Perhaps most conspicuously it's seen in the
visions brought on by psychotropic drugs. Otherworld images and
spiritual transformation were a frequent effect of therapeutic LSD
studies carried out in the 1960s, when patients were often said to describe a spiritual awakening, sometimes involving visions of transcendental realms, deceased relatives and mythical figures. Typically the
subjects became convinced of their immortality, sensing the unity of
all things and the existence of a timeless reality beyond the physical
world, sometimes extending to a belief in the reality of reincarnation.
It's worth noting that a similar psychotropic substance – *soma* – is
credited with having produced many of the insights in the Hindu
Rig Veda, the world's oldest religious text. But these 'entheogens' are
far from being the only way to stimulate a religious trance: adepts of
all persuasions use techniques such as fasting, flagellation, chanting,
dancing, whirling or drumming to achieve visions and ecstasies.[43]

Clearly there's some physical trigger for religious-type experiences, and this naturally reinforces the view that religion can and
should be explained in purely naturalistic terms. Each new study
that links meditative states – or transcendental feelings, or other
aspects of religious experience – to specific cerebral events tends
to be greeted by atheists as the final nail in the coffin of religion:
intimations of another world are just 'something that happens in the
brain'. Michael Persinger's claim to be able to stimulate such things
artificially in controlled conditions, although entirely unconvincing
to researchers, has been especially influential in this regard.

I understand why sceptics reason like this, but the logic is not
as coercive as they think. Neurological processes are implicated in
all conscious activity and there's no reason to suppose that having
a religious experience is any different; nothing 'bypasses' the brain.
And the ability of science to correlate religious feelings with what
happens in the brain, in ever greater detail, does not in itself enforce

a physicalist interpretation, or militate against a form of mind–body dualism. We have not reached the point at which we can rule out, on scientific rather than ideological grounds, the possibility that brain centres are not alone responsible for generating thoughts and ideas, but may be interacting with an as yet unidentified external source.

It's unfashionable to argue in this way, of course, but as we have seen it's also unfashionable to consider paranormal and religious experience, or for that matter other aspects of consciousness that do not easily fit the physicalist paradigm.[44] Indeed, the established connections between religious experience and abnormal brain states positively encourage the idea that there exists some greater reality – Mind at Large, as Aldous Huxley termed it in *The Doors of Perception* – and that the brain partly functions as a 'reducing valve' that transforms it down to a level we can handle. Its functioning, clearly, can be compromised by various means – hallucinogens and fasting, for instance, or involuntarily through stress, heightened emotion, mental illness, fever, or for that matter, cardiac arrest and the temporary suspension of normal brain operations.[45]

Part of the same family as near-death and mystical experiences is that mediumistic activity known as 'channelling'. The claim is that discarnate entities communicate either by writing directly through the medium's hand or mind (a process known as automatic writing) or by taking possession of the medium's body in a trance state and speaking with her voice. The obscure metaphysics and flamboyant personages with silly names can make channelling hard to take seriously, but it really does not seem to be play-acting – at least not always. Automatic writing is an odd but verified phenomenon: in a relaxed state a person's hand may suddenly take on a life of its own and write religious, philosophical or artistic material at breakneck speed, which, when read back, may prove to be complex yet coherent, without relating in any way to the individual's habitual ideas, concerns and interests. Or else the writer records words and ideas that flood into her mind and which, again, appear to come from an external source.[46]

What's interesting about this is that, whether it's sober or fantastical, the material tends to be *didactic* – intended to positively influence readers' personal growth and development. The elements are fairly consistent. This world is said to be a sort of school which we are born into in order to have experiences, and to which we have to keep returning until certain lessons have been learned. The underlying moral message is constantly repeated. Look at what is wrong in your behaviour, and fix it. Be compassionate towards other people; forget about yourself. Don't waste time trying to make a fortune, or becoming famous, or seeking other people's approval. You can fulfil your intended purpose by living a modest or quiet life, by overcoming difficulties and challenges and serving other people. Control your thoughts and speech, and let no slander pass your lips. Curb your impatience. Start now.

10 *What does evolutionary psychology say?*

However sceptical we may be about religion there's a bottom line in this: a tendency to have these sorts of experiences is *part of the human condition*. Something happens to some people on rare occasions that causes them to see visions or to have insights about the nature of reality, the effect of which is to change behaviours, their own and other people's. I find this fascinating, and I want to know why it happens. And I'm puzzled that it holds so little interest for scientific commentators.

Scientists tend to see the origins of religion in errors of reasoning, and the idea of God as a pre-scientific, mystical explanation of the universe, now redundant since science performs that role far more effectively itself.[47] In this analysis, conscious self-awareness emerged in hominids as a side effect of the reasoning ability that evolved by natural selection as an aid to survival. It was when humans started to become aware of the environment that they recognized the need for causal mechanisms, and to satisfy it they imagined gods, invisible beings who held up the sun, caused the thunder and made the crops grow, and so on.

This by now conventional thinking carries an advantage for scientists such as Richard Dawkins who are also campaigning atheists in that the error is potentially reversible: once humans recognize that it *is* an error they can put it right. That might be one reason why religious-type experiences tend to be overlooked: they complicate the atheistic view which to many people is both scientifically persuasive and morally preferable. In *The God Delusion*, Dawkins acknowledges that some people may be influenced by a personal revelation, but advises them not to expect anyone else to take their word for it who has 'the slightest familiarity with the brain and its powerful workings'.[48]

But that still leaves a rather large question unanswered – why *does* the brain do this? Why do these revelations occur? What is their source? I found it natural to start thinking in terms of some kind of evolutionary adaptation, and I could not understand why those Darwinist commentators such as Dawkins, Daniel Dennett and others who speculate creatively about the origins of religious belief are not more interested in this.

What evolutionary psychologists *have* done is develop theories to account for the development of a moral sense, and these are at least partly relevant. Why, they ask, if we are driven by our genes to compete with other people for resources in order to survive and procreate, are we nevertheless prepared to go out of our way to help them, for instance rushing to give money to earthquake victims? What is the origin of love, empathy and compassion, which religions consider so important?

As is well known, Darwinism supplies two main answers: *kin altruism,* where parents put their children's welfare first to promote the survival of their own genes, and *reciprocal altruism* where help is offered to an unrelated member of the community on the basis that it will one day be returned, and thus benefit the giver.[49] Computer models have demonstrated that offering to co-operate is always the best strategy for personal success. The essential point is that this strategy will only work if individuals in a particular community are able to distinguish between those who keep their bargain, and are to be favoured in the future, and those who welsh on it and must be shunned. It was in evolving this psychological faculty that concepts of fairness and justice – the Golden Rule - came into being among the first humans. As they started to congregate in large groups, social and moral norms became codified in sacred texts, the origin of religious institutions whose essential purpose was to exert social control.

The secular argument then would be that there's a powerful imperative for humans to co-operate as a means to increase opportunities for survival and procreation, and that the command to do so is triggered by neurological events of various kinds. Those who experience it first hand become influencers through religions and the media, and it radiates through society by a memetic process.

It's a start, but it doesn't answer all my questions. Looked at closely, reciprocal altruism falls way short of the demands of religious teachers, whether of the traditional or the New Age variety. Jesus Christ, to take a prominent example, did not advocate a *quid pro quo* you-scratch-my-back type of morality, but a full-on, turn-the-other-cheek self-abnegation: 'give to everyone who asks you, and do not ask for your property back from the man who robs you.'[50] Such absolute selflessness could never be an effective survival strategy, since the giver gets nothing back and makes himself utterly vulnerable – surely not the kind of behaviour that would have been selected by any known evolutionary mechanism. The paradox we are left with is that an instruction which can potentially bubble up from the subconscious requires us to behave in a way that in superficial terms favours genetic continuity, but on closer examination is seen to be actually suicidal.

Perhaps we could argue for some kind of misfunction, as an evolutionist thinker might do in such circumstances. What motivates the saints, seers and prophets is an abnormally exaggerated form of what among the masses is merely an underlying tendency; such individuals should be viewed as freaks. They have experienced an overdose, as also happens sometimes to people whose brains are disturbed by fever, drugs, extreme physical effort or trauma. In other words, a tendency to extreme altruism is only *quantitatively* different from that self-interested altruism which humanity exhibits in general, not distinct in its underlying cause and nature. Perhaps, but for me this is just adding extra layers of speculation, and falls far short of an explanation of just what is occurring in the near-death experience.

11 *'When I was big'*

A complicating factor in much channelled material is the insistence on the reality of reincarnation. Life is not a one-shot affair, it is said, but something that we may experience many times. Some near-death experiencers report a sense of having lived before, and this also arises sometimes in mystical experiences or visions induced by hallucinogens. People very occasionally claim to remember incidents from what they take to be past lives, and surprisingly detailed and convincing memories can be elicited under hypnosis.

On its own, a mere sense of having lived before hardly constitutes evidence of that. Where it starts to get interesting is when the memories of a past life are found to correspond to facts that are later discovered, especially if it can be shown to be unlikely that the details might have been learned in normal ways. But it's difficult to establish this; cryptomnesia – the recall of information come across in the past, books read long ago, or long-forgotten facts – has been demonstrated in some cases, and the epidemic of false memories of childhood sexual abuse in the 1980s was a disturbing reminder of the effects of suggestion. So it's always possible that memory recall, particularly under hypnosis, is some kind of fantasy projection.[51]

On the other hand, with very young children these alternatives are less probable, and there's a large research literature dealing with such cases. The children, as soon as they can speak, start talking about 'when I was big', and express an urgent desire to visit a husband or wife or parents or children in a distant town, any or all of which they may name. They may also talk about the house in which they used to live, their previous occupation, life circumstances and manner of death, which in a disproportionate number of cases they describe as having occurred by violence.

What makes this phenomenon so significant is that many of the statements can be verified: the family the children name may be found to be living in a house that corresponds to their description, and the person they claim to have been did recently die – details that ordinarily they could have no way of knowing. Researchers at the University of Virginia say they have a file of some two thousand seven hundred cases, many of them collected by Ian Stevenson, who worked as a professor of psychiatry there for many years and spent much time travelling in Asia, the Middle East and other parts of the world to investigate such claims.[52]

This 1988 case from Sri Lanka is typical.[53] At three years of age, a girl named Thusitha Silva began to talk about having been pushed into a river by a boy at a town called Kataragama; the boy was mute, she said. She identified her father in this previous life as a farmer named Rathu Herath; he owned a flower shop, was bald and wore a sarong (her present father wore trousers). These details gave a solid lead to the local investigator employed by Stevenson. There had been no attempt by the parents to follow them up and no prior contact between the two families to confuse the issue. Kataragama was over two hundred kilometres away, a small town consisting almost entirely of temples for pilgrims. After going there and asking around, the investigator was able quite quickly to find a flower seller named Rathu Herath who had a mute son. Yes, Herath said, as it happened he *had* once also had a daughter, but some years ago she had accidentally fallen into the river when playing with her brother, and drowned.

Ten of thirteen verifiable statements made by Thusitha corresponded accurately with this man's family. Within a few months the child had made a further seventeen statements, of which two were unverifiable but all the others were found to be correct for the family of the drowned girl.

Some of these statements were too general to be significant, such as the fact that the family's house had a thatched roof and that there were crocodiles in the river. But there were quite specific details that corresponded to the situation of the previous personality. For instance, Thusitha remembered dogs who were tied up and fed meat; this would have been unusual in a country where most dogs are strays, but it turned out the family had neighbours who hunted and who fed meat to a dog they kept chained in their yard. She was also able to describe some of the rituals carried out by worshipping pilgrims, such as smashing coconuts on the ground at the temple, which a child living in a distant village would not ever have witnessed.

Stevenson also argues that birthmarks and congenital defects can be occasionally associated with memories of violent death, and often correspond closely to the claimed manner of dying. In a typical example, a boy is born with a odd stippled brown mark across his throat, As soon as he starts to speak he describes having been murdered by having his throat cut.[54]

A Burmese case involved a child named Ma Win Tar who was born in 1962 with severe defects of both hands.[55] These led to the amputation of several fingers; other of her fingers were either missing or showed constriction rings, as if they had been bound by rope.

There was also a prominent ring around her left wrist that consist-ed of three separate depressions, which, again, looked like grooves made by a rope wound round the arm. All this became significant when, at age three the little girl started to talk, at which time she stated that she had been a Japanese soldier who had been captured by Burmese villagers, tied to a tree and burned alive. She gave no name, and no facts that could be verified. However her description corresponded to the fate of some Japanese soldiers in Burmese vil-lages in the spring of 1945.

Ma was fervent in her insistence that she was Japanese, and re-garded herself as a foreigner, which led to quarrels with her fam-ily. Her behaviour was unusual for a Burmese, but appropriate for the previous life she claimed to remember. She liked to dress as a boy, with short hair, shirts and trousers (Burmese boys, by contrast, normally start by wearing shorts, then graduate to the ankle-length garment known as a *longyi*). She complained too that Burmese food was too spicy, and showed a liking for sweet foods and pork.

Stevenson is particularly interested in the Igbo of Nigeria who believe in *ogbanje* or 'repeater babies' that die deliberately to tor-ment their parents. Such babies may go on being born to the same parents and dying soon after, unless they are prevented from doing so. The Igbo believe they can discourage this by making some minor mutilation, like cutting off a portion of a finger.

This sounds like a rather abhorrent superstition yet, intriguingly, Stevenson says he has identified cases in which children are born with this type of defect that seems to correspond with something that was done to a previous baby that died in the family. The natu-ral explanation for the defect would be sickle-cell anaemia, however Stevenson argues this is unlikely to explain the high incidence of it and its close relation to the mutilation practice.[56]

12 *Wilson et al vs Stevenson*

These claims brought Stevenson a lot of flak from sceptics, for whom reincarnation is no kind of explanation. How, they ask, can one take seriously the idea of continuing to live after death without brain or sense organs; of returning as a baby having previously lived to a mature age; and, as often appears to happen, choosing to be born in poor and overpopulated countries where life is likely to be wretched?

A common criticism is that Stevenson's cases are anecdotal, in the sense that the claims and the investigations of them have been completed long before he arrives on the scene. Shortcomings in his research methods and reasoning in a few individual cases are held to weaken the credibility of all the rest. There are also complaints about his apparent commitment to the reincarnation hypothesis, which might indicate that he is biased. It has been suggested that if one starts looking around for an individual whose life circumstances match those of another person, one will quickly find them.[57]

Fraud again is a popular explanation. In *Reincarnation? The Claims Investigated* (1981), British historian Ian Wilson takes the line that Stevenson was 'cruelly misled' by a series of 'tall stories and acting performances'.[58] Wilson notes that most of the memories are recalled by children in Asian countries like India where the culture accepts reincarnation, and thinks that their parents may have had a motive for perpetrating the hoax. After analysing the data Wilson concludes that the parents of the children claiming to have lived before were mostly in a lower socio-economic class than the families of the claimed previous personality, and they might therefore have hoped for some financial gain.

Wilson also criticizes Stevenson for failing to adequately consider alternative non-paranormal ideas. Perhaps there's such a thing as maternal impressions, where the fetus in some way absorbs some of the mental imagery of the mother. He is concerned that there's no logical pattern in the data, for instance that it gives no guidance about the length of time between incarnations, which may be as long as five years or as little as two weeks. The data also show inconsistent patterns between cultures in terms of changing sex and the interval between lives. If reincarnation was a fact and not a fancy, he believes, memories of previous lives should display the same features across all cultures.

Similar ideas have been mooted by other critics.[59] For instance an alternative to outright fraud might be that an unconscious self-deception occurs, one that is moulded by cultural patterns. One could start with the possibility of cryptomnesia, the child's recall of information picked up from chance meetings with family acquaintances, for instance, or from visits by strangers in the parents' absence. In theory the child could then unconsciously select details of an overheard conversation, which is why they would later be found to correspond with actual events and people. Or else the parents might find significance in something the child says, and interpret it as a past-life memory. They might then seek out a family who they think fits the case; together the two families may embroider the statements in their own minds, perhaps encouraging the child to confirm their ideas by prompting it to recognize other individuals or people in photographs.

A quite different approach sees the child's memories as genuine but questions whether they originate with the child. One idea is that memories can be stored genetically and can in some circumstances be inherited. Or perhaps memories have a life of their own, explicable in some quasi-physical sense as enduring in the environment after their owner's death. Some commentators have talked of survival in terms of a 'psychic factor', a sort of lingering energy or particle field that the human organism might leave behind after dying. For instance it has been suggested that this field may become activated in the consciousness of a medium, giving rise to the appearance of spirit communication.[60] Perhaps a newborn might be affected, at least temporarily, by such a field. The memories might take root in its mind and grow to the extent that the child would not be able to distinguish between them and his own experience. Only when he sees that they have no relevance to his actual circumstances would they start to fade. This field might even cause distinguishing marks, in the same way that a powerful hypnotic suggestion can cause burn marks to appear on a person's skin.[61]

13 *How conclusive are the criticisms?*

I too wondered about the inconsistencies in Stevenson's data. It is suspicious that apparent instances of rebirth in a particular country tend to take the form that is expected in that locality: some with gender changes between lives, some without; some with long gaps between incarnations, others with short gaps or none; a few born exclusively into the same family as the previous personality, but most to other families.

It is perhaps also a shortcoming that Stevenson tends to favour the reincarnation hypothesis, as it puts him at an automatic disadvantage when trying to convince his peers in the academic community. I didn't always agree with him about the significance of certain recollections, and in one or two cases I felt he exposed himself to criticism by unnecessarily convoluted reasoning.[62] I'd have to add that the idea of reincarnation, more than some other things we have been looking at, fills me with apprehension, as I think it does to many people, and I'd be relieved if I thought Stevenson's claims could be adequately explained away.

On the other hand Stevenson was no breathless New Ager: his approach conformed to conventional academic standards, being full, detailed, and presented in a scholarly and unsensational manner. He worked by having colleagues on the spot, who could follow up reports that came in by word of mouth or press reports. The data consists of numerous interviews with the child, the child's parents, other family members, friends and neighbours; and then with the family and friends of the claimed previous personality. Where possible, the business of tracing the family of the previous personality was undertaken by the investigators themselves, before the pitch had been muddied. Stevenson was also quite cautious about drawing conclusions, properly stressing that reincarnation is the last hypothesis we should accept and only after we have eliminated all other possibilities. He discussed the major alternatives in relation to each case and did not ever claim that any case proves reincarnation. It's also the case that other researchers have replicated his findings.[63]

I agreed that Stevenson didn't pay much attention to some of the alternatives that critics like Wilson suggest, such as the ability of the fetus to absorb the mother's mental imagery. But then I reflected that he probably saw no point in advancing ideas which are as conceptually problematical as reincarnation itself; for which there's no independent evidence; and which could only apply in certain cases, in this instance those where the remembered events took place in the mother's vicinity. Much the same applies to the popular idea of genetic memory: you can talk plausibly about the possibility of memory traces being passed through DNA to surface in the infant's mind, as faint whispers and intimations of past events, a sense of *déjà vu* perhaps. But it's hard to see this as more than a very partial explanation, given that the dead person whose life the child appears to be recalling is rarely related to the child; that in many cases he or she died before reaching child-bearing age; and furthermore that the child may appear to have specific memories of an interlude between dying and being reborn.

The idea that the matches between the child's memories and the previous life of the person he or she claimed to be are very general, and might emerge as soon as one starts looking for them, is exactly what might suppose – but only if one doesn't bother to look closely at the research. Take the case of Sunil Dutt Saxena in Stevenson's Indian collection. When Sunil started to speak he mentioned that he had been married, and named the town where he previously lived. In his statements, the previous personality emerged as affluent, with a big house, servants, and what in those days were luxury items such as a fridge and a radio. This is all pretty general stuff. He further claimed to have owned a factory and to have been married four times, which narrows it down a bit. But he also talked of having founded a college named after himself, and identified the principal, who he said had been one of his best friends – the sort of detail which is too exact to apply to more than one person. As it happens all these details – the general, not so general, and the very specific ones – did in fact apply to a deceased individual in the town who Sunil named.[64] In the same volume, there is the case of Jagdish Chandra, who at age three talked of having lived a previous life, and among other things mentioned the names of the former personality's father and brother. He stated that the brother had died of poisoning, and identified the exact location of a safe where the father kept his cash – again, these details were all traced to a person who was recently deceased.[65]

Looking closely at scores of reports of this kind, and bearing in mind the quantity and specificity of the matching details, it was hard to see it as an artefact of over-eager researchers. If it was false it would be much more likely to be a deliberate fraud. But it struck me that the critics are pretty casual in imputing various motives and abilities to infants. The memories typically start to become apparent as soon as the child can talk, which can be as early as eighteen months. It's not obvious to me that very young children, at least up until the age of three or four, might consider it in their interests to abandon their mummy and daddy and go to live with strangers. Infants are not going to know that other people have a different or a better life, and are not able to conceptualize what this might be, let alone know how to achieve it for themselves. One might protest that, on the contrary, many of the children in Stevenson's cases had a very clear idea of a better life compared to their present reduced circumstances, but that's surely the anomaly that has to be explained.

If the deception is the parents' idea, they are obviously going to have to drill the child to deceive investigators. But having experience of small children I found this rather hard to imagine:

> *Father*: Now listen Shreya, when a man comes and asks questions you must say that your name is Thusitha and that you come from Katagarama.
>
> *Child*: But I am Shreya Daddy.
>
> *Father*: Yes, I know my child, but to this man I want you to say it's Thusitha.
>
> *Child*: Why Daddy?
>
> *Father*: Because if you do I will give you a biscuit. Now will you try? We will practise one time. Imagine I am the stranger. Now. What is your name?
>
> *Child*: My. Name. Is. Shreya.
>
> *Father*: No no, I am the stranger and you are to say 'I am Thusitha'. Now try again.
>
> *Child*: But you are not the stranger you are Daddy.

And the children do not just casually mention details of this kind; Stevenson says he was startled by the actual behaviour they often showed, weeping as they talked about a previous life or angrily denouncing the murderers who ended it. A pretence of this depth in an infant is surely rather unlikely. So too, one might say, is reincarnation, but that doesn't resolve the problem. Still, let's suppose that if the parents have a toddler with the appropriate talent, they can get it up to the required level. We then encounter a curious problem. Why is this charade being acted, and what do the parents expect to get out of it?

The fraud idea involves Western stereotypes about stupid, grasping peasants, which anyone with a knowledge of the developing world will consider questionable, to put it mildly. Indian villagers do not find it funny or cute when their three-year-old says things like, 'This house is dirty, I'm getting out of here' or compares their cooking unfavourably with that of another mummy. They won't think it quaint or interesting or to their financial advantage if, as sometimes happens, the child starts to accuse local people of having murdered the person he remembers having been. And while reincarnation is widely believed it's far from universally welcomed: claims that involve a change of religion, sex or caste are greatly disliked, as one might expect.

Nor is the economic motive as obvious as the critics think. Later and larger samples than Wilson's don't support the idea that claims of a previous life are connected with hopes for material advantage: in nearly half of one group of seventy-nine Indian cases the previous personality belonged to a lower socioeconomic class, sometimes living in wretched circumstances, while for a third of cases there was no change. Only a minority showed any upward movement and in many cases it was not enough to constitute evidence of greed.[66] Taken all together it's not surprising that studies show couples taking steps to suppress their child's past-life memories, beating him or, if they have the money, taking him to consult a psychiatrist.[67]

Might the motive for the deceit be found among the relatives of the previous personality? Perhaps, but then how would they have gained sufficient access to another family's child to set the trick up? These are rarely close neighbours, and typically they are in distant locations. Conversely, if the claim originates with the child's parents, it's by no means the case that the target family is going to be particularly motivated to foster the child; in fact, they are the first to suspect fraud. The very least they are going to do is test the child, which in documented cases they do thoroughly, observing his or her reactions and ability to recognize relevant people in person or in photographs. The fact that the child may have highly accurate knowledge of the intimate details of the family history and may correctly identify people that he or she could never have seen before, often using intimate pet names, is what convinces them. But what then? Even if, as often happens, the relations of the previous personality eventually accept the truth of the claim, they are not getting their loved one back; he or she is still in the body of someone else's child in another village, or even another part of the country altogether, and has embarked on a different life, one in which they are not involved.

Returning one more time to cryptomnesia, it's questionable on close examination whether a convincing case could be built on a few details that were heard once or twice. The child's story typically involves descriptions of people and places, names, relationships and incidents that would require a good deal of exposure to some rather obvious source of information. Yet these sources are looked for by investigators and on the whole they are not found. Also self-deception doesn't go far in explaining veridical details of events and affairs which, it can be demonstrated, are not known to the parents and which they couldn't reasonably be expected to know, but which can nevertheless be checked and found to be accurate. This would apply to cases such as that of the drowned girl Thusitha, where investigators reach the scene before the parents have a chance to check out the child's statements themselves, and where the two localities are too far apart for any subliminal information channel to exist. Finally, self-deception doesn't fully explain the phobias – of water, fire or weapons, and so on – that match the nature of the death of the supposed previous personality, for instance drowning, murder or death in battle.

In making these reflections I was influenced, as elsewhere, by the rough and ready nature of the critics' arguments. Some, like Wilson, had clearly given some thought to the problem, but others equally obviously had not. Terence Hines, for instance, says Stevenson's methods are inadequate for ruling out 'simple imaginative story-telling', a pretty sure sign that he hasn't actually read the research, or at least is relying on the fact that his readers have not.[68] And here too, objections are chucked at the problem with little regard for consistency: the same people who denounce the investigators as fools for believing the frivolous claims of greedy villagers can later be found speculating in terms of particle physics to explain what they now seem to be treating as a genuinely anomalous memory transfer.

14 *Is this our destiny?*

As I say, not being personally at all comfortable about the idea of being born again, I would be relieved if these claims turned out to be mistaken. There's something disturbing about these young boys and girls being haunted by the memory of the people they used to be, and the lives they made for themselves – the men and women they loved, the children they parented, the money and status they acquired – finding themselves about to go through the same thing all over again. Is this humans' true destiny. Could it happen to *us*?

The problem is how to explain it away. Finding fault with Stevenson does it for some people, I have noticed, but it doesn't work for me. His methods were not above reproach, but he was generally conscientious and aware of the potential pitfalls, and other researchers have been gathering exactly the same kind of data. The children's statements are too insistent and particular, and correspond too closely with the reality, to be shrugged off, and critics have offered no convincing model based on fraud or error. And the sheer quantity of this data is also extraordinary. If it were just a matter of one or two cases one would be bound to dismiss it as an oddity. But as with many of the topics I have talked about, it's the accumulated effect of reading several scores of documented cases – and knowing that there are several hundreds more of comparable quality in a database of nearly three thousand general cases of the kind – that creates the impression of a genuine and hitherto unacknowledged phenomenon, whatever its true cause.

Some sceptics are reassured by the fact that the data applies predominantly to countries and cultures that believe in reincarnation. We all die, the reasoning goes, and if reincarnation is a fact then we are all reborn, in which case there would be an equal number of cases in the US and Europe. The fact that countries with a Christian heritage don't produce these cases is a strong indication that the phenomenon is a cultural artefact. And why would cases of rebirth correspond to the *beliefs* about rebirth in a particular country if it were not an effect of the imagination?

Against this, it is becoming increasingly clear that children in the West *do* occasionally have these sorts of memories, and if the phenomenon has taken much longer to surface it's perhaps because there's no cultural acceptance of reincarnation, so no context for the memories to take hold in the public consciousness. Crisis apparitions and near-death experiences were widely experienced before active research made them known, and something of the kind may also be the case here. What is different about Western cases is that the children's memories, although surprisingly accurate as regards historical details they could not be expected to know anything about – a two-year-old describing details from the Pacific War in 1944–45, for instance[69] – are far less frequently traced to identifiable individuals.

There is in fact another, perhaps rather surprising, way of accounting for the differences between different cultures, and also for that matter, those that arise in the near-death experience. However this will need to wait until we have put everything into a larger context and tried to determine what we make of it all – the subject of the next and final chapter.

～

SEVEN

PSI
IN THE WORLD

'Science seems to me to teach in the highest and strongest manner the great truth which is embodied in the Christian conception of entire surrender to the will of God. Sit down before fact as a little child, be prepared to give up every preconceived notion, follow humbly wherever and to whatever abysses nature leads, or you shall learn nothing.'
Thomas Henry Huxley

I began my journey wondering whether people who describe a psychic episode are mistaken, or deluded, or the victims of a hoax – as sceptics insist. These things obviously happen, and it must be the place to start when considering paranormal claims. But I no longer doubt that there is here also a distinct and meaningful kind of human experience, one that science is slowly and fitfully getting to grips with.

This is of course a subjective opinion, but on this issue and at this time, surely, there can be no other kind. I'd also insist it's an informed and entirely *rational* position. Yes, people can be absurdly credulous: the popular appetite for sensational tales is evident in tabloid newspapers, satellite television programmes and a host of murky, illiterate websites. But I've learned that a belief in psi and related anomalous phenomena is not always merely a response to uncanny personal experiences or the claims of professional psychics; it also comes from responsible research and experiment, that empirical process which we rely on for our understanding of how the world works. And it astonishes me that so little of what has been established about these things is generally known. After a century and a half of investigation, if we talk about it all we are still like children asking each other after lights out 'Do you believe in ghosts?' The knowledge is there, however inconclusive, but we have chosen to disregard it.

I'm fascinated by this extraordinary disconnect. Why is our society so ignorant about psychic research? Of course the question invites all kinds of retorts: it's not a proper science; parapsychologists haven't made their case; telepathy is scientifically impossible; and so on. But beyond these conventional responses there may be another, very familiar reason: the suspicion we tend to harbour towards radical new ideas, and the difficulties we experience trying to reconcile them with the known and familiar. And really, in this case, how could it be otherwise? Paranormal claims surely pose a challenge not just to our notions of what is possible, but also to what we can *accept*, and to our idea of the kind of world we want this to be.

For if psi is real and not imagined, we may say to ourselves, if minds truly *can* communicate wordlessly with other minds, or see into the future, or cause objects to move capriciously, then what does that say about our belief in an ordered, lawful universe? Does it not strike at the heart of the secular and scientific narrative that we have only recently constructed, and that encourages both technological progress and personal freedoms? Surely it will bring back the worst superstitious practices, from which we thought we had liberated ourselves. And if it's more than telepathy, if mediums really do talk to the dead, does this not powerfully validate religious belief, a force that seems to many to threaten our hopes for future progress?

Such considerations must surely be behind the extraordinarily visceral reactions that the idea of psi tends to evoke. Healthy scepticism is a must, and bizarre claims have to be challenged to the uttermost. But there is something about the scientific response to psychic research that goes well beyond this.

It is surely a matter for wonder the way some well-known scientists insist there is not one *scintilla* of evidence for paranormal claims, when there exist thousands of reports of spontaneous psychic phenomena, many of them documented in large-scale surveys and corroborated to a large degree; when hundreds of controlled psi experiments have produced striking results; when scores of separate investigations of psychics and mediums have concluded that at least some are doing something genuinely inexplicable in conventional terms; and all this has been reported, analyzed and debated at enormous length by scientists, philosophers and intellectuals in books and specialist peer-reviewed journals in many countries for over a century. To be sure, I sometimes wonder whether disbelievers aren't just using the term 'evidence' in its narrowest sense, meaning 'conclusive proof'. But I don't think they are. They don't often bother to dispute the evidence. They say there isn't any.

This is deeply curious to watch. I'm thinking, for instance, of Lewis Wolpert, a professor of developmental biology at London University and a former chairman of the Committee for the Public Understanding of Science. When Wolpert – gamely standing next to Rupert Sheldrake to argue the case against telepathy in front of an audience of believers – seems unable to grasp Sheldrake's arguments, is indifferent to his research, and can't even bring himself to watch his video presentation, one senses a mind up against a mental barrier, unable to accommodate something so profoundly antithetical to a lifetime's conditioned thinking.[1]

Wolpert seems vaguely aware of what the claims are but is unable to engage with them in a meaningful way. In his recent book *Six Impossible Things Before Breakfast* he makes a series of familiar assertions. Critics who have examined ganzfeld experiments consider them flawed. Mediums work by cold reading. A fake psychic stunt by Michael Shermer was 'very impressive and persuasive'. Studies by Richard Wiseman provide ordinary explanations for hauntings and mediums. Stories about poltergeists are legion, but why do psychics never do useful things, like change lead into gold or prevent ageing?[2]

The scientist doesn't say much about these things, but canters through the list as though the mere mention of them will carry his case. I get no sense that he understands at all what it is he is explaining away. If he knows about Roll's investigation of the Miami disturbances, or Hodgson's work with Piper, or Gurney's *Phantasms* or the Stargate remote-viewing experiments, or Sabom's or Van Lommel's work on near-death experiences, or any of the other research that powerfully suggests the operation of psychic functioning, he is keeping it to himself. He might have referred to the work and ideas of parapsychologists, but instead displays an innocent trust in debunking sceptics. Who, really, was impressed by Shermer's psychic stunt, apart from his audience of disbelievers? And yes it's true, as Wiseman demonstrates, that Victorian séance mediums played tricks in the dark, but it's trivial, as no one could dispute it – the compelling evidence was gained in conditions of good light.

Again, it's not that caution and scepticism are not hugely necessary in dealing with paranormal claims, but that commentary on this level is too weak to be of any real value. It purports to clarify, but in fact misleads. That is also the case with Richard Dawkins, who must know about parapsychologists' experimental work, and if he wished could also inform himself about their field research, upon both of which the case for psi largely rests. Yet one searches his work in vain for any serious reference to either; he mostly prefers to laugh and point.

And I know from my own experience how persuasive the critics can be. Approaching the subject as a novice, I thought it unlikely that scientists of the calibre of Sagan and Dawkins could be wrong about something so potentially significant. In their own fields their insight and passion are hugely inspiring. I was disillusioned to discover that their sense of certainty about this subject did not result from any serious investigation. It just doesn't engage their interest. They parade a few facts and allegations, speculate off the top of their heads and make declarations in an authoritative manner that suggests to the uninitiated they know what they are talking about.[3] Their analysis, if that is the right word, largely lacks either familiarity with the subject or viable insights, yet such are their reputations it may be praised and repeated by readers, journalists and reviewers as if it actually meant something.

It's shameful, too, to see reputable scientists so completely taken in by James Randi's Million Dollar Challenge. Not the least successful of the conjuror's illusions has been his ability to pose as a neutral arbiter on this subject while simultaneously cheering his audience with his contempt for 'woo-woo'. In supporting him so uncritically, sceptical scientists have elevated the prejudices of an entertainer over the findings of researchers who are doing the real work.

Certainly, I can understand why so many sceptics and scientists are persuaded that psi does not exist by the fact that no-one has won Randi's prize. Had I not undertaken my own research, I might have thought so as well. Randi himself laments that none of the stars in the psychic firmament – John Edward or Uri Geller, for instance – has entered for it, which might indeed suggest that they don't dare risk being caught out by the master; such tests as they have submitted to have been carried out by scientists, whose powers of observation are allegedly inferior.[4] Another view, of course, is that, unlike the naïve individuals who actually do apply for the prize, they have more sense than to put themselves in the hands of a crusading sceptic who considers them the scum of the earth.

But my main point is to question how a single individual has acquired such a remarkable degree of influence. Surely this is a job for *science*. Of course there's a role for stage magicians to play in investigating some psychic claims, as parapsychologists readily acknowledge. Why should they not do the job together? Then again, professional psychics and people with 'special abilities' are just a small part of the picture, and to consider them the only source of the phenomenon is unduly restrictive. To offer an analogy: the difference between parapsychology and Randi's prize is the difference between a fleet of boats heading out to sea equipped with radar and large nets, and one man sitting beside a muddy stream waiting for fish to jump into his lap.

As I have suggested, it helps to look at the problem from the opposite point of view. If something such as telepathy were true, *how would we know?* Only when we seriously consider this can we start to appreciate the extraordinary challenge parapsychologists face in convincing their mainstream colleagues. If we are tempted to respond that it's an unreasonable question, on the grounds that such a thing could not possibly occur, then we are half way to understanding why such claims remain unacknowledged.

In the end, it's easy *not* to know about something. If it is perfectly camouflaged, sitting quietly in the background, hardly drawing attention to itself, and if, in addition, we are appalled by the idea of it, and would get anxious if we thought it was really there, then obviously we will never find it. We will continue to adopt a defensive posture, dismissing vague reports that come to our ears now and then with a smile and a wave of the hand.

2 *Psi and science*

At the head of this chapter I cited a favourite quote, by Thomas Henry Huxley, on the need to sit down before fact 'as a little child' – prepared to see the world with fresh eyes. He, of course, was arguing for science and against religious belief; he had no time at all for psychic research. But in some ways his remark might equally be directed at sceptics of the paranormal. Psychic experience – or psychic-*seeming*, at least – *is* fact, and it needs to be examined without preconceptions if it is to be properly understood. In reality this sort of openness is very hard to achieve. We aren't innocent children, alive to any new ideas and experiences that come our way; on the contrary, by the time we reach thirty most of us are primed to repel anything that does not fit with that bundle of facts, assumptions, preconceptions, prejudices and half-truths that we call a worldview.

Scientists surely are no exception to this, however eminent; once their minds are made up they can be particularly susceptible to rigid thinking. And to be fair, it would be hard for an evolutionary biologist suddenly to agree to start questioning the principles that inform his entire life's work, any more than the theologians with whom Huxley battled over the subject of evolution were about to abandon their Christian dogmas. A respect for the objective truth, and a passion to identify it, however unpalatable, are vanishingly rare: most of us, most of the time, busily arrange the facts to suit our self-interest.

Even the most imaginative scientists can exhaust their capacity to respond to challenging new ideas. Albert Einstein was hostile to the claims of quantum scientists, which we consider to be odd in the genius who discovered relativity. But there are yet more egregious examples. Lord Kelvin, a leading figure in late nineteenth-century physics, insisted that the newly-invented radio technology had no future; he also thought that x-rays would prove to be a hoax.[5] A well-known astronomer claimed to have 'proved scientifically' that flight was impossible just weeks before the Wright brothers first took to the skies.[6] And when Thomas Edison invented the electric light bulb, a professor wrote to a newspaper to protest on behalf of 'true science' that Edison's experiments were a 'fraud upon the public', while another opined that he obviously didn't understand electricity at all.[7]

Against this, one could argue that a consensus is eventually reached in most things, and the best evidence will always win out.

For all its manifest weirdness, quantum mechanics is demonstrably true. X-rays are reliable medical aids, aeroplanes fly, electric light illuminates, and so on. Psi is quite clearly not in that category, and perhaps never will be; for all the declarations by some paranormalists that its discovery will usher in a new world of possibilities – of which I am personally sceptical – this is not about new technology. Instead, like Darwin's ideas about evolution, psi offers a radical perspective on human existence, and exactly for that reason, like evolution, it is fiercely fought over, a battleground for competing ideologies.

Parapsychologists are natural disciples of the philosopher Thomas Kuhn, who argued that scientific change is an essentially revolutionary process. A particular 'paradigm' – a framework of assumptions – may eventually collapse under the pressure of observed anomalies and in so doing give way to a radically different interpretation, most famously the Copernican shift from an earth-centric to a helio-centric view of the universe.

The new paradigm typically emerges not because supporters of the old one become converted, Kuhn thought, but because they eventually give way to a new generation which takes more readily to new ideas.[8] Or as the quantum pioneer Max Planck remarked, scientific progress 'proceeds funeral by funeral'. Unsurprisingly, parapsychologists look forward to a similarly radical shift towards a view of the universe in which their own discipline is fully recognized.

How would this occur? The history of science suggests that apparently outlandish ideas – which, like psi, are based on observed anomalies – are accepted only when a mechanism or underlying cause can be demonstrated. In 1912 Alfred Wegner put forward his theory of continental drift as a logical explanation of observed data, but it was derided by geologists until the development of plate tectonics in the 1960s. Similarly, in the late eighteenth century the Italian physiologist Lazzaro Spallanzani established experimentally that bats use their ears to guide them in the dark. However, the explanation promoted by other scientists, and generally accepted, was that they used nerves in their wingtips to avoid bumping into objects, even though this was based entirely on conjecture. Spallanzani's findings were only vindicated in the twentieth century when the principle of navigation by echo-location was discovered.[9]

Another view would be that the breakthrough is not going to come from new evidence, or from some dramatically successful new experimental protocol that someone may one day come up with, but rather from better knowledge of the existing research. It would mean that scientists cease to rely only on debunking conjurors and psychologists for information, and start to familiarize themselves with parapsychologists' data and arguments. Here at least the Internet is providing the conditions for progress; there's no need any longer to travel to specialist libraries, as many of the primary sources can be found online, along with comment and debate. So anyone who wants to get to grips with the subject can now do so with far less effort than would have been required ten years ago.[10]

Encouragingly, books are starting to appear by scientifically literate writers that give parapsychology the kind of intelligent, rational attention I believe it merits. Two recent ones stand out: Elizabeth Lloyd Mayer's *Extraordinary Knowing,* which I briefly referred to earlier, and *Outside the Gates of Science: Why It's Time for the Paranormal to Come in from the Cold* by the science fiction writer Damien Broderick.[11] Significantly, as is often the case, both writers' interest in psychic research seems to have been triggered by experiencing psi close up. For them it was no longer just an abstraction or something that other people claim, as it is for sceptics; it clearly happened and they wanted to understand it better.

It's notable that both Mayer and Broderick maintain a clear boundary. Their interest is in psi: that is, telepathy, clairvoyance, precognition and psychokinesis. They are not much interested in allied claims that consciousness survives death, which they rather quickly dismiss. They see a distinction between personal experience that can be validated by recent scientific experiments, on the one hand, and on the other the activities of mediums, of which they appear to remain suspicious. That reflects the feelings of many parapsychologists themselves: it's hard enough to draw other scientists' attention to successful psi experiments without the added burden of being associated with research into ghosts and mediums, and some would prefer that the discipline formally disassociated itself from the question of survival altogether.[12]

If the study of psi could be somehow detached from its esoteric baggage, and be isolated as a purely scientific project, it might go some way to making parapsychology less controversial. In fact I think it's at least possible that, as the literature of psychic research and experimental parapsychology become better known – as also the logical absurdities that can arise when anomalous experiences are 'explained away' – psi-research will start to attract more attention within the academic community, particularly among those whose disciplines can make a direct contribution: physicists, statisticians, psychologists, physicians, anthropologists, philosophers, sociologists and historians, among others.

The expectation would be that an expanded science will one day satisfactorily explain psi, perhaps in terms of quantum theory and multiple universes.[13] Or perhaps artificial intelligence experts, joining forces with neuroscientists, will successfully recreate human consciousness in all its complexity, confirming that the computational approach to the brain is essentially correct. One day robots may be so advanced they will actually be conscious, ego-driven beings like ourselves, as some artificial intelligence enthusiasts insist has to happen.[14] Who knows, when these self-aware machines break down, perhaps they too will have visions of an afterlife, which will then be proved to have been all along a mere aberration of the enormously complex informational system we call the mind.

3 *Doubts about survival of consciousness*

This thinking would be problematic for those who are used to thinking of ghosts and spirits and suchlike as evidence of life after death. But should they accept that the appearance of humans surviving death is just that, an illusion that we naively misunderstand?

Doubts about survival of consciousness were rife even among those early researchers like Frederic Myers who were disposed to believe it. For these were rational thinkers; the veridical information that forced them to accept the reality of psi did not extend to doing the same for survival.[15] The evidence in that respect was never entirely coercive: while that information presents itself as coming from surviving spirits of the recently deceased – however convincingly – it's extremely difficult to prove it does not actually originate in the minds of living people.

In séance situations this wasn't just a possibility, it clearly happened. A sitters' particular interests and preoccupations often emerged in the communications; for instance if a personality identifying itself as Charles Dickens communicated, it might well be discovered that one of the sitters had recently been reading *Bleak House*; it was as though the material in the front of her memory provided the content for an unconscious confabulation. There are notable instances of 'spirits' communicating in sittings whose identities had simply been made up for the occasion,[16] as well as historical figures whose personalities – as conveyed by their speech and behaviour – conformed to an erroneous public idea of what they were like that differed from the reality.[17] This sort of thing has alarming implications for the rest of the research.

It was apparent from the proxy sittings and book tests that mediums could at least sometimes access true information by means other than person-to-person telepathy. But these experiments still didn't exclude the possibility of the information being stored in some cosmic databank, which the medium might access by some sort of unconscious free-ranging process. By the 1930s, when Joseph Rhine and his associates were demonstrating psi to be potentially a general human faculty – and not merely the gift of a few freaks – it was being argued that *any* information that appeared to come from a deceased spirit could more economically be explained purely in terms of the psychic faculties of the medium and other living individuals, whether known or unknown. This reasoning has come to be known as the 'super-ESP' or 'super-psi' theory and, despite its fantastical character, the lack of understanding of psi's underlying causes makes it difficult to rule out entirely.[18]

Sceptics can also point to the failure of any medium to gain unequivocal proof of survival, proof of a kind that might put the matter beyond doubt. Various people have left behind codes or messages that they promised to try to convey through a medium after they are deceased, but no code has so far been unambiguously cracked.[19] If mediums really are in touch with the dead, this failure requires explanation.

Psi can be used to explain away other phenomena that look like survival. We have seen how the movement of objects during poltergeist episodes can be regarded as an effect of living minds, and the same may be true also of apparitions: Louisa Rhine argued from her 1950s survey that these are best considered a psychic illusion generated by the percipient. Out-of-body perception, too, whether in healthy people or in hospital patients, can possibly be explained as a psi-mediated hallucination, in which the veridical information is gained by clairvoyance, while the other features – the tunnel, the meetings with deceased relatives and angels – are simply a dramatic production that helps the ego assuage its fear of annihilation.

Or perhaps a deceased person's mind does survive, but only for a while, in the same way that ripples continue to form on the surface of a pond after a stone has been thrown into it. What we naively take to be spirit communications are actually the automatic reflexes of the psychic organism winding down.[20] As I mentioned earlier, something like this might explain children's memories of past lives, as floating wisps of dead people's memories that float around in space and somehow get into the minds of newborns, who then claim them as their own.

To a believer in survival all this might seem far-fetched. But to a sceptic – in this context, someone who accepts the reality of psi but not of survival – it's a way out, achieved through the reasonable application of Occam's razor. According to this thinking, a world that encompasses psi certainly needs to be described in different scientific terms to those we are used to, but it is not necessarily any less naturalistic. But a world in which humans come and go as immortal spirits is an utterly different proposition, one that appears to validate religious belief and all the baggage that comes with it.

Furthermore, we cannot overlook the fact that, to the rational mind, the notion of surviving death is quite fantastic. Our sense of self is bound up with our personality, our thoughts and memories. Yet personality seems to depend on the brain; relatives of someone with Alzheimer's or a brain injury often observe that he or she has become a quite different person to the one they once knew. Logically, then, it makes sense to suppose that the demise of the brain extinguishes the personality altogether.

And, anyway, what exactly is supposed to survive in the absence of the body? Leaving aside the question of where an afterlife might be situated, it's quite baffling as to what kind of experiences we might have. As philosopher Julian Baggini points out, we don't know how this very 'unhuman' form of life could be the vehicle for the continuation of our very human selves. 'Life as a disembodied soul is a very different kind of existence from the one we have now,' Baggini says, 'and it is unclear how such an afterlife could be a continuation of this life at all. Rather it would seem to be a radical break, with some very different kind of entity coming into existence after we die. Something would live after our death, but it is not clear it would be us.'[21]

4 *Arguments in favour of survival*

This is all true, yet those who prefer to take the evidence at face value have some arguments on their side.[22] One that many people have been struck by is the appearance of Frederic Myers, Edmund Gurney and others in the psychic research community, following their deaths in the beginning of the twentieth century, trying to communicate to their surviving colleagues the fact of their continued existence. This unexpected development came to light when certain women who practised automatic writing and who lived in different parts of the world – including the medium Leonora Piper in America, Rudyard Kipling's sister Alice Fleming in India, and the writer and social activist Dame Edith Lyttelton in Britain – began finding what appeared to be messages from these men in their scripts. For the most part these were not conventional 'spirit communications' of the kind that mediums pass on in sittings, but erudite allusions to classical Greek and Latin literature, in which these men had all been well versed. Intriguingly, the snippets made no sense on their own, but when pieced together later at the Society for Psychical Research they created a coherent and meaningful whole. The point, clearly, was to try to rule out any suggestion that the messages might be the spurious product of a single medium's mind, vastly increasing the likelihood that they came from discarnate sources. This web of 'cross-correspondences' was so complex and striking that it convinced most of their colleagues of the deceased researchers' continued existence. Even some sceptics have been impressed by it.[23]

Then there's the fact that spiritualist circles have sometimes found themselves in contact with an unseen personality unknown to any of their members, whose account of itself is subsequently found to correspond closely to someone who actually lived. These so-called 'drop-in communicators' gave the impression of having chanced upon the circle and taken the opportunity to interact; the detailed information they give – name, place of residence, circumstances of their life and death – checks out in documentary sources.[24] The phenomenon might possibly be dismissed as a hoax, but it would be an extremely complex one, given the obscurity of the sources, while the independent indications that mediumship is a paranormal process militates against it. Cryptomnesia is a possible explanation in some cases, from a medium or sitter having once been exposed to a newspaper article or obituary and unconsciously retaining some details, but there are others in which this can be ruled out.

Arguments in favour of survival can also be made from other categories of experience. Repressed emotion in living people is quite likely to be a cause of some poltergeist incidents, such as the case of Tina Resch. But there have been documented instances in which no single individual appeared to observers to be the focus of the disturbance, and others in which there did seem to be an active external intelligence. Here there's a sense that the movements are purposeful and intended to attract attention, which inclines some investigators to think that discarnate entities are involved.[25] A small but growing category of research focuses on apparent attempts by the recently deceased to communicate the fact of their survival by displacing objects in rooms occupied by friends and family members.[26]

As we saw, 'crisis' hallucinations point to some telepathic disturbance at the moment of death, but don't necessarily indicate that the individual survived beyond it. Somewhat more suggestive are simultaneous sightings of someone known to be dead by two or more people, or an apparition that is later recognized in photographs – although these are less common. There are also interesting inferences to be made from reports of apparitions of living people, which sometimes apparently can be induced experimentally, as I described in Chapter Five. An apparition projected by a living person of himself or herself to a friend or family member in a distant location – whether intentionally or not – has been shown to be precisely similar, across a broad range of characteristics, to an apparition of a person who is recognized and known to have been dead for days, weeks or years.[27] If such episodes are subjective hallucinations, then that's to be expected of course. But if we accept, on the basis of the veridical information these episodes contain, that they are *not* subjective hallucinations, then the concordance increases the likelihood that they are *both* projections of living minds, even if one of them is discarnate and normally imperceptible to us.

The fact that all these things *look* so much like survival perhaps also needs to be taken into account. Among them, the unexplained minor 'poltergeist' incidents experienced by a family shortly after a bereavement; the apparition of the person that appears at the moment of his or her death; repeated and evidential contacts appearing to come from the recently deceased through mediums; the hospital patient who feels a glorious sense of life apart from her body and encounters deceased relatives. All these in different ways suggest survival of consciousness. If they don't mean what they seem to mean, then what *do* they mean?

The least we can say is that, as a by-product of consciousness, the human species has created an enormously complex, life-like illusion that the ego in some way survives the death of the body. And this illusion is far more realistic than sceptics, with their scanty knowledge of the research, will be able to recognize.

Mediums, for instance, do not just convey information that a deceased person would have known, but also that person's character and mannerisms. They come up with typical jokes and asides and reveal highly specific preoccupations, which one would think are more difficult to identify, and would in any case require real acting ability. There are documented cases of interactions between living and deceased family members continuing for years through mediums, and if this interaction *was* illusory one wonders why it did not eventually become obvious.[28] How could people not grasp that the entity they were talking to was never anything more than an animated memory, a marionette of the medium's imagination? It does not seem coherent to talk of a memory, or a shade, or some enduring psychological disposition – or however else we describe it – demonstrating will and emotion, and exciting a sense of recognition in living friends or relatives.

It's the manner of its delivery that often convinces sitters as much as the content itself, as in this example from a Leonora Piper sitting:

> Then came the greeting from my father and a description of the life there, and of his first day there, and that his only unhappiness was that he could not tell me how well it was with him. He had found so many of his friends there—his father and mother and my mother. He spoke of the home here and of my step-mother, and of much known to him alone. He spoke of the life at some length and in words and manner peculiar to himself. My father had been a great student, with an intense love of books, and always expressed his thoughts with a piquant, caustic, ready eloquence, as rare as it was peculiar to himself. Anyone who had ever heard my father speak could not mistake the beautiful and rounded phraseology of his address to us. It could be no one but my father.[29]

If it is not the father communicating, we would have to acknowledge that the medium, besides ransacking the sitter's memory, is showing extraordinary powers of dramatic reconstruction. There is a sense of artistry here, of an intelligence striving to create an appearance of verisimilitude, and without any obvious means of identifying the model that it needs to match.

Often it's the little details that pull you up. I'm thinking for instance of the young couple who believe themselves to be in contact, through an entranced medium, with their recently deceased young daughter. The child inquires after a favourite toy horse, and then, when they produce it at a second sitting, retorts it was actually not that little horsey she meant but the *big* one, which she describes and they then recall.[30] If that little girl's mind, memory and personality have not survived death, then what *is* happening here? What is the point of this exchange, if not to make the illusion more convincing than it might otherwise be? *And who or what is making that calculation?*

5 *But is it conceivable?*

If these ideas are unfamiliar to you, it's not surprising; the research has not in the past been easily accessible and remains little known. When the subject of survival comes up most of us naturally fall back on conventional religious ideas and preconceptions.

Philosopher Julian Baggini, for one, argues that belief in life after death can only be based on faith, since the evidence and good reasons required for a rational argument that it exists are lacking. True, mediums sometimes make correct statements, he says, but then there are bound to be occasional uncanny coincidences and lucky guesses. If there were genuine communication between the living and the dead, he thinks, there would surely be many more accurate and otherwise inexplicable communications. The fact that they are so rare suggests they are not genuine, but frauds, guesses, and coincidences.[31]

But Baggini appears here simply to be following the intellectual consensus that survival of death is a discredited concept. He could not reasonably talk in this way if he had read the investigative literature of psychic research. And why would he have read it, as long as it is considered dubious and unscientific? The relevant books and journals won't be in the libraries he frequents: he would have to go out of his way to find them. And if he then became interested, and wanted to talk about it, who around him would be willing to take him seriously?

On the other hand, the near-death experience has been a big subject of discussion in recent years, and it surprises me a little that this, too, has hardly modified secular certainties. After all, the phenomenon provides a striking empirical justification for afterlife belief and poses all kinds of challenges for science. Clearly, it does not satisfy our questions about what long-term experiences we might have after death: it's widely taken for granted that there's nothing we can usefully say about that, as we can't visualize it. There's no data and it's pointless to speculate. But that is not necessarily the case: there exists a quite large body of material said to have been 'channelled' by deceased individuals through professional mediums – also through ordinary people who have developed some mediumistic ability, usually by automatic writing – which offers detailed information about the afterlife state.[32]

These texts, at the very least, falsify the widely-held view that survival of consciousness can't be conceived of or rationally discussed. Christians and Muslims do not bother much with details of afterlife: it's difficult to attach sense to churchy expressions like being 'caught up in God's glory', and the Quran's promise of banquets and virgins only satisfies the most primitive appetites. Spiritualist literature, by contrast, offers quite a lot of detail. Agreed, the notion of dead people writing books is problematic, and these scripts need to be treated with caution. We're bound to assume on some level that their living scribes simply imagine they are getting information from an external source, if not actually making it up. But whether true or not, the ideas are interesting, and if, as I have argued, mediumship is a psychic phenomenon, and not an effect of cold reading or out-and-out fraud, it makes sense to add them into the mix.

What the communicators describe is a sense of continuity, in a sort of replica existence of what they are used to. They are still *people*, relating with each other, and their impression of solidity is no less strong than ours, they insist. They have no sense that their bodies and their surroundings are not real, any more than they did while living in this world. Yet in some strange way this quasi-physical environment is malleable; external events are directly mediated by their thoughts. To create an object or a situation simply requires a flip of the imagination; to think of having a cup of tea is to find oneself holding it in one's hand – there is no intermediate process of going into the kitchen to put on a kettle.

I can remember once thinking how ludicrous this is, the idea that mediums have of dead folk pottering around their houses and doing mundane things like drinking tea. It seemed banal and a bit sad. But having spent some time reading and re-reading the scripts – and often between the lines – it now looks to me to be a more complex proposition than at first appears. I suspect much of the problem is that we latch onto trivial details because they are what is meaningful to us. In fact a lot of the communicators stress that the appearance of continuity in outward forms is just that, an appearance, and not necessarily one that persists for long. In a subjective thought-world, the exterior that one experiences is largely an expression of collective memory and habits of thought. In this environment, an emotionally well-adjusted individual would thrive, while one is who habitually depressed, angry or emotionally repressed, or has entrenched criminal tendencies, might encounter something far more bleak and unpleasant.

From here I began to see how these ideas relate to conventional religious concerns. Traditional theism is shaped by the political and social contours of the ancient world, with God conceived as the all-powerful ruler who admits loyal supporters to the inner sanctum and banishes traitors to the dungeons. The insight of modern religious thinking is that, on the contrary, progress is won not through allegiance to a deity but by spiritual growth, and this is abundantly reflected here. Moral virtue is not a currency to be exchanged for a ticket to paradise, but rather the development of mental habits that make a heaven out of existence. It is not a transaction; we are simply being encouraged to create the conditions for our own future well-being.

Of course, it's still very hard to imagine what being dead is actually like, how one fills the time, and so on. For many people – and this is a problem especially for scientists and intellectuals – the worry is that afterlife would be a vegetative existence, where rational pursuits are no longer possible. It doesn't help that communicators tend to be quite evasive about their external reality and what they do: most of their discourse is characterized by a sort of abstract preachiness. I found this frustrating, and it added to my general suspicions that the speakers aren't what they claim to be.

But I also noticed they talk constantly about *feeling*, and eventually I recognized the possible relevance of that. We feel in all sorts of ways – joy, exhilaration, frustration, anger, grief – and from all sorts of causes – a love affair, a bereavement, a fight with a life partner or work colleague, a race won, a contract clinched, and so on – but these are usually ripples on the otherwise placid surface of daily existence, the exception, not the rule. Most of us, most of the time, aren't conscious of feeling very much at all. In this other existence, by contrast, feeling is said to have become central. Theirs is not the experience of reasoning and acting, but of experiencing the inner reality of themselves, of what they are and what they have become, and the external forms that creates.

If we try making this mental switch we can perhaps start to glimpse what being dead might feel like – and also why it's so very hard to explain. Recall a past moment of great satisfaction: the world takes on a rosy glow; we read in people and objects the inner contentment that we feel. Nothing can disturb us; we are above it all, smiling inwardly. Then imagine that state sustained indefinitely, in constantly changing forms. That fits too with communicators insisting that their sense of time is quite different from ours. Time ceases to be relevant: it is not a case of events experienced one after another, but of an eternal 'now'. And where for most of us these states of heightened emotion are temporary, there they become the permanent reality. The conclusion would be that what, to our ears, sounds like tiresome sermonizing may contain the essential instructions as to how this future state of exaltation is to be achieved, and how to avoid the converse reality – sustained discomfort or worse.

Underlying all this is the implication that communicators initially do not understand that much of what they take to be real consists of thought forms, or that they are aware how suggestible their minds have become. The individuals who believe they are living in their houses and carrying on much as before have not progressed far beyond the basic level. This susceptibility to illusion might also explain some of the things that puzzled psychic researchers about communicators, for instance why they sometimes claimed fictitious identities or vouched for the genuineness of surviving 'spirits' whose identities had been made up; in such cases their minds were being influenced by ideas in the mind of the medium and sitters.

We tend to assume that with the idea of an afterlife we are dealing with a single reality and that post-mortem existence can be explained in terms that apply to everyone. But perhaps we should consider post-mortem existence to be like the life we are living now, in which we share the same biological and terrestrial reality with other humans, but experience wildly differing environments and circumstances. If it is true that minds survive with their memories, it must also be the case that the beliefs held by these minds largely survive as well – in all their chaotic variety. In other words, there are here the conditions for the survival of different social groups and communities, whose members subscribe to a common set of ideas about themselves and about their relation to each other and to their environment, but which do not necessarily accord with those of other groups.

This is a possible approach to explaining those characteristics of psychic phenomena which to sceptical analysts seem obviously to imply a cultural conditioning. The fact that near-death experiences vary in content between ages and cultures would indicate not that humans have different conceptions of what an afterlife should be – and that the experience is therefore shaped by their imaginations

– but rather the reverse, that the post-mortem experience they undergo reflects the surviving cultural characteristics of their society or ethnic group. Similarly with reincarnation: if cultural variations continue to apply in the early stages of post-mortem existence, an individual who found himself suddenly bereft of life – murdered or killed in an accident – and wanted quickly to return, or was pressured into it, might do so in ways that conform with his own ideas, and those of the discarnate community in which he found himself, of how such things are done.

These sorts of considerations might help illuminate an issue that I left unresolved in the last chapter: why is it that in some out-of-body experiences – those described by James Randi and Susan Blackmore, specifically – features of the environment that looked realistic at the time were afterwards found to be at odds with reality. On the face of it, we have no choice but to consider such experiences as illusory, and in Blackmore's case this insight has helped to form the basis of a determinedly materialist approach to the whole phenomenon. But if we can accept the logic of survival (a big 'if' of course) then we have another category to work with: a state of consciousness, the 'astral' (as it is commonly described in specialist literature) in which the external environment, although objectively real, is also influenced by the beholder's memory and imagination.

6 *Psi and superstition*

Returning to this world, I want to explore in more detail the issues I touched on right at the beginning of this chapter: How can we reconcile ourselves to the implications of psi? And in what sense, specifically, might a growing general belief in the reality of psychic phenomena amount to the retrograde step that some scientists fear?

To argue that sceptics' arguments against psi are poorly informed is not to dismiss all their underlying concerns as unfounded. On the contrary, there are live issues here. Does an endorsement of psi imply a relaxation of scientific standards? How far should we go in this respect? If we accept the reality of psi, then why not also of homeopathy, or any other health treatment that lacks any conceivable basis in known science? After all, like psi, these alternative therapies can often point to at least some positive studies. Why not make a case also for astrology, or creationism, or for that matter any of the other stuff that fills paranormal encyclopaedias: Big Foot, Bible codes, Dianetics, palmistry, crop circles, alien abductions, ley lines, reflexology, and so on?

In an age which we like to think is rational, at least compared to previous eras, humans are still surprisingly prone to fearful and irrational behaviour. The appalling consequences of false-memory syndrome in the 1980s, in which some regression therapists falsely persuaded their patients that they had been abused by their parents, are a warning that even in our enlightened age we can still fall victim to dangerous delusions. Similarly, the rush by overzealous health professionals to diagnose so-called 'Munchausen by proxy' – a condition said to involve abuse of children by their mothers – is now acknowledged to have destroyed perfectly normal families. It hardly needs to be pointed out that the utterly subjective basis upon which these tragic decisions were made also fuelled the witchcraft persecutions of the sixteenth and seventeenth centuries, an occurrence we are naturally appalled and disgusted by, but which we believe to be ancient history.

We can't shrug off the fact that a scientific endorsement of psi might potentially open the door to the worst kinds of superstition. Take psychokinesis. How do we know when it is active and when it is merely imagined? The very idea implies that people and machines may be vulnerable to human mentation – something no one can calmly contemplate. It's one thing if it happens and we don't know about it. That's to say, full-blown, grade-A poltergeist episodes of the kind that make it onto the six o'clock news may be extremely rare, but minor episodes could be occurring more frequently, and just not rising above the threshold of public awareness. As University of Maryland philosopher Stephen Braude points out, psychic interactions of which we have no notion at all may be happening all the time.[34] We may unconsciously by our thoughts be doing things like influencing the cycle of traffic lights or even causing a despised work colleague's computer to crash.

As long as these interactions are imperceptible, and science says they can't happen, we are protected from the implications. But that could change dramatically if psychokinesis received a degree of validation. To acknowledge an invisible external influence – whether or not it is explicable in scientific terms – is effectively to suggest that a person may hex an enemy, causing harm or even death. It does not have to be true; if the possibility is endorsed by a central authority it introduces a new element in human relations, and powerfully fuels suspicion and fear, the slander that can be thought and declared but never proved – just as happens in African societies that remain infected by *juju* beliefs, with deadly consequences for innocent people. In this sense, science would come to sanction primitive magic – an unthinkable prospect.

Then if psi is held to equate with the survival of consciousness after death, this carries implications for a raft of social issues. If an essential living principle pre-exists in some form before incarnating in the world as a human being, and continues to live afterwards, and may quickly reincarnate, how does this impact on social policy? Is abortion really murder as conservative Christians insist? How should we view cloning or the use of genetic science to eliminate disabilities? What about euthanasia? Is it wrong to end a life prematurely, even to limit human suffering? If we think we cannot die, then why attach any value to earthly existence at all? We can quietly bump off our elderly relatives to get our hands on the inheritance, on the grounds that it won't cause them any real harm and may even be doing them a favour. For that matter we can check ourselves into a termination clinic when we think we have had enough of earthly toils, in the expectation not of annihilation, but a new life of comfort and ease.

These worries are hypothetical in the absence of any serious interest in psi among the opinion-forming elite. Clearly I cannot offer even halfway definitive answers; the point of raising the issues at all is to acknowledge the barriers, perhaps mainly unconscious, that stand in the way of accepting psi as a fact of life. Any paradigmatic shift could not be a matter just for science: it would involve personal, social and political adjustments as well.

However there are a few points that I think are worth making. With regard to scientific authority, I agree that we should proportion our belief according to the evidence. To acknowledge that the evidence for psi is suggestive does not in itself automatically invite reconsideration of other controversial claims, such as astrology and homeopathy. I confess to being intrigued by indications of a relationship between birth signs and personality, and one major study partly validates it.[35] But that's not much to go on, and inconsistencies about the division of the zodiac surely militate against any idea of a physical influence caused by the planets. Homeopathy apparently helps many people, to the extent that even some general practitioners recommend it, but its claimed basis is more provocative to conventional science even than psi.[36]

As for creationism, in its recently adopted guise as intelligent design (the Biblical 'young-earth' variant being presumably beyond rational discussion), it is hardly in the same class. For me, creationists actually have more in common with psi-sceptics than they do with parapsychologists. Creationists don't like Darwinism for ideological reasons, so they debunk it by picking holes, arguing for instance that the eye is far too complex to have evolved by natural selection. Like the CSI (CSICOP) they are generously funded, in their case by conservative religious institutions. Their reasoning is indifferently supported, while biologists can offer elaborate, well-substantiated arguments to explain how the eye might have evolved, just as parapsychologists can easily confound casually proposed 'normal' alternatives for their telepathic data.[37] And the fact that parapsychologists have an abundant source of phenomena to study also gives them something else in common with evolutionary scientists – in stark contrast to creationists, who are pretty much parasitical on their opponents' research.

So to accept psi on scientific grounds is not necessarily to open the door to other entities that appear superficially to belong to the same family. On whether it's *right* to accept psi, if by so doing we open a Pandora's box of superstitious practices, I'd ask: Do we have a choice? Are we getting this the right way round? If the evidence is persuasive, as it arguably is to those who immerse themselves in it, surely it's something we have to come to terms with.

Believing as I do that psi exists, and that the conditions are ripe for this to be more widely understood, I have come to think of it as one of that family of awesome challenges that humanity faces in the twenty-first century. Take nuclear power and genetic science, both products of scientific understanding; in very different ways each has frightening implications, as unstable states strive to acquire doomsday weapons and the prospect of genetic manipulation calls into question the very idea of what it means to be human. But these genies can't be coaxed back into their bottles; we're stuck with them, and we have to try to act responsibly, to encourage others to do so too, and be ready to act firmly if the need arises.

A parallel of a different kind might be made with recreational drug dependence, where the possibility of legalization is increasingly being raised as a means to mitigate a major source of crime and violence. That itself is a step into the unknown and carries certain risks, but as some governments start to move in this direction – and more will surely follow – the responsibility for avoiding what is freely available will eventually become mainly the individual's.

In these and other issues, humans will have no choice but to adapt to the fruits of their industry and knowledge. There's also a point to be made here about how these matters are governed. Every field of activity has its experts, those scientists, managers and professionals who understand it and can assess the risks and opportunities and provide appropriate advice. That's not to say that they speak with one voice, or pull in the same direction, but at least the public knows that there are people who understand the complexities, and where necessary can provide appropriate counsel.

Now consider the case of parapsychology. This is a community of investigators and researchers who have a fair idea of what psi is, when and where it is to be found, and – something that in this particular context is absolutely crucial – where it is likely to be illusory or bogus. But these experts are ridiculed and marginalized by other 'experts' whose insistence that it is *all* illusory and bogus does not resonate in any useful way with the uncanny experiences that people occasionally report. In the absence of any scientific consensus, such people are left to figure it out for themselves, and it's perhaps not surprising that their conclusions are often confused and erroneous. If you think about it, this free-for-all is an extraordinary state of affairs, especially in an age when just about every other aspect of our existence is closely monitored. And since sceptics' organizations strive so mightily to bring it about, they arguably bear a share of responsibility for what they claim most to deplore.

7 *Psi and religion*

In practical terms, psi is not merely a facet of human experience; it is a potential gateway to religious belief. Although psi-literate people see psi and survival as distinct entities, they are but a small minority; in the public mind one implies the other. Oddly, this applies to sceptics as well. For both groups, a ghost is either the manifestation of a surviving spirit or it is an illusion; the in-between concept of a telepathic hallucination is probably not one that either would recognize.

Psi's potentially religious basis is one of the main reasons why it is forcefully contested by sceptic thinkers like Paul Kurtz, the humanist philosopher and founder of the CSI (CSICOP). In making the case against the Fox sisters he wants to disabuse spiritualists of their illusions. But suppose it went the other way, and the academic community were one day to acknowledge that the Fox family experienced a genuine anomaly and that psi is real, and in so doing conferred greater credibility on belief in an afterlife? In that case, perhaps the fears of Kurtz and like-minded sceptics would be fully realized. The idea of secularity would be weakened, to the extent that it might eventually cease to have any real meaning.

You don't have to be a sceptic or an atheist to recognize the social and political implications of this. As a quasi-religious creed, secular or scientific humanism has a relatively small, though significant following in developed countries. But as a philosophical concept, secularity plays a unifying role in our governance and institutions, emphasizing our common humanity and our shared interest in an ordered, sustainable and prosperous existence. According to the secular ideal, individuals may think and say what they like, as long as they don't interfere with this central project, or try to force their varying metaphysical beliefs on other people: the separation of church and state is a fundamental element of the western democratic system.

Yet this ideal has been coming under sustained attack as traditionalist Christianity intrudes in such matters as abortion, medical technology and the teaching of evolution, and Islamic fanatics persuade ignorant folk to blow themselves up, along with their innocent fellows, in exchange for some notional martyr's reward in heaven. In this context, to accept as scientifically proven certain mental phenomena that to some minds validate religious doctrines would run entirely counter to the secular project.

But we would also need to ask, precisely *which* doctrines would this reinforce: Those of the Abrahamic religions that invoke faith and scriptural authority? Or those of the eastern-influenced mystical tradition that looks more to direct experience and is arguably less understood in the developed world?

The answer, surely, is the second of these; to conservative Christians and Muslims any acknowledgement of psi's reality would merely intensify the estrangement from secular scientific materialism that many already feel. Psi and spiritualism are anathema to many Christians, especially, who point to the Biblical proscription against communication with spirits, on the grounds that they are really demons, and who reject the notion popularized by near-death experiences that the gates of paradise are as open to ordinary unrepentant folk as they are to the 'saved'.[38] What's more, the vast majority of doctrinaire Christians do not accept the idea of reincarnation that is at the heart of the Buddhist and Hindu traditions, which, for their part, fully acknowledge *siddhis* – psychic powers – as phenomena that can occur on the spiritual path (although they are considered to lack any intrinsic value).[39]

To scientists and sceptics of course, there is no real distinction to be made here. Anything that validates religious belief invites all kinds of woolly, superstitious thinking, they argue. Yet for mystically inclined folk, at least, that validation has already taken place – nearly a century ago, when the pioneers of quantum mechanics revealed consciousness to be implicated in matter, and the universe to be 'more like a great thought than a great machine'.[40] That process has accelerated in our own time as the physicists, while remaining suspicious of psychic claims (and in some cases vocally hostile) speculate about multiple universes and dimensions in a way that seems to many to support a mystical worldview.[41] (It hardly needs to be said that a great many medical professionals and scientists are conventionally religious, or in other ways recognize a confluence of the scientific and the sacred.[42] And parapsychologists, it's worth adding, insist that scientists in other disciplines very often reveal to them, in private one-to-one conversations, a belief in the reality of psychic phenomena that they dare not admit to openly.)

My point is to question the perception that science and religion are opposite and mutually incompatible entities. In current debates they tend to be presented as Titans engaged in a struggle to the death, upon which the survival of the species depends. An alternative view is that – in a purely moral sense, and despite the perceived chasm between them – scientific materialism and mystical religion share the same essential basis: their *humanism*. I don't want to make too much of this: the uncompromising supernaturalism of eastern mystical philosophy is wildly at odds with the materialist basis of secular humanism. But in their different ways, both take an empirical stance – one through a subjective response to experience, the other by objective experiment. And in terms of their moral orientation they are arguably alike too; indeed, the psychological 'this-world' concerns of Buddhism attract atheists such as Susan Blackmore, who can apparently derive value from its mental discipline while ignoring its ideas about rebirth.

One might conceivably do the same with those 'personalities' – whether real or on some level imagined – who deliver their sermons through mediums and automatic writers: ignore all the talk about a 'greater reality' and a 'future life' and focus instead on the advice about how to live a *better* life. My impression is – and I think it's fair to say this sets spiritualism apart from institutional Western religions – they would not greatly mind, as they seem little interested in beliefs and creeds. They have not much to say about God, ritual, worship or prayer; nor do they talk of 'sin' that will earn punishment in the next life; they refer instead to 'unwise choices', to be learned from and made anew. Asked directly what credentials they can offer, and why they should be considered objectively real, they do not demand faith or blind belief, but point to the advice they are giving. Does it make sense? Would it be *rational* to follow it?

One could go further and argue that a secularity that allowed itself to become influenced by spirituality would arguably become a far more powerful force against religious obscurantism than one shaped by scientific materialism alone. And realistically, this convergence is surely the more likely future scenario, however widely the prospect is presently feared by committed secularists.

Certainly it's hard to disagree with much of what atheists complain about in organized religion. We can argue fiercely about whether more people were killed by religious conflicts than by secular despots like Hitler and Stalin, and so on, but it's indisputable that religious literalism and intolerance continue to be powerfully destructive influences in human affairs.

Yet all the evidence is that humans are hard-wired to be religious, and campaigning atheists are surely wrong to insist that religious thinking can one day simply be eradicated by improved scientific education. This error, I believe, is a consequence of their failure adequately to consider reports of mystical and religious experience. Evolutionary psychologists occasionally make ritual references to William James and *The Varieties of Human Experience,* but without apparently grasping the extraordinary challenge this material poses for our understanding of the mind.[43] It's not clear how a brain architecture capable in rare and special circumstances of affording a glimpse of what people take to be the ultimate nature of reality, and which they call *God*, can simply be reprogrammed to recognize it all as an illusion.

And while it's natural for secularists to see the widespread interest in psi and mystical religion as a hangover from a bygone age – a reaction against the cheerless vision offered by materialist science – an alternative view is that it's a progressive development, and one to which science has contributed by its empirical method of observation and experiment.

Finally, let's consider that future generations looking back to our era may see the two worldviews of science and religion not locked together in mortal combat, but co-operating to achieve the same ultimate goal.

8 *My views on survival*

If I ask myself how seriously I take the idea of consciousness surviving death I find myself hesitating. I look around and see beings like myself, coming and going, absorbed in their affairs, and wonder – what *are* we really? Lumbering robots driven by our genes, an accident of nature?[44] Or, at the other extreme, visitors from some distant dimension, our memories erased so that we cannot recall the strange mission we are supposed to be on.

If the writer of *The Selfish Gene* thought his idea sounded like science fiction, how much more so does this supernatural version. It's disconcerting to think that my whole life is being recorded on some cosmic surveillance camera – for training and monitoring purposes, as it were – and that I will eventually undergo some kind of debriefing session. It's bizarre, and I'm bound to ask: *Why?* What's the point of it all? What greater interest is served by our struggles and sufferings? Why not simply accept the scientific insight that the universe is self-creating and cares not a jot for humanity's feelings, which are merely the odd outcome of an evolutionary process. In certain moods one longs for absolute peace, and imagines that in death one will finally find it, even if that simply means going to sleep and not ever waking up.

How easy it is, too, to imagine that this picture that psi and spiritualism provide of surviving death – surely more intelligible to the modern mind than traditional notions involving such things as bodily resurrection and eternal salvation or damnation – is an effect of the imagination and of developing human culture, itself a product of human mentation. It's impossible not to be struck by the way that these new ideas have emerged in parallel with social development, where threats have largely given way to persuasion, rulers are viewed with openly expressed scepticism, and self-improvement is considered a worthy goal. According to this view, the jibe about wishful thinking would be pretty much right; a more sophisticated version than the atheist gives credit for, perhaps, but wishful thinking nonetheless.

It's natural at first glance to suppose that the 'personalities' that express themselves through mediums and automatic writing are the inventions of their scribes. I believe the phenomenon is too well documented for that to be true, but I did find myself trying always to frame it in terms that I could attach sense to. I gravitated rationally towards the 'obvious' explanation: that they are not literally apart from us – they are *ourselves* in an exotic disguise, or our *higher selves*, in New Age parlance. Perhaps, I reflected, they are an expression of Jung's collective human psyche; what some humans say or write in trance states has its origin in some age-old memory, captured in the architecture of the brain, something we carry in our genes, the distilled wisdom that humans have gathered through long millennia of experience.

But following this through I became increasingly distracted by a rather odd paradox. These voices that speak to us adopt a tone of high morality. In the new kind of existence that awaits us, they say, any kind of lie or deceit is impossible; they urge us to start at once making total honesty part of the fabric of our lives. The insight is spelled out repeatedly and urgently in channelled communications, and for people who have been through the near-death experience it has become an absolutely natural thing to do. However if as far as we as individuals are concerned *nothing* will happen after we die – in the fullest meaning of the word – then all the time we are telling ourselves a big fat lie. That part of ourselves that claims to be speaking unvarnished truth *is itself a deception*

It's not just that this doesn't make sense, it looks to me suspiciously like the kind of weird anomaly that results when debunkers try to explain away psychic claims, magically transforming children into expert conjurors, for instance. The highly persuasive nature of the best survival evidence also requires explanation. It's easy to brush it away as wishful thinking if you don't know much about it, but if you see it close up, its sheer realism can be spine-chilling. I allow myself to doubt that the human mind, for all its astonishingly creative and histrionic powers, extends to that level of crafty collective labour.

I agree these are subjective arguments, and that even for many people who do have good knowledge of the relevant data they are therefore not logically coercive. As long as seeming evidence of survival *might* be a product of the human unconscious mind it is not conclusive. And however personally convinced I am by some of the best evidence, I can see that others might find contrary arguments more persuasive.

At the same time there's the historical perspective to take into account. The argument about survival is not taking place in a philosophically neutral environment: on the contrary, it's only a few generations since science dethroned God as the centre of humanity's conceptual universe, and the aftershocks of this momentous change continue to reverberate. To take an illustrative example, however sincerely Joseph Rhine may have believed that psi in living people might explain phenomena suggestive of survival, to argue this way must surely also have been a tactical move: to win acceptance, psi had to be presented as a scientific entity, a product of the natural world. It would have been the same consideration, incidentally, that caused his wife Louisa, who researched spontaneous psi phenomena such as apparitional episodes, to try to frame them – in my view with limited success – in non-survivalist terms.

In the 1930s, the heyday of logical positivism and behaviourism, the Rhines' position was entirely understandable; the intellectual climate demanded no less than that. But it was surely based on an illusion, one that sceptics have never been fooled by. Like them, I do not see how the data on telepathy – not to speak of clairvoyance, precognition and psychokinesis, which are even more challenging – can conceivably be reconciled with the conventional view of the brain as the product purely of biological evolution. Nor are these things obviously compatible with the computational approaches that currently dominate cognitive psychology and neuroscience. This is a major reason why the idea of psi is so fiercely resisted; it doesn't fit with what else we take to be true.

Here I part company with those who believe psi can eventually be explained within a modified and expanded version of scientific materialism. I'm glad that some people *do* think this; psi is much easier to debate if it is not automatically seen to be destructive of current assumptions. And of course the principle of Occam's razor positively requires that we start from this point.

Nor do I mean that there can never be a scientific explanation of psi, and that it will forever remain a mystery, belonging in the despised category of 'miracles and magic'. On the contrary, I believe that one day we will understand the principles behind it. I do however maintain that the science that explains it could not be science in its present form. If the majority of scientists were to acknowledge that it exists, this would be because the materialist paradigm had metamorphosed into something rather different, a process that psi would have helped to bring about. And since scientific materialism underpins its structures, secular society in turn would have undergone a fundamental alteration in its philosophical outlook, and in its ideas about the origins and development of life.

There would then be a reversal of the situation as it now stands. As individuals we could indeed continue to be secular – to insist that the idea of a divine reality behind existence is an illusion, and with it the notion of the personal survival of death – but we would not necessarily be able any longer to claim the unequivocal backing of science in this. We would adopt it as a matter of atheistic preference, because we dislike supernaturalist ideas and get along better without them.

Or to put it another way, we would finally have to acknowledge – which I believe is often actually the case – that we invoke Occam's razor not just for the less complex explanation *but for the lesser of two evils.* Now in this changed intellectual environment, how much sense would it make to continue to deny that survival occurs? With materialism fatally undermined, what ideological reason would we have for continuing to reject it?

In sum, I believe that the existence of psi as an aspect of human consciousness is not an argument against survival, as Rhine and others argued, but, on the contrary, *powerfully reinforces it.*

I concede that to contemplate the idea of survival of consciousness persisting after death requires a certain kind of imagination, and for that reason is perhaps easier for some people than for others. I may be unusual in this respect, but to me the idea of living in a different state of being is neither frightening nor strange. That may partly be because in the past I experimented with hallucinogens such as LSD and mescaline, and have a lively understanding of just how radically one's consciousness can be altered – and our normal daily concerns made to seem vanishingly unimportant[45] – but also because I find I can readily empathize with people who have experienced near-death states, apparitions and mystical visions, and believe that what they report is relevant to our situation in a way that some people clearly can't accept. Perhaps also an element of my involuntary, somewhat perfunctory Christian schooling has stayed with me, which makes it easier for me to respond to

God-talk than it is for people who have never been exposed to it, or ever had occasion to examine its relevance.

I'd go further and suggest that there's an element of faith in this. Not to be misunderstood, I should say at once that this is not what I take to be religious faith, and certainly not in any Kierkegaardian sense of a 'leap of faith', which, wedded as I am to the plodding process of questioning and investigation, I doubt I would be capable of. It has nothing to do with the dogmas of scriptural Christianity, many aspects of which, again, I'm as baffled about as any atheist, let alone the perilous paths that some radical Islamists feel called on to follow. It's a faith in the validity of my own reasoning (not dissimilar, surely, from the faith that scientists and philosophers have in theirs) and in the quality of my empathetic judgements about people and the experiences they report. And yes, it's also a faith that afterlife – a very different form of life certainly – will not be an alien environment but on the contrary, will seem absolutely natural.

For myself there remains an element of doubt – how could there not? But for all practical purposes I find I have come to accept the proposition that survival of death is part of the human situation – as yet dimly glimpsed and poorly understood. I think and work and walk in the belief that in the moments that follow my last breath, whatever the circumstances, I will remain in a certain sense as alive and mindful as before, a thinking sentient being, retaining the memory of my experiences. Furthermore, having come this far, I cannot reject the notion – however unsettling it might be – that this thing I call 'me' is an expression of countless incarnations and that there will be many more of them unless I take steps here and now to stop it happening. My priority now is to explore these ideas and their relevance to my own life.

All that said, I continue to respect humanists who devoutly believe existence to be a meaningless accident. A considered and ethical position is better than indifference. To be sure, I think there is something rather self-regarding in the way they congratulate themselves, as they often do, for 'looking the universe unflinchingly in the eye', chucking away the 'crutch of religion', and so on. But I feel real awe for those people who calmly face imminent death, sometimes at a tragically young age, with the conviction that it means their complete annihilation, unmitigated by any spiritual consolation. I can't be certain that in such circumstances I'd be capable of such dignity and forbearance.

At the same time, I wonder whether this heroism is really demanded of us. Atheists insist we err to believe that life has meaning apart from that which we create for ourselves but, as at least some of them recognize, it's not obvious why this should be liberating. I'd suggest that for most people the idea that death spells extinction is not a well-considered moral position, but a burden, dully perceived and dutifully born, that leaves a vacuum in the centre of their being. I'm of course not talking about the majority of people on this planet, those who follow religions blithely uncaring about the strictures of heathen scientists. I'm thinking of those people who put their trust in science, who accept naturalistic accounts because they appear to be the outcome of a rigorous empirical process, and who take at face value the debunkings of psychic claims, unable to recognize the personal, professional and ideological motivations that drive them.

9 *Last thoughts*

A friend, an atheist, once listened patiently as I described my research and then exclaimed 'But Rob, if all this is true, *why is it not known?*' She could not conceive how science might have overlooked something so fundamental.

It was a good question, and in different ways most of this book has been an attempt to answer it. The truth about psi is not known because it clashes with what we take to be true, because we fear it, and because we believe, unthinkingly and erroneously, that we can always explain it away. It's not known because the way that our minds work, as well as sometimes generating the illusion of it, often masks the reality. It's not known because, being both rare and immaterial, a property of consciousness, it fails the criteria demanded by materialist science. Finally (and perhaps most crucially), it's not known because it appears to validate religious belief at a time when much of humanity is desperate to eliminate a perceived cause of tribal divisions.

As beings adrift in this strange world, forced into existence through no conscious choice of our own, we are heavily dependent on the guidance we give each other. The controversy about the paranormal may seem like a petty dispute on the fringes of academia, but it's not insignificant: it could impact on people's lives and the health and progress of our society in the most fundamental way imaginable. If we are to have confidence in the direction we follow, it needs to be based on the very best in science and scholarship. That requires curiosity and open-mindedness, a willingness to debate and a dedication to finding the truth. On an issue of such importance we should test our guides, ask for their qualifications, and judge how reliable they are likely to be.

And really, what is there to fear in acknowledging our psychic nature? It's the basis of an optimistic philosophy, one that offers hope and guidance, provides meaningful alternatives to the pursuit of wealth and status, urges social co-operation, exposes the futility of religiously motivated violence, and encourages the breaking down of ethnic, religious and nationalist barriers. These are all things that our world surely needs more of. Perhaps understanding it better will also promote a more humane view of death. One of secular society's least attractive characteristics is its exaggerated worship of youth, and that horror of decay that causes us often to put the elderly and dying out of sight and mind. A philosophy that sees life as a learning experience and death as a transition to the next stage, one would think, could help assuage anxiety and encourage a less fearful response to life's burdens.

It has special relevance, too, for the manner in which we ourselves will one day depart this life. If post-mortem survival is a fact it's worth thinking what it might mean to die without having even an inkling of what may be about to occur. We may witness – clearly and with full force – the grief of family and friends, yet be powerless to reveal the truth that would console them. We will enter into a new stage of existence largely unprepared, and with little concept of how our actions and behaviour may have determined our future experiences. How will we then feel about the engine of knowledge in which we put our trust, that it was unable to reveal to us this most fundamental of matters?

If, on the other hand, some people feel discouraged by science – its bleak reductionism, its brusque negation of the spiritual and the psychic – they should remember that scientists and intellectuals *have* studied this matter and their conclusions are broadly in agreement with what many people intuitively feel to be true. Had they not done so – had there been no investigations of mediums and psychics, no psi experiments, no surveys of spontaneous phenomena such as apparitions and out-of-body experiences – a book like this could never have been written. The sceptics would then be right: the idea of psi would be a purely personal affair, based on faith or on individual experience.

The problem is perhaps not that science is not doing its job, but rather that the process is incomplete. The scale of the challenge is enormous. The Enlightenment project was never a matter of a single generation; there is surely no reason to suppose it has run its course or that further astonishing and disorienting revelations do not lie ahead. The process of coming to terms with an aspect of consciousness that could give birth to a new worldview may take a century or more to complete.

Looked at in this way, we are creatures of history, players in an enterprise from whose outcome future generations will perhaps benefit, while we as individuals grapple with uncertainty, just as we benefit from technologies that our ancestors did not even dream of. Of course we worry about the world that our descendents (or who knows, our reincarnated selves) will inhabit. It may be so utterly disfigured by war, drought, flood and famine that anarchy will reign and no further intellectual progress will be possible.

To be sure, new scientific advances may help save our planet from the ravages it faces. But if humanity is to escape decline or sudden annihilation, the one thing it truly cannot do without is goodwill, a willingness to put personal and national interests aside for the common good. If empirical observation confirms what many people intuitively believe to be true, that within us lies a common source of wisdom that can help guide us through the adventure of life, that is something we surely need to accept and understand.

SUGGESTIONS FOR
FURTHER READING

Still unsure what to believe? Then why not do as I did? Read the research and see what *you* think.

The companion website provides more information around the topics covered here, and others besides (www.randisprize.net). It contains brief reviews of the books I read, as well as links to scientific research papers and scholarly articles relating to recent psi research. You can also access earlier psychic research material: extracts from *Phantasms of the Living* and other books of the period, papers on mediums Leonora Piper and Gladys Leonard, examples of poltergeist and apparitional incidents, and so on.

If you have leisure to delve in depth, you could subscribe to one of the research organisations such as the Parapsychological Association or the Society for Psychical Research (SPR). The SPR has a useful library in Kensington, London, and provides complete on- and off-line access to its own and other research journals (www.spr.ac.uk). Its catalogue (also on the website) gives brief summaries of all the papers, book reviews and correspondence published since 1882, and gives a good introduction to the subject.

There is a lot of material to be found online. The *Journal of Scientific Exploration* is free to download; books out of copyright can be read or downloaded; and Googling authors and topics can often bring up complete papers from other sources.

A rich seam of articles on topics on survival can be found at www. survivalafterdeath.org.uk. Among those represented are William James, Frederic Myers, Oliver Lodge, Carl Jung and Charles Richet, also later commentators such as Arthur Koestler, C.D. Broad, J.B. Rhine, David Scott Rogo, Stephen Braude, and many others. The site also carries a comprehensive list of links to other resource sites.

Rupert Sheldrake's website (www.sheldrake.org) is an important resource, containing material relating to his research and his interactions with sceptics.

As you become familiar with the background you can contribute to online discussion forums such as Michael Prescott's Blog (http://michaelprescott.typepad.com) or my own Paranormalia (www.paranormalia.com), which offer comment and analysis on psi-related subjects, and generate vigorous debate in the comments thread.

Skeptical Investigations, despite its somewhat misleading name, carries articles that challenge sceptics (www.skepticalinvestigations.org). For sceptics' views, visit James Randi Educational Foundation (www.randi.org) and the *Skeptical Inquirer* at the CSI (www.csicop.org).

If you have a query about any of the topics in *Randi's Prize,* you can send me an email (address on the website). I can't guarantee to answer it personally, but I'll try to address it on the site's blog.

NOTES AND REFERENCES

Throughout these notes, the *Journal of the Society for Psychical Research* and *the Proceedings of the Society for Psychical Research* are abbreviated to *Journal SPR* and *Proceedings SPR,* respectively. Website addresses were valid at April 2010. Publisher details are provided on first citation only, but can also be found in the *Bibliography*.

Introduction

1. 'Aliens are not among us', *Sunday Mirror*, 8 February 1998.

2. *Flim-Flam! Psychics, ESP, Unicorns and Other Delusions* (Buffalo, NY: Prometheus, 1982), p. 326.

3. Michael Shermer, *Why People Believe Weird Things* (New York: Henry Holt, 1997).

Chapter One: Naughty Adolescent Syndrome

Opening quote: William Barrett, 'Poltergeists, Old and New', *Proceedings SPR* **25**, 1911, p. 393.

1. Carl Sagan, *The Demon-Haunted World: Science as a Candle in the Dark* (London: Hodder Headline, 1996), p. 28.

2. Richard Dawkins, *Unweaving the Rainbow* (London: Penguin, 1999), p. xiii.

3. *Unweaving the Rainbow,* p. 129.

4. *The Demon-Haunted World*, pp. 224–28.

5. Guy Lyon Playfair, *This House is Haunted* (New York: Stein and Day, 1980).

6. Its website still uses the old address www.csicop.org. The decision to retire the acronym CSICOP may have been influenced by the fact that it lends itself to the term 'psi-cop', gleefully employed by detractors. For a detailed, somewhat jaundiced account of the organization's early years see George P. Hansen, *The Trickster and the Paranormal* (Philadelphia, PA: Xlibris, 2001), pp. 148–61.

7. Above, Introduction, note 2.

8. Paul Kurtz, *The Transcendental Temptation* (Buffalo, NY: Prometheus, 1887).

9. Joe Nickell, *Looking for a Miracle: Weeping Icons, Relics, Stigmata, Visions and Healing Cures* (Amherst, NY: Prometheus, 1993).

10. Terence Hines, *Pseudoscience and the Paranormal: A Critical Examina-

tion of the Evidence (Buffalo, NY: Prometheus, 1988), pp. 62–65. *The Amityville Horror* was slated in a review by parapsychologist Robert L. Morris, head of the Koestler Parapsychology Unit at the University of Edinburgh (Kendrick Frazier, *Paranormal Borderlands of Science* (Buffalo, NY: Prometheus, 1981), pp. 170–76).

11. Hines, *Pseudoscience and the Paranormal,* pp. 62–64. The Borley case was reported by Harry Price in *The Most Haunted House in England: Ten Years' Investigation of Borley Rectory* (London: Longmans, Green and Co, 1940). Price's claims were questioned by SPR members and parapsychologists: Eric Dingwall, Kathleen M. Goldney, Trevor Henry Hall, 'The Haunting of Borley Rectory. A critical survey of the evidence', *Proceedings SPR* 51, 1955, pp. 1–180.

12. *Anomalistic Psychology: A Study of Extraordinary Phenomena of Behavior and Experience* (Hillsdale, N.J: Lawrence Erlbaum, 1982), p. 412.

13. See the SPR's website: www.spr.ac.uk.

14. Barrett, 'Poltergeists, Old and New', pp. 377–412. See also Frank Podmore, 'Report on the Worksop Disturbances', *Journal SPR* 1, 1884, pp. 199–212; Frederic W.H. Myers, 'On Alleged Movements of Objects, Without Contact, Occurring Not in the Presence of a Paid Medium', *Proceedings SPR* 7, 1892, pp. 383–94. For a more recent case see David Fontana, 'A Responsive Poltergeist: A Case from South Wales', *Journal SPR* 57, 1991, pp. 385–403.

15. Besides Playfair's *This House Is Haunted*, details of the Enfield incidents and some sceptical reactions are given by Guy Lyon Playfair and Maurice Grosse in 'Enfield Revisited: The Evaporation of Positive Evidence', *Journal SPR* 55, 1988, p. 208–19.

16. Matthew Manning, *The Link* (London: Ballantine, 1976).

17. William Roll, *The Poltergeist* (New York: Signet, 1972); D. Scott Rogo, *On the Track of the Poltergeist* (San Antonio: Anomalist Books, 1986); Alan Gauld and A.D. Cornell, *Poltergeists* (London: Routledge and Kegan Paul, 1979); Hans Bender, 'Modern Poltergeist Research: A Plea for an Unprejudiced Approach', in J. Beloff (ed.) *New Directions in Parapsychology* (London: Elek, 1974), pp. 131–34.

18. See for instance Andrew Lang, 'The Poltergeist, Historically Considered', *Proceedings SPR* 17, 1902, pp. 305–26, and Hereward Carrington and Nandor Fodor, *Haunted People – The Story of the Poltergeist Down Through the Centuries* (New York: Dutton, 1951). Historical descriptions can also be found in Gauld and Cornell's *Poltergeists*, and A.R.G. Owen's *Can We Explain the Poltergeist?* (New York: Garrett Publications, 1964). A useful resource is Michael Goss, *Poltergeists: An Annotated Bibliography of Works in English, Circa 1880–1975* (Metuchen, NJ: Scarecrow Press, 1979). An overview of the German literature is Annekatrin Puhle, 'Ghosts, Apparitions

and Poltergeist Incidents in Germany Between 1700 And 1900', *Journal SPR* 63, 1999, pp. 292–305. For a collection of anecdotal accounts see John and Anne Spencer, *The Poltergeist Phenomenon: An Investigation into Psychic Disturbance* (London: Headline, 1996).

19. 'Poltergeists', in Benjamin B. Wolman (ed.), *The Handbook of Parapsychology* (Jefferson, NC: McFarland and Co, 1986).

20. *Pseudoscience and the Paranormal*, p. 65.

21. Some early cases reported in the SPR *Journal* decided in favour of trickery. See for instance, *Journal SPR* 3, 1888, p. 272; 'The Waterford Ghost', *Journal SPR* 5, 1892, pp. 227–8; 'An Early Record of a Poltergeist Case', *Journal SPR* 24, 1927, pp. 26–7; V.J. Woolley, 'Some Investigations into Poltergeists', *Journal SPR* 26, 1930, pp. 104–07. However such cases are substantially outnumbered in the SPR literature by those where trickery was partially or wholly ruled out.

22. See for instance 'Some Mysterious Rappings Explained', *Journal SPR* 13, 1908, pp. 218–19.

23. In support of this theory, G.W. Lambert argued that the geographical distribution of the occurrences favour coastal regions, especially tidal estuaries; that they tend to occur in winter rather than summer; and that they correlate significantly with meteorological and local geological conditions, also in some coastal cases with the tides. He concluded that disturbances caused by underground water are misinterpreted from fear and superstition into 'miraculous' effects. 'Poltergeists: A Physical Theory', *Journal SPR* 38, 1955, pp. 49–71. Gauld and Cornell criticized this theory on a number of grounds, among them that geophysical forces could not produce the kinds of phenomena that are reported. 'The Geophysical Theory of Poltergeists', *Journal SPR* 41, 1961, pp. 129–46.

24. See for instance Peter Eastham, 'Ticking Off a Poltergeist', *Journal SPR* 55, 1988, pp. 80–83.

25. See for instance Roll, *The Poltergeist*, pp. 107–14.

26. Scott Rogo describes a 1974 Los Angeles case where he was sure he had witnessed several examples of genuine poltergeist activity at the beginning of his investigation, but also felt that the 13-year old girl at the centre of the disturbances had fraudulently caused some of the later ones, beginning with the arrival of television cameras. *On the Track of the Poltergeist*, p. 44.

27. For discussions of the underlying psychodynamics see Jan Ehrenwald, *The ESP Experience: A Psychiatric Validation* (New York: Basic Books, 1978), pp. 130–41; and Roll, *The Poltergeist*, pp. 169–98.

28. James Randi, 'The Columbus Poltergeist Case', in Kendrick Frazier, *Science Confronts the Paranormal* (Buffalo, NY: Prometheus Books, 1986), p. 152.

29. ibid., p. 156.

30. Milbourne Christopher, *Seers, Psychics and ESP* (London: Cassell, 1970), pp. 149–60. See a more detailed description in Roll, *The Poltergeist*, pp. 13–25.

31. The fullest, most recent sceptical version of the Fox sisters that I know of is given by Ruth Brandon in *The Spiritualists: The Passion for the Occult in the Nineteenth and Twentieth Centuries* (London: Weidenfeld and Nicolson, 1983), pp. 1–41. Similarly oriented summaries can be found in Kurtz, *The Transcendental Temptation*, pp. 322–9, and in most sceptic accounts of 19th century spiritualism. Brian Inglis provides relevant details mostly overlooked by sceptics: *Natural and Supernatural* (London: Hodder and Stoughton, 1977), pp. 204–209. See also a recent biography of the Fox sisters by Barbara Weisberg, *Talking to the Dead: Kate and Maggie Fox, and the Rise of Spiritualism* (San Francisco: Harper, 2005).

32. The statement is quoted in E.W. Capron, *Modern Spiritualism: Its Facts and Fanaticisms, Its Consistencies and Contradictions* (Boston: Bela Marsh, 1855), pp. 39–43. See also E.E. Lewis, *A Report of the Mysterious Noises Heard in the House of Mr John D. Fox* (Canandaigua, NY: E.E. Lewis, 1848), which contains the statements of 22 witnesses.

33. 'Spiritualism Exposed: Margaret Fox Kane Confesses to Fraud', *New York World*, October 21, 1888, in Paul Kurtz (ed.), *A Skeptic's Handbook of Parapsychology* (Buffalo, NY: Prometheus, 1985), p. 226.

34. ibid., p. 229.

35. Capron, *Modern Spiritualism*, p. 421.

36. Gauld and Cornell, *Poltergeists*, p. 226.

37. Capron, *Modern Spiritualism*, p. 39.

38. Maurice Grosse and Mary Rose Barrington, 'Report on Psychokinetic Activity Surrounding a Seven-Year-Old Boy', *Journal SPR* 65, 2001, pp. 207–17.

39. Playfair and Grosse, 'Enfield Revisted', p. 208.

40. Owen, *Can We Explain the Poltergeist?*, pp. 148–49.

41. Some other examples: Observing a case in a farmhouse near Eniskillen in Ireland, William Barrett writes, 'The younger children were apparently asleep, and Maggie was motionless; nevertheless, knocks were going on everywhere around; on the chairs, the bedstead, the walls and ceiling. The closest scrutiny failed to detect any movement on the part of those present that could account for the noises, which were accompanied by a scratching or tearing sound ('Poltergeists, Old and New', p. 396). In a nineteenth-century episode, reported in an American magazine article, an Irish maid in a Massachusetts household seemed to be the focus of noises that sounded like someone rapping sharply on a piece of wooden furniture, although nobody was seen to be doing so; they were also heard while the girl was sleeping

in bed (H.A. Willis, 'A Remarkable Case of Psychical Phenomena', *Atlantic Monthly*, August 1868; summarized in Gauld and Cornell, *Poltergeists*, p. 69). In Hopfgarten near Weimar a series of knockings were heard in the room of a dying woman, that sounded like blows with the fist or knuckles rapping on furniture. They were sometimes heard in two places at once and no visible cause could be discovered ('The Hopfgarten Poltergeist Case', *Journal SPR* 20, 1921, pp. 199–207). And in a Swiss case in 1863, a lawyer described 'a repeated peculiar rapping of 10–12 blows, which came very quickly towards the end, as if someone, tapping nervously on a door with his finger, demanded instant admission.' (Gauld and Cornell, *Poltergeists*, p. 9.) The phenomenon also turns up in earlier historical cases, such as a house in Tedworth in 1661 where 'a very great knocking' was reported, a persistent 'strange noise and a hollow sound', which at one point 'returned with mighty violence and applied it self wholly to my youngest children, whose bedsteeds it would beat, when there have been many strangers as well as ourselves present in the roome, that we did at every blow expect they would have fallen to pieces...' (Gauld and Cornell, *Poltergeists*, pp. 46–7).

42. Gauld and Cornell, *Poltergeists*, pp. 51–52.

43. ibid., p. 24.

44. 'Automatic Phenomena' *Journal SPR* 13, 1907, pp. 15–16.

45. Barrett, 'Poltergeists, Old and New', p. 393–94.

46. Playfair, *This House is Haunted*, p. 208.

47. Playfair and Grosse, 'Enfield Revisited', p. 210.

48. W.G. Roll and J.G. Pratt, 'The Miami Disturbances', *Journal of the American Society for Psychical Research* 65, 1971, pp. 409–54.

49. Playfair, *This House is Haunted*, p. 46.

50. Cited in Scott Rogo, *On the Track of the Poltergeist*, p. 12. Scott Rogo was present when a plastic compact case was hurled against the wall and made a loud bang, but did not bounce away, and was seen resting against the wall, undamaged (pp. 30–31).

51. These details were published recently in William Roll and Valerie Storey, *Unleashed: Of Poltergeists and Murder, The Curious Story of Tina Resch* (New York: Simon and Schuster, 2004). Roll had originally declined to write up the case, feeling he had said all he wanted to say about poltergeists, but renewed his interest years later as a result of certain tragic circumstances in Tina Resch's later life: she was arrested and convicted of the murder of her child, for which she is currently serving a prison sentence. Roll was sympathetic, and tried to arrange proper legal defence for her. Randi suggests that by 'encouraging' Tina's 'delinquency', Roll should share the blame for her later circumstances.

52. ibid., p. 4.

53. In a 1957 'raps' case, having eliminated other possibilities, Gauld and Cornell took up the floorboards to see if a hoaxer might have concealed an apparatus beneath them. 'Our examination of the structure of the floor convinced us that knocking devices could have been laid under it only by removing boards from the floor of [the] bedroom or from the ceiling of the washroom; and that no boards had been removed from either of these places.' A.D. Cornell and A. Gauld, 'A Fenland Poltergeist', *Journal SPR* 40, 1960, p. 348. In Enfield, Playfair left a concealed tape recorder running and went to the pub. On his return, he was told that several incidents had taken place in his absence. On privately playing the tape, he heard sounds that corresponded closely to what the family had described; their comments appeared to be reactions of genuine alarm, and offered no hint that they were practising a hoax. Playfair, *This House is Haunted,* pp. 60–61.

54. Roll and Pratt, 'The Miami Disturbances', also in Roll, *The Poltergeist*, pp. 115–47.

55. Bender, 'An Investigation of "Poltergeist Occurrences" in Rosenheim', pp. 376–83. Summaries can be found in Scott Rogo, *On the Track of the Poltergeist*, pp. 56–7, and J. Beloff (ed.), *New Directions in Parapsychology* (London: Elek Science, 1974).

56. Anon. *An Authentic, Candid, and Circumstantial Narrative, of the Astonishing Transactions at Stockwell, in the County of Surrey* (London: J. Marks, 1772). Cited in Gauld and Cornell, *Poltergeists,* p. 86.

57. ibid., pp. 86–87.

58. William Hone, *The Every Day Book* (London: William Tegg, 1826), cited in Gauld and Cornell, *Poltergeists,* p. 87.

59. The witnesses were puzzled by Ann's calm demeanour during the occurrence, and this has since been considered evidence of her guilt. Another possibility, pointed out by Owen, is that she had been troubled by such episodes before, and had got used to them; her employer would not have known of this if she came from outside the locality. *Can We Explain the Poltergeist,* p. 56.

60. Roll, *The Poltergeist*, p. 173.

61. Owen, *Can We Explain the Poltergeist?* p. 74.

62. ibid., p. 75.

63. Grosse and Playfair, 'Enfield Revisted', p. 216.

64. Matthew Manning and Teresa Rose, *One Foot in the Stars: The Story of the World's Most Extraordinary Healer* (Shaftesbury, Dorset: Element, 1999), pp. 78–79. For other examples of fictional media 'exposés', see Carrington, *The American Seances with Eusapia Palladino*, pp. 40–41; Ian Stevenson, *Unlearned Language: New Studies in Xeneglossy* (Charlottesville, VA: University Press of Virginia, 1984), pp. 140–41; Jule Eisenbud, *The World of Ted*

Serios: 'Thought-ographic' Studies of an Extraordinary Mind (Jefferson, NC and London: McFarland, 1966/1989), pp. 226–28. Piet Hein Hobeins complains of inadequate reporting by Bender at Rosenheim, but balances his criticism with the following: 'In 1978 the criminologist Dr. Herbert Schäfer told the press that Heiner Scholz, focus person of the celebrated Bremen case of 1965–66, had made a complete confession. Bender and his colleague Johannes Mischo have pointed out serious flaws in the fragmentary press accounts of this exposé. Schäfer never published a complete report of his findings, nor has he publicly replied to the parapsychologists' counter arguments.' 'Sense and Nonsense in Parapsychology', in Frazier (ed.), *Science Confronts the Paranormal*, p. 39.

65. Christopher, *Seers, Psychics and ESP*, p. 147.

66. ibid., p. 148.

67. ibid., p. 7.

68. Weisberg, *Talking to the Dead*, p. 238.

69. 'The youngest girl is about twelve years old... The other girl, who is in her fifteenth year...' Capron, *Modern Spiritualism,* p. 40. Hines gives 13 and 11 (*Pseudoscience and the Paranormal*, p. 21), as does Brandon in *The Spiritualists*, p. 1, and Lynne Kelly, *The Skeptic's Guide to the Paranormal* (New York: Thunder's Mouth Press, 2004), p. 52. Zusne and Jones have 15 and 12 (*Anomalistic Psychology,* p. 271). One of the few to follow the ages given in the confession text is C.E.M. Hansel, *ESP and Parapsychology: A Critical Re-Evaluation* (Buffalo: Prometheus, 1980), p. 55, probably because he then goes on to quote relevant passages from it, which the others do not. Paul Kurtz cites a short direct quote that ends: 'When I began this deception, I was too young to know right from wrong', but makes no reference to the age discrepancy, even though he had earlier drawn attention to this in a footnote. He cites ages of 11 and 9, oddly relying on the *Encyclopaedia Britannica* (11 edition). *Transcendental Temptation,* pp. 322, 327.

70. Kurtz, *A Skeptic's Handbook of Parapsychology*, pp. 226–29.

71. Simon Hoggart and Michael Hutchinson, *Bizarre Beliefs* (London: Richard Cohen Books, 1995), p. 189.

72. Milton A. Rothman, *The Science Gap: Dispelling the Myths and Understanding the Reality of Science* (Buffalo, NY: Prometheus, 1992), p. 129.

73. This comes from Roll (*Unleashed,* pp. 120–21), and I would hesitate to repeat what might well be hostile gossip, were it not so exactly the way that Randi often talks and behaves.

74. David Hume, 'Of Miracles', in L. Selby-Bigge and P. Nidditch (eds.), *An Enquiry Concerning Human Understanding* (Oxford: Clarendon, 1975) pp. 109–31. For a useful discussion on the implications and limits of Hume's approach see Phil Dowe, *Galileo, Darwin and Hawking: The Interplay of Sci-*

ence, Reason and Religion (Grand Rapids, Michigan: W.B. Eerdmans, 2005), pp. 82–98.

75. Scott Rogo criticizes the modern tendency to explain all such episodes in terms of repressed emotion in a living person, arguing that some cases give every appearance of involving a discarnate intelligence. *On the Track of the Poltergeist,* pp. 145–66. See also Alfonso Martinez Taboas and Carlos S. Alvarado, 'An Appraisal of the Role of Aggression and the Central Nervous System in RSPK Agents', *Journal of the American Society for Psychical Research*, 1984, 78, pp. 55–69.

76. See Jeff Wagg, 'JREF Challenge FAQ' at www.randi.org/site. 'Between 1964 and 1982, Randi declared that over 650 people had applied. Between 1997 and February 15, 2005, there had been a total of 360 official, notarized applications. Applications continue to pour in!' See also below, Chapter Three, note 6, for two recent examples of psychics who, exceptionally, *were* accepted for testing.

77. An Iranian living in the UK claimed a supernatural ability as follows: 'No lion, whatever its size, no matter how wild or how hungry, will bite me'. When apprised of the practical difficulties of testing this claim, he changed it to: 'No dog, whatever its size, no matter how wild or how hungry, will bite me'. The application processor writes: 'True to the specifics of his claim, we instructed this applicant to contact us the moment he had every dog on earth together in one place and ready for testing. I told him that we were "good to go". I received some nasty emails in response, then a brief series of emails in which the applicant bemoaned the absence of a dog pound warden in the UK who would grant him easy access to the wild dog cage. Then nothing' (see http://forums.randi.org/showthread.php?t=30405).

Chapter Two: Eusapia Palladino and the Phantom Narrative

Opening quotes: Inglis, Natural and Supernatural, pp. 226. Charles Richet, *Concerning the Phenomena of Materialisation (The Villa Carmen Phenomena).* Extracts from *The Annals of Psychical Science*, October/November 1905, p. 146.

1. Russell Targ and Harold Puthoff, 'Information transmission under conditions of sensory shielding', *Nature* 251, 18 October 1974, pp. 602–07.

2. William Crookes, 'Notes into an Enquiry into the Phenomena of Spiritualism during the Years 1870–1873', *Quarterly Journal of Science*, 1874. See also below, note 22.

3. Descriptions of psychic research activity by all four scientists can be found in Inglis, *Natural and Supernatural*. Chris Carter discusses Zöllner's work with Henry Slade in *Parapsychology and the Skeptics: A Scientific Argument for the Existence of ESP* (Pittsburg, PA: Sterling House, 2007). Crookes's psychic research is also discussed in Deborah Blum, *Ghost Hunt-*

ers: The Victorians and the Hunt for Proof of Life after Death (London: Arrow Books, 2007).

4. The slanders were made anonymously by the psychologist W.B. Carpenter in 'Spiritualism and its Recent Converts', *Quarterly Review,* 131, 1871, pp. 301–53. Carpenter gave his identity away by favouring in his article psychological theories of which he was the chief champion.

5. According to the poet William Allingham, Wallace 'never doubts any statement whatever in favour of 'Spiritualism', and has an answer to every objection.' Russell M. Goldfarb and Clare R. Goldfarb, *Spiritualism and Nineteenth Century Letters* (Cranbury, NJ: Associated University Presses, 1978), p. 113.

6. *Flim-Flam!,* p. 131.

7. 'J.M. Maskelyne at Cambridge', *Daily Chronicle,* 29 October 1895.

8. Andrija Puharich, at one time Geller's principal mentor/investigator, was a medical electronics expert who had developed a radio that could be concealed in a tooth. The *New Scientist* argued the case in detail, backed up with drawings (Joseph Hanlon, 'Looking in Uri's Mouth' in 'Uri Geller and Science', *New Scientist* 64, 17 October 1974, pp. 170–85.)

9. Randi provides a drawing that locates the hole in the wall as being 34 inches above the floor, apparently relying on hostile testimony from a participant in the experiments (*Flim-Flam!* p. 139). A parapsychologist who visited the scene some time later pointed out that the hole was actually at floor-level, as one would expect if its purpose was to carry audio cables; it was also covered by a metal plate. D. Scott Rogo, *Psychic Breakthroughs Today* (Wellingborough, Northamptonshire: Aquarian, 1987), pp. 221–24.

10. Frank Podmore, *Modern Spiritualism* (London: Methuen, 1902), Vol II, Book 4, Chapter 3.

11. Inglis, *Natural and Supernatural* (above, Chapter One, note 31); Ruth Brandon, *The Spiritualists* (above, note Chapter One, note 27).

12. Peter Lamont's generally sympathetic book about Daniel Home spells out various possible positions without appearing to favour any of them. See *The First Psychic: The Peculiar Mystery of a Notorious Victorian Wizard* (London: Little, Brown, 2005), pp. 273–75. By contrast, journalist Jonathan Margolis commits to a personal belief, though moderately stated, in the genuineness of Uri Geller's feats: *Uri Geller: Magician or Mystic?* (London: Orion, 1998).

13. H.J. Irwin, 'Charles Bailey: A biographical study of the Australian apport medium', *Journal SPR* 54, 1987, pp. 97–118.

14. Above, *Opening quotes.*

15. See for instance Hereward Carrington, *The Physical Phenomena of Spiritualism, Fraudulent and Genuine* (London: T. Werner Laurie, 1908). For first-

person confessions of hoaxing see Edward D. Lunt, *Mysteries of the Séance and Tricks and Traps of Bogus Mediums* (Boston, MA; Lunt Bros., 1903) and more recently M. Lamar Keene's *The Psychic Mafia* (New York: St Martin's Press, 1976). Several mediums investigated by psychic researchers were considered by them to be fraudulent. See for instance Stanley L. Krebs, 'A Description of Some Trick Methods Used by Miss Bangs, of Chicago', *Journal SPR* 10, 1901, pp. 5–16; Oliver Lodge, 'On a Sitting with Mr and Mrs Tomson', *Journal SPR* 14, 1910, pp. 365–70; Eric J. Dingwall, 'The Case of the Medium Pasquale Erto', *Journal SPR* 21, 1924, pp. 278–80; 'The Cases of Mr Moss and Mr Munnings', *Journal SPR* 23, 1926, pp. 71–5; K.H.E. Jong, 'The Trumpet-Medium, Mrs S. Harris', *Journal SPR* 16, 1914, pp. 266–70. Fake materializing mediums were exposed in: 'Exposure of the Medium Husk', *Journal* 5, 1891, p. 46; 'Sittings with Mr Chambers', *Journal SPR* 12 1905, pp. 197–203; and 'Exposure of Mr Eldred', *Journal SPR* 12, 1906, pp. 242–52.

16. Hugo Münsterberg, 'Report on a Sitting with Eusapia Palladino', *Metropolitan Magazine*, February 1909. A transcript of the relevant section can be found in Hansel, *ESP and Parapsychology*, p. 62.

17. R. Hodgson, E. Gurney, F.W.H. Myers *et al.*, 'Report of the Committee Appointed to Investigate Phenomena Connected with the Theosophical Society', *Proceedings SPR* 3, 1885, pp. 201–400. Richard Hodgson and S.J. Davey, 'The Possibilities of Mal-Observation and Lapse of Memory From a Practical Point of View', *Proceedings SPR* 4, 1887, pp. 381–495.

18. 'J.N. Maskelyne at Cambridge', *Daily Chronicle*, 29 October 1895.

19. Conan Doyle became an evangelist for spiritualism in his later years, arguing that séance phenomena was so clearly supernatural as to be beyond doubt. See his *The History of Spiritualism* (London: Echo Library, 1926/2006), which can also be read online at: www.classic-literature.co.uk. Conan Doyle became friendly with the illusionist and anti-spiritualist crusader Harry Houdini in his later years; see Brandon, *The Spiritualists*, pp. 167–73.

20. Michael Faraday, 'Experimental Investigation of Table-Moving', *The Athenaeum*, July 2, 1853, pp. 801–802. Faraday's explanation is mentioned by most critics who deal with nineteenth century séance claims, in some detail by Hansel, *ESP and Parapsychology*, pp. 189–90.

21. Carrington, *The American Seances with Eusapia Palladino*, p. 70.

22. Some of the main sources about Home are William Crookes, 'Notes of Séances with D.D. Home', *Proceedings SPR* 6, 1889, pp. 98–127; W.F. Barrett and F.W.H. Myers, 'Review of 'D.D. Home, His Life and Mission', *Journal SPR* 4, 1889, pp. 101–16; Earl of Dunraven, 'Experiences in Spiritualism with D.D. Home', *Proceedings SPR* 35, 1926, pp. 1–289.

23. Frederic Myers describes table-turning claims, including a Brazilian spiritist circle where a table 'acted like a restless, living creature endowed with human intelligence' in 'On Alleged Movements of Objects, Without

Contact, Occurring Not in the Presence of a Paid Medium, Part 1', *Proceedings SPR* 7, 1891, pp. 146–98. The table-turning fad of 1853 throughout Europe is described by Inglis, *Natural and Supernatural,* pp. 216–20. In 1869, the Dialectical Society, a rationalist debating club, carried out forty table turning sessions, of which thirty-four were productive. In one session, the table moved four times in one minute up to a distance of one foot, when the members' feet were out of range and their hands were extended four inches about the surface. *Report on Spiritualism of the Committee of the London Dialectical Society* (London, 1873). Quoted in Inglis, *Natural and Supernatural*, pp. 246–7; and Alan Gauld, *The Founders of Psychic Research* (London: Routledge and Kegan Paul, 1968), pp. 84–86. For a more recent experience see Stephen E. Braude, *Immortal Remains: The Evidence for Life after Death* (New York: Rowman and Littlefield Publishers, 2003), pp. ix-x.

24. Myers, 'On Alleged Movements of Objects', p. 159.

25. ibid., p. 157.

26. K.J. Batcheldor, 'Report on a Case of Table Levitation and Associated Phenomena', *Journal SPR* 43, 1966, pp. 329–56. See also I.M. Owen and M.H. Sparrow, 'Generation of paranormal physical phenomena in connection with an imaginary communicator', *New Horizons* 1, 1974. pp. 6–13. Also I.M. Owen, *Conjuring up Philip* (New York: Harper and Row, 1977).

27. J.N. Maskelyne, 'Mr. Maskelyne and the spiritualists', *Pall Mall Gazette*, 23 April 1885, p. 2.

28. Edwin Lee, *Animal Magnetism* (London: Longmans, Green and Co, 1866), p. 163. A sceptic tried to explain away Robert-Houdin's statements in support of Didier, averring, for instance that the words 'after this sad ceremony' could be found in virtually any book, and that the look of of stupefaction on the conjuror's face after witnessing Didier's feats was actually one of suppressed laughter. Bertrand Méheust, *Un Voyant Prodigieux: Alexis Didier, 1826–1866* (Paris: *Les Empêcheurs de penser on rond, 2003), pp.* 249–69. See a useful summary by Mary Rose Barrington, 'The clairvoyant, the magician and the proto-psi-cop', *Paranormalia.com,* 23 March 2010.

29. Cesare Lombroso, *After Death – What? Spiritistic Phenomena and Their Interpretation* (Boston, MA: Small, Maynard and Co., 1909), pp. 312–13. For this and other examples see also George P. Hansen, 'Magicians Who Endorsed Psychic Phenomena', *The Linking Ring,* 70/8, 1990, pp. 52–54. See also Uri Geller's website for magicians and mentalists who endorse him: http://site.uri-geller.com/en/what_magicians_say

30. Richard Hodgson, 'Indian Magic and the Testimony of Conjurors', *Proceedings SPR*, 9, 1894, p. 359. Kellar is said subsequently to have duplicated other of Eglinton's feats, but not the levitation, which he continued to be puzzled by. Hodgson himself was sceptical, as described above.

31. Richard Wiseman, 'The Feilding Report: A Reconsideration', *Journal*

SPR 58, 1991, pp. 129–52. See also Mary Rose Barrington. 'Palladino and the Invisible Man Who Never Was', *Journal SPR* 58, 1992, pp. 324–40; and David Fontana, 'The Feilding Report and the Determined Critic', *Journal SPR* 58, 1992, pp. 341–50. See further discussion below.

32. A good introduction to Palladino is a biography by Hereward Carrington, *Eusapia Palladino and Her Phenomena* (London: T. Werner Laurie, 1909). See also his later volume *The American Séances With Eusapia Palladino* (New York: Garrett, 1954). For a short summary of Palladino's career, with a detailed list of references, see Carlos S. Alvarado, 'Gifted Subjects' Contributions to Psychic Research: The Case of Eusapia Palladino', *Journal SPR* 59, 1993, pp. 269–92. See below for other key sources. During her lifetime there was some confusion about the spelling of Palladino's name, which sometimes appears with one 'l' but more commonly with two, which is how she signed it and how it appears on her birth certificate. See Carlos S. Alvarado, 'Palladino Or Paladino? On the Spelling of Eusapia's Surname', *Journal SPR* 52, 1984, pp. 315–16.

33. Carrington, *Eusapia Palladino and Her Phenomena*, pp. 32–33.

34. Oliver Lodge, 'Experience of Unusual Physical Phenomena Occurring in the Presence of an Entranced Person (Eusapia Pal[l]adino)', *Journal SPR* 6, 1894, pp. 306–60.

35. Richard Hodgson, 'The Value of the Evidence for Supernormal Phenomena in the Case of Eusapia Pal[l]adino', *Journal SPR* 7, 1895, pp. 36–79.

36. ibid., p. 56.

37. Details of the SPR's Cambridge sittings are in Alice Johnson, 'Eusapia Pal[l]adino', *Journal SPR* 7, 1895, pp. 148–59. For a re-appraisal of the negative verdict see Manfred Cassirer, 'Palladino at Cambridge', *Journal SPR* 52, 1983, pp. 52–58.

38. See for instance the exchange between Edward Tylor and Alfred Russel Wallace, summarized in Inglis, *Natural and Supernatural,* pp. 300–302. Hallucination is also considered in detail, and rejected, in the case of Palladino: Everard Feilding, W.W. Baggally, and Hereward Carrington, 'Report on a Series of Sittings with Eusapia Palladino', *Proceedings SPR* 23, 1909, p. 342–44. See also Count P-P. Solovovo, 'The Hallucination Theory as Applied to Certain Cases of Physical Phenomena', *Proceedings SPR* 21, 1909, pp. 436–82, Alice Johnson's reply, 'The Education of the Sitter', *Proceedings SPR* 21, 1909, pp. 483–511, and Oliver Lodge's reply to Johnson, 'The Education of an Observer', *Journal SPR* 14, 1909, pp. 253–60.

39. Count P-P. Solovovo, 'M. Courtier's Report on the Experiments with Eusapia Palladino at the Paris Institut General Psychologique and Some Comments Thereon', *Proceedings SPR* 23, 1909, pp. 570–89.

40. Susan Quinn, *Marie Curie: A Life* (Cambridge, MA: Da Capo, 1995), p. 208.

41. ibid., p. 226. Pierre Curie died shortly after writing this in 1906, run over by a carriage in the street.

42. See Carrington, *The Physical Phenomena of Spiritualism, Fraudulent and Genuine;* W.W. Baggally, 'Sittings with Carancini', *Journal SPR* 14, 1909, pp. 193–211.

43. Feilding *et al.*, 'Report on a Series of Sittings with Eusapia Palladino', p. 309–569.

44. ibid., p. 332.

45. ibid., p. 348.

46. J. Jastrow, 'The Unmasking of Paladino', *Colliers*, May 14, 1910, and 'The Case of Paladino', *Review of Reviews*, July 1910. See also Joseph Rinn, *Sixty Years of Psychical Research* (New York: The Truth Seeker Company, 1950), pp. 278–91.

47. Feilding et al, 'Report on a Series of Sittings with Eusapia Palladino', p. 333.

48. The habitual claim by debunkers to have approached psychic investigations with more care than their opponents deserves close scrutiny, as this gem on Uri Geller suggests. 'Two psychologists, David Marks and Richard Kammann ... carefully monitored Geller's visit to New Zealand. Marks was permitted to test Geller in his hotel room. He had placed a previously prepared drawing of a sailboat in a sealed envelope and handed it to Uri. Marks was surprised when Geller was able to duplicate the figure... Later Marks retrieved the discarded envelope and found that Geller had evidently peeled it open when Marks was in the bathroom and the other observer was distracted by a phone call. He apparently peeked into the envelope to see the drawing.' Paul Kurtz, 'Spiritualists, Mediums, and Psychics: Some Evidence of Fraud', in Kurtz (ed.), *A Skeptic's Handbook of Parapsychology*, p. 214. So during this 'careful monitoring', one of the two observers left the room while the other took a phone call, leaving Geller unattended.

49. Carrington, *The American Seances with Eusapia Palladino*, p. 113.

50. Hansel, *ESP and Parapsychology*, p. 62.

51. Inglis, *Natural and Supernatural*, p. 394.

52. Feilding *et al.*, 'Report on a Series of Sittings with Eusapia Palladino', p. 462–63.

53. Wiseman, 'The Feilding Report: A Reconsideration', pp. 141, 146, 149.

54. The main proponent of this approach is Trevor H. Hall who, in one book, speculated that the premature death of a leading SPR researcher, Edmund Gurney, from a medication overdose was not accidental, as had been generally supposed, but suicide motivated by shame at discovering that he had been deceived in telepathy experiments. *The Strange Case of Edmund Gurney* (London: Duckworth, 1964). This scenario would have been unlikely on many counts, not least that Gurney and his colleagues had dismissed the claim

of deception as implausible. On the topic of William Crookes's surprising claims about Florence Cook, Hall argues that the girl's parents conspired to make her seem younger than she actually was, so that no one would suspect her of fraud. He supports this by describing his inability to trace Cook's birth registration, concluding that the actual date of her birth has been enveloped in 'a fog of mystery that has so far proved impenetrable.' *The Spiritualists* (London: Duckworth, 1962), p. 2. However, parapsychologists located Cook's birth certificate with little difficulty, and the age difference turned out to be no more than a year, which could hardly have made a difference. R.G. Medhurst and K.M. Goldney, 'William Crookes and the Physical Phenomena of Mediumship', *Proceedings SPR* 54, 1964, p. 62.

55. In his 1973 biography of the Boston medium Mina Crandon, Thomas Tieze assembled snippets of gossip in order to explain away the endorsement of her by Hereward Carrington. 'Carrington asked her to sell her house and elope with him... she and her husband were hardly on speaking terms... at that time she was making advances to every man in sight... Houdini showed me photographic evidence...' To make quite sure we have got the point, Tieze added the following oily innuendo: 'I was informed by another old colleague of Carrington's that the famed researcher was fond of reminiscing about this love affair with Mina – complete with such details as time, place, and quality of their sexual encounters. Although I do not repose absolute confidence in this story, at least we may suppose that Carrington was enthralled by Mina. Whatever bearing this sort of thing has upon the factual details of a science at that time so dependent upon the personal equation must be left for the reader to ponder.' Thomas R. Tieze, *Margery the Medium* (Harper and Row, 1973), p. 59.

56. Brandon, *The Spiritualists*, p. 130.

57. *The Spiritualist*, 15 July 1870, p. 82 and 15 August 1870, p. 90, in R.G. Medhurst, *Crookes and the Spirit World* (London: Souvenir Press, 1972), p. 138. Crookes reported the results of his investigations in three letters to *The Spiritualist*, 6 February 3 April and 5 June 1874, reprinted in Medhurst, *Crookes and the Spirit World*, pp. 130–41.

58. This is an unpublished statement made in 1949 to the SPR by Francis G.H. Anderson, now in the SPR archives, following a private communication made by him to an SPR member in 1922. For a full description see Hall, *The Spiritualists*, pp. 99–104. Objections to Hall's case were set out by Medhurst and Goldney, 'William Crookes and the Physical Phenomena of Mediumship', pp. 25–157.

59. 'Crookes was a crook and the medium was his mistress', remarks Antony Flew in *The Logic of Mortality* (Oxford: Blackwell, 1987), pp. 166–67. Also Steven Hoffmaster, 'How not to be a scientist: Science and Sir William Crookes', *Skeptical Inquirer* 15, 1990.

60. See C.D. Broad, 'Cromwell Varley's Electrical Tests with Florence Cook', *Proceedings SPR* 54, 1963, pp. 158–72.

61. *Annals of Psychical Science*, April 1906, pp. 201–205. In a similar incident, a French witness described seeing a form, which for a brief period had been a girl calling herself Lucie, subside at his feet like a house of cards: 'Lucie disappeared by degrees in two seconds at most as she had come, but this time some twenty inches in front of the curtains beside which I was standing. The curtains did not move ... Just as the last white spot was disappearing from the carpet where the figure had been, I stooped down and put my hand upon it, but could feel nothing'. Charles Richet, *Thirty Years of Psychical Research: Being a Treatise on Metapsychics* (London: W. Collins, 1923), p. 474. For other descriptions of materialization, see Donald West, 'The Trial of Mrs Helen Duncan', *Proceedings SPR* 48, 1946, pp. 32–64; Manfred Cassirer, 'Helen Victoria Duncan: A Reassessment', *Journal SPR* 53, 1985, pp. 138–4; Henry S. Olcott, *People From The Other World* (Hartford, Connecticut: American Publishing Company, 1875); W.P. Adshead, *Dr Monck in Derbyshire* (London: J. Burns, 1877); W. J. Crawford, *The Psychic Structures at the Goligher Circle* (London: John M. Watkins, 1921; and Gustave Geley, *Clairvoyance and Materialisation* (London: T. Fisher Unwin, 1927). See also E.J. Dingwall, 'An Amazing Case: The Mediumship of Carlos Mirabelli', *Journal of the American Society for Psychical Research* 24, 1930, pp. 296–306. For first-person accounts by materializing mediums see Einer Nielsen, *Solid Proofs of Survival* (London: Spiritualist Press, 1950); E. d'Esperance, *Shadow Land* (London: George Redway, 1898); and Tom Harrison, *Life After Death: Living Proof* (Saturday Night Press Publications, 2004).

62. Brandon, *The Spiritualists*, p. 135.

63. D.H. Rawcliffe, *The Psychology of the Occult* (London: Derricke Ridgway, 1952), p. 326.

64. ibid., p. 323.

65. For an early example of overstatement see Camille Flammarion, *Death and Its Mystery: Before Death, Proofs of the Existence of the Soul* (London: T. Fisher Unwin, 1909). Victor Zammit directs some fairly intemperate polemic at sceptics: http://www.victorzammit.com/skeptics/index.html

66. Myers's chief work is his posthumously published *Human Personality and Its Survival of Bodily Death* (London: Longmans, 1903), in which he argues for the existence of a subliminal aspect of human consciousness appearing in dreams, in the revelations of genius, and in the kind of states germane to psychic research such as automatic writing, trance states and apparitional visions. The book is a step-by-step exploration of these various aspects, which he held demonstrate the links between human consciousness and a state that exists beyond conscious perception, with which it reunites at the death of the body. For a general account of the background to his life and work see Gauld, *The Founders of Psychical Research*. Gauld has also contributed a chapter to

the more recent *Irreducible Mind: Toward a Psychology for the 21ˢᵗ Century* by Edward F. Kelly, Emily Williams Kelly, Adam Crabtree, Alan Gauld, Michael Grosso and Bruce Greyson (Lanham, MD: Rowman and Littlefield Publisher, 2007), in which Myers's thought is examined in the context of a wide variety of more recent data (for more details see below Chapter Six, note 44). A sceptical view of Myers and early psychic research is provided by Janet Oppenheim, *The Other World: Spiritualism and Psychical Research in England, 1850–1914* (Cambridge: Cambridge University Press, 1985).

67. Richet acknowledges the reality of séance materialization, but when it comes to explanations considers the 'spiritist hypothesis' involving the spirits of the dead as 'the least likely of any'. *Thirty Years of Psychical Research*, pp. 622–23. See also Charles Richet, 'The Difficulty of Survival from the Scientific Point of View', *Proceedings SPR* 34, 1924, pp. 107–12.

68. Rawcliffe, *The Psychology of the Occult*, p. 15.

69. See for instance Hugo Münsterberg, *Psychology and Life* (London: Archibald Constable, 1899).

70. Harry Houdini, *A Magician Among The Spirits* (New York: Harper, 1924), p. 243.

71. Randi, *Flim-Flam!*, pp. 222, 217, 227.

72. 'Consensus will probably remain elusive. Looking at the Fox sisters' story is like peering through a kaleidoscope: the configuration is never fixed; it changes depending on the angle of the prism and the way the pieces seem to fall … Whether they were nothing more than marvellous conjurers or (I am especially puzzled by Kate), something other, I enjoy the mediums too much to be critical of them…' *Talking to the Dead*, p. 270–71.

73. For instance Geoffrey Best, *Mid-Victorian Britain 1851–75* (London: Fontana, 1979), and Stewart Wolf, *Brain, Mind And Medicine: Charles Richet and the Origins of Physiological Psychology* (Piscataway, NJ: Transaction Publishers, 1993). The latter's blurb points out that as well as being a scientist Richet was a 'poet, playwright, historian, bibliographer, political activist, classical scholar, and a pioneer in aircraft design', but makes no mention of his considerable interest in psychic research.

74. Deborah Blum's *Ghost Hunters* (above, note 3) is a notably full and sympathetic account of nineteenth-century psychic research by a Pulitzer Prize-winning science writer, but it stops short of committing to a belief that the phenomena were genuine.

75. The SORRAT mediumistic circle formed in the 1960s aimed to validate psychokinesis, levitation, apports, apparitions, and communication with entities in fraud-proof conditions, but its activities were considered unconvincing by parapsychologists. John Thomas Richards, *SORRAT: A History of the Neihardt Psychokinesis Experiments, 1961–1981* (Metuchen, NJ: Scarecrow Press, 1982). A circle in Scole in Norfolk was the subject of a three-

year investigation by SPR investigators, and attracted widespread interest and support, although their conviction that it stood as good evidence of paranormality was contested by some other SPR members. Montague Keen, Arthur Ellison and David Fontana, 'The Scole Report', *Proceedings SPR* 58, 1999.

Chapter Three: Communicators

Opening quote: *Many Voices: The Autobiography of a Medium* (New York: Putnam, 1968), preface.

1. The show, produced and hosted by Edward, ran from 1999 to 2004, and is regularly repeated on Living TV in the UK. See also John Edward, *Crossing Over: The Stories Behind the Stories* (New York: Princess Books, 2001).

2. For a detailed description of cold reading, see Ray Hyman, *The Elusive Quarry* (Buffalo, NY: Prometheus, 1989), pp. 403–19.

3. Perhaps the best known case of this kind concerns Arthur Ford, a reputable American medium of the mid-twentieth century, whose possessions were found after his death to include evidence of intelligence-gathering on people, such as newspaper cuttings and obituaries. See Allen Spraggett with William Rauscher, *Arthur Ford: The Man Who Talked with the Dead* (New York: W.W. Norton, 1973).

4. This charge was made against Doris Stokes by Ian Wilson (*The After Death Experience* (London: Sidgwick & Jackson, 1987), pp. 71–79 and against John Edward by Leon Jaroff (described by Edward in *Crossing Over*, pp. 245-53).

5. Peter FitzSimons, *Sydney Morning Herald*, 23 January 2003.

6. Derek Ogilvie, who claims an ability to communicate with infants telepathically, failed tests carried out by Professor Chris French at Goldsmith's College, University of London, and later by James Randi. The tests were televised by Channel 4, *Extraordinary People: The Million Dollar Mind Reader,* 27 September 2008. Patricia Putt also failed Randi's test: 'Patricia Putt: Score for Sceptics', *Paranormalia.com*, 25 May 2008. Both these cases appear to contradict the claim that no applicant has been formally tested, none having passed the preliminaries.

7. The key papers on Piper are as follows: F.W.H. Myers, 'A Record of Observations of Certain Phenomena of Trance', *Proceedings SPR* 6, pp. 436–660, the record of investigations undertaken during a ten-week visit by Piper to England in 1889–90; Richard Hodgson, 'A Record of Observations of Certain Phenomena of Trance', *Proceedings SPR* 8, 1892, pp. 1–168; Richard Hodgson, 'A Further Record of Certain Phenomena of Trance', *Proceedings SPR* 13, 1898, pp. 284–582. A third paper was planned but never written owing to Hodgson's sudden death in 1905. See also James H. Hyslop, 'A Further Record of Observations of Certain Trance Phenomena', *Proceedings*

SPR 16, 1901, pp. 1–649, a report and analysis of 17 sittings by an American researcher. Other sources containing commentary on Piper are given below. For sources on Leonard see below.

8.   Hodgson, 'A Record of Observations', p. 128.

9.   ibid., p. 4.

10. Inglis, *Natural and Supernatural,* p. 147.

11. Myers *et al.*, 'A Record Of Observations', p. 642.

12. Hodgson, 'A Record of Observations', p. 116

13. ibid., p. 60.

14. ibid., p. 129.

15. ibid., p. 121.

16. A rare exception is Ruth Brandon, who, however, misleadingly centres her analysis on a single failed sitting: *The Spiritualists,* pp. 211–12. Psychologist C.E.M. Hansel attempts a critique of Leonard in *ESP and Parapsychology,* pp. 66–8 (discussed below).

17. 'Mrs. Z., a lady who was mourning for a near relation, gave so many hints that Mr. Myers, in the course of taking notes, guessed much more of the facts than Phinuit succeeded in giving. Phinuit, as occasionally happened, seemed so obstinately bent upon some erroneous ideas of his own that he would pay no attention to Mrs. Z.'s leading questions.' Myers *et al.*, 'A Record of Observations', p. 646.

18. Hodgson, 'A Record of Observations', p. 91.

19. William James, *Psychological Review,* July 1898, pp. 421–22.

20. Frank Podmore, 'Discussion of the Trance-Phenomena of Mrs Piper 1, *Proceedings SPR* 14, 1898, p. 75

21. Zusne and Jones, *Anomalistic Psychology, 2nd edition 1989,* p. 214.

22. Rinn, *Sixty Years of Psychical Research,* pp. 173–74.

23. Eleanor Sidgwick, 'A Contribution to the Study of the Psychology of Mrs Piper's Trance Phenomena, *Proceedings SPR* 28, 1915, pp. 1–652.

24. Amy Tanner, *Studies in Spiritism* (Buffalo, NY: Prometheus, 1910/1994), p. 181.

25. Leonora Piper, *New York Herald*, 20 October 1901. Quoted in Rinn, *Sixty Years of Psychical Research*, pp. 195–98. For a discussion see 'The Newspapers on Mrs Piper', *Journal SPR* 10, 1901, pp. 142–43, 150–52.

26. Other critics mention Piper's statement as a means to build up suspicions about mediums, but evade the obvious questions: what exactly was she confessing to, and how does it support their argument? See for

instance Brandon, *The Spiritualists,* pp. 232–5, and Andrew Neher, *The Psychology of Transcendence* (New York: Dover, 1990), p. 218.

27. There is a large literature on Leonard in the proceedings and journals of the SPR between 1918 and 1949. See for instance, Radclyffe-Hall and Una Troubridge, 'On a Series of Sittings with Mrs Osborne Leonard', *Proceedings SPR* 30, 1920, pp. 339–554; Eleanor Sidgwick, 'An Examination of Book-Tests Obtained in Sittings with Mrs Leonard', *Proceedings SPR* 31, 1921, pp. 241–416; Mrs W.H. Salter (Helen Verrall). 'A Further Report on Sittings with Mrs Leonard', *Proceedings* 32, 1922, pp. 1–143; and C. Drayton Thomas, 'A Consideration of a Series of Proxy Sittings', *Proceedings SPR* 41, 1932, pp. 139–185. For biographical background, see Gladys Osborne Leonard's memoir, *My Life in Two Worlds* (London: Cassells, 1931), and Rosalind Heywood, 'Mrs Gladys Osborne Leonard: A Biographical Tribute', *Journal SPR* 45, 1969, pp. 95–105.

28. Radclyffe-Hall and Troubridge, 'On a Series of Sittings with Mrs Osborne Leonard', p. 343–44.

29. Eleanor Sidgwick, 'An Examination of Book-Tests Obtained in Sittings With Mrs Leonard', *Proceedings SPR* 31, 1921, pp. 286–89.

30. Eleanor Sidgwick, 'On the Element of Chance in Book-Tests *Proceedings SPR* 33, 1923, pp. 606–20.

31. C. Drayton Thomas, 'A Proxy Experiment of Significant Success', *Proceedings SPR* 45, 1939, pp. 257–306.

32. H.F. Saltmarsh, 'Report on the Investigation of Some Sittings with Mrs Warren Elliott', *Proceedings SPR* 39, 1930, pp. 47–184. A later statistical analysis of Elliott sittings effectively ruled out in this case the hypothesis of chance working to give the effect of veridicality: H.F. Saltmarsh and S.G. Soal, 'A Method of Estimating the Supernormal Content of Mediumistic Communications', *Proceedings SPR* 39, 1931, pp. 266–73.

33. See Verrall, 'A Further Report on Sittings with Mrs Leonard', pp. 11–13.

34. Hansel, *ESP and Parapsychology,* pp. 66–68.

35. Oliver Lodge, *Raymond, or Life and Death* (London: Methuen, 1916), pp. 105–16.

36. Steven Hoffmaster similarly misses the point. 'Sir Oliver Lodge and the Spiritualists' in Frazier, *Science Confronts the Paranormal,* pp. 79–87.

37. Hansel, *ESP and Parapsychology*, pp. 68–69.

38. ibid., p. 69.

39. 'If you wish to upset the law that all crows are black, you must not seek to show that no crows are; it is enough if you prove one single crow to be white.' William James, 'What Psychical Research Has Accomplished', in *The Will to Believe and Other Essays in Popular Philosophy* (New York: Dover Publica-

tions, 1897/1956), p. 319. Karl Popper, *Conjectures and Refutations* (London: Routledge, 1963).

40. K. Oldfield, 'Philosophers and Psychics: The Vandy episode', *Skeptical Inquirer,* 25 (6) Nov/Dec 2001. His article is a critique of A.R. Miller, 'Survival and diminished consciousness', *Journal of Philosophical Research* 23, 1998, pp. 479–96. A detailed rebuttal of Oldfield was made by Montague Keen, 'The Case of Edgar Vandy: Defending the Evidence', *Journal SPR* 66, October 2002, pp. 247–59. The original case was reported by Kathleen Gay, 'The Case of Edgar Vandy', *Journal SPR* 39, 1957, pp. 1–64.

41. C.D. Broad, *Lectures on Psychical Research* (London: Routledge and Kegan Paul, 1962), pp. 349–83.

42. Gay, 'The Case of Edgar Vandy', p. 29.

43. ibid., p. 29.

44. This and the following notes 45–47 refer to shortened versions of summaries provided by Broad: *Lectures on Psychical Research,* pp. 360–61.

45. ibid., p. 361–62.

46. ibid., p. 363–34.

47. ibid., p. 372.

48. Gary E. Schwartz and Linda G.S. Russek, 'Evidence of Anomalous Information Retrieval between Two Mediums: Telepathy, Network Memory Resonance, and Continuance of Consciousness', *Journal SPR* 65, 2001, pp. 257–75; Gary E. Schwartz *et al.*, 'Accuracy and Replicability of Anomalous Information Retrieval: Replication and Extension', *Journal SPR* 66, 2002, pp. 144–56.

49. G.E. Schwartz, S. Geoffrion, S. Jain, S. Lewis and L.G. Russek, 'Evidence of Anomalous Information Retrieval Between Two Mediums: Replication in a Double-Blind Design', *Journal SPR* 67, 2002, pp. 115–130. Gary E. Schwartz with William L. Simon, *The Afterlife Experiments* (New York: Pocket Books, 2002).

50. 'May the Schwartz Be with You, the Tooth Fairy's Existence Proven by Science!', Commentary, March 23, 2001 on http://www.randi.org/jr/03–23–2001.html

51. http://survivalscience.50megs.com/torandi.htm

52. Richard Wiseman and Ciaran O'Keefe, 'A Critique of Schwartz *et al.*'s After-Death Communication Studies', *Paranormal Review*, 20, 2001. Also in *Skeptical Inquirer,* November/December 2001.

53. Ray Hyman, 'How Not to Test Mediums: Critiquing the Afterlife Experiments', *Skeptical Inquirer,* 27/1, Jan/Feb 2003, p. 22 (also at www.csicop.org).

54. Ray Hyman, 'Hyman's Reply to Schwartz's 'How *Not* To Review Mediumship Research', *Skeptical Inquirer,* May/June 2003, p. 64.

55. Gary E. Schwartz, 'How *Not* To Review Mediumship Research', *Skeptical Inquirer*, 27(3), May/June 2003, pp. 58–61; http://www.enformy.com/Gary-rehymanReview.htm. See also G. E. Schwartz, 'Accuracy and replicability of anomalous after-death communication across highly skilled mediums: a call for balanced evidence-based skepticism', *The Paranormal Review* 20, 2001.

56. Hyman, 'Hyman's Reply to Schwartz's 'How *Not* To Review Mediumship Research', p. 63.

Chapter Four: Uncertain Science

Opening quotes: Martin Gardner, *The Whys of a Philosophical Scrivener* (New York: Quill, 1983), p. 60. Charles Honorton, 'Rhetoric over substance: The impoverished state of skepticism', *Journal of Parapsychology* **57**, 1993, p. 194. Alan Turing, Computing Machinery and Intelligence, *Mind* **59**, October 1950.

1. J.B. Rhine, *New Frontiers of the Mind* (London: Faber and Faber, 1938), pp. 18–20.

2. ibid., pp. 50–68. For a useful overview see S.H. Mauskopf and M.R. McVaugh, *The Elusive Science: Origins of experimental psychical research* (Baltimore: John Hopkins University Press, 1980).

3. Alan Turing, the pioneer of computing, included telepathy in a list of characteristics that computers would have to demonstrate if they were to reach the human level of intelligence, a detail now usually overlooked in discussions of his test. 'Computing, machinery and intelligence', *Mind*, 59, pp. 433–60. Albert Einstein, in a short preface to Upton Sinclair's *Mental Radio* (Charlottesville: Hampton Roads, 1930/2001), a description of successful telepathy experiments between Sinclair and his wife, thought it 'out of the question' that the author was carrying on a conscious deception, but wondered if the observations might be explained in terms of 'unconscious hypnotic influence from person to person' rather than telepathy; p. xi. Norbert Winer, a pioneer of cybernetics, argued that telepathy would become an integral part of psychology, and that investigation would 'not be corrupted by the unscientific assumption that we are dealing with phenomena with no physical correlates.' In Arthur Koestler, *Roots of Coincidence* (London: Vintage, 1973), pp. 18–19.

4. In Britain, psi research is being carried out in ten universities besides Northampton, including Liverpool Hope, Coventry and Goldsmiths (which however takes a moderately sceptical approach, led by Professor Chris French). Projects are being run by Ph.D. graduates of the Koestler Parapsychology Unit at the University of Edinburgh's Department of Psychology, of whom there are now more than thirty. See 'The Psi-seeding of

Academe', *Paranormalia.com*, 15 March 2008.

5. The term 'pathological science' was coined by Irving Langmuir in a talk in 1953 (see 'Pathological Science', in *Physics Today* 42(10), 1989, pp. 36–48). He applied it to cases where scientists were tricked by subjective effects and wishful thinking into seeing non-existent effects. One example he cites is the affair of the 'N-Rays' that René-Prosper Blondlot claimed to have discovered in 1903. An American physicist visited Blondlot's laboratory and by means of covert experiment established that Blondlot's observations were subjective and demonstrably erroneous. For a discussion see Wallace Sampson, ' "Alternative Medicine": How it Demonstrates Characteristics of Pseudoscience, Cult, and Confidence Game', in Paul Kurtz (ed.), *Skeptical Odesseys* (Buffalo, NY: Prometheus, 2001), pp. 259–67.

6. Peter Atkins, quoted in M. Henderson,'Theories of telepathy and afterlife cause uproar at top science forum', *The Times,* 6 September 2006, p. 22. This was one of several hostile comments by leading scientists on the decision by the British Association for the Advancement of Science to invite presentations on telepathy and near-death experiences at its festival of science held at the University of East Anglia in Norwich in 2006. A similar controversy occurred in 2001, when the Royal Mail issued stamps commemorating the centenary of the founding of the Nobel Prize. In a contribution to its accompanying booklet, Brian Josephson, a University of Cambridge physicist, suggested that quantum theory might one day explain processes still not understood within conventional science such as telepathy, an endorsement of psi's reality that other scientists took fierce exception to. See also below, Chapter 7 note 41.

7. Dawkins, *Unweaving the Rainbow,* p. 147.

8. Comments following 'Losing My Religion', *Paranormalia.com,* August 17 2009. David Lorimer describes a story told to him by a Manchester taxi driver, who was woken one night soon after going to sleep feeling as though he had been hit on the head. The next day he learned that his brother had, at this time, fallen down the stairs and banged his head. David Lorimer, 'Distant feelings', *Network* 71, 1999, p. 19, quoted in Guy Lyon Playfair, *Twin Telepathy: The Psychic Connection* (London: Vega, 2002), p. 34.

9. See for instance Charles Richet, 'Further Experiments in Hypnotic Lucidity or Clairvoyance', *Proceedings SPR* 6, 1889, pp. 66–83, describing how he used ten packs of fifty-two cards each with an experimental subject 'Leonie B', and tabulated the results.

10. J.B. Rhine and J.G. Pratt, 'A Review of the Pearce-Pratt Distance Series of ESP Tests', *Journal of Parapsychology,* 18/3, 1954, pp. 165–77.

11. In its early years the SPR reported on informal experiments of the 'guessing game' type, eg. J. Page Hopps, 'Some New Experiments in Thought-Transference, *Journal SPR* 1, 1884, pp. 111–2, in which two young women were successfully willed to perform certain pre-agreed actions and to find

objects. Also, Anton Schmoll, 'Experiments in Thought-Transference', *Proceedings SPR* 4, 1886, pp. 324–37, in which a person sitting in a corner with his or her back to the room receives accurate impressions of shapes and objects that others in the centre of the room are attempting to transmit telepathically. A much-quoted later example concerns Gilbert Murray, an Oxford professor, who described instances of personal telepathic awareness, some occurring spontaneously and others in experiments with his family. Murray described the involvement of sense impressions, for instance of smell and sight, in becoming aware of scenes and situations. 'Presidential Address', *Proceedings* 29, 1916, pp. 46–63; and A.W. Verrall, 'Report On A Series Of Experiments In 'Guessing', *Proceedings* 29, 1916, pp. 64–110. An early successful example of remote viewing was carried out between two women, first when they were separated by a distance of 20 miles, and later when one was in France and the other in England. Clarissa Miles and Hermione Ramsden, 'Experiments In Thought-Transference', *Proceedings* 21, 1908, pp. 60–93. Brief abstracts of further examples can be found in the SPR catalogue.

12. See note 3, above.

13. M. Ullman and S. Krippner, *Dream Studies and Telepathy: an experimental approach* (New York: Parapsychology Foundation, 1970).

14. For a detailed description of the ganzfeld procedure see H.J. Irwin, *An Introduction to Parapsychology* (Jefferson, NC and London: McFarland and Co, 1999), p. 97, or Dean Radin, *Entangled Minds* (New York: Simon & Schuster, 2006), pp. 115–18.

15. A. Parker, A. Persson and A. Hauler, 'Using Qualitative Ganzfeld Research for Theory Development: Top–Down Processes in Psi-Meditation', *Journal SPR* 64, 2000, p. 70. The paper includes other examples.

16. Jessica Utts, 'Replication and meta-analysis in parapsychology', *Statistical Science* 6, 1991, p. 374.

17. Russell Targ and Harold E. Puthoff, *Mind Reach* (NY: Delacorte, 1977), pp. 50–52.

18. Jim McMoneagle, *The Stargate Chronicles: Memoirs of a Psychic Spy* (Charlottesville: Hampton Roads, 2002), pp. 114–20.

19. Robert G. Jahn and Brenda J. Dunne, *Margins of Reality* (London: Harcourt Brace Jovanovich, 1987), p. 164.

20. Carroll Nash analyzed the results of ESP tests published between 1882 and 1939, extracted from J.G. Pratt et al's, *Extra-Sensory Perception After Sixty Years: A Critical Appraisal of the Research in Extra-Sensory Perception* (New York: Holt, 1940). He found the scoring rate to be negatively correlated to the length of the experiment (*Journal SPR* 55, 1989, pp. 412–6). Nash noted a trend for scores to recover towards the end of a run or series, which points to motivational inconsistency rather than a natural regression back to the mean.

21. Gertrude Schmeidler, 'Predicting good and bad scores in clairvoyance experiments: A final report', *Journal of the American Society for Psychical Research* 37, 1943, pp. 210–21; and 'Separating the Sheep from the Goats', *Journal of the American Society for Psychical Research*, 39, 1945, pp. 47–50.

22. Jahn and Dunne, *Margins of Reality*, p. 104–19. See also Helmut Schmidt, 'Clairvoyant Tests with a Machine', *Journal of Parapsychology*, 33, 1969, p. 305, and 'A PK Test with Electronic Equipment', *Journal of Parapsychology*, 34, 1970, pp. 176–87.

23. J.B. Rhine, *New Frontiers of the Mind* (London: Faber & Faber, 1938), p. 129.

24. Blackmore is currently Visiting Professor in the School of Psychology, University of Plymouth. For a personal perspective on her unsuccessful search for psi, see 'Why I Have Given Up' in Paul Kurtz (ed.), *Skeptical Odysseys: Personal Accounts by the World's Leading Paranormal Inquirers* (Buffalo, NY: Prometheus, 2001), pp. 85–94, and her memoir *In Search of the Light: Adventures of a Parapsychologist* (Buffalo, NY: Prometheus, 1987). Parapsychologist Rick Berger questions Blackmore's claim never to have found evidence of psi. Having analyzed her work he concluded that 'The claim of 'ten years of psi research' actually represents a series of hastily constructed, executed, and reported studies that were primarily conducted during a 2-year period'. Seven out of twenty-one experiments were statistically significant, but she explained these away on the grounds of flaws. Following the publication of Berger's critique, Blackmore conceded that no conclusions about the existence or otherwise of psi could be determined from her work. However Carter points out that despite making this concession in her academic writings Blackmore maintained her original stance in the popular press. *Parapsychology and the Skeptics*, pp. 69–73.

25. Kurtz says he used Zener cards and the ganzfeld method to test for psi, but achieved positive results in none of the many tests conducted (*Skeptical Odesseys*, pp. 68–69).

26. Even some of psi's advocates believe that they are affected by the experimenter effect. The philosopher John Beloff, who established the Koestler Chair of Parapsychology at Edinburgh University, was disappointed never to achieve a positive result in his own experiments. John Beloff, *The Relentless Question: Reflections on the Paranormal* (London: McFarland, 1988), p. 8. For a brief discussion of the experimenter effect, see Irwin, *An Introduction to Parapsychology*, pp. 84–86. A more detailed consideration is given by John Palmer, 'The challenge of experimenter psi', *European Journal of Parapsychology* 13, 1997, pp. 110–25. See also Radin, *Entangled Minds*, p. 285. Caroline Watt and Richard Wiseman argue that it is 'vital that parapsychologists and psychologists researching [psi] realize that their participants' performance may be affected by the experimental context' and that 'the experimenter's own beliefs and idiosyncrasies in interacting with participants may affect participants so as to elicit, or to obscure, a relationship between paranormal belief and cognitive ability'

('Experimenter Differences in Cognitive Correlates of Paranormal Belief and in PSI', *Journal of Parapsychology* 66/4, 2002, pp. 371–85).

27. Rupert Sheldrake speculates that animals evolved an ability to sense when they were being watched as a means to escape predators. *The Sense of Being Stared At and Other Aspects of the Extended Mind* (London: Arrow, 2004), pp. 148–65.

28. For an overview of theoretical approaches, including his own based on quantum 'entanglement', see Radin, *Entangled Minds*, pp. 240–74.

29. Rhine, *New Frontiers of the Mind,* p. 130.

30. Notably Jessica Utts, professor of statistics at the University of California, whose views are discussed further in this chapter.

31. The cheating claim was first made explicit by George R. Price, 'Science and the Supernatural', *Science* 122, 1955, pp. 359–67. Hansel's detailed scenario is in *ESP and Parapsychology*, pp. 111–23, first published in 1966.

32. See Charles Honorton, 'Review of Hansel, "ESP: A Scientific Evaluation"', *Journal of Parapsychology* 31, 1967, pp. 76–82; and 'Beyond the Reach of Sense: Some comments on C.E.M. Hansel's *ESP and Parapsychology: A Critical Re-evaluation*', *Journal of the American Society for Psychical Research* 75, 1981, pp. 155–66.

33. The original experiments with the Creery sisters are described in W.F. Barrett, E. Gurney and F.W.H. Myers, 'First Report on Thought-Reading', *Proceedings SPR* 1, 1882, pp. 34–64, and E. Gurney, F.W.H. Myers and W.M. Barrett 'Second Report on Thought-Transference', *Proceedings SPR* 1, 1882, pp. 70–97. The discovery of cheating is described in 'Note Relating to Some of the Published Experiments in Thought-Transference, *Proceedings SPR* 5, 1888, pp. 269–70.

34. Douglas Blackburn, 'Confessions of a Telepathist: Thirty-Year Hoax Exposed', *Daily News* (London), 1 September 1911, pp. 115–32; quoted in Kurtz (ed.), *A Skeptic's Handbook of Parapsychology*, p. 238.

35. J.B. Rhine, 'A new case of experimenter unreliability', *Journal of Parapsychology* 38, 1974, pp. 218–25.

36. B. Markwick, 'The Soal-Goldney experiments with Basil Shackleton: New evidence of data manipulation,' *Proceedings SPR* 56, 1978, pp. 250–77.

37. James Randi, 'The Project Alpha Experiment: Part 1. The First Two Years', *Skeptical Inquirer* 7/4, 1983, pp. 24–35; reprinted in Frazier, *Science Confronts the Paranormal,* pp. 158–65. 'The Project Alpha Experiment: Part 2. Beyond the Laboratory', *Skeptical Inquirer* 8/1, 1983, pp. 36–45. For critiques of the hoax see Marcello Truzzi, 'Reflections on "Project Alpha": Scientific Experiment or Conjuror's Illusion?' *Zetetic Scholar* 12/13, 1987, pp. 73–98, and M.A. Thalbourne, 'Science versus Showmanship: A History of the Randi Hoax', *Journal of the American Society for Psychical Research*, 89, 1995, pp. 344–66. A suspected attempt to dupe parapsychologists at the Koes-

tler Parapsychology Unit at the University of Edinburgh failed. A seventeen-year-old youth claimed an ability to bend metal objects by willpower, but failed to show evidence of PK under thoroughly-controlled conditions. Eventually a hidden camera caught him engaging in fraudulent activity and he later confessed to being a practising magician. Deborah L. Delanoy, 'Work With a Fraudulent PK Metal-Bending Subject', *Journal SPR* 54, 1987, pp. 247–56.

38. Hyman, *The Elusive Quarry*, p. 245.

39. ibid., p. 255 (the comment was made by philosopher Stephen Braude).

40. D. Druckman and J.A. Swets (eds.), *Enhancing Human Performance: Issues, Theories and Techniques* (Washington: National Academy, 1988), p. 22.

41. J.A. Palmer, C. Honorton and J. Utts, 'Reply to the National Research Council study on parapsychology', *Journal of the American Society for Psychical Research* 83, 1989, pp. 31–49.

42. David Marks, 'Sensory Cues Invalidate Remote Viewing Experiments', *Nature* 292, 1981, p. 177; also David F. Marks and Richard Kammann, *The Psychology of the Psychic*, pp. 26–41; and David F. Marks, 'Remote Viewing Revisited', in Frazier, *Science Confronts the Paranormal*, pp. 110–21.

43. Hyman, *The Elusive Quarry*, p. 20–62.

44. Charles Honorton, 'Meta-analysis of psi ganzfeld research: A response to Hyman', *Journal of Parapsychology* 49, 1985, pp. 51–91. See also D. Radin, E. May and M.J. Thomson, 'Psi experiments with random number generators: Meta-analysis Part 1' in D.H. Weiner and D.I. Radin (eds.), *Research in Parapsychology,* 1985 (Metuchin, NJ: Scarecrow Press, 1986), pp. 14–17.

45. D.S. Saunders, 'On Hyman's Factor Analyses', *Journal of Parapsychology*, 49, 1985, pp. 86–88. See also J.M. Utts 'Replication and meta-analysis in parapsychology', *Statistical Science* 6, 1991, pp. 363–403; and R.L. Atkinson, R.C. Atkinson, E.E. Smith and D.J. Bem, *Introduction to Psychology,* 10th edn. (New York: Harcourt Brace Jovanovich, 1990).

46. Radin, *Entangled Minds,* pp. 111–13.

47. David Marks, *The Psychology of the Psychic: A penetrating scientific analysis of claims of psychic abilities* (Buffalo, NY: Prometheus, 2000), p. 63.

48. ibid., p. 104.

49. Playfair, *Twin Telepathy,* pp. 111–15. See also Guy Lyon Playfair, 'The Twin Thing', *Paranormalia.com,* 19 February 2010.

50. Radin, *Entangled Minds,* pp. 19–20.

51. Rupert Sheldrake, *A New Science of Life* (London: Granada, 1983).

52. John Maddox, 'A book for burning?' *Nature* 293, 24 September 1981, pp. 245–46.

53. Rupert Sheldrake, 'The sense of being stared at: experiments in schools', *Journal SPR* 62, 1998, pp. 311–23. For a brief summary of Sheldrake's research conclusions and rebuttals to sceptics see Sheldrake, *The Sense of Be-*

ing Stared At, and Other Aspects of the Extended Mind, pp. 320–25. For an overview of the research see Rupert Sheldrake, 'The Sense of Being Stared At, Part I: Is it Real or Illusory?' *Journal of Consciousness Studies* 12, 2005, pp. 22–3 (available online at http://www.sheldrake.org/ArticlesandPapers/papers/staring/pdf/JCSpaper1.pdf).

54. Rupert Sheldrake, 'Experiments on the sense of being stared at: The elimination of possible artefacts', *Journal SPR* 65, 2001, p. 122–37.

55. R. Wiseman and M. Smith, 'A further look at the detection of unseen gaze', *Proceedings of the Parapsychological Association 37th Annual Convention* (Columbus, OH: Parapsychological Association, 1994), pp. 465–78.

56. Sheldrake, 'Experiments on the sense of being stared at: The elimination of possible artefacts', pp. 124–25.

57. R. Wiseman and M. Schlitz, 'Experimenter effects and the remote detection of staring', *Journal of Parapsychology* 61, 1997, pp. 199–207.

58. Sheldrake, *The Sense of Being Stared At,* p. 325.

59. R.A. Baker, 'Can we tell when someone is staring at us?' *Skeptical Inquirer* 24 (2), 2000, pp. 34–40.

60. Rupert Sheldrake, 'Research on the Feeling of Being Stared At', *Skeptical Inquirer,* March/April 2000, pp. 58–61.

61. D. Marks and J. Colwell. 'The psychic staring effect: An artefact of pseudo randomization', *Skeptical Inquirer* 41, September/October 2000. See also, J. Colwell, S. Schröder and B. Sladen, 'The ability to detect unseen staring: A literature review and empirical tests', *British Journal of Psychology* 91, 2000, pp. 71–85.

62. Sheldrake, 'Research on the Feeling of Being Stared At', pp. 58–61.

63. Rupert Sheldrake, *Seven Experiments That Could Change the World: A Do-It-Yourself Guide to Revolutionary Science* (London: Fourth Estate, 1994), p. 12.

64. Rupert Sheldrake and Pamela Smart, 'Psychic Pets: A Survey in North-West England', *Journal SPR* 61, 1998, pp. 353–64; David J. Brown and Rupert Sheldrake, 'Perceptive Pets: A Survey in North-West California', *Journal SPR* 62, 1998, pp. 396–406.

65. Rupert Sheldrake and Pamela Smart, 'A Dog that Seems to Know When His Owner is Returning: Preliminary Investigations', *Journal* 62, 1997–98, pp. 220–32. This research is also described in Sheldrake, *Dogs That Know When Their Owners Are Coming Home.* A fuller study that included videotaped experiments is described in Rupert Sheldrake and Pamela Smart, 'A Dog That Seems to Know When His Owner Is Coming Home: Videotaped Experiments and Observations', *Journal of Scientific Exploration* 14/2, 2000, pp. 233–55.

66. R. Sheldrake, 'Commentary on a paper by Wiseman, Smith and Milton on the 'psychic pet' phenomenon', *Journal SPR* 63, 1999, p. 307.

67. ibid., p. 306.

68. ibid., *passim*.

69. R. Wiseman, M. Smith, and J. Milton, 'The "psychic pet" phenomenon: A reply to Rupert Sheldrake', *Journal SPR* 64, 2000, pp. 46–49.

70. R. Wiseman, M. Smith, and J. Milton. 'Can animals detect when their owners are returning home? An experimental test of the "psychic pet" phenomenon', *British Journal of Psychology* 89, 1998, pp. 453–62.

71. ibid., p. 461.

72. Zoologist and dog lover Miriam Rothschild, interviewed by *The Times*, attributed her dogs' knowing when she was coming home to their ability to pick up the sound of her car leaving the main road seven or eight miles away and distinguish it from the sound of all the other cars. 'I did initially think they were psychic, but in the beginning I was completely taken in.' Sanjida O.Connell, 'Are Pets Psychic?', *The Times*, London, 21 November 1998.

73. Sheldrake, 'Commentary on a paper by Wiseman, Smith and Milton on the 'psychic pet' phenomenon' , p. 309. Also, Sheldrake and Smart, 'A Dog That Seems to Know When His Owner Is Coming Home: Videotaped Experiments and Observations, pp. 242–43.

74. ibid., pp. 249–51. Sheldrake dryly heads the section that describes Wiseman's debunking experiments, 'An Independent Replication'.

75. 'Magic Tricks and Psychic Dogs', Interview on The Science Show, The Australia Broadcasting Corporation, February 9, 2002: http://www.abc.net.au/rn/scienceshow/stories/2002/472790.htm

76. Wiseman *et al.*, 'The "psychic pet" phenomenon: A reply to Rupert Sheldrake', p. 46–47.

77. Alex Tsakiris, a moderate sceptic, questioned Wiseman about his approach in an interview podcast (http://www.skeptiko. com/11-dr-richard-wiseman-on-rupert-sheldrakes-dogsthatknow/). Tsakiris has also chaired a podcast discussion between Sheldrake and Wiseman (http://www.skeptiko. com/rupert-sheldrake-and-richard-wiseman-clash/).

78. Sheldrake, *The Sense of Being Stared At*, pp. 24–7, 299–304.

79. K. Christopher, 'The "Psychic" Parrot and Best-Kept Secrets', *Skeptical Inquirer* 15 February 2001. The blurred line between scientific enquiry and sceptical propaganda is also to be seen in the investigation by Wiseman and Hyman of Natasha Demkina. See M.R. Barrington, 'Respected Scientists: The Natasha Demkina case', www.skepticalinvestigations.org.

80. D.J. Bem and C. Honorton. 'Does psi exist? Replicable evidence for an anomalous process of information transfer', *Psychological Bulletin* 115/1,

1994, pp. 4–18. For a readable introduction to the meta-analysis and its use in parapsychology see Dean Radin, *The Conscious Universe: The Scientific Truth of Psychic Phenomena* (New York: Harper Collins, 1997), pp. 51–58. A good detailed summary of the ganzfeld debate by a parapsychologist is John Palmer, 'ESP in the Ganzfeld: Analysis of a Debate', in James Alcock, Jean Burns and Anthony Freeman (eds.), *Psi Wars: Getting to Grips with the Paranormal* (Exeter: Imprint Academic, 2003), pp. 51–68.

81. J. Milton and R. Wiseman, 'Does psi exist? Lack of replication of an anomalous process of information transfer', *Psychological Bulletin* 125, 1999, pp. 387–91. See also L. Storm and S. Ertel, 'Does psi exist? Comments on Milton and Wiseman's 1999 meta-analysis of ganzfeld research', *Psychological Bulletin* 127, 2001, pp. 424–33; J. Milton and R. Wiseman, 'A Response to Storm and Ertel', *Journal of Parapsychology* 66/2, 2002, pp. 183–86.

82. J. Milton, 'Should ganzfeld research continue to be crucial in the search for a replicable psi effect? Part I. Discussion paper and an introduction to an electronic-mail discussion', *Journal of Parapsychology* 63, 1999, pp. 309–33.

83. Daryl J. Bem, John Palmer, Richard S Broughton, 'Updating the ganzfeld database: A victim of its own success', *Journal of Parapsychology* 65, 2001, pp. 207–18.

84. M.J. Willin, 'A ganzfeld experiment using musical targets', *Journal SPR* 61, 1996, pp. 1–17; 'A ganzfeld experiment using musical targets with previous high scorers from the general population, *Journal SPR* 61, 1996, pp. 103–106.

85. K. Dalton, 'Exploring the Links: Creativity and psi in the ganzfeld', in *The Parapsychological Association 40th Annual Convention: Proceedings of Presented Papers* (Durham, NC: Parapsychological Association, 1997), pp. 119–34.

86. Radin, *Entangled Minds*, p. 120. For a discussion of shortcomings in the Milton-Wiseman meta-analysis see C.A. Roe, 'The role of altered states of consciousness in extrasensory experiences', in M. Smith (ed.), *Developing perspectives on anomalous experience* (Jefferson, NC: McFarland and Co., 2009).

87. Richard Wiseman, Matthew Smith, Diana Kornbrot, 'Exploring possible sender-to-experimenter acoustic leakage in the PRL autoganzfeld experiments', *Journal of Parapsychology* 60, 1996, pp. 97–128.

88. ibid., p. 126.

89. Successful early remote-viewing experiments are described in M.J. Schlitz and E. Gruber, 'Transcontinental remote viewing', *Journal of Parapsychology* 44, 1980, pp. 305–17; M.J. Schlitz and J. Haight, 'Remote viewing revisited: An intrasubject replication', *Journal of Parapsychology* 48, 1984, pp. 39–49. For a narrative of the military Stargate program (sometimes also 'Star Gate') by a remote viewer see McMoneagle, *The Stargate Chronicles;*

also Edwin C. May 'The American Institutes for Research Review of the Department of Defense's Star Gate Program: a commentary,' *Journal of Scientific Exploration* 10, 1996, pp. 89–107.

90. Jessica Utts, 'An Assessment of the Evidence for Psychic Functioning,' *Journal of Parapsychology* 59, 1995, pp. 289–320.

91. Ray Hyman, 'Evaluation of Program on Anomalous Mental Phenomena,' *Journal of Parapsychology* 1995, p. 334.

92. Jessica Utts, 'Response to Ray Hyman's report "Evaluation of the Program on Anomalous Mental Phenomena",' *Journal of Parapsychology* 59, 1995, pp. 353–56.

93. Charles Honorton offers a strong rebuttal of the 'lack of cumulativeness' argument, along with other sceptical approaches, in 'Rhetoric over substance: The impoverished state of skepticism,' *Journal of Parapsychology* 57, 1993, pp. 191–214.

94. S. Schouten, 'Are we making progress?' In L. Coly and J. McMahon, (eds.), *Psi research methodology: A re-examination* (New York: Parapsychology Foundation, 1993), pp. 295–322. In an emotional public attack on parapsychology in 1979, the physicist and Nobel laureate John Wheeler decried the waste of funds, which he estimated to be up to $20 million per year, being spent by as many as 200 workers. Parapsychologists' own survey the previous year revealed the actual size of funding to be a tiny fraction of that figure, around $550,000. Hansen reckons that at the beginning of the twenty-first century there were no more than ten full time parapsychologists in the US, all privately funded (*The Trickster and the Paranormal*, p. 200). At this time the worldwide circulation of the *Journal of Parapsychology*, the main journal in the field, was eight hundred, compared with a circulation of fifty thousand for the CSI (CSICOP) magazine *Skeptical Inquirer*. Sheldrake, *The Sense of Being Stared At*, p. 334.

95. It's right to highlight the two known cases of experimenter fraud in parapsychology relating to Soal and Levy, but it is pertinent also to point out that fraud is common in many sciences, compared with which this level of incidence is by no means high. See Horace Freeland Judson, *The Great Betrayal: Fraud in Science* (London: Harcourt, 2004). Hyman also makes great play with two nineteenth-century cases of fraud, arguing that they were devastating to the discipline's credibility. However the story here is more complex than one would suspect from the way sceptics describe it. It's uncontested that two of the Creery sisters developed a code to cheat, but not surprising that they should have done so, as by the time it was discovered they had been submitting themselves for investigation for six years. What started as an entertaining game among young children would surely have become tedious for adolescents who, at the same time, might not have wanted to let the family down by failing to produce positive results.

(Above, note 33). In later life, Douglas Blackburn publicly disavowed the telepathic connections with his colleague Smith that had apparently been demonstrated during experiments carried out when they were young men, thinking that Smith was dead. However Smith was not dead, and vigorously disputed the claim, as did the researchers, who pointed out that the cheating scenarios described by Blackburn were crude, and could not conceivably have gone undetected. An alternative explanation for this incident is that Blackburn wished in later life to disassociate himself from what he now viewed as a youthful indiscretion. (Above, note 34).

Chapter Five: Experience and Imagination (I)

Opening quotes: Walter Franklin Prince, *The Enchanted Boundary* (Boston: Boston Society For Psychic Research, 1930), p. 2; Elizabeth Lloyd Mayer, *Extraordinary Knowing: Science, Skepticism, and the Inexplicable Powers of the Human Mind* (New York: Bantam Dell, 2007), p. 104.

1. See for instance Thomas Gilovich, *How We Know What Isn't So: The Fallibility of Human Reason in Everyday Life* (Simon and Schuster: New York, 1991); Graham Reed, *The Psychology of Anomalous Experience* (Buffalo, NY: Prometheus, 1988); John F. Schumaker, *Wings of Illusion: The Origin, Nature and Future of Paranormal Belief* (Buffalo, NY: Prometheus, 1990); Massimo Piatelli-Palmarini, *Inevitable Illusions: How Mistakes of Reason Rule Our Mind* (Hoboken, NJ: John Wiley and Sons, 1996); Nicholas Capaldi, *The Art of Deception: An Introduction to Critical Thinking* (Buffalo, NY: Prometheus, 1987).

2. Gilovich, *How We Know What Isn't So,* pp. 11–17, 54–56.

3. See for instance James A. Alcock, *Parapsychology: Science or Magic?* (Oxford: Pergamon Press, 1981), pp. 93–94.

4. ibid., p. 64. Also of interest is Hines, *Pseudoscience and the Paranormal* and Marks and Kammann, *The Psychology of the Psychic*. In *The Psychology of Transcendence* Neher attempts a more positive appraisal of transcendent experience, but still from a basically sceptical position;

5. Alcock, *Parapsychology: Science or Magic?* p. 75.

6. ibid., p. 84.

7. ibid., p. 85.

8. ibid., p. 87.

9. Zusne and Jones, *Anomalistic Psychology,* pp. 128–30.

10. ibid., p. 131.

11. See for instance Susan Blackmore, 'Psychic Experiences: Psychic Illusions', *Skeptical Inquirer* 16, 1992, pp. 367–76. Also, Nicolas Humphrey, *Soul Searching: Human Nature and Supernatural Belief* (London: Chatto and Windus, 1995), p. 46.

12. Zusne and Jones, *Anomalistic Psychology*, pp. 186–90. For a discussion of

gender in attitudes to the paranormal see David J. Hess, *Science in the New Age: The Paranormal, Its Defenders and Debunkers, and American Culture* (Madison, WI: University of Wisconsin, 1993). A study of UFO witnesses found no evidence of weaker critical judgement than other people; Keul Alex, and Ken Phillips, 'Assessing the Witness: Psychology and the UFO Reporter' in Hilary Evans with John Spencer, (eds.), *UFOs 1947–1987* (London: Fortean Tomes, 1987), pp. 230–77.

13. A 1999 study found no evidence for differences in critical-thinking ability between believers and disbelievers. Chris Roe, 'Critical thinking and belief in the paranormal: A re-evaluation', *British Journal of Psychology* 90, 1999, pp. 85–98. See also M. Hughes, 'Perceived accuracy of fortune-telling and belief in the paranormal', *Journal of Social Psychology* 141/1, 2001, pp. 159–60.

14. See for instance Sheryl Wilson and Theodore X. Barber, 'The Fantasy-Prone Personality: Implications for Understanding Imagery, Hypnosis and Parapsychological Phenomena' in A. Shiekh (ed.), *Imagery: Current Theory, Research, and Application* (New York: John Wiley, 1983), pp. 340–87.

15. Zusne and Jones, *Anomalistic Psychology*, 2nd edition 1989, p. 10.

16. Alcock, *Parapsychology: Science or Magic?* p. 82.

17. Zusne and Jones, *Anomalistic Psychology*, pp. 44–47.

18. ibid., pp. 61–65.

19. E. Gurney, F.W.H. Myers, F. Podmore, *Phantasms of the Living*, 2 volumes (London: Trubner, 1886), pp. 375–77. Both volumes can be read on the SPR's website (www.spr.ac.uk).

20. H. Sidgwick, A. Johnson, F.W.H. Myers, F. Podmore and E. Sidgwick. 'Report on the Census of Hallucinations', *Proceedings SPR* 10, 1894, pp. 25–422. Had they ever, when awake, had the impression of seeing or hearing or of being touched by anything which, so far as they could discover, was not due to any external cause?

21. Later British and American collections include Eleanor Sidgwick, 'Phantasms of the Living (1886–1922)', *Proceedings SPR* 33, 1922, pp. 23–429; D.J. West, 'A Mass Observation Questionnaire on Hallucinations, *Journal SPR* 34, 1984, pp. 187–96; J. Palmer, 'A community mail survey of psychic experiences', *Journal of the American Society for Psychical Research* 73, 1979, pp. 221–51; R.L. Kohrn, 'A survey of psi experiences among members of a special population' *Journal of the American Society for Psychical Research*, 74, 1980, pp. 395–411; E. Haraldsson, 'Apparitions of the Dead: A Representative Survey in Iceland,' in W. Roll (ed.), *Research in Parapsychology*, 1980 (Metuchen, NJ: The Scarecrow Press, 1981), pp. 3–5.

22. Louisa E. Rhine, 'Hallucinatory Psi Experiences I. An Introductory Survey', *Journal of Parapsychology* 20, 1956, p. 244; Louisa E. Rhine, 'Hallucinatory Psi Experiences II. The initiative of the percipient in hallucinations of the living, the dying, and the dead', *Journal of Parapsychology* 21, 1957, pp. 13–46;

S.A. Schouten, 'Analysing Spontaneous Cases: A replication based on the Sannwald Collection', *European Journal of Parapsychology* 4, 1981, pp. 9–48.

23. For assessments of the background and characteristics to apparitions see Celia Green and Charles McCreery, *Apparitions* (London: Hamish Hamilton, 1975), and Andrew MacKenzie, *Hauntings and Apparitions* (London: Heinemann, 1982). For cultural attitudes see R. C. Finucane, *Appearances of the Dead: A Cultural History of Ghosts* (London: Junction, 1982).

24. Gurney *et al. Phantasms of the Living*, Vol. I, p. 188-9.

25. ibid., p. 194-5.

26. ibid., Vol. II, p. 45.

27. Rhine, 'Hallucinatory Psi Experiences I. An Introductory Survey', p. 244.

28. Sidgwick et al, 'Census of Hallucinations', pp. 245–51. The researchers' calculations are also described in Broad, *Lectures in Psychical Research*, pp. 245–51.

29. Gurney et al, *Phantasms of the Living*, pp. 381–83. The Census showed that in ninety-five out of two hundred and fifty-three cases where the witness of an apparition had a companion the second person also saw it. For comments on collectively perceived apparitions see G.N.M. Tyrrell, *Apparitions* (London: SPR/Duckworth, 1943/1953), and Hornell Hart and Ella B. Hart, 'Visions and Apparitions Collectively and Reciprocally Perceived', *Proceedings SPR* 41, 1933, pp. 205–49.

30. R.C. Morton, 'Record of a Haunted House', *Proceedings SPR* 8, 1892, pp. 317–18.

31. Myers, *Human Personality and its Survival of Bodily Death,* p. 208–09. (This and following references are to the single volume, abridged version).

32. ibid., p. 208–09.

33. Myers describes three cases, ibid., pp. 163–66.

34. ibid., pp. 181–82.

35. Gurney et al, *Phantasms of the Living,* pp. 389–93.

36. ibid., Vol. 1, p. 129.

37. See Ian Stevenson, 'Cryptomnesia and Parapsychology', *Journal SPR* 52, 1983, pp. 1–30.

38. Gilovich, *How We Know What Isn't So*, pp. 156–82.

39. Blackburn, 'Confessions of a Telepathist' in Kurtz (ed.), *A Skeptic's Handbook of Parapsychology*, p. 238.

40. D.J. West, 'The Investigation of Spontaneous Cases', *Proceedings SPR* 48, 1948, p. 277.

41. Zusne and Jones, *Anomalistic Psychology*, Ist edition 1982, p. 281.

42. John E. Coover, 'Metapsychics and the Incredulity of Psychologists: Psy-

chical Research Before 1927' in Kurtz, *A Skeptic's Handbook*, pp. 241–73.

43. Quoted in Inglis, *Natural and Supernatural*, pp. 227–29.

44. E. Gurney and F.W.H. Myers, 'Visible Apparitions', *Nineteenth Century* 16, July 1884, pp. 89–91. Quoted in Coover, 'Metaphysics and the Incredulity of Psychologists', Kurtz, *A Skeptic's Handbook of Parapsychology*, pp. 268–71.

45. *Nineteenth Century* 16, 1884, p. 451. Quoted in Kurtz, *A Skeptic's Handbook of Parapsychology*, p. 271.

46. Neher, *The Psychology of Transcendence*, p. 139.

47. *Nineteenth Century* 16, 1884, p. 451.

48. James H. Hyslop, 'Professor Newcomb and Occultism', *Journal of the American Society for Psychical Research* 3, 1909, p. 271.

49. Hansel, *ESP and Parapsychology*, p. 47.

50. Elizabeth Lloyd Mayer, *Extraordinary Knowing*, pp. 1–3.

51. Hal E. Puthoff and Russell Targ, 'A Perceptual Channel for Information Transfer Over Kilometer Distances: Historical Perspective and Recent Research', *Journal of Electrical and Electronic Engineering* 64/3, 1976, pp. 329–54. Quoted in Mayer, *Extraordinary Knowing*, p. 133. Some scientists have shown greater awareness of psi-dissonance. Mathmetician Warren Weaver once said of psi research, 'I find this whole field intellectually a very painful one. I cannot reject the evidence and I cannot accept the conclusions.' Minutes from the 'Great Issues of Conscience in Modern Medicine' conference at Dartmouth, September 8–10, 1960 (Dartmouth College Library, Rauner Special Collections Library). Parapsychologist Charles Tart writes: 'The vehement denial of the existence of psi, as in the case of some pseudocritics whose behaviour suggests they are protecting their "faith" against heresy, strongly suggests that fear of psi is quite strong in them at an unconscious level. Insofar as psi is an aspect of reality, its denial is inherently psychopathological.' 'Acknowledging and dealing with the fear of psi', *Journal of the American SPR* 78, April 1984, pp. 137.

52. Above, Quotes

53. Alcock, *Parapsychology: Science or Magic*, p. 191.

54. Humphrey, *Soul Searching*, p. 224.

55. For more discussions see Tart, 'Acknowledging and dealing with the fear of psi'; R.A. McConnell, 'The resolution of conflicting beliefs about the ESP evidence', *Journal of Parapsychology* 41, 1977, pp. 198–214, and J. Wren-Lewis 'Resistance to the study of the paranormal', *Journal of Humanistic Psychology* 14(2), 1974, pp. 41–48.

56. 'Every supernatural phenomenon I investigated crumbled to nothing before my gaze,' wrote Dr John Taylor, professor of mathematics at King's College, London. *Science and the Supernatural* (London: Temple Smith,

1980), p. viii. This represented a complete rejection of his previously stated conviction in the reality of psychic phenomena, derived from his investigations of Uri Geller and other individuals. *Superminds* (London: Pan, 1976).

Chapter Six: Experience and Imagination (II)

Opening quote: Sam Harris, *The End of Faith*, p. 221.

1. James Randi, 'Randi at CalTech: A Report from the Paranormal Trenches', *Skeptic* 1(1), 1992, pp. 22–31.

2. Susan J. Blackmore, *Beyond the Body* (London: Heinemann, 1982), p. 3.

3. Robert Monroe, *Journeys Out Of The Body* (New York: Doubleday, 1971); Sylvan Muldoon and Hereward Carrington, *The Projection of the Astral Body* (London: Rider, 1929/1968); J.H.M. Whiteman, *The mystical life: An outline of its nature and teachings from the evidence of direct experience* (London: Faber, 1961). See also: Caroline D. Larsen, *My Travels in the Spirit Worlds* (Rutland, VT: Tuttle, 1927) and Yram, *Practical Astral Projection* (New York: Weiser, 1926/1974). Anecdotal accounts of spontaneous out-of-body experiences are given by Robert J. Crookall, *The Study and Practice of Astral Projections* (New Hyde Park, NJ: University Books, 1966) and Celia Green *Out-Of-The-Body Experiences* (Oxford: Institute of Psychophysical Research, 1968).

4. Alcock, *Parapsychology: Science or Magic?*, p. 84.

5. C.C. French, 'Dying to know the truth: visions of a dying brain, or false memories?' *Lancet* 358, 2001, pp. 2010–11. The alternative view held by researchers is that the patients were not immediately able to talk about their experience. See below, page 262.

6. Russell Noyes, Jr. and Roy Kletti, 'The Experience of Dying From Falls' in Richard A. Kalish (ed.), *Death, Dying, Transcending* (Amityville, NY: Baywood, 1980), pp. 129–36. These and other arguments are explored in Susan Blackmore, *Dying to Live: Near-Death Experiences* (Amherst, NY: Prometheus, 1993). See also Ronald K. Siegel, 'The Psychology of Life After Death' in Bruce Greyson and Charles P. Flynn (eds), *The Near-Death Experience: Problems, Prospects, Perspectives* (Springfield,. IL: Charles C. Thomas, 1984), pp. 78–120.

7. Stanislav Grof and Joan Halifax, *The Human Encounter With Death* (London: Souvenir, 1977); R.E.L. Masters and Jean Houston, *The Varieties of Psychedelic Experience* (London: Turnstone, 1966/1973).

8. Andrew Newberg, Eugene D'Aquili, Vince Rause, *Why God Won't Go Away: Brain Science and the Biology of Belief* (New York: Random House: 2001). Michael A. Persinger, *Neuropsychological Bases of God Beliefs* (Westport, CT: Praeger, 1987), and *The Paranormal: Part II, Mechanisms and Models* (New York: MSS Information Corporation, 1974).

9. *Dying to Live,* pp. 83–86.

10. Raymond Moody, *Life after Life* (Atlanta, GA: Mockingbird, 1975). The phenomenon had also previously been discussed by Elizabeth Kübler-Ross, *On Death and Dying* (New York: Macmillan, 1971).

11. Kenneth Ring, *Life At Death: A Scientific Investigation of the Near-Death Experience* (New York: Coward, McCann and Geoghegan, 1980); Melvin Morse, *Closer to the Light: Learning from the Near-Death Experiences of Children* (Raleigh, NC: Ivy Book, 1991); Michael Sabom, *Recollections of Death* (New York: Harper and Row, 1982) and *Light and Death: One Doctor's Fascinating Account of Near-Death Experiences* (Grand Rapids, MI: Zonervan, 1998).

12. Pim van Lommel, Ruud van Wees, Vincent Meyers, Ingrid Eifferich, 'Near-death experience in survivors of cardiac arrest: A prospective study in the Netherlands,' *The Lancet* 358, 2001, pp. 2039–45. Penny Sartori carried out a long-term prospective study in a clinic between 1997 and 2003, in which symbols were placed on top of the cardiac monitor at each patient's bedside, which could only be viewed from an out-of-body perspective. Seven out of thirty-nine cardiac arrest survivors reported a near-death experience, but none saw the images. *The Near-death Experiences of Hospitalized Intensive Care Patients: A Five-year Clinical Study* (Lampeter, UK: Edwin Mellen Press, 2008). For a brief discussion, see 'Just Coincidence' online at *Paranormalia.com,* 13 June 2008.

13. D. Scott Rogo, 'Ketamine and the Near-Death Experience', *Anabiosis* 4, 1984, pp. 87–96.

14. For scientific arguments against anoxia and hypercarbia as general explanations of the near-death experience see Peter Fenwick and Elizabeth Fenwick, *The Truth in the Light: An Investigation over 300 Near-Death Experiences* (London: Headline, 1995).

15. Fenwick, *The Truth in the Light*, pp. 53, 86.

16. Michael Sabom points out that when opiates were injected into cancer patients to reduce pain, the effect took between twenty-two and seventy-three hours to wear off. And in the therapy treatment the effect was of pleasant somnolence, compared with the hyper-alertness characteristic of the near-death experience. Sabom, *Recollections of Death*, pp. 171–73.

17. Kelly *et al.*, *Irreducible Mind*, p. 418.

18. Sabom, *Light and Death*, pp. 44.

19. See John Palmer, 'The out-of-body experience: A psychological theory', *Parapsychological Review* 9, 1978, pp. 19–22, and H.J. Irwin, *Flight of Mind* (London and New York: Scarecrow Press, 1985).

20. In support of this argument Blackmore cites J.M. Evans, 'Patients' expe-

riences of awareness during general anaesthesia' in *Consciousness, Awareness and Pain in General Anaesthesia* (ed.), M. Rosen and J.N. Lunn (London: Butterworths, 1987), pp. 184–92. But see below, note 24.

21. Blackmore, *Dying To Live,* p. 134.

22. Sabom, *Recollections of Death,* p. 65.

23. ibid., p. 70.

24. 'The phenomenology of such awakenings … is altogether different from that of NDEs, and often extremely unpleasant, frightening, and even painful… The experiences are typically brief and fragmentary, and primarily auditory or tactile, and not visual; for example the patient may report hearing noises or snippets of speech, or briefly feeling sensations associated with intubation or with specific surgical procedures.' Kelly *et al.*, *Irreducible Mind,* p. 387.

25. Blackmore, *Dying to Live*, p. 116.

26. Glen O. Gabbard and Stuart W. Twemlow, *With the Eyes of the Mind* (Westport, CT: Praeger, 1984), pp. 223–25.

27. Blackmore, *Dying to Live*, p. 118.

28. Kimberly Clark, 'Clinical Interventions with Near-Death Experiencers', in Bruce Greyson and Charles P. Flynn (eds.), *The Near-Death Experience: Problems, Prospects, Perspectives* (Springfield, IL: Charles P. Thomas, 1984), pp. 242–55.

29. Blackmore, *Dying to Live*, p. 128.

30. ibid., p. 128.

31. Kenneth Ring has pursued this line of enquiry: Kenneth Ring and Sharon Cooper, *Mindsight: Near-Death and Out-Of-Body Experiences in the Blind* (Pali Alto, CA: Institute of Transpersonal Psychology, 1999).

32. Ring, *Heading Toward Omega*, pp. 54–75.

33. ibid., pp. 159–60.

34. ibid., p. 159.

35. ibid., p. 175. Ring has focused in detail on this 'learning' aspect, examining the subsequent transformational effect on experiencer's lives. *Lessons From the Light* (Portsmouth, NH: Moment Point Press, 1998).

36. Shermer, *Why People Believe Weird Things,* pp. 78–80.

37. Carol Zaleski, *Otherworld Journeys: Accounts of Near-Death Experience in Medieval and Modern Times* (Oxford: Oxford University Press, 1987) pp. 197, 202.

38. I do not include in this category well-known individuals whose atheism was a matter of public record before they reported a near-death experience which, although somewhat untypical, appeared at least partly to modify

their beliefs. In June 1988 the humanist philosopher A.J. Ayer suffered a four-minute cardiac arrest while in hospital. He later described an experience in which he felt he was being pulled toward a red light, which was "exceedingly bright, and also very painful," encountered the ' "ministers" of the universe', and attempted to cross a river, which he took to be the Styx, which borders the underworld in Greek mythology. He concluded, 'My recent experiences have slightly weakened my conviction that my genuine death, which is due fairly soon, will be the end of me, though I continue to hope that it will be. They have not weakened my conviction that there is no god' (see http://commonsenseatheism.com/wp-content/uploads/2009/11/Ayer-What-I-Saw-When-I-Was-Dead.pdf). A doctor who had attended him in hospital later claimed Ayer had in fact confided to him at the time, 'I saw a Divine Being. I'm afraid I'm going to have to revise all my various books and opinions'. See William Cash, 'Did atheist philosopher see God when he 'died'? *National Post,* 3 March 2001. Novelist Fay Weldon has described a near-death experience in which she found herself being pulled towards the 'Gates of Paradise', finding them to be 'very vulgar, very middle-class with very rich colours and double glazed'. In Stuart Jeffries, 'Lie Back and Think of Jesus', *The Guardian* 5 September 2006.

39. William James, *The Varieties of Religious Experience* (London: Penguin, 1902/1983; Raynor C. Johnson, *Watcher on the Hills* (Norwich: Pelegrin Trust/Pilgrim Books, 1959/1988); Alister Hardy *The Spiritual Nature of Man: A Study of Contemporary Religious Experience* (Oxford: Clarendon Press, 1979). Individual experiences have been collected for many years by the The Religious Experience Research Centre of the Alister Hardy Trust, now at the University of Wales, Lampeter: www.lamp.ac.uk/aht.

40. Johnson, *Watcher on the Hills,* p. 23.

41. See F.C. Happold, *Mysticism* (London: Penguin, 1963/90).

42. See for instance Newberg and D'Aquili, *Why God Won't Go Away.*

43. Examples of the literature on these topics are: David Terry Bradford, *The Experience of God: Portraits in the Phenomenological Psychopathology of Schizophrenia* (New York: Peter Lang, 1984); Andrew Weil, 'Pharmacology of Consciousness: A Narrative of Subjective Consciousness', in S. Hameroff, A.W. Kaszniak and A.C. Scott, (eds.), *Towards A Science of Consciousness: The First Tucson Discussion and Debates* (Cambridge, MA: Massachusetts Institute of Technology, 1996), pp. 677–89; Grof and Halifax, *The Human Encounter With Death*; Masters and Houston, *The Varieties of Psychedelic Experience*, above, note 7; R.K. Siegel and L.J. West (eds), *Hallucination: Behaviour, Experience and Theory* (Los Angeles: University of California, 1975); Robert Forte (ed.), *Entheogens and the Future of Religions* (Thousand Oaks:, CA: Pine Forge Press, 2001); R.G. Wasson, *Persephone's Quest: En-*

theogens and the Origins of Religion (New Haven, CT: Yale University Press, 1992).

44. The year 2007 saw the publication of *Irreducible Mind* (above, Chapter Two, note 66), a sustained and well-evidenced argument for a form of mind–body dualism, authored by Edward F. Kelly and Emily Williams Kelly, research professors in the Department of Psychiatric Medicine at the University of Virginia, with contributions by Alan Gauld, Adam Crabtree, Bruce Greyson and Michael Grosso. This volume of nearly eight hundred pages reviews the existing scientific data on a variety of anomalous mental phenomena, including psychophysiological influence (faith healing, the placebo effect, stigmata, etc), memory, genius and near-death and mystical experience, building on the work and thought of Frederic Myers. Edward Kelly declares: 'We believe that the empirical evidence marshalled in this book is sufficient to falsify all forms of biological naturalism, the current physicalist consensus on mind-brain relations' (p. 605). See my reviews at *Paranormalia.com* (19 May 2008 and 21 April 2009, also Michael Prescott's review of 28 March 2007 (http://michaelprescott.typepad.com).

45. William James used the term 'permissive' (as illustrated by the trigger of a crossbow that has a releasing function), or 'transmission' (for instance as light being refracted through a prism, or air passing through an organ pipe). Frederic Myers posited a psychological 'membrane' that controls the passage of psychological elements and processes between the supraliminal and subliminal regions of consciousness. He saw the boundaries as being fluid, or 'permeable', with a constant exchange of material between regions. *Irreducible Mind*, pp. 603–38.

46. Jane Roberts writes: 'Between one normal minute and the next, a fantastic avalanche of radical new ideas burst into my head with tremendous force... My body sat at the table, my hands furiously scribbling down the words and ideas that flashed through my head. Yet I seemed to be somewhere else, at the same time, traveling through things.' Jane Roberts, *The Seth Material* (London: Bantam, 1981), p. 11. Meredith Young states: 'Without warning, my right hand began to move across the manila pad. I opened my eyes and stared at my hand as it continued to move quite without my assistance, the pencil making large random arcs on the paper. I watched in amazement as my hand moved in slow, steady rhythms across the paper... There was absolutely no conscious thought directing the motion. It just continued in an autonomous back-and-forth pattern as I watched, feeling awestruck and silently detached from the process.' Meredith L. Young, *Agartha: A Course in Cosmic Awareness* (Bath: Gateway, 1987), p. 27. Automatic writing could often initially be elicited with the use of a 'planchette', a pencil holder on rollers. For examples of what he classified as 'motor automatisms' among the general population see Myers, *Human Personality*, pp. 229–38. For mediumistic examples see Jon Klimo, *Channeling: Investigations on Receiving Information from Paranormal Sources*

(Berkely, CA: New Atlantic Books, 1998). A psychiatric study of the phenomenon in a therapeutic, non-paranormal context is Anita Muhl, *Automatic Writing: An Approach to the Unconscious* (New York: Garrett Publications, 1963). See also Hodgson, 'A Further Record of Observations of Certain Phenomena of Trance,' for a description of Piper's automatic writing.

47. For example Matthew Alper speculates: 'Perhaps a series of neurological connections emerged in our species that compelled us to perceive ourselves as "spiritually" eternal. Once we perceived ourselves as possessing an element of the infinite and eternal within us … we were now "wired" to believe that our conscious self, what we came to refer to as our spirit or soul, would persist for ever, thus rendering us immortal, a concept that has endured universally among nearly every single culture from the dawn of humankind. *The 'God' Part of the Brain: A Scientific Interpretation of Human Spirituality and God* (New York: Rogue Press, 2001), p. 106.

48. *The God Delusion* (London: Bantam, 2006), p. 92.

49. William D. Hamilton, 'The Evolution of altruistic behaviour', *american naturalist* 97, 1963, pp. 354–56. R.L. Trivers, 'The evolution of reciprocal altruism', *Quarterly Review of Biology* 46, 1971, pp. 35–57. See also Matt Ridley, *The Origins of Virtue: Human Instincts and the Evolution of Cooperation* (London: Viking, 1996) and Robert Wright, *The Moral Animal: Why We Are the Way We Are* (London: Abacus, 1996).

50. The Gospel According to Luke Chapter 6, Verse 30.

51. For cases of possible cryptomnesia see Ian Wilson, *Reincarnation? The Claims Investigated* (Harmondsworth, Middlesex: Penguin, 1981), pp. 102–19. In the Bridey Murphy case, one of the earliest of the kind, a mid-twentieth century Chicago woman was apparently regressed to the life of a nineteenth century Irishwoman. Sceptics claimed the obscure details of domestic life that she revealed might have been learned by her as a child from a neighbour. These claims have been criticized as misleading, and motivated by newspaper rivalry. See Morey Bernstein, *The Search for Bridey Murphy* (New York: Doubleday, 1956; C. J. Ducasse, *A Critical Examination of the Belief in a Life After Death* (Springfield, Ill: Charles C. Thomas, 1961), pp. 276–99 and Wilson, *Reincarnation?*, pp. 56–71. For an overview of Stevenson's work, see James G. Matlock, 'Past Life Memory Case Studies' in Stanley Krippner (ed.), *Advances in Parapsychological Research 6* (London: McFarland, 1990), pp. 184–267. More research sources are given below, *passim*. Against the cryptomnesia theory, Helen Wambach, a regression hypnotherapist, claimed that obscure details of domestic life during remote historical periods, described by her clients in more than 2000 sessions – relating to clothes, food, eating utensils and so on – proved to correspond exactly with known facts, even when these were against expectation: *Reliving Past Lives* (London: Hutchinson, 1978). For other arguments in favour of a paranormal process suggestive of rein-

carnation see Hans TenDam, *Exploring Reincarnation* (London: Arkana: 1990). For other verbatim reports by hypnotised subjects see Michael Newton, *Journey of Souls: Case Studies of Life Between Lives* (Woodbury, MN: Llewellyn Publications, 1994). Two of the more interesting claims of past life memory recall in adults are described in Arthur Guirdham, *The Cathars and Reincarnation* (London: Spearman, 1970) and Jenny Cockell, *Yesterday's Children* (London: Piatkus, 1993).

52. Stevenson's first book on the subject was *Twenty Cases Suggestive of Reincarnation* (Charlottesville, VA: University of Virginia Press, 1966). This was followed by four volumes containing examples from different parts of the world: *Cases of the Reincarnation Type Vol. I: Ten Cases in India* (1975), *Cases of the Reincarnation Type Vol. II: Ten Cases in Sri Lanka* (1978), *Cases of the Reincarnation Type Vol. III: Twelve Cases in Lebanon and Turkey* (1980), and *Cases of the Reincarnation Type Vol. IV: Twelve Cases in Thailand and Burma* (1983), all published by the University of Virginia Press. A general introduction is his *Children Who Remember Previous Lives: A Question of Reincarnation* (Charlottesville, VA: University of Virginia Press, 1987). The heavy emphasis on Asian cases is balanced by his more recent *European Cases of the Reincarnation Type* (Jefferson, MC: McFarland and Co., 2003).

53. I. Stevenson and G. Samararatne, 'Three new cases of the reincarnation type in Sri Lanka with written records made before verifications', *Journal of Scientific Exploration* 2/2 1988, pp. 217–38.

54. I. Stevenson, *Reincarnation and Biology: A Contribution to the Etiology of Birthmarks and Birth Defects. Volume 1: Birthmarks and Reincarnation and Biology: A Contribution to the Etiology of Birthmarks and Birth Defects; Volume 2: Birth Defects and Other Anomalies* (New York: Praeger, 1997). A shortened version is *Where Reincarnation and Biology Intersect.* (Westport, CT: Praeger, 1997).

55. *Reincarnation and Biology*, pp. 124–25.

56. Stevenson, *Children Who Remember Previous Lives*, pp. 253–55.

57. Leonard Angel, 'Reincarnation: Overview of the work of Ian Stevenson (1918–2007)', *The Skeptic* 21/1, 2008.

58. Wilson, *Reincarnation?* p. 45.

59. One of the best known critics of reincarnation is Paul Edwards. *Reincarnation: A Critical Examination* (Buffalo, NY: Prometheus Books, 1996).

60. Broad, *Lectures on Psychical Research*, pp. 414–30; also Whately Carington, 'Experiments on the paranormal cognition of drawings. IV, Section B: A theory of paranormal cognition and allied phenomena', *Proceedings SPR* 47, 1944, pp. 155–228.

61. See for instance Gardner Murphy, 'A Caringtonian Approach to Ian Steven-

son's "Twenty Cases Suggestive of Reincarnation", *Journal of the American Society for Psychical Research* 47, 1944, pp. 155–228 and 67, 1973, pp. 117–129. Also Ruth Reyna, *Reincarnation and Science* (Delhi: Sterling, 1973). For the limitations of this approach see Ian Stevenson, 'Carington's psychon theory as applied to cases of the reincarnation type: a reply to Gardner Murphy', *Journal of the American Society for Psychical Research* 67, 1973, pp. 130–46.

62. I'm thinking here of the Lebanese case of Imad Elawar in *Twenty Cases*, critiqued by Leonard Angel, *Enlightenment East and West* (New York: State University of New York Press, 1994).

63. See for instance Antonia Mills, 'A replication study: three cases of children in Northern India who are said to remember a previous life', *Journal of Scientific Exploration* 3, 1989, pp. 133–84, and Jurgen Keil, 'New cases in Burma, Thailand, and Turkey: A limited field study replication of some aspects of Ian Stevenson's research', *Journal of Scientific Exploration* 5, 1991, pp. 27- 60.

64. *Cases of the Reincarnation Type Vol. I,* pp. 107–43.

65. ibid., pp. 144–75.

66. For arguments against parental involvement see S. Pasricha, 'Are reincarnation-type cases shaped by parental guidance? An empirical study concerning the limits of parents' influence on children', *Journal of Scientific Exploration* 6, 1992, pp 167–180, and Antonia Mills, 'Moslem cases of the reincarnation type in Northern India: A test of the hypothesis of imposed identification, Part II', *Journal of Scientific Exploration* 4, 1990, pp. 189–202.

67. Matlock, 'Past Life Memory Case Studies', p. 227.

68. Hines, *Pseudoscience and the Paranormal*, p. 74.

69. Andrea Leininger and Bruce Leininger, *Soul Survivor: The Reincarnation of a World War II Fighter Pilot* (New York: Grand Central Publishing, 2009). The forum at Carol Bowman Past Life Center (http://www.childpastlives.org/) contains a number of anecdotal descriptions of children's past life memories.

Chapter Seven: Psi in the World

Opening quote: Huxley, letter to Charles Kingsley, 23 September 1860.

1. On 15 January 2004, Rupert Sheldrake and Lewis Wolpert debated the existence of telepathy at a public meeting. The full text of the debate can be found on Sheldrake's website: http://www.sheldrake.org/controversies/RSA_text.html. It includes the following statement by Sheldrake: 'Well, I noticed that when the parrot film was showing, Lewis wasn't looking at it! That film was shown on television ... and in early stage of our investigations, he did the same then. They asked a sceptic to commentate. Lewis appeared on the screen and he said, "Telepathy is just junk ... there is no evidence whatsoever for any personal, animal or thing being telepathic." The filmmakers were surprised that he

hadn't actually asked to see the evidence before he commented on it...'

2. *Six Impossible Things Before Breakfast* (London: Faber and Faber, 2006), pp. 151–56.

3. Carl Sagan speculated that the near-death experience is a memory of birth: going up a tunnel (the vagina) to a bright light (the lights of the operating theatre). *Broca's Brain* (London: Hodder & Stoughton, 1979), pp. 304–08. More knowledgeable critics acknowledge that this idea has superficial plausibility at best (eg. Blackmore, *Dying To Live*, p. 79).

4. See 'Randi's personal FAQ' following Wagg, 'JREF Challenge FAQ' (available at www/randi.org/site).

5. Richard Milton, *Alternative Science: Challenging the Myths of the Scientific Establishment* (Rochester, Vermont: Park Street Press, 1996), pp. 111, 183.

6. ibid., p. 11.

7. ibid., p. 18.

8. T.S. Kuhn, *The Structure of Scientific Revolutions* (Chicago: University of Chicago Press, 1962).

9. R. Galambos, 'The avoidance of obstacles by flying bats', *Isis* 34, 1942, pp. 132–40. For a summary see Guy Lyon Playfair 'How Skepticism Blocks Progress: Cuvier and Spallanzani', http://www.skepticalinvestigations.org/observer/bats.htm

10. See *Suggestions for Further Reading* at the end of Chapter Seven. More information, including links to online sources, can be found on the companion website http://www.randisprize.com.

11. Mayer, see Chapter Five, Quotes. Damien Broderick, *Outside the Gates of Science: Why It's Time for the Paranormal to Come in from the Cold* (Philadelphia, PA: Running Press, 2007).

12. See for instance Harvey Irwin, 'Is scientific investigation of post-mortem survival an anachronism? The demise of the survival hypothesis', *Australian Journal of Parapsychology* 2(1), 2002, pp. 19–27.

13. For views for and against multiple universes see Bernard Carr (ed.), *Universe or Multiverse?* (Cambridge: Cambridge University Press, 2007). For arguments against the multiverse being employed as an atheistic tool see Neil A. Manson (ed.), *God and Design: The Teleological Argument and Modern Science* (London: Routledge, 2003).

14. Ray Kurzweil, *The Age of Spiritual Machines: Howe We Will Live, Work, and Think in the New Age of Intelligent Machines* (London: Orion, 1999).

15. For negative assessments of data suggestive of survival by psi-literate writers see E.R. Dodds, 'Why I Do Not Believe in Survival', *Proceedings SPR* 42, 1934, pp. 147–72; J.B. Rhine, 'The Question of the Possibility of Proving Survival', *Journal SPR* 28, 1933, pp. 35–45; Gardner Murphy, 'Difficulties Confronting the Survival Hypothesis', *Journal American SPR*, 39, 1945, pp. 66–94.

16. A well-known instance is the investigation described in Owen, *Conjuring Up Philip,* in which experimenters first invented a deceased aristocrat named Philip, and then succeeded in generating séance phenomena, which were ostensibly used by this character as a means to communicate, confirming the details of his life that they had earlier made up. See also Chapter 2, note 26). See also Amy E. Tanner *Studies in Spiritism* (London and New York: Appleton and Co., 1910), a debunking based on six séances attended by Tanner, a sceptical psychologist, and her tutor G. Stanley Hall. The pair's aim was to demonstrate that the voices speaking through Piper were multiple personalities, which they achieved by ignoring the veridicality that interested the psychic researchers (Tanner complained of the 'triviality and dreariness' of the communicators' statements and that it was impossible to get down 'all the remarks and other circumstances which might explain them'). Hall worked hard to confuse the 'control' speaking through Piper, in this case ostensibly the deceased Richard Hodgson, and succeeded in getting him to agree that a living individual named Bessie Beals was in fact dead. Andrew Lang and Eleanor Sidgwick criticised contradictions, inaccuracies and misrepresentations in Tanner's work in separate reviews. Andrew Lang, 'Open Letter to Dr Stanley Hall', *Proceedings SPR* 25, 1911, pp. 90–101, and Eleanor Sidgwick, ' 'Studies In Spiritism' by Dr Tanner', *Proceedings SPR* 25, 1911, pp. 102–108. See a short online discussion at *The Daily Grail* (http://www.dailygrail.com/node/5786). Investigator S.G. Soal describes a communicator named John Ferguson whom he at first associated with a genuine personality but later realized was reproducing in the sittings ideas and incidents which had their origin as conjectures in his own mind. 'A Report on Some Communications Received Through Mrs Blanche Cooper', *Proceedings SPR* 35, 1926, pp. 471–594. For other similar cases see H.A. Dallas, 'Communications from the Still Incarnate at a Distance from the Body', *Occult Review* 40, 1924, pp. 87–92; F. C.S. Schiller, 'A Case of Apparent Communication through a Person Living, but Suffering from Senile Dementia', *Journal SPR* 21, 1923, pp. 87–92; and C.D. Thomas 'The Beard Case', *Journal SPR* 23, 1926, pp. 123–34.

17. Philosopher Stephen Braude points to the case of Alessandro Cagliostro, a controversial eighteenth-century mystic, who appeared to communicate in a series of sittings held in 1914. This produced a curious inconsistency. The 'Cagliostro' who came through was a swashbuckling, lascivious character, who cursed and swore and seemed preoccupied with sex. Yet these personality traits corresponded not at all with the historical Cagliostro described in contemporary records, but with the slanderous propaganda circulated by his enemies in the Catholic Church. *Immortal Remains*, pp. 39–43.

18. Alan Gauld, 'The "Super-ESP" Hypothesis', *Proceedings SPR* 53, 1960,

pp. 226–46 and *Mediumship and Survival* (London: Heinemann, 1982). Also Stephen E. Braude, 'Survival or Super-Psi?', *Journal of Scientific Exploration* 6, 1992, pp. 127–44 (which includes an exchange with Ian Stevenson) and *Immortal Remains, passim.*

19. See for instance 'F.W.H. Myers's Posthumous Message', *Proceedings SPR* 52, 1958, pp. 1–32; 'A Test of Survival', *Proceedings* 48, 1946, pp. 253–63; and 'Has Dr Thouless Survived Death?' *Journal SPR* 53, 1985, pp. 135–36.

20. Broad, *Lectures on Psychical Research,* p. 430.

21. Julian Baggini, *What's It All About? Philosophy and the Meaning of Life* (London: Granta, 2004), p. 52.

22. Some positive assessments of data suggestive of survival are David Fontana, *Is There an Afterlife? A Comprehensive Overview of the Evidence* (Ropley, Hampshire: O Books, 2005); Ducasse, *A Critical Examination of the Belief in a Life After Death;* Richard Almeder, *Death and Personal Survival* (Lanham, MD: Rowman and Littlefield, 1992); David Lorimer, *Survival?: Body, Mind and Death in the Light of Psychic Experience* (London: Arkana, 1988); and Carl B. Becker, *Paranormal Experience and Survival of Death* (New York: State University of New York Press, 1993).

23. See for instance Janet Oppenheim, *The Other World* (Chapter Two, note 66,) pp. 133–34. The cross-correspondences generated a vast literature in the SPR publications, mostly between 1902 and 1930. Some of the most important cases are described in J.G. Piddington, 'A Series of Concordant Automatisms', *Proceedings SPR* 22, 1908, pp. 19–416; Alice Johnson, 'Reconstruction of Some "Concordant Automatisms"', *Proceedings SPR* 27, 1914, pp. 1–156; Gerald Balfour, 'The Ear Of Dionysius: Further Scripts Affording Evidence of Personal Survival', *Proceedings SPR* 29, 1918, pp. 197–244; Jean Balfour, 'The 'Palm Sunday' Case: New Light on an Old Love Story', *Proceedings SPR* 52, 1958, pp. 79–267. For a summary see H.F. Saltmarsh, *Evidence of Personal Survival From Cross-Correspondences* (London: G. Bell, 1938).

24. Alan Gauld, 'A Series of 'Drop-in' Communicators', *Proceedings SPR* 55, 1972, pp. 273–340.

25. See for instance Ian Stevenson, 'Are Poltergeists Living or Are They Dead?' *Journal of the American Society for Psychical Research* 66, 1972, pp. 233–52.

26. See for instance Louis Legrand, *After Death Communication: Final Farewells* (Woodbury, MN: Llewellyn Publications, 1997). Psychologist David Fontana describes incidents that occurred shortly after the death of a close colleague, a fellow writer on psychic topics, which he interpreted as attempts to draw attention to his survival. 'Three Experiences Possibly Suggestive of Survival', *Journal SPR* 64, 2000, pp. 39–45.

27. Hornell and Ella B. Hart, 'Visions and Apparitions Collectively and Reciprocally Perceived', *Proceedings SPR* 41, 1933, pp. 205–49.

28. Charles Drayton Thomas, in his long-term investigations of Gladys Leonard, communicated on a regular basis with personalities he believed to be his deceased father and sister. See for instance C. Drayton Thomas, 'Newspaper Tests', *Journal SPR* 20, 1921, pp. 89–107, and 'The 'Modus Operandi' of Trance-Communication According to Descriptions Received Through Mrs Osborne Leonard', *Proceedings SPR* 38, 1928, pp. 49–100. In a book-length study of Leonora Piper the American researcher James Hyslop described extensive communications with a personality he believed to be his deceased father. J.H. Hyslop, 'A Further Record of Observations of Certain Trance Phenomena', *Proceedings SPR*, 16, 1901, pp. 1–649. David Kennedy describes in his 1987 memoir how his recently deceased wife Ann became for a while a continuing, invisible presence in his life. One day he fell asleep in his chair and was in danger of missing a church service. A medium whom he had previously consulted, who lived thirty miles away, phoned to say that Ann was prompting him to call her husband and wake him up. Later when he was doing his laundry, a different medium rang to say his wife was telling him to put the black pullover in as well, and also – referring to the previous incident – to buy an alarm clock. At other times the communicator he believed to be his wife helped him to trace lost objects, expressed mock horror at his having voted Tory, thanked him for some red roses he put in front of her photograph, and generally provided a sense of a continuing, loving presence. None of this is proof of her having survived death, as Kennedy is careful to note, but he finds the impression of it highly persuasive. David Kennedy, *A Venture in Immortality* (Gerrards Cross, Bucks: Colin Smythe, 1987).

29. Hodgson, 'A Record of Observations of Certain Phenomena of Trance', p. 123.

30. Hodgson, 'A Further Record of Observations of Certain Phenomena of Trance', pp. 387–88.

31. *What's It All About?* p. 51. Detailed criticisms of the concept of disembodied existence are made by Terence Penelhulme, *Survival and Disembodied Existence* (London: Routledge and Kegan Paul, 1976); Peter Geach, *God and the Soul* (New York: Routledge and Kegan Paul, 1969); and Antony Flew, *The Logic of Mortality* (Oxford: Blackwell, 1987). See also A.J. Ayer, *The Concept of a Person and Other Essays* (London: Macmillan, 1963) and Peter Strawson, *Individuals: An Essay in Descriptive Metaphysics* (London: Methuen, 1959).

32. Well-known examples of the genre are Albert Pauchard, *The Other World* (Norwich: Pelegrin Trust/Pilgrim, 1952/87); Geraldine Cummins, *The Road to Immortality* (London: Ivor Nicholson and Watson, 1932); Helen Greaves,

Testimony of Light (Saffron Walden, Essex: C.W. Daniel, 969/1988); Wellesley Tudor Pole, *Private Dowding* (Norwich: Pilgrims Book Services, 1917/1984); Jane Sherwood, *Post-Mortem Journal* (Saffron Walden, Essex: C.W. Daniel), 1964/1991); Jasper Swain, *On the Death of My Son* (London: Turnstone, 1974).

33. John Poynton cautions against the temptation to corroborate out-of-body experiences by comparing them with apparent physical observation, which he argues eventually leads to immense ontological difficulties. He suggests it can only make sense to think of the experience taking place in a nonphysical world, even if it closely *duplicates* the physical world. Poynton draws on the thought of the late Michael Whiteman, an emeritus professor of applied mathematics who had extensive psychical and mystical experience of his own, along with an expert knowledge of classical mystical texts. See J.C. Poynton, 'Making sense of psi: Whiteman's multilevel ontology, *Journal SPR* 59, 1994, pp. 401–12.

34. *Immortal Remains,* p. 13.

35. Michel Gauquelin, *Neo-Astrology: A Copernican Revolution* (London: Penguin, 1992).

36. Homeopathy is coming under increasing pressure in the UK, with attempts to stop the National Health Service providing it with funding. A growing trend among sceptics is to consider that its reported successes are in fact due to the placebo effect. See Ben Goldacre, *Bad Science* (London: HarperCollins, 2009).

37. For scientists arguing in support of creationism see William A. Dembski and Michael Ruse, *Intelligent Design: The Bridge Between Science and Technology* (Fortress Press, 2007); Michael J. Behe, *Darwin's Black Box: The Biochemical Challenge to Evolution* (New York: Simon and Schuster, 1998), and Michael Denton, *Evolution: A Theory in Crisis* (London: Ebury Press, 1985).

38. For a fundamentalist Christian critique of the near-death experience see John Ankerberg and John Weldon, *The Facts on Life After Death* (Eugene, Oregon: Harvest House, 1992). Clerics were prominent among those who debunked the Fox sisters and other nineteenth-century mediums. The Anglican Church was hostile to spiritualism until the mid-twentieth century: the findings of an investigation commissioned by the Archbishop of Canterbury Cosmo Lang, that some spirit mediums could really contact the dead, were suppressed by Lang until a leak forced their publication some years later. The report's authors stated: 'It is clearly true that the recognition of the nearness of our friends who have died and of their presence in the spiritual life and of their continuing concern for us cannot do otherwise, for those who have experienced it, than add a new immediacy and richness to their belief in the Communion of Saints.' *The Church of England and Spiritualism: Majority Report of The Church of England Committee of Inquiry* (London: Psychic Press, 1948).

39. For modern spiritualist views of reincarnation see Paul Beard, *Hidden Man* (Norwich: Pilgrim Books, 1986); P. Riva (ed.), *Light From Silver Birch* (London: Psychic Press, 1984) and Newton, *Journey of Souls.*

40. James H. Jeans, *The Mysterious Universe* (New York: Macmillan, 1930), p. 158.

41. It has been pointed out that David Deutsch, an Oxford University quantum physicist, considers telepathy to be 'complete nonsense' while at the same time promoting ideas about parallel universes and time-travel that many consider to be equally speculative. 'A Who's Who of Media Skeptics', Skepticalinvestigations.org. Bernard Carr, professor of mathematics and astronomy at Queen Mary, University of London, and a former SPR president, discusses the relationship between physics and psi-research in 'Worlds apart? Can psychical research bridge the gulf between matter and mind? *Proceedings SPR* 59, 2008.

42. A forum is The Scientific and Medical Network (www.scimednet.organisation).

43. See, for instance, Robert Wright, *The Evolution of God* (London: Little, Brown, 2009), pp. 40–41.

44. In a famous passage, Richard Dawkins conceived of replicators 'swarm[ing] in huge colonies, safe inside gigantic lumbering robots, sealed off from the outside world, communicating with it by tortuous indirect routes, manipulating it by remote control. They are in you and me; they created us, body and mind; and their preservation is the ultimate rationale for our existence.' *The Selfish Gene* (Oxford: Oxford University Press, 1976/89), p. 19.

45. When Aldous Huxley took mescaline he found himself repeating, 'This is how one ought to see, how things really are.' But there were reservations, he added. 'For if one always saw like this, one would never want to do anything else.' *Doors of Perception* (Harmondsworth, Middlesex: Penguin, 1954/1972), p. 30.

BIBLIOGRAPHY

This is a list of all printed sources referred to in the main text and in the *Notes and References*. The term '*Society for Psychical Research*' in journal titles has been abbreviated to '*SPR* ' throughout.

Adshead, W.P. (1877). *Dr Monck in Derbyshire*. London: J. Burns.

Alcock, J.A. (1981) *Parapsychology: Science or Magic?* Oxford: Pergamon Press.

Almeder, R. (1992). *Death and Personal Survival,* Lanham, MD: Rowman and Littlefield.

Alper, M. (2001). *The 'God' Part of the Brain: A Scientific Interpretation of Human Spirituality and God*. New York: Rogue Press.

Alvarado, C.S. (1984). 'Palladino or Paladino? On the Spelling of Eusapia's Surname'. *Journal SPR* **52**, 315–16.

Alvarado, C.S. (1993). 'Gifted subjects' contributions to psychical research: The Case of Eusapia Palladino'. *Journal SPR* **59**, 269–92.

Angel, L. (1994). *Enlightenment East and West*. New York: State University of New York Press.

Angel, L. (2008). 'Reincarnation: Overview of the work of Ian Stevenson (1918–2007)'. *The Skeptic* 21(1).

Ankerberg, J. and Weldon, J. (1992). *The Facts on Life After Death*. Eugene, OR: Harvest House.

Anon. (1772). *An Authentic, Candid, and Circumstantial Narrative, of the Astonishing Transactions at Stockwell, in the County of Surrey*. London: J. Marks.

Atkinson, R.L., Atkinson, R.C., Smith, E.E., and Bem, D.J. (1990). *Introduction to Psychology,* 10th edn. New York: Harcourt Brace Jovanovich.

Ayer, A.J. (1963). *The Concept of a Person and Other Essays*. London: Macmillan.

Baggally, W.W. (1909). 'Sittings With Carancini'. *Journal SPR* 14, 193–211.

Baggini, J. (2004). *What's It All About? Philosophy and the Meaning of Life*. London: Granta.

Baker, R.A. (2000). 'Can we tell when someone is staring at us?' *Skeptical Inquirer* **24**(2), 34–40.

Balfour, G. (1918). 'The Ear of Dionysius: Further Scripts Affording Evidence of Personal Survival'. *Proceedings SPR* 29, 197–244.

Balfour, J. (1958). 'The "Palm Sunday" Case: New Light on an Old Love Story'. *Proceedings SPR* 52, 79–267.

Barrett, W. (1911). 'Poltergeists, Old and New'. *Proceedings SPR* **25**, 377–412.

Barrett, W. and Myers, F.W.H. (1889). 'Review of 'D.D. Home, His Life and Mission'. *Journal SPR* 4, 101–16.

Barrett, W., Gurney, E. and Myers, F.W.H. (1882). 'First Report on Thought-Reading'. *Proceedings SPR* 1, 34–64.

Barrington, M.R. (1992). 'Palladino and the Invisible Man who never was'. *Journal SPR* 58, 324–40.

Batcheldor, K.J. (1966). 'Report on a Case of Table Levitation and Associated Phenomena'. *Journal SPR* 43, 329–56.

Beard, P. (1986). *Hidden Man*. Norwich: Pilgrim Books.

Becker, C.B. (1993). *Paranormal Experience and Survival of Death*. New York: State University of New York Press.

Behe, M.J. (1998). *Darwin's Black Box: The Biochemical Challenge to Evolution*. New York: Simon and Schuster.

Beloff, J. (1988). *The Relentless Question: Reflections on the Paranormal*. London: McFarland.

Beloff, J., ed. (1974). *New Directions in Parapsychology*. London: Elek Science.

Bem, D.J. and Honorton, C. (1994). 'Does psi exist? Replicable evidence for an anomalous process of information transfer'. *Psychological Bulletin* 115(1), 4–18.

Bem, D.J., Palmer, J. and Broughton, R.S. (2001). 'Updating the ganzfeld database: A victim of its own success,' *Journal of Parapsychology* 65, 207–18.

Bender, H. (1974). 'Modern Poltergeist Research - A Plea for an Unprejudiced Approach', in J. Beloff (ed.) *New Directions in Parapsychology*. London: Elek, pp. 131–34.

Bernstein, M. (1956). *The Search for Bridey Murphy*. New York: Doubleday.

Best, G. (1979). *Mid-Victorian Britain 1851–1875*. London: Fontana.

Blackburn, D. (1911). 'Confessions of a Telepathist: Thirty-Year Hoax Exposed'. *Daily News (London)*, 1 September, 115–32.

Blackmore, S. (1982). *Beyond the Body*. London: Heinemann.

Blackmore, S. (1987). *In Search of the Light: Adventures of a Parapsychologist*. Buffalo, NY: Prometheus.

Blackmore, S. (1992). 'Psychic Experiences: Psychic Illusions'. *Skeptical Inquirer* 16, 367–76.

Blackmore, S. (1993) *Dying to Live: Near-Death Experiences*. Amherst, NY: Prometheus.

Blackmore, S. (2001). 'Why I have given up', in P. Kurtz (ed.) *Skeptical Odysseys: Personal Accounts by the World's Leading Paranormal Inquirers*. Buffalo, NY: Prometheus, pp. 85–94.

Blum, D. (2007). *Ghost Hunters: The Victorians and the Hunt for Proof of Life after Death*. London: Arrow Books.

Bradford, D.T. (1984). *The Experience of God: Portraits in the Phenomenological Psychopathology of Schizophrenia*. New York: Peter Lang.

Brandon, R. (1983). *The Spiritualists: The Passion for the Occult in the Nineteenth and Twentieth Centuries*. London: Weidenfeld and Nicolson.

Braude, S. (1992). 'Survival or super-psi?' *Journal of Scientific Exploration* **6**, 127–44.

Braude, S. (2003). *Immortal Remains: The Evidence for Life after Death*. New York: Rowman and Littlefield.

Broad, C.D. (1962). *Lectures on Psychical Research*. London: Routledge and Kegan Paul.

Broad, C.D. (1963). 'Cromwell Varley's Electrical Tests with Florence Cook'. *Proceedings SPR* 54, 158–72.

Broderick, D. (2007). *Outside the Gates of Science: Why It's Time for the Paranormal to Come in from the Cold*. Philadelphia, PA: Running Press.

Brown, D.J. and Sheldrake, R. (1998). 'Perceptive pets: A survey in North-West California'. *Journal SPR* 62, 396–406.

Capaldi, N. (1987). *The Art of Deception: An Introduction to Critical Thinking*, Buffalo. New York: Prometheus.

Capron, E.W. (1855). *Modern Spiritualism: Its Facts and Fanaticisms, Its Consistencies and Contradictions*. Boston: Bela Marsh.

Carington, W. (1944). 'Experiments on the Paranormal Cognition of Drawings. IV, Section B: A Theory of Paranormal Cognition and Allied Phenomena'. *Proceedings SPR* 47, 155–228.

Carpenter, W.B. (1871). 'Spiritualism and its recent converts'. *Quarterly Review* 131, 301–53.

Carr, B., ed. (2007). *Universe or Multiverse?* Cambridge: Cambridge University Press.

Carr, B. (2008). Worlds apart? Can psychical research bridge the gulf between matter and mind? *Proceedings SPR* 59, 1–96.

Carrington, H. (1908). *The Physical Phenomena of Spiritualism, Fraudulent and Genuine*. London: T. Werner Laurie.

Carrington, H. (1909). *Eusapia Palladino and Her Phenomena*. London: T. Werner Laurie.

Carrington, H. (1954). *The American Seances with Eusapia Palladino*. New York: Garrett.

Carrington, H. and Fodor, N. (1951). *Haunted People – The Story of the Poltergeist Down Through the Centuries*. New York: Dutton.

Carter, C. (2007). *Parapsychology and the Skeptics: A Scientific Argument for the Existence of ESP*. Pittsburg, PA: Sterling House.

Cash, W. (2001). 'Did atheist philosopher see God when he 'died'? *National Post*, 3 March.

Cassirer, M. (1983). 'Palladino at Cambridge'. *Journal SPR* 52, 52–58.

Cassirer, M. (1985). 'Helen Victoria Duncan: A Reassessment'. *Journal SPR* **53**, 138–44.

Christopher, K. (2001). 'The "Psychic" Parrot and Best-Kept Secrets'. *Skeptical Inquirer,* 15 February 2001.

Christopher, M. (1970). *Seers, Psychics and ESP*. London: Cassell.

Church of England (1948). *The Church of England and Spiritualism: Majority Report of the Church of England Committee of Inquiry*. London: Psychic Press.

Clark, K. (1984). 'Clinical interventions with near-death experiencers', in B. Greyson and C.P. Flynn (eds.) *The Near-Death Experience: Problems, Prospects, Perspectives*. Springfield, IL: Charles P. Thomas, pp. 242–55.

Cockell, J. (1993). *Yesterday's Children*. London: Piatkus.

Colwell, J., Schröder, S. and Sladen, B. (2000). 'The ability to detect unseen staring: a literature review and empirical tests'. *British Journal of Psychology* 91, 71–85.

Connell, S.O. (1998). 'Are Pets Psychic?' *The Times (London)*, 21 November.

Coover, J.E. (1985). 'Metapsychics and the incredulity of psychologists: psychical research before 1927', in P. Kurtz (ed.) *A Skeptic's Handbook of Parapsychology*. Buffalo, NY: Prometheus, pp. 241–73.

Cornell A.D. and Gauld, A. (1960). 'A Fenland Poltergeist'. *Journal SPR* **40**, 343–58.

Crawford, W.J. (1921). *The Psychic Structures at the Goligher Circle*. London: John M. Watkins.

Crookall, R.J. (1966). *The Study and Practice of Astral Projections*. New Hyde Park, NJ: University Books.

Crookes, W. (1874). 'Notes of an Enquiry into the Phenomena Called Spiritual During the Years 1870–1873'. *Quarterly Journal of Science,* January.

Crookes, W. (1889). 'Notes of Séances with D.D. Home'. *Proceedings SPR* **6**, 98–127.

Cummins, G. (1932). *The Road to Immortality*. London: Ivor Nicholson and Watson.

Daily Chronicle (1895). 'J.M. Maskelyne at Cambridge'. *Daily Chronicle* 29 October.

Dallas, H.A. (1924). 'Communications from the Still Incarnate at a Distance from the Body'. *Occult Review* 40, 87–92.

Dalton, K. (1997). 'Exploring the links: Creativity and psi in the ganzfeld', in *The Parapsychological Association 40th Annual Convention: Proceedings of Presented Papers*. Durham, NC: The Parapsychological Association, 119–34.

Dawkins, R. (1976/1989). *The Selfish Gene*. Oxford: Oxford University Press.

Dawkins, R. (1986). *The Blind Watchmaker*. London: Longman.

Dawkins, R. (1998). 'Aliens are not among us'. *Sunday Mirror*, 8 February.

Dawkins, R. (1999). *Unweaving the Rainbow*. London: Penguin.

Dawkins, R. (2006). *The God Delusion*. London: Bantam.

Delanoy, D.L. (1987). 'Work with a Fraudulent PK Metal-Bending Subject'. *Journal SPR* 54, 247–56.

Dembski, W.A. and Ruse, M. (2007). *Intelligent Design: The Bridge Between Science and Technology*. Augsburg Fortress, MN: Fortress Press.

Denton, M. (1985). *Evolution: A Theory in Crisis*. London: Ebury Press.

d'Esperance, E. (1898). *Shadow Land*. London: George Redway.

Dingwall, E.J. (1924). 'The Case of the Medium Pasquale Erto'. *Journal SPR* 21, 278–80.

Dingwall, E.J. (1930). 'An Amazing Case: The Mediumship of Carlos Mirabelli'. *Journal American SPR* 24, 296–306.

Dingwall, E., Goldney, K.M. and Hall, T.H. (1955). 'The Haunting of Borley Rectory. A Critical Survey of the Evidence'. *Proceedings SPR* 51, 1–180.

Dodds, E.R. (1934). 'Why I Do Not Believe in Survival'. *Proceedings SPR* **42**, 147–72.

Dowe, P. (2005). *Galileo, Darwin and Hawking: The Interplay of Science, Reason and Religion*. Grand Rapids, MI: W.B. Eerdmans.

Doyle, A.C. (1926/2006). *The History of Spiritualism*. London: Echo Library.

Druckman, D. and Swets, J.A., eds. (1988). *Enhancing Human Performance: Issues, Theories and Techniques,* Washington: National Academy Press.

Ducasse, C.J. (1961). *A Critical Examination of the Belief in a Life After Death*. Springfield, IL: Charles C. Thomas.

Dunraven, Earl of (1926). 'Experiences in Spiritualism with D.D.Home'. *Proceedings SPR* 35, 1–289.

Eastham, P. (1988). 'Ticking Off a Poltergeist'. *Journal SPR* 55, 80–83.

Edward, J. (2001). *Crossing Over: The Stories Behind the Stories*. New York: Princess Books.

Edwards, P. (1996). *Reincarnation: A Critical Examination. Buffalo, NY*: Prometheus Books.

Ehrenwald, J. (1978). *The ESP Experience: A Psychiatric Validation*. New York: Basic Books.

Eisenbud, J. (1966/1989). *The World of Ted Serios: 'Thoughtographic' Studies of an Extraordinary Mind*. Jefferson, NC and London: McFarland.

Evans, J.M. (1987). 'Patients' experiences of awareness during general anaesthesia', in M. Rosen and J.N. Lunn (eds.) *Consciousness, Awareness and Pain in General Anaesthesia*. London: Butterworths, pp.184-92

Faraday, M. (1853). 'Experimental investigation of table-moving'. *The Athenaeum*, 2 July.

Feilding, E., Baggally, W.W., and Carrington, H. (1909). 'Report on a Series of Sittings with Eusapia Palladino,' *Proceedings SPR* 23, 309–569.

Fenwick, P. and Fenwick, E. (1995). *The Truth in the Light: An Investigation of Over 300 Near-Death Experiences*. London: Headline.

Finucane, R.C. (1982). *Appearances of the Dead: A Cultural History of Ghosts*. London: Junction.

FitzSimons, P. (2003). *Sydney Morning Herald*, 23 January.

Flammarion, C. (1909). *Death and Its Mystery: Before Death, Proofs of the Existence of the Soul*. London: T. Fisher Unwin.

Flew, A. (1987). *The Logic of Mortality*. Oxford: Blackwell.

Fontana, D. (1991). 'A responsive poltergeist: A case from South Wales'. *Journal SPR* **57**, 385–403.

Fontana, D. (1992). 'The Feilding report and the determined critic'. *Journal SPR* 58, 341–50.

Fontana, D. (2000). 'Three experiences possibly suggestive of survival'. *Journal SPR* 64, 39–45.

Fontana, D. (2005). *Is There an Afterlife? A Comprehensive Overview of the Evidence*. Ropley, Hants: O Books.

Forte, R., ed. (2001). *Entheogens and the Future of Religions*. Thousand Oaks, CA: Pine Forge Press.

Frazier, K. (1981). *Paranormal Borderlands of Science*. Buffalo, NY: Prometheus.

Frazier, K. (1986). *Science Confronts the Paranormal*. Buffalo, NY: Prometheus.

French, C.C. (2001). 'Dying to know the truth: Visions of a dying brain, or false memories?' *Lancet* 358, 2010–11.

Gabbard, G.O. and Twemlow, S.W. (1984). *With the Eyes of the Mind*. Westport, CT: Praeger.

Galambos, R. (1942). 'The avoidance of obstacles by flying bats'. *Isis* **34**, 132–40.

Gardner, M. (1983). *The Whys of a Philosophical Scrivener*. New York: Quill.

Garrett, E. (1968). *Many Voices: The Autobiography of a Medium*. *New York: Putnam*.

Gauld, A. (1960). 'The "Super-Esp" Hypothesis'. *Proceedings SPR* **53**, 226–46.

Gauld, A. (1968). *The Founders of Psychical Research*. London: Routledge and Kegan Paul.

Gauld, A. (1972). 'A Series of "Drop-in" Communicators'. *Proceedings SPR* **55**, 273–340.

Gauld, A. (1982). *Mediumship and Survival*. London: Heinemann.

Gauld, A. and Cornell, A.D. (1961). 'The Geophysical Theory of Poltergeists'. *Journal SPR* 41, 129–46.

Gauld, A. and Cornell, A.D. (1979). *Poltergeists*. London: Routledge and Kegan Paul.

Gauquelin, M. (1992). *Neo-Astrology: A Copernican Revolution*. London: Penguin.

Gay, K. (1957). 'The Case of Edgar Vandy'. *Journal SPR* **39**, 1–64.

Geach, P. (1969). *God and the Soul*. New York: Routledge and Kegan Paul.

Gilovich, T. (1991). *How We Know What Isn't So: The Fallibility of Human Reason in Everyday Life*. New York: Simon and Schuster.

Goldacre, B. (2009). *Bad Science*. London: Harper Collins.

Goldfarb, R.M. and Goldfarb, C.R. (1978). *Spiritualism and Nineteenth Century Letters*. Cranbury, NJ: Associated University Presses.

Goss, M. (1979). *Poltergeists: An Annotated Bibliography of Works in English, Circa 1880–1975*. Metuchen, NJ: Scarecrow Press.

Greaves, H. (1969/1988). *Testimony of Light*. S Walden, Essex: C.W. Daniel.

Green, C. (1968). *Out-Of-The-Body Experiences*. Oxford: Institute of Psychophysical Research.

Green, C. and McCreery, C. (1975). *Apparitions*. London: Hamish Hamilton.

Grof, S. and Halifax, J. (1977). *The Human Encounter With Death*. London: Souvenir.

Grosse, M. and Barrington, M.R. (2001). 'Report on psychokinetic activity surrounding a seven-year-old boy'. *Journal SPR* 65, 207–17.

Guirdham, A. (1970). *The Cathars and Reincarnation*. London: Spearman.

Gurney, E., Myers, F.W.H. and Barrett, W.M. (1882). 'Second Report on Thought-Transference'. *Proceedings SPR* 1, 70–97.

Gurney, E. and Myers, F.W.H. (1884). 'Visible Apparitions'. *Nineteenth Century* 16, July.

Gurney, E., Myers, F.W.H. and Podmore, F. (1886). *Phantasms of the Living (Two vols.)*. London: Trubner.

Gustave, G. (1927). *Clairvoyance and Materialisation*. London: T. Fisher Unwin.

Hall, T.H. (1962). *The Spiritualists*. London: Duckworth.

Hall, T.H. (1964). *The Strange Case of Edmund Gurney*. London: Duckworth.

Hameroff, S., Kaszniak, A.W. and Scott, A.C., eds. (1996). *Towards A Science of Consciousness: The First Tucson Discussion and Debates*. Cambridge, MA: Massachusetts Institute of Technology.

Hamilton, W.D. (1963). 'The evolution of altruistic behaviour'. *American Naturalist* 97, 354–56.

Hanlon, J. (1974). 'Uri Geller and Science'. *New Scientist* 64, 170–85.

Hansel, C.E.M. (1980). *ESP and Parapsychology: A Critical Re-Evaluation*. Buffalo, NY: Prometheus.

Hansen, G.P. (1990). 'Magicians Who Endorsed Psychic Phenomena'. *The Linking Ring* 70(8), 52–54.

Hansen, G.P. (2001). *The Trickster and the Paranormal*. Philadelphia, PA: Xlibris Corporation.

Happold, F.C. (1963/1990). *Mysticism*. London: Penguin.

Haraldsson, E. (1981). 'Apparitions of the dead: A representative survey in Iceland,' in W. Roll (ed.) *Research in Parapsychology 1980*. Metuchen, NJ: Scarecrow Press.

Hardy, A. (1979). *The Spiritual Nature of Man: A Study of Contemporary Religious Experience*. Oxford: Clarendon Press.

Harris, S. (2005). *The End of Faith: Religion, Terror, and the Future of Reason*. London: Simon and Schuster.

Harrison, T. (2004). *Life After Death: Living Proof. New York:* Saturday Night Press Publications.

Hart, H. and Hart, E.B. (1933). 'Visions and Apparitions Collectively and Reciprocally Perceived'. *Proceedings SPR* 41, 205–49.

Henderson, M. (2006). 'Theories of telepathy and afterlife cause uproar at top science forum', *The Times*, 6 September.

Hess, D.J. (1993). *Science in the New Age: The Paranormal, Its Defenders and Debunkers, and American Culture*. Madison, WI: University of Wisconsin.

Heywood, R. (1969). 'Mrs. Gladys Osborne Leonard: A Biographical Tribute'. *Journal SPR* 45, 95–105.

Hines, T. (1988). *Pseudoscience and the Paranormal: A Critical Examination of the Evidence*. Buffalo, NY: Prometheus.

Hobeins, P.H. (1986) 'Sense and nonsense in parapsychology', in K. Frazier (ed.) *Science Confronts the Paranormal*. Buffalo, NY: Prometheus, 28–39.

Hodgson, R. (1892). 'A Record of Observations of Certain Phenomena of Trance'. *Proceedings SPR* **8**, 1–168.

Hodgson, R. (1894). 'Indian Magic and the Testimony of Conjurors'. *Proceedings SPR* **9**, 354–66.

Hodgson, R. (1898). 'A Further Record of Certain Phenomena of Trance'. *Proceedings SPR* **13**, 284–582.

Hodgson, R. and Davey, S.J. (1887). 'The Possibilities of Mal-Observation and Lapse of Memory From a Practical Point of View'. *Proceedings SPR* **4**, 381–495.

Hodgson, R., Gurney, E., Myers, F.W.H., *et al.* (1885). 'Report of the Committee Appointed to Investigate Phenomena Connected with the Theosophical Society'. *Proceedings SPR* **3**, 201–400.

Hodgson, R. (1895). 'The Value of the Evidence for Supernormal Phenomena in the Case of Eusapia Pal[l]adino'. *Journal SPR* 7, 36–79.

Hoffmaster, S. (1986). 'Sir Oliver Lodge and the Spiritualists', in K. Frazier, *Science Confronts the Paranormal*. Buffalo, NY: Prometheus, pp. 79–87.

Hoffmaster, S. (1990). 'How not to be a scientist: Science and Sir William Crookes', *Skeptical Inquirer* 15.

Hoggart, S. and Hutchinson, M. (1995). *Bizarre Beliefs*. London: Richard Cohen Books.

Hone, W. (1826). *The Every Day Book*. London: William Tegg.

Honorton, C. (1967). 'Review of Hansel "ESP: A Scientific Evaluation"'. *Journal of Parapsychology* 31, 76–82.

Honorton, C. (1981). 'Beyond the Reach of Sense: Some comments on C.E.M. Hansel's "ESP and Parapsychology: A Critical Re-Evaluation". *Journal American SPR* **75**, 155–66.

Honorton, C. (1985). 'Meta-analysis of psi ganzfeld research: A response to Hyman'. *Journal of Parapsychology* 49, 51–91.

Honorton, C. (1993). 'Rhetoric over substance: The impoverished state of skepticism'. *Journal of Parapsychology* **57**, 191–214.

Hopps, J.P. (1884). 'Some New Experiments in Thought-Transference'. *Journal SPR* **1**, 111–12.

Houdini, H. (1924). *A Magician Among the Spirits*. New York: Harper.

Hughes, M. (2001). 'Perceived accuracy of fortune-telling and belief in the paranormal'. *Journal of Social Psychology* 141(1), 159–60.

Hume, D. (1975). 'Of miracles', in L. Selby-Bigge and P. Nidditch (eds.) *An Enquiry Concerning Human Understanding*. Oxford: Clarendon.

Humphrey, N. (1995). *Soul Searching: Human Nature and Supernatural Belief*. London: Chatto and Windus.

Huxley, A. (1954/1972). *Doors of Perception*. Harmondsworth, Middlesex: Penguin.

Hyman, R. (1989). *The Elusive Quarry*. Buffalo, NY: Prometheus.

Hyman, R. (1995). 'Evaluation of the Program on Anomalous Mental Phenomena'. *Journal of Parapsychology* 59, 321–51.

Hyman, R. (2003). 'How Not to Test Mediums: Critiquing the Afterlife Experiments'. *Skeptical Inquirer*, **27**(1), 20–30.

Hyman, R. (2003). 'Hyman's Reply to Schwartz's 'How *Not* To Review Mediumship Research'. *Skeptical Inquirer*, **27**(3), 61–64.

Hyslop, J.H. (1901). 'A Further Record of Observations of Certain Trance Phenomena'. *Proceedings SPR* 16, 1–649.

Hyslop, J.H. (1909). 'Professor Newcomb and Occultism'. *Journal American SPR* 3, 255–89.

Inglis, B. (1977). *Natural and Supernatural*. London: Hodder and Stoughton.

Irwin, H. (2002). 'Is scientific investigation of post-mortem survival an anachronism? The demise of the survival hypothesis'. *Australian Journal of Parapsychology* **21**, 19–27.

Irwin, H.J. (1985). *Flight of Mind*. London and New York: Scarecrow Press.

Irwin, H.J. (1987). 'Charles Bailey: A Biographical Study of the Australian Apport Medium'. *Journal SPR* 54, 97–118.

Irwin, H.J. (1999). *An Introduction to Parapsychology,* Jefferson, NC and London: McFarland and Co.

Jahn, R.G. and Dunne, B.J. (1987). *Margins of Reality*. London: Harcourt Brace Jovanovich.

James, W. (1897/1956). 'What psychical research has accomplished', in *The Will to Believe and Other Essays in Popular Philosophy*. New York: Dover Publications, pp. 299–327.

James, W. (1902/1983). *The Varieties of Religious Experience*. London: Penguin.

Jastrow, J. (1910). 'The Unmasking of Paladino'. *Colliers*, 14 May.

Jeans, J.H. (1930). *The Mysterious Universe*. New York: Macmillan.

Jeffries, S. (2006). 'Lie Back and Think of Jesus'. *The Guardian,* 5 September 2006.

Johnson, A. (1895). 'Eusapia Pal[*l*]adino'. *Journal SPR* 7, 148–59.

Johnson, A. (1909). 'The Education of the Sitter'. *Proceedings SPR* 21, 483–511.

Johnson, A. (1914). 'Reconstruction of Some "Concordant Automatisms"'. *Proceedings SPR* 27, 1–156.

Johnson, R.C. (1959/1988). *Watcher on the Hills*. Norwich: Pelegrin Trust/Pilgrim Books.

Jong, K.H.E. (1914). 'The Trumpet-Medium, Mrs S. Harris'. *Journal SPR* 16, 266–70.

Judson, H.F. (2004). *The Great Betrayal: Fraud in Science*. London: Harcourt.

Keen, M. (2002). 'The case of Edgar Vandy: Defending the evidence'. *Journal SPR* 66, 247–59.

Keen, M., Ellison, A. and Fontana, D. (1999). 'The Scole Report'. *Proceedings SPR* 58, 150–392.

Keene, M.L. (1976). *The Psychic Mafia*. New York: St Martin's Press.

Keil, J. (1991). 'New cases in Burma, Thailand, and Turkey: A limited field study replication of some aspects of Ian Stevenson's research'. *Journal of Scientific Exploration* 5, 27– 60.

Kelly, E.F., Kelly, E.W., Crabtree, A., Gauld, A., Grosso, M. and Greyson, B. (2007). *Irreducible Mind: Toward a Psychology for the 21ˢᵗ Century*. Lanham, MD: Rowman and Littlefield Publisher.

Kelly, L. (2004). *The Skeptic's Guide to the Paranormal*. New York: Thunder's Mouth Press.

Kennedy, D. (1987). *A Venture in Immortality*. Gerrards Cross, Bucks: Colin Smythe.

Keul, A. and Phillips, K. (1987). 'Assessing the witness: Psychology and the

UFO reporter', in H. Evans and J. Spencer (eds.) *UFOs 1947–1987*. London: Fortean Tomes, pp. 230–37.

Klimo, J. (1998). *Channeling: Investigations on Receiving Information from Paranormal Sources*. Berkeley, CA: New Atlantic Books.

Koestler, A. (1973). *Roots of Coincidence*. London: Vintage.

Kohrn, R.L. (1980). 'A Survey of Psi Experiences Among Members of a Special Population', *Journal of the American SPR* 74, 395–411.

Krebs, S.L (1901). 'A Description of Some Trick Methods Used by Miss Bangs of Chicago'. *Journal SPR* 10, 5–16.

Kübler-Ross, E. (1971). *On Death and Dying*. New York: Macmillan.

Kuhn, T.S. (1962). *The Structure of Scientific Revolutions*. Chicago, IL: University of Chicago Press.

Kurtz, P. (1885). 'Spiritualism Exposed: Margaret Fox Kane Confesses to Fraud', in P. Kurtz (ed.) *A Skeptic's Handbook of Parapsychology*. Buffalo, New York: Prometheus, 225–33.

Kurtz, P. (1985). 'Spiritualists, mediums, and psychics: some evidence of fraud', in P. Kurtz (ed.) *A Skeptic's Handbook*. Buffalo, NY: Prometheus, pp. 177–223.

Kurtz, P., ed. (1985). *A Skeptic's Handbook*. Buffalo, NY: Prometheus.

Kurtz, P. (1887). *The Transcendental Temptation*. Buffalo, NY: Prometheus.

Kurtz, P., ed. (2001). *Skeptical Odysseys: Personal Accounts by the World's Leading Paranormal Inquirers*. Amherst, NY: Prometheus

Kurzweil, R. (1999). *The Age of Spiritual Machines: How We Will Live, Work, and Think in the New Age of Intelligent Machines*. London: Orion.

Lambert, G.W. (1955). 'Poltergeists: A Physical Theory'. *Journal SPR* 38, 49–71.

Lamont, P. (2005). *The First Psychic: The Peculiar Mystery of a Notorious Victorian Wizard*. London: Little, Brown.

Lang, A. (1902). 'The Poltergeist, Historically Considered'. *Proceedings SPR* 17, 305–26.

Lang, A. (1911). 'Open Letter to Dr Stanley Hall'. *Proceedings SPR* 25, 90–101.

Langmuir, I. (1989). 'Pathological science'. *Physics Today* 42(10), 36–48.

Larsen, C.D. (1927). *My Travels in the Spirit Worlds*. Rutland, VT: Tuttle.

Lee, E. (1866). *Animal Magnetism*. London: Longmans, Green and Co.

Legrand, L. (1997). *After Death Communication: Final Farewells*. Woodbury, MN: Llewellyn Publications.

Leininger, A. and Leininger, B. (2009). *Soul Survivor: The Reincarnation of a World War II Fighter Pilot*. New York: Grand Central Publishing.

Leonard, G.O. (1931). *My Life in Two Worlds.* London: Cassells.

Lewis, E.E. (1848). *A Report of the Mysterious Noises Heard in the House of Mr John D. Fox.* Canandaigua, NY: E.E. Lewis.

Lodge, O. (1894). 'Experience of Unusual Physical Phenomena Occurring in the Presence of an Entranced Person Eusapia Pal[*l*]adino'. *Journal SPR* **6**, 306–60.

Lodge, O. (1909). 'The Education of an Observer'. *Journal SPR* **14**, 253–60.

Lodge, O. (1910). 'On a Sitting With Mr and Mrs Tomson'. *Journal SPR* **14**, 365–70.

Lodge, O. (1916). *Raymond, or Life and Death.* London: Methuen.

Lombroso, C. (1909). *After Death – What? Spiritistic Phenomena and Their Interpretation.* Boston, MA: Small, Maynard and Co.

London Dialectical Society (1873). *Report on Spiritualism of the Committee of the London Dialectical Society.* London: London Dialectical Society.

Lorimer, D. (1988). *Survival?: Body, Mind and Death in the Light of Psychic Experience.* London: Arkana.

Lorimer, D. (1999). 'Distant feelings'. *Network* **71**.

Lunt, E.D. (1903). *Mysteries of the Séance and Tricks and Traps of Bogus Mediums.* Boston, MS: Lunt Bros.

MacKenzie, A. (1982). *Hauntings and Apparitions.* London: Heinemann.

Maddox, J. (1981). 'A book for burning?' *Nature* 293, 245–46.

Manning, M. (1976). *The Link.* London: Ballantine.

Manning, M. and Rose, T. (1999). *One Foot in the Stars: The Story of the World's Most Extraordinary Healer,* Shaftesbury, Dorset: Element.

Manson, N.A., ed. (2003). *God and Design: The Teleological Argument and Modern Science.* London: Routledge.

Margolis, J. (1998). *Uri Geller: Magician or Mystic?* London: Orion.

Marks, D. (1981). 'Sensory Cues Invalidate Remote Viewing Experiments'. *Nature* 292, 177.

Marks, D. (1986). 'Remote viewing revisited', in K. Frazier (ed.) *Science Confronts the Paranormal.* Buffalo, NY: Prometheus, pp. 110–21.

Marks, D. (2000). *The Psychology of the Psychic: A Penetrating Scientific Analysis of Claims of Psychic Abilities.* Buffalo, NY: Prometheus.

Marks, D. and Kammann, R. (1980). *The Psychology of the Psychic: A penetrating scientific analysis of claims of psychic abilities.* Amherst, NY: Prometheus.

Marks, D. and Colwell, J. (2000). 'The psychic staring effect: An artefact of pseudo randomization,' *Skeptical Inquirer* 41.

Markwick, B. (1978). 'The Soal–Goldney experiments with Basil Shackleton: New evidence of data manipulation', *Proceedings SPR* 56, 250–77.

Maskelyne, J.N. (1885). 'Mr. Maskelyne and the spiritualists'. *Pall Mall Gazette*, 23 April.

Masters, R.E.L. and Houston, J. (1966/1973). *The Varieties of Psychedelic Experience*. London: Turnstone.

Matlock, J.G. (1990). 'Past Life Memory Case Studies' in Stanley Krippner (ed.) *Advances in Parapsychological Research 6*. London: McFarland, pp. 184–267.

Mauskopf, S.H. and McVaugh, M.R. (1980). *The Elusive Science: Origins of Experimental Psychical Research*. Baltimore: John Hopkins University Press.

May, E.C. (1996). The American Institutes for Research review of the Department of Defense's Star Gate Program: A commentary', *Journal of Scientific Exploration* 10, 89–107.

Mayer, E.L. (2007). *Extraordinary Knowing: Science, Skepticism, and the Inexplicable Powers of the Human Mind*. New York: Bantam Dell.

McConnell, R.A. (1977). 'The resolution of conflicting beliefs about the ESP evidence'. *Journal of Parapsychology* 41, 198–214.

McMoneagle, J. (2002). *The Stargate Chronicles: Memoirs of a Psychic Spy*, Charlottesville: Hampton Roads.

Medhurst, R.G. (1972). *Crookes and the Spirit World*. London: Souvenir Press.

Medhurst, R.G. and Goldney, K.M. (1964). 'William Crookes and the Physical Phenomena of Mediumship'. *Proceedings SPR* 54, 25–156.

Méheust, B. (*2003). Un Voyant Prodigieux: Alexis Didier, 1826–1866. Paris: Les Empêcheurs de penser on rond.*

Miles, C. and Ramsden, H. (1908). 'Experiments in Thought-Transference'. *Proceedings SPR* 21, 60–93.

Miller, A.R. (1998) 'Survival and diminished consciousness'. *Journal of Philosophical Research* 23, 479–96.

Mills, A. (1989). 'A replication study: three cases of children in Northern India who are said to remember a previous life'. *Journal of Scientific Exploration* 3, 133–84.

Mills, A. (1990). 'Moslem cases of the reincarnation type in Northern India: A test of the hypothesis of imposed identification, Part II'. *Journal of Scientific Exploration* 4, 189–202.

Milton, J. (1999). 'Should ganzfeld research continue to be crucial in the search for a replicable psi effect? Part I. Discussion paper and an introduction to an electronic-mail discussion'. *Journal of Parapsychology* 63, 309–35.

Milton, J. and Wiseman, R. (1999). 'Does psi exist? Lack of replication of an anomalous process of information transfer'. *Psychological Bulletin* 125, 387–91.

Milton, J. and Wiseman, R. (2002). 'A Response to Storm and Ertel'. *Journal of Parapsychology* 66(2), 183–86.

Milton, R. (1996). *Alternative Science: Challenging the Myths of the Scientific Establishment,* Rochester, VT: Park Street Press.

Monod, J. (1972). *Chance and Necessity: Essay on the Natural Philosophy of Modern Biology.* London: Collins.

Monroe, R. (1971). *Journeys Out of the Body.* New York: Doubleday.

Moody, R. (1975). *Life after Life.* Atlanta, GA: Mockingbird.

Morton, R.C. (1892). 'Record of a Haunted House'. *Proceedings SPR* **8**, 317–18.

Münsterberg, H. (1899). *Psychology and Life.* London: Archibald Constable.

Münsterberg, H. (1909). 'Report on a Sitting With Eusapia Palladino'. *Metropolitan Magazine*, February.

Muhl, A. (1963). *Automatic Writing: An Approach to the Unconscious.* New York: Garrett Publications.

Muldoon, S. and Carrington, H. (1929/1968). *The Projection of the Astral Body.* London: Rider.

Murphy, G. (1944). 'A Caringtonian Approach to Ian Stevenson's "Twenty Cases Suggestive of Reincarnation"'. *Journal American SPR* 47, 155–228.

Murphy, G. (1945). 'Difficulties Confronting the Survival Hypothesis'. *Journal American SPR* 39, 66–94.

Murray, G. (1916). 'Presidential Address'. *Proceedings SPR* 29, 46–63.

Myers, F.W.H. (1891). 'On Alleged Movements of Objects, Without Contact, Occurring Not in the Presence of a Paid Medium, Part 1'. *Proceedings SPR* 7, 146–98.

Myers, F.W.H. (1892). 'On Alleged Movements of Objects, Without Contact, Occurring Not in the Presence of a Paid Medium, Part 2'. *Proceedings SPR* 7, 383–94.

Myers, F.W.H. (1903). *Human Personality and Its Survival of Bodily Death.* London: Longmans.

Myers, F.W.H., Lodge, O. (Sir), Leaf, W. and James, W. (1890). 'A Record of Observations of Certain Phenomena of Trance'. *Proceedings SPR* **6**, 436–660.

Neher, A. (1990). *The Psychology of Transcendence.* New York: Dover.

Newberg, A. and D'Aquili, E. (2001). *Why God Won't Go Away: Brain Science and the Biology of Belief.* New York: Ballantine.

Newton, M. (1994). *Journey of Souls: Case Studies of Life Between Lives.* Woodbury, MN: Llewellyn Publications.

Nickell, J. (1993). *Looking for a Miracle: Weeping Icons, Relics, Stigmata, Visions and Healing Cures.* Amherst, NY: Prometheus.

Nielsen, E. (1950). *Solid Proofs of Survival.* London: Spiritualist Press.

Noyes, R. Jr and Kletti, R. (1980). 'The experience of dying from falls', in R.A. Kalish (ed.) *Death, Dying and Transcending.* Amityville, NY: Baywood, 129–36.

Olcott, H.S. (1875). *People From The Other World.* Hartford, CT: American Publishing Company.

Oldfield, K. (2001). 'Philosophers and Psychics: The Vandy episode'. *Skeptical Inquirer,* **25**(6).

Oppenheim, J. (1985). *The Other World: Spiritualism and Psychical Research in England, 1850–1914. Cambridge:* Cambridge University Press.

Owen, A.R.G. (1964). *Can We Explain The Poltergeist?* New York: Garrett Publications.

Owen, I.M. (1977). *Conjuring Up Philip.* New York: Harper and Row.

Owen, I.M. and Sparrow, M.H. (1974). 'Generation of paranormal physical phenomena in connection with an imaginary communicator'. *New Horizons* **1**, 6–13.

Palmer, J. (1978). 'The out-of-body experience: A psychological theory'. *Parapsychological Review* 9, 19–22.

Palmer, J. (1979). 'A Community Mail Survey of Psychic Experiences'. *Journal American SPR* **73**, 221–51.

Palmer, J. (1997). 'The challenge of experimenter psi'. *European Journal of Parapsychology* 13, 110–25.

Palmer, J. (2003). 'ESP in the Ganzfeld: Analysis of a debate', in J. Alcock, J. Burns and A. Freeman (eds.) *Psi Wars: Getting to Grips with the Paranormal.* Exeter: Imprint Academic, 51–67.

Palmer, J.A., Honorton. C. and Utts, J. (1989). 'Reply to the National Research Council Study on Parapsychology'. *Journal American SPR* **83**, 31–49.

Parker, A., Persson, A., and Hauler, A. (2000). 'Using qualitative ganzfeld research for theory development: Top-down processes in psi-meditation'. *Journal SPR* 64, 65–81.

Pasricha, S. (1992). 'Are reincarnation type cases shaped by parental guidance? An empirical study concerning the limits of parents' influence on children'. *Journal of Scientific Exploration* 6, 167–80.

Pauchard, A. (1952/1987). *The Other World.* Norwich: Pelegrin Trust/Pilgrim.

Penelhulme, T. (1976). *Survival and Disembodied Existence.* London: Routledge and Kegan Paul.

Persinger, M.A. (1974). *The Paranormal: Part II, Mechanisms and Models.* New York: MSS Information Corporation.

Persinger, M.A. (1987). *Neuropsychological Bases of God Beliefs.* Westport, CT: Praeger.

Piatelli-Palmarini, M. (1996). *Inevitable Illusions: How Mistakes of Reason Rule Our Mind,* Hoboken, NJ: John Wiley and Sons.

Piddington, J.G. (1908). 'A Series of Concordant Automatisms'. *Proceedings SPR* **22**, 19–416.

Playfair, G.L. (1980). *This House is Haunted.* New York: Stein and Day.

Playfair, G.L. (2002). *Twin Telepathy: The Psychic Connection.* London: Vega.

Playfair, G.L. and Grosse, M. (1988). 'Enfield Revisited: The Evaporation of Positive Evidence'. *Journal SPR* **55**, 208–19.

Podmore, F. (1884). 'Report on the Worksop Disturbances'. *Journal SPR* 1, 199–212.

Podmore, F. (1898). 'Discussion of the Trance-Phenomena of Mrs Piper 1. *Proceedings SPR* 14, 50–78.

Podmore, F. (1902). *Modern Spiritualism, Vol II.* London: Methuen.

Pole, W.T. (1917/1984). *Private Dowding.* Norwich: Pilgrims Book Services.

Popper, K. (1963). *Conjectures and Refutations.* London: Routledge.

Poynton, J.C. (1994). Making sense of psi: Whiteman's multilevel ontology. *Journal SPR* **59**, 401–12.

Pratt, J.G., Rhine, J.B., Smith, B.M., Stuart, C.E. and Greenwood, J.A. (1940/1996). *Extra-Sensory Perception after Sixty Years.* Boston: Bruce Humphries.

Price, G.R. (1955). 'Science and the Supernatural'. *Science* **122**, 359–67.

Price, H. (1940). *The Most Haunted House in England: Ten Years' Investigation of Borley Rectory.* London: Longmans, Green and Co.

Prince, W.F. (1930).*The Enchanted Boundary.* Boston: Boston Society for Psychic Research.

Puhle, A. (1999). 'Ghosts, apparitions and poltergeist incidents in Germany between 1700 and 1900'. *Journal SPR* 63, 292–305.

Puthoff, H.E. and Targ, R. (1976). 'A Perceptual Channel for Information Transfer Over Kilometer Distances: Historical Perspective and Recent Research,' *Journal of Electrical and Electronic Engineering* 64, **3** March, 329–54.

Quinn, S. (1995). *Marie Curie: A Life*. Cambridge, MA: Da Capo Press.

Radclyffe-Hall and Troubridge, U. (1920). 'On a Series of Sittings With Mrs Osborne Leonard'. *Proceedings SPR* 30, 339–554.

Radin, D.I. (1997). *The Conscious Universe: The Scientific Truth of Psychic Phenomena*. New York: HarperCollins.

Radin, D.I. (2006). *Entangled Minds: Extrasensory Experiences in a Quantum Reality*. New York: Simon and Schuster.

Radin, D., May, E.C. and Thomson, M.J. (1986). 'Psi experiments with random number generators: Meta-analysis. Part 1', in D.H. Weiner and D.I. Radin (eds.) *Research in Parapsychology 1985*. Metuchin, NJ: Scarecrow Press, pp. 14–17.

Randi, J. (1982). *Flim-Flam! Psychics, ESP, Unicorns and Other Delusions*. Buffalo, NY: Prometheus.

Randi, J. (1983). 'The Project Alpha Experiment: Part 1. The First Two Years'. *Skeptical Inquirer* 7(4), 24–35.

Randi, J. (1983). 'The Project Alpha Experiment: Part 2. Beyond the Laboratory'. *Skeptical Inquirer* 8(1), 36–45.

Randi, J. (1986). 'The Columbus poltergeist case', in K. Frazier (ed.) *Science Confronts the Paranormal*. Buffalo, NY: Prometheus Books, 145–57.

Randi, J. (1992). 'Randi at Caltech: A Report from the Paranormal Trenches'. *Skeptic* 1(1).

Rawcliffe, D.H. (1952). *The Psychology of the Occult*. London: Derricke Ridgway.

Reed, G. (1988). *The Psychology of Anomalous Experience*. Buffalo, NY: Prometheus.

Reyna, R. (1973). *Reincarnation and Science*. Delhi: Sterling Publishers.

Rhine, J.B and Pratt, J.G. (1954). 'A Review of the Pearce–Pratt Distance Series of ESP Tests'. *Journal of Parapsychology* 18(3), 165–77.

Rhine, J.B. (1933). 'The Question of the Possibility of Proving Survival. *Journal SPR* 28, 35–45.

Rhine, J.B. (1938). *New Frontiers of the Mind*. London: Faber and Faber.

Rhine, J.B. (1974). 'A new case of experimenter unreliability'. *Journal of Parapsychology* 38, 218–25.

Rhine, L.E. (1956). 'Hallucinatory Psi Experiences I. An Introductory Survey'. *Journal of Parapsychology* 20, 233–56.

Rhine, L.E. 'Hallucinatory Psi Experiences II. The initiative of the percipient in hallucinations of the living, the dying, and the dead'. *Journal of Parapsychology* 21, 13–46.

Richards, J.T. (1982). *SORRAT: A History of the Neihardt Psychokinesis Experiments, 1961–1981*, Metuchen, NJ: Scarecrow Press.

Richet, C. (1889). 'Further Experiments in Hypnotic Lucidity or Clairvoyance'. *Proceedings SPR* **6**, 66–83.

Richet, C. (1905). 'Concerning the Phenomena of Materialisation: The Villa Carmen Phenomena.' *The Annals of Psychical Science* **6**, October and November.

Richet, C. (1923). *Thirty Years of Psychical Research: Being a Treatise on Metapsychics*. London: W. Collins.

Richet, C. (1924). 'The Difficulty of Survival from the Scientific Point of View'. *Proceedings SPR* **34**, 107–12.

Ridley, M. (1996). *The Origins of Virtue: Human Instincts and the Evolution of Cooperation*. London: Viking.

Ring, K. (1980). *Life At Death: A Scientific Investigation of the Near-Death Experience*. New York: Coward, McCann and Geoghegan.

Ring, K. (1998). *Lessons From the Light*. Portsmouth, NH: Moment Point Press.

Ring, K. and Cooper, S. (1999). *Mindsight: Near-Death and Out-Of-Body Experiences in the Blind*. Pali Alto, CA: Institute of Transpersonal Psychology.

Rinn, J. (1950). *Sixty Years of Psychical Research*. New York: The Truth Seeker Company.

Riva, P., ed. (1984). *Light from Silver Birch*. London: Psychic Press.

Roberts, J. (1981). *The Seth Material*. London: Bantam.

Roe, C.A. (1999). 'Critical thinking and belief in the paranormal: A re-evaluation'. *British Journal of Psychology* 90, 85–98.

Roe, C.A. (2009). 'The role of altered states of consciousness in extrasensory experiences', in M. Smith (ed.) *Developing Perspectives on Anomalous Experience*. Jefferson, NC: McFarland and Co.

Rogo, D.S. (1984). 'Ketamine and the Near-Death Experience'. *Anabiosis* **4**, 87–96.

Rogo, D.S. (1986). *On the Track of the Poltergeist*. San Antonio: Anomalist Books.

Rogo, D.S. (1987). *Psychic Breakthroughs Today*. Wellingborough, Northants: Aquarian.

Roll, W. (1972). *The Poltergeist*. New York: Signet.

Roll, W. (1986). 'Poltergeists', in B. Wolman (ed.), *The Handbook of Parapsychology,* Jefferson, NC: McFarland and Co.

Roll, W. and Pratt, J.G. (1971). 'The Miami Disturbances'. *Journal American SPR* **65**, 409–54.

Roll, W. and Storey, V. (2004). *Unleashed: Of Poltergeists and Murder, The Curious Story of Tina Resch*. New York: Simon and Schuster.

Rothman, M.A. (1992). *The Science Gap: Dispelling the Myths and Understanding the Reality of Science*. Buffalo, NY: Prometheus.

Sabom, M. (1982). *Recollections of Death*. New York: Harper and Row.

Sabom, M. (1998). *Light and Death: One Doctor's Fascinating Account of Near-Death Experience,* Grand Rapids, MI: Zonervan.

Sagan, C. (1979). *Broca's Brain*. London: Hodder and Stoughton.

Sagan, C. (1996). *The Demon-Haunted World: Science as a Candle in the Dark*. London: Hodder Headline.

Saltmarsh, H.F. (1930). 'Report on the Investigation of Some Sittings with Mrs Warren Elliott'. *Proceedings SPR* 39, 47–184.

Saltmarsh, H.F. (1938). *Evidence of Personal Survival from Cross-Correspondences*. London: G. Bell.

Saltmarsh, H.F. and Soal, S.G. (1931). 'A Method of Estimating the Supernormal Content of Mediumistic Communications'. *Proceedings SPR* 9, 266–73.

Sampson, W. (2001). '"Alternative medicine": How it demonstrates characteristics of pseudoscience, cult, and confidence game', in P. Kurtz (ed.) *Skeptical Odesseys*. Buffalo, NY: Prometheus, 259–67.

Sartori, P. (2008). *The Near-Death Experiences of Hospitalized Intensive Care Patients: A Five Year Clinical Study.,* Lampeter, UK: Edwin Mellen Press.

Saunders, D.S. (1985). 'On Hyman's factor analyses'. *Journal of Parapsychology* 49, 86–88.

Schiller, F.C.S. (1923). 'A Case of Apparent Communication through a Person Living, but Suffering from Senile Dementia'. *Journal SPR* 21, 87–92.

Schlitz, M.J. and Gruber, E. (1980). 'Transcontinental remote viewing,' *Journal of Parapsychology* 44, 305–17.

Schlitz, M.J. and Haight, J. (1984). 'Remote viewing revisited: An intrasubject replication'. *Journal of Parapsychology* 48, 39–49.

Schmeidler, G. (1943). 'Predicting Good and Bad Scores in Clairvoyance Experiments: A final report'. *Journal American SPR* 37, 210–21.

Schmeidler, G. (1945). 'Separating the Sheep from the Goats'. *Journal American SPR* 39, 47–50.

Schmidt, H. (1969). 'Clairvoyant Tests with a Machine'. *Journal of Parapsychology* **33**, 300–06.

Schmidt, H. (1970). 'A PK Test with Electronic Equipment'. *Journal of Parapsychology* 34, 176–87.

Schmoll, A. (1886). 'Experiments in Thought Transference'. *Proceedings SPR* 4, 324–37.

Schouten, S. (1981). 'Analysing spontaneous cases: A replication based on the Sannwald Collection'. *European Journal of Parapsychology* 4, 9–48.

Schouten, S. (1993). 'Are we making progress?', in L. Coly and J. McMahon (eds.) *Psi Research Methodology: A Re-Examination*. New York: Parapsychology Foundation, 295–322.

Schumaker, J.F. (1990). *Wings of Illusion: The Origin, Nature and Future of Paranormal Belief*. Buffalo, NY: Prometheus.

Schwartz, G.E. (2001). 'Accuracy and replicability of anomalous after-death communication across highly skilled mediums: a call for balanced evidence-based skepticism'. *The Paranormal Review* 20.

Schwartz, G.E. (2003). 'How *Not* To Review Mediumship Research'. *Skeptical Inquirer,* May/June, 58–61.

Schwartz, G.E. and Russek, L. (2001). 'Evidence of anomalous information retrieval between two mediums: Telepathy, network memory resonance, and continuance of consciousness'. *Journal SPR* 65, 257–75.

Schwartz, G.E. and Simon, W.L. (2002). *The Afterlife Experiments*. New York: Pocket Books.

Schwartz, G.E., Russek, L. and Barentsen, C. (2002). 'Accuracy and Replicability of Anomalous Information Retrieval: Replication and Extension'. *Journal SPR* 66, 144–56.

Schwartz, G.E., Geoffrion, S., Jain, S., Lewis, S. and Russek, L.G. (2003). 'Evidence of anomalous information retrieval between two mediums: Replication in a double-blind design'. *Journal SPR* 67, 115–130.

Selby-Bigge, L. and Nidditch, P., eds. (1975). *An Enquiry Concerning Human Understanding*. Oxford: Clarendon.

Sheldrake, R. (1983). *A New Science of Life*. London: Granada.

Sheldrake, R. (1994). *Seven Experiments That Could Change the World*. London: Fourth Estate.

Sheldrake, R. (1999). 'Commentary on a paper by Wiseman, Smith and Milton on the "psychic pet" phenomenon'. *Journal SPR* **63**, 306–311.

Sheldrake, R. (1999). *Dogs that Know When Their Owners are Coming Home*. London: Hutchinson.

Sheldrake, R. (1999). 'The sense of being stared at: Experiments in schools. *Journal SPR* **62**, 311–323.

Sheldrake, R. (2000). 'Research on the feeling of being stared at'. *Skeptical Inquirer,* March/April, 58–61.

Sheldrake, R. (2001). 'Experiments on the sense of being stared at: The elimination of possible artefacts'. *Journal SPR* 65, 122–37.

Sheldrake, R. (2004). *The Sense of Being Stared At, and Other Aspects of the Extended Mind*. London: Arrow Books.

Sheldrake, R. (2005). 'The sense of being stared at, Part I: Is it real or illusory?' *Journal of Consciousness Studies* 12, 10–31.

Sheldrake, R. and Smart, P. (1997). 'A dog that seems to know when his owner is returning: Preliminary investigations'. *Journal SPR* 62, 220–32.

Sheldrake, R. and Smart, P. (1998). 'Psychic pets: A survey in North-West England'. *Journal SPR* 61, 353–64.

Sheldrake, R. and Smart, P. (2000). 'A dog that seems to know when his owner is coming home: Videotaped experiments and observations'. *Journal of Scientific Exploration* 14(2), 233–55.

Shermer, M. (1997). *Why People Believe Weird Things*. New York: H. Holt.

Sherwood, J. (1964/1991). *Post-Mortem Journal*. Saffron Walden, Essex: C.W. Daniel.

Sidgwick, E. (1911). '"Studies in Spiritism" by Dr Tanner'. *Proceedings SPR* **25**, 102–08.

Sidgwick, E. (1915). 'A Contribution to the Study of the Psychology of Mrs Piper's Trance Phenomena. *Proceedings SPR* 28, 1–652.

Sidgwick, E. (1921). 'An Examination of Book-Tests Obtained in Sittings With Mrs Leonard'. *Proceedings SPR* 31, 241–416.

Sidgwick, E. (1923). 'Phantasms of the Living 1886–1922'. *Proceedings SPR* **33**, 23–429.

Sidgwick, H., Johnson, A., Myers, F.W.H., Podmore, F. and Sidgwick, E. (1894). 'Report on the Census of Hallucinations'. *Proceedings SPR* 10, 25–422.

Siegel, R.K. (1980). 'The psychology of life after death'. *American Psychologist* 35, 911–50.

Siegel, R.K. and West, L.J., eds. (1975). *Hallucination: Behaviour, Experience and Theory*. Los Angeles: University of California.

Sinclair, U. (1930/2001). *Mental Radio,* Charlottesville: Hampton Roads.

Soal, S.G. (1926). 'A Report on Some Communications Received Through Mrs Blanche Cooper'. *Proceedings SPR* 35, 471–594.

Society for Psychical Research (1888). 'Note Relating to Some of the Published Experiments in Thought-Transference'. *Proceedings SPR* **5**, 269–70.

Society for Psychical Research (1891). 'Exposure of the Medium Husk'. *Journal SPR* **5**, 46.

Society for Psychical Research (1892). 'The Waterford Ghost'. *Journal SPR* **5**, 227–28.

Society for Psychical Research (1901). 'The Newspapers on Mrs Piper'. *Journal SPR* 10, 142–43.

Society for Psychical Research (1905). 'Sittings With Mr Chambers'. *Journal SPR* **12**, 197–203.

Society for Psychical Research (1906). 'Exposure of Mr Eldred'. *Journal SPR* **12**, 242–52.

Society for Psychical Research (1907). 'Automatic Phenomena'. *Journal SPR* **13**, 15–16.

Society for Psychical Research (1908). 'Some Mysterious Rappings Explained'. *Journal SPR* **13**, 218–19.

Society for Psychical Research (1921). 'The Hopfgarten Poltergeist Case'. *Journal SPR* **20**, 199–207.

Society for Psychical Research (1926). 'The Cases of Mr Moss and Mr Munnings'. *Journal SPR* **23**, 71–5.

Society for Psychical Research (1927). 'An Early Record of a Poltergeist Case'. *Journal SPR* **24**, 26–7.

Society for Psychical Research (1946). 'A Test of Survival'. *Proceedings SPR* **48**, 253–63.

Society for Psychical Research (1958). 'F.W.H. Myers's Posthumous Message'. *Proceedings SPR* **52**, 1–32.

Society for Psychical Research (1985). 'Has Dr Thouless Survived Death?' *Journal SPR* **53**, 135–36.

Solovovo, Count P.-P. (1909). 'The Hallucination Theory as Applied to Certain Cases of Physical Phenomena'. *Proceedings SPR* **21**, 436–82.

Solovovo, Count P.-P. (1909). 'M. Courtier's Report on the Experiments with Eusapia Palladino at the Paris Institut General Psychologique and Some Comments Thereon'. *Proceedings SPR* **23**, 570–89.

Spencer, J. and Spencer, A. (1996). *The Poltergeist Phenomenon: An Investigation into Psychic Disturbance*. London: Headline.

Spraggett, A. and Rauscher, W. (1973). *Arthur Ford: The Man Who Talked with the Dead*. New York: W.W. Norton.

Stevenson, I. (1966). *Twenty Cases Suggestive of Reincarnation*. Charlottesville, VA: University of Virginia Press.

Stevenson, I. (1972). 'Are Poltergeists Living or Are They Dead?' *Journal of the American Society for Psychical Research* 66, 233–52.

Stevenson, I. (1973). 'Carington's psychon theory as applied to cases of the reincarnation type: a reply to Gardner Murphy'. *Journal American SPR* 67, 130–46.

Stevenson, I. (1975). *Cases of the Reincarnation Type, Volume I: Ten Cases in India. Charlottesville,* VA: University of Virginia Press.

Stevenson, I. (1978). *Cases of the Reincarnation Type, Volume II: Ten Cases in Sri Lanka. Charlottesville,* VA: University of Virginia Press.

Stevenson, I. (1980). *Cases of the Reincarnation Type, Volume III: Twelve Cases in Lebanon and Turkey.* Charlottesville, VA: University of Virginia Press.

Stevenson, I. (1983). *Cases of the Reincarnation Type, Volume IV: Twelve Cases in Thailand and Burma* Charlottesville, VA: University of Virginia Press.

Stevenson, I. (1983).' Cryptomnesia and Parapsychology'. *Journal SPR* **52**, 1–30.

Stevenson, I. (1984). *Unlearned Language: New Studies in Xeneglossy.* Charlottesville, VA: University Press of Virginia.

Stevenson, I. (1987). *Children Who Remember Previous Lives: A Question of Reincarnation.* Charlottesville, VA: University of Virginia Press.

Stevenson, I. (1997). *Reincarnation and Biology: A Contribution to the Etiology of Birthmarks and Birth Defects.* Volume 1: *Birthmarks and Reincarnation and Biology: A Contribution to the Etiology of Birthmarks and Birth Defects.* Volume 2: *Birth Defects and Other Anomalies. Westport,* CT: Praeger.

Stevenson, I. (1997). *Where Reincarnation and Biology Intersect.* Westport, CT: Praeger.

Stevenson, I. (2003). *European Cases of the Reincarnation Type.* Jefferson, NC: McFarland and Co.

Stevenson, I. and Samararatne, G. (1988). 'Three new cases of the reincarnation type in Sri Lanka with written records made before verifications'. *Journal of Scientific Exploration* **2**(2), 217–38.

Storm, L. and Ertel, S. (2001). 'Does psi exist? Comments on Milton and Wiseman's 1999 meta-analysis of ganzfeld research'. *Psychological Bulletin,* 127.

Strawson, P. (1959). *Individuals: An Essay in Descriptive Metaphysics.* London: Methuen.

Swain, J. (1974). *On the Death of My Son.* London: Turnstone.

Taboas, A.M. and Alvarado, C.S. (1984). 'An Appraisal of the Role of Aggression and the Central Nervous System in RSPK Agents'. *Journal American SPR* **78**, 55–69.

Tanner, A. (1910/1994). *Studies in Spiritism*. Buffalo, NY: Prometheus.

Targ, R. and Puthoff, H. (1974). 'Information transmission under conditions of sensory shielding'. *Nature* 251, 602–607.

Targ, R. and Puthoff, H. (1976). 'A Perceptual Channel for Information Transfer Over Kilometer Distances: Historical Perspective and Recent Research', *Journal of Electrical and Electronic Engineering* 64(3), 329–54.

Targ, R. and Puthoff, H. (1977). *Mind Reach*. New York: Delacorte.

Tart, C. (1984). 'Acknowledging and Dealing with The Fear of Psi'. *Journal American SPR* 78, April, 133–43.

Taylor, J. (1976). *Superminds*. London: Pan.

Taylor, J. (1980). *Science and the Supernatural*. London: Temple Smith.

TenDam, H. (1990). *Exploring Reincarnation*. London: Arkana.

Thalbourne, M.A. (1995). 'Science versus Showmanship: A History of the Randi Hoax'. *Journal of the American SPR* 89, 344–66.

Thomas, C.D. (1921). 'Newspaper Tests'. *Journal SPR* **20**, 89–107.

Thomas, C.D. (1926). 'The Beard Case'. *Journal SPR* **23**, 123–34.

Thomas, C.D. (1928). 'The 'Modus Operandi' of Trance-Communication According to Descriptions Received Through Mrs Osborne Leonard'. *Proceedings SPR* 38, 49–100.

Thomas, C.D. (1932). 'A Consideration of a Series of Proxy Sittings'. *Proceedings SPR* 41, 139–185

Thomas, C.D. (1939). 'A Proxy Experiment of Significant Success'. *Proceedings SPR* 45, 257–306.

Tieze, T.R. (1973). *Margery the Medium*. New York: Harper and Row.

Trivers, R.L. (1971). 'The evolution of reciprocal altruism'. *Quarterly Review of Biology* 46, 35–57.

Truzzi, M. (1987). 'Reflections on "Project Alpha": Scientific Experiment or Conjuror's Illusion?' *Zetetic Scholar* **12**(13), 73–98.

Turing, A. (1973). 'Computing, machinery and intelligence'. *Mind* **59**, 433–60.

Tyrrell, G.N.M. (1943/1953). *Apparitions*. London: SPR/Duckworth.

Ullman, M. and Krippner, S. (1970). *Dream Studies and Telepathy: An Experimental Approach*. New York: Parapsychology Foundation.

Utts, J. (1991). 'Replication and meta-analysis in parapsychology'. *Statistical Science* 6, 363–403.

Utts, J. (1995). 'An assessment of the evidence for psychic functioning'. *Journal of Parapsychology* 59(4), 289–320.

Van Lommel, P., van Wees, R., Meyers, V. and Elfferich, I. (2001). 'Near-death experience in survivors of cardiac arrest: a prospective study in the Netherlands,' *The Lancet* 358, 2039–45.

Verrall, A.W. (1916). 'Report on a Series of Experiments in "Guessing"'. *Proceedings SPR* 29, 64–110.

Verrall, H. (1922). 'A Further Report on Sittings with Mrs Leonard'. *Proceedings SPR* 32, 1–143.

Wambach, H. (1978). *Reliving Past Lives*. London: Hutchinson.

Wasson, R.G. (1992). *Persephone's Quest: Entheogens and the Origins of Religion*. New Haven, CT: Yale University Press.

Watt, C. and Wiseman, R. (2002). 'Experimenter Differences in Cognitive Correlates of Paranormal Belief and in PSI'. *Journal of Parapsychology* 66(4), 371–85.

Weil, A. (1996). 'Pharmacology of consciousness: A narrative of subjective experience', in S.R. Hameroff, A.W. Kaszniak and A.C. Scott (eds.) *Towards A Science of Consciousness: The First Tucson Discussion and Debates*. Cambridge, MA: MIT, 677–89.

Weisberg, B. (2005). *Talking to the Dead: Kate and Maggie Fox, and the Rise of Spiritualism,* San Francisco: Harper.

West, D.J. (1946). 'The Trial of Mrs Helen Duncan'. *Proceedings SPR* 48, 32–64.

West, D.J. (1948). 'The Investigation of Spontaneous Cases'. *Proceedings SPR* 48, 277.

West, D.J . (1984). 'A Mass Observation Questionnaire on Hallucinations. *Journal SPR* 34, 187–96.

Whiteman, J.H.M. (1961). *The mystical life: An outline of its nature and teachings from the evidence of direct experience*. London: Faber.

Willin, M.J. (1996). 'A ganzfeld experiment using musical targets'. *Journal SPR* 61, 1–17.

Willin, M.J. (1996). 'A ganzfeld experiment using musical targets with previous high scorers from the general population. *Journal SPR* 61, 103–108.

Willis, H.A. (1868). 'A Remarkable Case of Psychical Phenomena'. *Atlantic Monthly*, August.

Wilson, S. and Barber, T.X. (1983). 'The fantasy-prone personality: Implications for understanding imagery, hypnosis and parapsychological phenomena', in A. Shiekh (ed.) *Imagery: Current Theory, Research, and Application*. New York: John Wiley, 340–87.

Wilson, I. (1981). *Reincarnation? The Claims Investigated*. Harmondsworth, Middlesex: Penguin, 102–19.

Wilson, I. (1987). *The After Death Experience*. London: Sidgwick and Jackson.

Wiseman, R. (1991). 'The Feilding report: A reconsideration'. *Journal of the SPR* **58**, 129–52.

Wiseman, R. and O'Keefe, C. (2001). 'A critique of Schwartz *et al.*'s after-death communication studies'. *Paranormal Review* 20.

Wiseman, R. and Schlitz, M. (1997). 'Experimenter effects and the remote detection of staring'. *Journal of Parapsychology* 61, 199–207.

Wiseman, R. and Smith, M. (1994). 'A further look at the detection of un-seen gaze'. *Proceedings of the Parapsychological Association's* 37th Annual Convention. Columbus, OH: Parapsychological Association, pp. 465–78.

Wiseman, R., Smith, M. and Kornbrot, D. (1996). 'Exploring possible sender-to-experimenter acoustic leakage in the PRL autoganzfeld experiments,' *Journal of Parapsychology* 60, 97–128.

Wiseman, R., Smith, M. and Milton, J. (1998). 'Can animals detect when their owners are returning home? An experimental test of the "psychic pet" phenomenon'. *British Journal of Psychology* 89, 453–62.

Wiseman, R., Smith, M., and Milton, J. (2000). 'The "psychic pet" phenomenon: A reply to Rupert Sheldrake'. *Journal SPR* 64, 46–47.

Wolf, S. (1993). *Brain, Mind and Medicine: Charles Richet and the Origins of Physiological Psychology*. Piscataway, NJ: Transaction Publishers.

Wolman, B., ed. (1986). *The Handbook of Parapsychology*. Jefferson, NC: McFarland and Co.

Wolpert, L. (2006). *Six Impossible Things Before Breakfast*. London: Faber and Faber.

Woolley, V.J. (1930). 'Some Investigations into Poltergeists'. *Journal SPR* **26**, 104–07.

Wren-Lewis, J. (1974). 'Resistance to the study of the paranormal'. *Journal of Humanistic Psychology* 142, 41–48.

Wright, R. (1996). *The Moral Animal: Why We Are the Way We Are*. London: Abacus.

Wright, R. (2009). *The Evolution of God*. London: Little, Brown.

Young, M.L. (1987). *Agartha: A Course in Cosmic Awareness*, Bath: Gateway.

Yram (1926/1974). *Practical Astral Projection*. New York: Weiser.

Zaleski, C. (1987). *Otherworld Journeys: Accounts of Near-Death Experience in Medieval and Modern Times*. Oxford: Oxford University Press.

Zusne, L. and Jones, W. (1982). *Anomalistic Psychology: A Study of Extraordinary Phenomena of Behavior and Experience*. Hillsdale, NJ: Lawrence Erlbaum.

Zusne, L. and Jones, W. (1989). *Anomalistic Psychology: A Study of Magical Thinking* (2nd edition). Hillsdale, NJ: Lawrence Erlbaum.

INDEX

Page numbers in italics are in the Notes and References section